Cracking the

SSAT®

& ISEE®

2017 Edition

By the Staff of The Princeton Review

PrincetonReview.com

Penguin
Random
House

The Princeton Review
24 Prime Parkway, Suite 201
Natick, MA 01760
E-mail: editorialsupport@review.com

Published in the United States by Penguin Random House LLC, New York, and in Canada by Random House of Canada, a division of Penguin Random House Ltd., Toronto.

Terms of Service: The Princeton Review Online Companion Tools ("Student Tools") for the retail books are available for only the two most recent editions of that book. Student Tools may be activated only twice per eligible book purchased for two consecutive 12-month periods, for a total of 24 months of access. Activation of Student Tools more than twice per book is in direct violation of these Terms of Service and may result in discontinuation of access to Student Tools Services.

ISBN: 978-1-101-91973-6
eBook ISBN: 978-1-101-91974-3
ISSN: 1090-0144

SSAT is a registered trademark of the Secondary School Admission Test Board, and ISEE is a registered trademark of the Educational Records Bureau, neither of which sponsors nor endorses this product.

The Princeton Review is not affiliated with Princeton University.

Editor: Sarah Litt
Production Editor: Beth Hanson
Production Artist: Deborah A. Silvestrini

Printed in the United States of America on partially recycled paper.

10 9 8 7 6 5 4 3 2 1

2017 Edition

Editorial

Rob Franek, Senior VP, Publisher
Casey Cornelius, VP Content Development
Mary Beth Garrick, Director of Production
Selena Coppock, Managing Editor
Meave Shelton, Senior Editor
Colleen Day, Editor
Sarah Litt, Editor
Aaron Riccio, Editor
Orion McBean, Editorial Assistant

Random House Publishing Team

Tom Russell, Publisher
Alison Stoltzfus, Publishing Manager
Melinda Ackell, Associate Managing Editor
Ellen Reed, Production Manager

Acknowledgments

The Princeton Review would like to thank Anne Morrow and V. Zoe Gannon for their hard work revising and developing test material for this book.

Contents

Register Your

1 Go to **PrincetonReview.com/cracking**

2 You'll see a welcome page where you can register your book using the following ISBN: 9781101919736

3 After placing this free order, you'll either be asked to log in or to answer a few simple questions in order to set up a new Princeton Review account.

4 Finally, click on the "Student Tools" tab located at the top of the screen. It may take an hour or two for your registration to go through, but after that, you're good to go.

If you are experiencing book problems (potential content errors), please contact EditorialSupport@review.com with the full title of the book, its ISBN number (located above), and the page number of the error. Experiencing technical issues? Please e-mail TPRStudentTech@review.com with the following information:

- your full name
- e-mail address used to register the book
- full book title and ISBN
- your computer OS (Mac or PC) and Internet browser (Firefox, Safari, Chrome, etc.)
- description of technical issue

Book Online!

Once you've registered, you can...

- Get extra practice with online drills for all levels

- Take a full-length Elementary-level SSAT exam

- Find any late-breaking information released about the SSAT and ISEE tests

- Get valuable advice about the college application process, including tips for writing a great essay and where to apply for financial aid

- Learn more about the college of your choice, and see how it ranks according to *The Best 379 Colleges*

- Sort colleges by whatever you're looking for, be it the Best Theater or Dorm, overall Quality of Life or Science Lab Facilities, or even Birkenstock-Wearing, Tree-Hugging, Clove-Smoking Vegetarians

- Check to see if there have been any reported typos in this edition

Look For These Icons Throughout The Book

 Online Practice Tests   More Great Books

A Parent's Introduction

HOW CAN I HELP?

Congratulations! Your child is considering attending a private secondary school, and by virtue of the fact that you hold this book in your hands, you have recognized that either the SSAT or the ISEE is an important part of the admissions process. Providing your child with the information contained in this book is an excellent first step toward a strong performance on the SSAT or the ISEE.

As a parent, however, you know well the fine line between support and intrusion. To guide you in your efforts to help your child, we'd like to offer a few suggestions.

Have a Healthy Perspective

Both the SSAT and the ISEE are standardized tests designed to say something about an individual student's chances for success in a private secondary school. Neither is an intelligence test; neither claims to be.

Set realistic expectations for your child. The skills necessary for a strong performance on these tests are very different from those a student uses in school. The additional stress that comes from being expected to do well generally serves only to distract a student from taking a test efficiently.

At the same time, beware of dismissing disappointing results with a simple, "My child doesn't test well." While it is undoubtedly true that some students test better than others, this explanation does little to encourage a student to invest time and effort into overcoming obstacles and improving his or her performance.

Know How to Interpret Performance

Both the SSAT and the ISEE use the same test to measure the performance of an eighth-grade student and an eleventh-grade student. It is impossible to interpret scores without considering the grade level of the student. Percentile rankings have much more value than do either raw or scaled scores, and percentiles are the numbers schools use to compare students.

Remember That This Is Not an English or a Math Test

There are both verbal and math questions on the SSAT and on the ISEE. However, these questions are often based on skills and concepts that are different from those used on a day-to-day basis in school. For instance, very few English teachers—at any level—spend a lot of time teaching students how to approach analogy or sentence completion questions.

This may be frustrating for parents, students, and teachers. But in the final judgment, our educational system would take a turn for the worse if it attempted to teach students to do well on the SSAT, the ISEE, or even the SAT. The fact that the valuable skills students learn in school don't directly improve test scores is evidence of a flaw in the testing system, not an indictment of our schools or those who have devoted their professional careers to education.

Realize That All Tests Are Different

Many of the general rules that students are accustomed to applying to tests in school do not apply to either the SSAT or the ISEE. Many students, for instance, actually hurt their scores by trying to work on every question. Although these tests are timed, accuracy is much more important than speed. Once your child learns the format and structure of these tests, he or she will find it easier to apply his or her knowledge to the test and will answer more questions correctly.

Provide All the Resources You Can

This book has been written to provide your child with a very thorough review of all the math, vocabulary, reading, and writing skills that are necessary for success on the SSAT and ISEE. We have also included online practice drills for each chapter and practice tests that simulate actual SSAT or ISEE examinations.

The very best practice test questions, however, are naturally the ones written by the organizations who write the real test questions—the Secondary School Admission Test Board (SSATB) for the SSAT and the Educational Resources Bureau (ERB) for the ISEE. We encourage you to contact both these organizations (addresses and phone numbers can be found on page 5) to obtain any resources containing test questions that you can use for additional practice.

One word of caution: Be wary of other sources of SSAT or ISEE practice material. There are a number of test preparation books available (from companies other than The Princeton Review, of course) that are woefully outdated. The ISEE changed quite substantially in 2010, and the SSAT implemented some changes in 2012; many books have not caught up with these changes. In addition, both the SSAT and the ISEE change with time in very subtle ways. Thus, we suggest supplementing the information in this book with ERB's "ISEE Student Guide," which you can find at www.erblearn.org, and "Preparing and Applying Guide for Independent School Admission and the SSAT" which you can order at www.ssat.org.

Make sure the materials you choose are, to the greatest extent possible, reflective of the test your child will take and not a test that was given years earlier. Also, try to avoid the inevitable confusion that comes from asking a student to follow two different sets of advice. Presumably, you have decided (or are about to decide) to trust The Princeton Review to prepare your child for this test. In doing so, you have made a wise decision. As we have said, we encourage you to provide any and all sources of additional practice material (as long as it is accurate and reflective of the current test), but providing other test preparation advice tends to muddy the waters and confuse students.

Be Patient and Be Involved

Preparing for the SSAT or the ISEE is like learning how to ride a bicycle. You will watch your child struggle, at first, to develop a level of familiarity and comfort with the test's format and content.

The vocabulary list in this book covers all test levels. If you would like a list targeted to younger levels, you can find them online when you register this book!

Developing the math, vocabulary, reading, and writing skills that your child will use on the SSAT or the ISEE is a long-term process. In addition to making certain that he or she is committed to spending the time necessary to work through the chapters of this book, you should also be on the lookout for other opportunities to be supportive. An easy way to do this is to make vocabulary development into a group activity. In the vocabulary chapters, we provide an extensive list of word parts and vocabulary words; learn them as a family, working through flash cards at the breakfast table or during car trips. You may even pick up a new word or two yourself!

Important: If your child is in a younger grade, you may want to offer extra guidance as he or she works through this book and prepares for the test. Because this book covers preparation for the full range of grade levels taking the tests (fourth through eleventh grades), some of the content review will be beyond the areas that your child is expected to know. It is an excellent idea to work through the book along with your younger child, so that he or she doesn't become intimidated by these higher level questions that should be skipped. Go online to see the suggested schedule.

A SHORT WORD ON ADMISSIONS

Be an Informed Parent
For the most accurate information about their admissions policies, don't hesitate to call the schools to which your child may apply.

The most important insight into secondary school admissions that we can offer is that a student's score on the SSAT or the ISEE is only one of many components involved in the admissions decision. While many schools will request SSAT or ISEE scores, all will look seriously at your child's academic record. Think about it—which says more about a student: a single test or years of solid academic performance?

In terms of testing, which is the focus of this book, some schools will specify which test they want applicants to take—the SSAT or ISEE. Others will allow you to use scores from either test. If you are faced with a decision of whether to focus on the SSAT, the ISEE, or both, we encourage you to be an informed consumer. This book contains practice tests for the ISEE and the SSAT, and your child should take both. Then, based on the requirements of your desired school and the results of the practice tests, you can decide which test best suits your child. The ISEE can be taken only once every six months, and the SSAT can be taken multiple times.

There are some differences in subject matter. The SSAT, for example, contains a section on analogies, which many students find difficult; the ISEE includes a section of sentence completions. On the other hand, Middle and Upper Level ISEE test takers will be faced with a number of quantitative comparison questions in the

Math section, and these can be tricky at first, especially for younger students.

Resources

SSAT

Secondary School Admission Test Board (SSATB)
609-683-4440
www.ssat.org
info@ssat.org

ISEE

Educational Records Bureau (ERB)
800-446-0320
www.erblearn.org
iseeoperations@erblearn.org

REGISTERING FOR THE SSAT

Before you go any further in preparing for the SSAT, you must complete one essential step: **Sign up for the SSAT**. The test is administered about eight times every year—generally in October, November, December, January, February, March, April, and June. Once you decide which test date you prefer, we encourage you to register as soon as possible. Testing sites can fill up; by registering early, you will avoid the possibility of having to take the test at an inconvenient or unfamiliar second-choice location. You can register online at www.ssat.org, or call the SSATB at 609-683-4440 to receive a registration form by mail.

The regular registration deadline for the test (at U.S. testing centers) is usually three weeks before the test date. You may return the registration form by mail along with the $127 registration fee ($80 for the Elementary Level test) for test centers in the United States and Canada (or $247 for international test centers), or you may submit your registration form by fax. If you register online, you can pay the fee with a credit card. In some cases, you may be able to obtain an SSAT fee waiver.

If you forget to register for the test or decide to take the SSAT at the last minute, there is a late registration deadline and, if it is within two weeks of the test date, a rush registration deadline (for U.S. testing centers). If you still have at least two weeks, you can register online late and pay an additional $45 late registration fee. After that point, it's an $85 rush registration fee.

Students who need special testing accommodations must apply for accommodations at least two weeks before the test. Sunday testing is available, but only for those students who are unable to take a Saturday test for religious reasons. There is no online registration or standby testing option for Sunday administrations.

Plan Ahead
Early registration will not only give you one less thing to worry about as the test approaches, but it will also help you get your first-choice test center.

REGISTERING FOR THE ISEE

Before you go any further in preparing for the ISEE, you must do one essential thing: **Sign up for the ISEE.** Your first step should be to get a copy of the most recent ISEE Student Guide, which comes from the Educational Records Bureau (ERB), the organization that writes and administers the ISEE. This publication is available directly from ERB (call 800-989-3721 or download it from the ERB website at www.erblearn.org) or from the schools to which you are applying. The test is administered on a regular basis, but test dates differ from one city to the next. The Student Guide lists all available test dates and test centers. The regular registration deadline for the test (at U.S. testing centers) is usually three weeks before the test date. The registration fee over the phone is $125, while the mail-in and online registration fees are $105. If you register online, you can use Visa, MasterCard, or American Express. If you miss the registration deadline, you may register up to two weeks before the test date for a $20 fee. You can also walk in and pay a $30 fee.

In locations where group testing is not readily available, it is possible to take the ISEE online at a Prometric testing center. The fee is $185.

A Student's Introduction

WHAT DO I DO WITH THIS BOOK?

You've got a hefty amount of paper and information in your hands. How can you work through it thoroughly, without spending eight hours on it the Saturday before the test?

Plan ahead.

Before you start, go online and download the study guide. We've broken down the contents of this book into 12 study sessions and suggested a timeline for you to follow. Some of these sessions will take longer than others, depending on your strengths and weaknesses. If any of them takes more than two hours, take a break and try to finish the session the following day. You may want to do one, two, or three sessions a week, but we suggest you give yourself at least a day or two in between each session to absorb the information you've just learned. The one thing you should be doing every day is quizzing yourself on vocabulary and making new flash cards.

If You Want to Start Early
If you have more than ten weeks to prepare, start with vocabulary building and essay writing. These skills only improve with time.

We also caution against thinking that you can work through this book during summer vacation, put it aside in September, and be ready to take the test in December. If you want to start that early, work primarily on vocabulary until about ten weeks before the test. Then you can start on techniques, and they'll be fresh in your mind on the day of the test. If you've finished your preparation too soon and have nothing to practice on in the weeks before the test, you're going to get rusty.

If you know you are significantly weaker in one of the subjects covered by the test, you should begin with that subject so you can practice it throughout your preparation.

At Each Session

At each practice session, make sure you have sharpened pencils, blank index cards, and a dictionary. Each chapter is interactive—all the drills can be found online; to fully understand the techniques we present, you need to be ready to try them out.

Get Your Pencil Moving
You'll get the most out of this book by trying out techniques as you read about them.

As you read each chapter, practice the techniques and do all the exercises. Check your answers in the Answer Key, which is also found online, as you do each set of problems, and try to figure out what types of errors you made to correct them. Review all of the techniques that give you trouble.

As you begin each session, review the chapter you completed during the previous session before moving on to a new chapter.

When You Take a Practice Test

We recommend some specific times to take practice tests in the following session outlines. Here are some guidelines for taking these tests.

- Time yourself strictly. Use a timer, watch, or stopwatch that will ring, and do not allow yourself to go over the allotted time for any section. If you try to do so on the real test, your scores will probably be canceled.
- Take a practice test in one sitting, allowing yourself breaks of no more than two minutes between sections. You need to build up your endurance for the real test, and you also need an accurate picture of how you will do.
- Always take a practice test using an answer sheet with bubbles to fill in, just as you will do for the real test. For the practice tests in this book, use the attached answer sheets. You need to be comfortable transferring answers to the separate sheet because you will be skipping around a bit.
- Each bubble you choose should be filled in thoroughly, and no other marks should be made in the answer area.
- As you fill in the bubble for a question, check to be sure you are on the correct number on the answer sheet. If you fill in the wrong bubble on the answer sheet, it won't matter if you've worked out the problem correctly in your test booklet. All that matters to the machine scoring your test is the No. 2 pencil mark.

The Day of the Exam

- Wake up refreshed from at least eight hours of sleep the night before.
- Eat a good breakfast.
- Arrive at the test center about a half hour early.
- Have with you all the necessary paperwork that shows you have registered for the test, four No. 2 pencils with erasers, and a working black pen. You may also want to bring juice or water and a small snack like a granola bar. The test center may not allow you to bring food or beverages into the room, but you can leave them in the hall, in case you have a chance to get them during a short break. Do not bring a cell phone or any books, papers, or calculators.
- Remind yourself that you do not have to work out every question on the test to get a good score. Don't let yourself become rushed. Pace yourself.

GENERAL TEST-TAKING TECHNIQUES FOR THE SSAT & ISEE

Pacing

Most people believe that to do well on a test, it is important to answer every question. While this is true of most of the tests you take in school, it is not true of many standardized tests, including the SSAT. On this test, it is very possible to score well without answering all of the questions; in fact, many students can improve their scores by answering fewer questions.

"Wait a second. I can get a better score by answering *fewer* questions?" Yes. You will be penalized only for the questions you answer incorrectly, not for the questions you skip. Because all of the questions are worth the same amount of points, it's just as good to get an easy question right as a hard one. So for the most part, you'll give your attention to problems you think you can answer, and decide which questions are too thorny to waste time on. This test-taking approach is just as important to score improvement as your knowledge of vocabulary and math rules!

In general, all math and verbal questions on the SSAT gradually increase in difficulty from first to last. (The one exception is the Reading section, where question difficulty is mixed.) This means that for most students, the longest and hardest problems are at the end of each section. For this reason, all students should focus the majority of their attention on the early easy and medium problems. Why rush through these and make careless errors, when you could spend time and get all of them right? Worry about the hard ones last—if you have time.

Points are not deducted for wrong answers on the Elementary Level test. Thus, do not leave any answers blank. Even so, pace yourself wisely to increase your accuracy on easy and medium questions.

The reason that this approach to pacing can actually *increase* scores is that skipped questions gain you zero points, whereas incorrect answers each reduce your raw score by a quarter-point. Because your raw score will decrease only if you answer a question incorrectly, skipping is the best strategy for a problem that has you completely stumped. Ideally, you will either get a question right or skip it (with some exceptions when you can guess intelligently and aggressively).

Skipping will be a major tool mostly for the hardest of questions. Guessing will be part of the whole test, so let's look at how guessing and skipping work together.

Guessing

When should you guess? Whenever you can eliminate even one wrong answer with certainty. Yes, really. We'll get to why in a minute. Eliminate four and you have the right answer by process of elimination. So eliminate the definitely wrong answers and guess! Be aggressive.

Over the course of the whole test, this strategy will increase your score. How? Well, let's look again at how SSAT questions are scored, right answers are rewarded, and wrong answers are penalized.

Correct answers: +1 point

Wrong answers: $-\dfrac{1}{4}$ point

Blank answers: 0 points

Suppose we asked you to place a bet on five flips of a coin. There's only one chance in five that it will come up heads, but if it does, you get a dollar. There's a four in five chance of tails; when it's tails, you pay us 25¢. Would you do it? Maybe yes, maybe no. If it came up heads once and tails four times, you'd get a dollar and then pay 25¢ four times, ending up with nothing. You wouldn't lose money, but you wouldn't win any, either. Similarly, there are five answer choices on every SSAT question, but only one right answer. So if you just guess randomly without eliminating anything first, you will be right about one time and wrong about four times for every five questions you do. That means that the one time you were right, you would get one full raw point (yay!), and you would lose a quarter-point four times (boo!). All of this would bring you right back to where you started.

$$1 - 4\left(\frac{1}{4}\right) = 0$$

So random guessing will pretty much keep your score flat. Here is where our guessing strategy comes in. What if, instead of a one-in-five chance of getting heads, the odds were one in four? This time, if four flips usually turned up one head ($1 for you) and three tails (pay out 75¢), you'd make a little money and come out on top. On an SSAT question, if you can eliminate one answer choice out of the five, you're in the same situation. You now have only four possible answers, and you will be right about once for every *three* times you are wrong. Now the penalty for wrong answers will have less impact. If you narrow it down to three choices, you'll get about one right for every two times you're wrong. Good odds? You bet. That's like making a dollar and losing 50¢. If you can do this throughout the test, you will gradually increase your score. That's why it pays to spend time eliminating the definitely wrong answers and then guessing aggressively.

$$1 - 3\left(\frac{1}{4}\right) = \frac{1}{4}$$

Want to use what you've just learned to improve your score? You've come to the right place. Guessing well is one of the most important skills this book can teach you. Strategic guessing and skipping, as simple as they seem, are very powerful score-boosters on standardized tests like the SSAT. Now, let's discuss one more major test-taking approach that should be a part of your game plan.

Process of Elimination

Here's a question you will not see on the SSAT, but which will show you how powerful Process of Elimination (POE) can be.

What is the capital of Malawi?

(A) New York
(B) Paris
(C) London
(D) Lilongwe
(E) Washington, D.C.

There are two ways to get this question right. First, you can know that the capital of Malawi is Lilongwe. If you do, good for you! The second is to know that the capital of Malawi is not New York, Paris, London, or Washington, D.C. You don't get more points for knowing the right answer from the start, so one way is just as good as the other. Try to get in the habit of looking at a question and asking, "What are the wrong answers?" instead of "What is the right answer?"

By using POE this way, you will eliminate wrong answers and have fewer answers from which to pick. The result is that you will pick right answers more often. In the example above, you're not even really guessing. You *know* that the other four answers are wrong, and that's as good as knowing the right answer. In fact, now you *do* know the capital of Malawi. That's the great thing about guessing on a standardized test like the SSAT—when you have trouble finding the correct answer, you can often eliminate the wrong ones and come out on top. Now let's look at the same idea in practice in another problem.

Which of the following cities is the capital of Samoa?

(A) Vila
(B) Boston
(C) Apia
(D) Chicago
(E) Los Angeles

You may not know the right answer off the top of your head, but which cities are not the capital of Samoa? You probably know enough about the locations of (B), (D), and (E) to know that Boston, Chicago, and Los Angeles are not the capital of Samoa.

So, what's a good answer to this question? (A) or (C).

What's the right answer? That is not the right question here. The better question is: Should I guess? And the answer is absolutely yes. Yes, yes, yes. You've done a great job of narrowing the answer down to just two choices. On any question where you've done this, you'll have a 50–50 chance. In other words, on average you'll get these questions right about half the time (+1 point) and wrong the other half $(-\frac{1}{4}$ point). Even though you'll get some (about half) of these wrong, your score will go up overall, by about 1 point for every 3 questions, and that can make all the difference. Always use POE and guess aggressively. Remember that you should skip the question if you can't eliminate anything at all.

A QUICK SUMMARY

These points about the SSAT are important enough that we want to mention them again. Make sure you understand them before you go any farther in this book.

- You do not have to answer every question on the test. Slow down!
- You will not immediately know the correct answer to every question. Instead, look for wrong answers that you can eliminate.
- Random guessing will not improve your score on the SSAT. However, educated guessing, which means that you eliminate two or (better) three of the five choices, is a good thing and will improve your score. As a general rule of thumb, if you invest enough time to read and think about the answer to a question, you should be able to eliminate at least one choice and make a good guess!

Part I
The Basics of
Both Tests

Chapter 1
Learning
Vocabulary

THE IMPORTANCE OF VOCABULARY

Both the ISEE and the SSAT test synonyms, and you need to know the tested words to get those questions right. While ISEE Sentence Completions and SSAT Analogies allow for a more strategic approach, the fact remains that knowing words is important to scoring points on these questions.

Having a strong vocabulary will also help you throughout your life: on other standardized tests, of course; in college; in your job; and when you read. Additionally, having a great vocabulary impresses people and makes you sound smarter.

Flash Cards
Making *effective* flash cards is important. We'll address how to do so shortly!

BUILDING A VOCABULARY

The best way to build a great vocabulary is to keep a dictionary and flash cards on hand and look up the new words you encounter. For each word you find, make a flash card, and review your flash cards frequently. We'll discuss effective ways of making flash cards shortly.

You will be more likely to encounter new words if you read a lot. Read newspapers, magazines, and books. If you think you don't like reading, you just haven't found the right material to read. Identify your interests—science, sports, current events, fantasy, you name it—and there will be plenty of material out there that you will look forward to reading.

Not sure what you should read? Ask a parent or favorite teacher. Below are just a few suggestions, but there are so many more.

Title	Area of Interest
Editorial and op-ed pages of *The Washington Post*, *The New York Times*, and *The Wall Street Journal*	News, politics, and economics
U.S. News and World Report	
The Economist	
The New Yorker	Culture and trends
Scientific American	Science
National Geographic (different editions for different age levels)	Science and environment
The Lord of the Rings by J.R.R. Tolkien	Fantasy and adventure
The Pillars of the Earth by Ken Follett	
The Adventures of Sherlock Holmes by Sir Arthur Conan Doyle	Mystery
Narrative of the Life of Frederick Douglass by Frederick Douglass	Autobiography
Out of Africa by Isak Dinesen	
2001: A Space Odyssey by Isaac Asimov	Science Fiction

You can also learn words through vocab-building websites, such as vocabulary.co.il or quizlet.com, which present drills in the form of addictive and rewarding games.

Finally, in the coming pages, you will find lists of words that you may see on the SSAT or ISEE, by level.

The vocabulary list in this chapter is for Upper Level. Lower, Elementary, and Middle Level vocabulary lists can be found online. But it's much more fun to learn words you might not know. Imagine how smart you'll sound!

Making Effective Flash Cards

Most people make flash cards by writing the word on one side and the definition on the other. That's fine as far as it goes, but you can do much better. An effective flash card will provide information that will help you remember the word. Different people learn words in different ways, and you should do what works best for you. Here are some ideas, along with a couple of examples.

Relating Words to Personal Experience

If the definition of a word reminds you of someone or something, write a sentence on the back of your flash card using the word and that person or thing. Suppose, for example, you have a friend named Scott who is very clumsy. Here's a flash card for a word you may not know:

Maladroit

Clumsy

Tripping over his own feet yet again, Scott is quite maladroit.

Relating Words to Roots

Many words are derived from Latin or Greek words. These words often have roots—parts of words—that have specified meanings. If you recognize the roots, you can figure out what the word probably means. Consider the word *benevolent*. It may not surprise you that "bene" means *good*; think *beneficial*. "Vol" comes from a word that means *wish* and also gives us the word *voluntary*. Thus *benevolent* describes someone who is good-hearted (good wish). Your flash card can mention the roots as well as the words *beneficial* and *voluntary* to help you remember how the roots relate to *benevolent*.

Often if you don't know the exact meaning of a word, you can make a good guess as to what the tone of the word is. For example, you may not know what "terse" means, but if a teacher said "My, you're being very terse today," you'd probably assume it meant something bad. Knowing the tone of words can be very helpful even if you can't remember the exact definition. As you go through your flash cards, you can separate them into three piles: positive, negative, and neutral. This will help you more rapidly recognize the tone of hard vocabulary.

Here are some roots that may show up in words on the SSAT or ISEE.

Root	Meaning	Example
ambi	both	ambidextrous
a/an/anti	not/against	amoral, antibiotics
anim	life	animated
auto	self	autograph
ben	good	beneficial
chron	time	chronology
cis/cise	cut/shorten	scissors, concise
cred	belief	credibility
de/dis	away from/not	deficient, dissent
equ	equal	equality, equate
fort	strength	fortress
gress	movement	progress
il/im/in	not	illegal, imperfect
laud	praise	applaud
loc/loq	speech	eloquent
mag/magna	great	magnify, magnificent
mal	bad	malicious
mis	wrong	mistake
ob	against	obstruct
pac	peace	pact, pacifier
path	feeling	sympathy, apathetic
phil/phile	love	philanthropy, bibliophile
ver	truth	verify
vit/viv	life	vital, revive

Other Methods

There are many other ways to remember words. If you are visually inclined, you might draw pictures to help you remember words. Others use mnemonics (a word that comes from a Greek word for memory), such as sound associations or acronyms (such as PEMDAS: Please Excuse My Dear Aunt Sally). Some people remember words if they speak the words and definitions out loud, in addition to writing flash cards. A great way to remember a word is to start using it in conversation. Ultimately, whatever works for you is the right approach!

Upper Level Vocabulary (SSAT and ISEE)

Includes Lower, Elementary, and Middle Level Vocabulary

Ab through An	An through Bl	Bl through Co
Abandon	Androgynous	Blunt
Abbreviation	Anguish	Bolster
Abdicate	Animosity	Bombastic
Abhor	Annex	Brandish
Abridge	Antagonistic	Brash
Abrupt	Antipathy	Brazen
Abundant	Anxious	Brittle
Abyss	Apprehension	Burgeon
Acclaimed	Approximate	Cache
Accord	Arbitrary	Callow
Acknowledge	Arid	Candid
Acrid	Ascertain	Capitulate
Acumen	Aspect	Capricious
Acute	Aspiration	Cascade
Adamant	Assail	Cater
Adapt	Assent	Cautious
Adept	Assert	Censor
Adhere	Assess	Chagrin
Adhesive	Assured	Chasm
Admire	Astonish	Chronic
Admonish	Attenuate	Chronicle
Adversary	Austere	Coalesce
Affiliation	Astute	Coerce
Agenda	Audible	Commodities
Aggrandize	Auspicious	Compassion
Aggravate	Authentic	Compel
Aggregate	Authoritative	Competent
Agile	Avarice	Composure
Ail	Banal	Comprehensive
Aimless	Barrage	Conceal
Akin	Barren	Concise
Alarmed	Barrier	Condemn
Allege	Bashful	Condescending
Aloof	Bastion	Condone
Alter	Bellicose	Confer
Altruism	Belligerent	Confine
Amalgamate	Bemoan	Conform
Ambiguous	Benevolent	Confound
Ambivalent	Benign	Congenial
Ameliorate	Bequest	Conjure
Amiable	Betray	Conniving
Amorphous	Bewilder	Consensus
Analyze	Biased	Conspicuous
Ancient	Blatant	Consume

Co through Di

Contemplation
Contented
Contradiction
Contrite
Controversial
Conventional
Copious
Cordial
Corpulent
Corrosion
Counsel
Counterfeit
Credible
Creed
Crucial
Cunning
Dawdle
Debate
Debt
Deceive
Decline
Decree
Defensive
Defiant
Deficient
Deft
Dejection
Deliberate
Delicate
Depict
Despair
Desolate
Detest
Detrimental
Deviate
Devotion
Dexterity
Dignity
Dilute
Differentiate
Disavow
Discreet
Disgraced
Dismayed

Di through Eu

Dispel
Disparage
Disperse
Display
Disputed
Dissect
Distasteful
Distort
Diversity
Docile
Domestic
Dominate
Dormant
Doubtful
Drastic
Dread
Drenched
Dubious
Duration
Eager
Economize
Egotist
Egress
Elegant
Elegy
Elongate
Eloquent
Embodiment
Embryonic
Emphasize
Endeavor
Enigma
Entrust
Envy
Ephemeral
Epitome
Equity
Equivalent
Eradicate
Erratic
Esoteric
Essential
Esteem
Euphemism

Ev through Fu

Evacuate
Evade
Evict
Exalt
Exasperate
Excavate
Excel
Exemplify
Exhilarating
Exile
Exquisite
Extend
Extent
Extinct
Extol
Extravagant
Facet
Fallacy
Fallow
Falter
Fathom
Fatigue
Feasible
Feeble
Feign
Feisty
Fickle
Flaccid
Flamboyant
Flatter
Fleeting
Flotsam
Flourish
Fluctuate
Foolhardy
Foreseen
Forge
Formulate
Fortunate
Foster
Fragile
Frank
Frugal
Fulcrum

Fu through In	In through Mo	Mo through Pe
Fundamental	Innovate	Molten
Furious	Inquiry	Moor
Furtive	Insight	Moral
Gap	Insinuate	Morose
Genial	Insipid	Muddled
Generous	Insolent	Mundane
Genuine	Integrity	Mystify
Germane	Intermission	Myth
Glean	Integrate	Nag
Glint	Intricate	Narcissism
Glutton	Inundate	Navigate
Graceful	Invoke	Negate
Gratified	Irate	Neglect
Grievances	Jeer	Noncommittal
Gullible	Jest	Nostalgic
Haphazard	Jubilant	Notorious
Hardship	Justify	Novel
Hasten	Keen	Novice
Haughty	Kinetic	Noxious
Hazard	Laudatory	Null
Hesitate	Lavish	Obfuscate
Hideous	Legacy	Obscure
Hinder	Lament	Obstacle
Hoard	Legend	Obstinate
Homely	Legitimate	Obstruct
Idiosyncrasy	Lenient	Obtuse
Ignoble	Liberate	Occupy
Illuminate	Limber	Ominous
Illustrate	Linger	Omit
Immaculate	Lofty	Opaque
Impasse	Loquacious	Optimistic
Imply	Lucrative	Opulent
Impulsive	Luminous	Ostentatious
Inane	Lure	Overbearing
Incident	Malicious	Overt
Incidental	Meager	Pacify
Incision	Meander	Pact
Incisive	Meddle	Palpable
Incite	Meek	Paltry
Indifferent	Menace	Paradigm
Indignant	Mentor	Parody
Infiltrate	Merge	Parsimonious
Ingenuity	Meticulous	Particle
Ingress	Mimic	Partisan
Inhabit	Mirage	Patron
Initial	Misery	Peak
Innate	Model (adjective)	Pedestrian (adj)
Innocuous	Modify	Permeate

Pe through Pl

Perpetuate
Perplexed
Persevere
Persist
Pragmatic
Precise
Precocious
Predicament
Prediction
Predominate
Prejudiced
Presume
Pretentious
Prevalent
Primary
Pristine
Prominent
Prone
Prophesy
Prototype
Provoke
Prudent
Pungent
Puny
Puzzled
Ratify
Ravenous
Raze
Recalcitrant
Reckless
Refute
Reject
Reluctant
Reminisce
Remote
Rendezvous
Renounce
Renown
Personify
Pervasive
Pessimistic
Petty
Pigment
Pilfer
Pinnacle
Pious
Placate
Plausible

Pl through Si

Plea
Plight
Plunder
Pompous
Porous
Qualm
Quiescent
Remonstrate
Replete
Replenish
Replica
Reprehensible
Repress
Reprimand
Reproach
Repudiate
Repugnant
Reservations
　(about something)
Residual
Resilience
Restore
Resume
Reticent
Reveal
Revere
Reverent
Robust
Rouse
Routine
Rue
Ruminate
Ruse
Rustic
Ruthless
Salvage
Satire
Savor
Sedate
Scant
Scarce
Scorn
Seclude
Seldom
Sequence
Shrewd
Simulate
Sincere

Si through Ut

Sinister
Solemn
Solitary
Somber
Soothe
Specific
Sporadic
Speck
Spirited
Spontaneous
Stagnate
Stature
Steadfast
Stoic
Stringent
Subside
Succinct
Sullied
Superb
Superfluous
Suppose
Surrogate
Tact
Tangible
Taper
Task
Taunt
Tenacious
Terse
Testify to
Thrive
Thwart
Timid
Tiresome
Toil
Torment
Tragedy
Trifle
Trite
Ultimate
Uncouth
Undermine
Underscore
Unique
Unruly
Uproot
Utilitarian
Utilize

Va through Vi	Vi through Wa	Wa through Ze
Vacillate	Vigilant	Wax (verb)
Vend	Vivacious	Weary
Veneration	Vivid	Wily
Versatile	Voracious	Wrath
Vetted	Vow	Writhe
Vibrant	Voyage	Zany
Viewpoint	Vulnerable	Zealous (or zeal)
Vigorous	Wane	

Chapter 2
Fundamental
Math Skills for
the SSAT & ISEE

INTRODUCTION

Whether you are taking the Lower Level ISEE or the Upper Level SSAT, there are some basic math skills that are at the heart of many of the questions on your test. For students taking the Lower or Elementary Level exams, the content in this section may be something you learned recently or are learning right now. You should go through this chapter very carefully and slowly. If you are having trouble understanding any of the content, you should ask your parents or teachers for help by having them explain it more thoroughly to you. For students taking the Middle and Upper Level tests, this chapter may serve more as a chance to review some things you have forgotten or that you need to practice a little. Even the most difficult questions on the Upper Level exams are built on testing your knowledge of these same skills. Make sure you read the explanations and do all of the drills before going on to either the SSAT or ISEE math chapter. Answers to these drills are provided in Chapter 3.

A Note to Lower, Elementary, and Middle Level Students

This section has been designed to give all students a comprehensive review of the math found on the tests. There are four sections: "The Building Blocks," "Algebra," "Geometry," and "Word Problems." At the beginnings and ends of some of these sections you will notice information about what material you should review and what material is only for Upper Level (UL) students. Be aware that you may not be familiar with all the topics on which you will be working. If you are having difficulty understanding a topic, bring this book to your teachers or parents and ask them for additional help.

Lose Your Calculator!

You will *not* be allowed to use a calculator on the SSAT or the ISEE. If you have developed a habit of reaching for your calculator whenever you need to add or multiply a couple of numbers, follow our advice: Put your calculator away now and take it out again after the test is behind you. Do your math homework assignments without it, and complete the practice sections of this book without it. Trust us, you'll be glad you did.

Write It Down

Write It Down; Get It Right! You don't get points for doing the math in your head, so don't do it!

Do not try to do math in your head. You are allowed to write in your test booklet. You *should* write in your test booklet. Even when you are adding just a few numbers together, write them down and do the work on paper. Writing things down not only helps to eliminate careless errors but also gives you something to refer back to if you need to double-check your work.

THE BUILDING BLOCKS

Math Vocabulary

Term	Definition	Examples
Integer	Any number that does not contain either a fraction or a decimal. Can be positive, negative, or zero.	14, 3, 0, –3
Whole number	Positive integers and zero	0, 1, 17
Positive number	Any number greater than zero	$\frac{1}{2}$, 1, 104.7
Negative number	Any number less than zero	$-\frac{1}{2}$, –1, –104.7
Even number	Any number that is evenly divisible by two. **Note:** Zero is an even number!	104, 16, 2, 0, –2, –104
Odd number	Any number that is not evenly divisible by two	115, 11, 1, –1, –11, –115
Prime number	Any number that is divisible by only 1 and itself. **Note:** One is **not** a prime number, but two **is**.	2, 3, 5, 7, 13, 131
Digit	The numbers from 0 through 9	0, 2, 3, 7. The number 237 has digits 2, 7, and 3.
Units (ones) digit	The digit in the ones place	For 281, 1 is in the units place.
Consecutive numbers	Any series of numbers listed in the order they appear on the number line	3, 4, 5 or –1, 0, 1, 2
Distinct numbers	Numbers that are different from one another	2, 7, and 19 are three distinct numbers; 4 and 4 are not distinct because they are the same number.
Divisible by	A number that can be evenly divided by another	12 is divisible by 1, 2, 3, 4, 6, 12.
Sum	The result of addition	The sum of 6 and 2 is 8 because 6 + 2 = 8.
Difference	The result of subtraction	The difference between 6 and 2 is 4 because 6 – 2 = 4.
Product	The result of multiplication	The product of 6 and 2 is 12 because 6 × 2 = 12.
Quotient	The result of division	The quotient when 6 is divided by 2 is 3 because 6 ÷ 2 = 3.
Remainder	The amount left over when dividing	17 ÷ 5 leaves a remainder of 2.
Factor	Any numbers or symbols that can be multiplied together to form a product	8 and 5 are factors of 40 because 8 × 5 = 40.

The Rules of Zero

Zero has some funny rules. Make sure you understand and remember these rules.

- Zero is neither positive nor negative.
- Zero is even.
- Zero is an integer.
- Zero multiplied by any number is zero.
- Zero divided by any number is zero.
- You cannot divide by zero ($9 \div 0 = undefined$).

The Times Table

Elementary Level
If you haven't learned the Times Table yet, this is a great opportunity to get ahead of your classmates!

Make sure you are comfortable with your multiplication tables up to 12. If you are having trouble with these, write some on flash cards. On one side of the card write down the multiplication problem, and on the other write down the answer. Now quiz yourself. You may also want to copy the table shown below so you can practice. For handy tips on using flash cards effectively, turn to the vocabulary chapter and read the section on flash cards.

	1	2	3	4	5	6	7	8	9	10	11	12
1	1	2	3	4	5	6	7	8	9	10	11	12
2	2	4	6	8	10	12	14	16	18	20	22	24
3	3	6	9	12	15	18	21	24	27	30	33	36
4	4	8	12	16	20	24	28	32	36	40	44	48
5	5	10	15	20	25	30	35	40	45	50	55	60
6	6	12	18	24	30	36	42	48	54	60	66	72
7	7	14	21	28	35	42	49	56	63	70	77	84
8	8	16	24	32	40	48	56	64	72	80	88	96
9	9	18	27	36	45	54	63	72	81	90	99	108
10	10	20	30	40	50	60	70	80	90	100	110	120
11	11	22	33	44	55	66	77	88	99	110	121	132
12	12	24	36	48	60	72	84	96	108	120	132	144

PRACTICE DRILL 1—MATH VOCABULARY

1. How many integers are there between –1 and 6 ? _____

2. List three consecutive odd integers. _____

3. How many odd integers are there between 1 and 9 ? _____

4. What is the tens digit in the number 182.09 ? _____

5. The product of any number and the smallest positive integer is:
   _____

6. What is the product of 5, 6, and 3 ? _____

7. What is the sum of 3, 11, and 16 ? _____

8. What is the difference between your answer to question 6 and your answer to question 7 ? _____

9. List three consecutive negative even integers: _____

10. Is 11 a prime number? _____

11. What is the sum of the digits in the number 5,647 ? _____

12. What is the remainder when 58 is divided by 13 ? _____

13. 55 is divisible by what numbers? _____

14. The sum of the digits in 589 is how much greater than the sum of the digits in 1,207 ? _____

15. Is 21 divisible by the remainder of 19 ÷ 5 ? _____

16. What are the prime factors of 156 ? _____

17. What is the sum of the odd prime factors of 156 ? _____

18. 12 multiplied by 3 is the same as 4 multiplied by what number?
    _____

19. What are the factors of 72 ? _____

20. How many factors of 72 are even? _____
    How many are odd? _____

When You Are Done
Check your answers in Chapter 3.

Working with Negative Numbers

It is helpful to think of numbers as having two component parts: the number itself and the sign in front of it (to the left of the number). Numbers that don't have signs immediately to the left of them are positive. So +7 can be, and usually is, written as 7.

Adding

If the signs to the left of the numbers are the same, you add the two numbers and keep the same sign. For example:

$$2 + 5 = (+2) + (+5) = +7 \text{ or just plain } 7$$

$$(-2) + (-5) = -7$$

If the signs to the left of the numbers are different, you subtract the numbers and the answer takes the sign of the larger number. For example:

$5 + (-2) = 5 - 2 = 3$, and because 5 is greater than 2, the answer is +3 or just plain 3.

$(-2) + 5 = 5 - 2 = 3$, and because 5 is greater than 2, the answer is +3 or just plain 3.

$(-5) + 2 = 5 - 2 = 3$, and because 5 is greater than 2, you use its sign and the answer is −3.

Subtracting—Middle and Upper Levels only

All subtraction problems can be converted to addition problems. This is because subtracting is the same as adding the opposite. "Huh?" you say—well, let's test this out on something simple that you already know. We know that $7 - 3 = 4$, so let's turn it into an addition problem and see if we get the same answer.

$$7 - 3 = (+7) - (+3)$$

Okay, so now we reverse only the operation sign and the sign of the number we are subtracting (the second number). The first number stays the same because that's our starting point.

$$(+7) + (-3)$$

Now use the rules for addition to solve this problem. Because the signs to the left are different, we subtract the two numbers $7 - 3 = 4$, and the sign is positive because 7 is greater than 3.

We have just proven that subtraction problems are really just the opposite of addition problems. Now let's see how this works in a variety of examples.

$3 - 7 = (+3) - (+7) = (+3) + (-7) = 7 - 3 = 4$ and, because 7 is greater than 3, the answer is -4.

$-9 - 3 = (-9) - (+3) = (-9) + (-3) = -12$

$13 - (-5) = (+13) - (-5) = (+13) + (+5) = +18$

$(-5) - (-8) = (-5) + (+8) = +3$

PRACTICE DRILL 2—ADDING AND SUBTRACTING NEGATIVE NUMBERS

1. $6 + (-14) =$

2. $13 - 27 =$

3. $(-17) + 13 =$

4. $12 - (-15) =$

5. $16 + 5 =$

6. $34 - (+30) =$

7. $(-7) + (-15) =$

8. $(-42) + 13 =$

9. $-13 - (-7) =$

10. $151 + (-61) =$

11. $(-42) - (-42) =$

12. $5 - (-24) =$

13. $14 + 10 =$

14. $(-5) + (-25) =$

15. $11 - 25 =$

When You Are Done
Check your answers in
Chapter 3.

Multiplying and Dividing

The rules for multiplying and dividing positive and negative integers are so much easier to learn and use than the rules for adding and subtracting them. You simply multiply or divide as normal, then determine the sign using the rules below.

Positive (÷ or ×) Positive   =   Positive

Negative (÷ or ×) Negative   =   Positive

Positive (÷ or ×) Negative   =   Negative

Negative (÷ or ×) Positive   =   Negative

Here are some examples.

$$6 \div 2 = 3 \qquad\qquad 2 \times 6 = 12$$

$$(-6) \div (-2) = 3 \qquad\qquad (-2) \times (-6) = 12$$

$$6 \div (-2) = -3 \qquad\qquad 2 \times (-6) = -12$$

$$(-6) \div 2 = -3 \qquad\qquad (-2) \times 6 = -12$$

If you are multiplying more than two numbers, simply work from left to right and deal with the numbers two at a time.

$$2 \times (-5) \times (-10) = 2 \times (-5) = -10 \text{ and now } (-10) \times (-10) = +100$$

Helpful Rule of Thumb
When multiplying numbers, simply count the number of negative signs. An even number of negative signs (−6 × −3) means that the product must be a positive number. An odd number of negative signs (2 × −5) means that the product must be negative.

PRACTICE DRILL 3—MULTIPLYING AND DIVIDING NEGATIVE NUMBERS

1. $20 \div (-5) =$

2. $(-12) \times 3 =$

3. $(-13) \times (-5) =$

4. $(-44) \div (-4) =$

5. $7 \times 9 =$

6. $(-65) \div 5 =$

7. $(-7) \times (-12) =$

8. $(-10) \div 2 =$

9. $81 \div 9 =$

10. $32 \div (-4) =$

11. $25 \times (-3) =$

12. $(-24) \times (-3) =$

13. $64 \div (-16) =$

14. $(-17) \times (-2) =$

15. $(-55) \div 5 =$

When You Are Done
Check your answers in Chapter 3.

ORDER OF OPERATIONS

How would you attack this problem?

$$16 - 45 \div (2 + 1)^2 \times 4 + 5 =$$

To solve a problem like this, you need to know which mathematical operation to do first. The way to remember the order of operations is to use PEMDAS.

$$
\begin{array}{l}
\text{Parentheses} \\
\text{Exponents} \\
\left.\begin{array}{l} \text{Multiplication} \\ \text{Division} \end{array}\right\} \\
\left.\begin{array}{l} \text{Addition} \\ \text{Subtraction} \end{array}\right\}
\end{array}
$$

Done at the same time from left to right { Multiplication / Division

Addition / Subtraction } **Done at the same time from left to right**

You can remember the order of operations by using the phrase below:

"Please Excuse My Dear Aunt Sally"

Now, let's give it a try.

$$16 - 45 \div (2 + 1)^2 \times 4 + 5 =$$

1. **Parentheses:**

$$16 - 45 \div \underline{(2 + 1)}^2 \times 4 + 5 =$$

$$16 - 45 \div (3)^2 \times 4 + 5 =$$

2. **Exponents:**

$$16 - 45 \div (3)^2 \times 4 + 5 =$$

$$16 - 45 \div 9 \times 4 + 5 =$$

3. **Multiplication and division (from left to right):**

    $16 - \underline{45 \div 9} \times 4 + 5 =$

    $16 - \underline{5 \times 4} + 5 =$

    $16 - 20 + 5 =$

4. **Addition and subtraction (from left to right):**

    $\underline{16 - 20} + 5 =$

    $-4 + 5 = \boxed{1}$

Just take it one step at a time and the math is easy!

PRACTICE DRILL 4—ORDER OF OPERATIONS

1. $10 - 3 + 2 =$

2. $15 + (7 - 3) - 3 =$

3. $3 \times 2 + 3 \div 3 =$

4. $2 \times (4 + 6)^2 \div 4 =$

5. $420 \div (10 + 5 \times 12) =$

6. $20 \times 5 \div 10 + 20 =$

7. $3 + 5 \times 10 \times (7 - 6) \div 2 - 4 =$

8. $10 \times (8 + 1) \times (3 + 1) \div (8 - 2) =$

9. $12 + (5 \times 2)^2 - 33 \div 3 =$

10. $200 - 150 \div 3 \times 2^3 =$

When You Are Done
Check your answers in Chapter 3.

Factors

Factors are all the numbers that divide evenly into your original number. For example, two is a factor of ten; it goes in five times. Three is not a factor of ten because ten divided by three does not produce an integer quotient (and therefore does not "go in evenly"). When asked to find the factors of a number, just make a list.

> The factors of 16 are
> > 1 and 16   (always start with 1 and the original number)
> > 2 and 8
> > 4 and 4
>
> The factors of 18 are
> > 1 and 18
> > 2 and 9
> > 3 and 6

Knowing some of the rules of divisibility can save you some time.

Larger Factors

There's an easy way to figure out if a number is divisible by larger numbers. Simply take the two smaller factors and check both. If a number is divisible by both 2 and 3, then it's divisible by 6.

A number is divisible by	If...
2	it ends in 0, 2, 4, 6, or 8
3	the sum of the digits is divisible by 3
4	the number formed by the last two digits is divisible by 4
5	it ends in 0 or 5
8	the number formed by the last three digits is divisible by 8
9	the sum of the digits is divisible by 9
10	it ends in 0

Factor Trees

To find the prime factors of a number, draw a factor tree.

Start by writing down the number and then drawing two branches from the number. Write down any pair of factors of that number. Now if one (or both) of the factors is not prime, draw another set of branches from that factor and write down a pair of factors for that number. Continue until you have only prime numbers at the end of your branches. Each branch end is a prime factor. Remember, 1 is NOT prime!

What are the distinct prime factors of 56? Well, let's start with the factor tree.

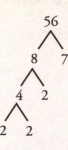

The prime factors of 56 are 2, 2, 2, and 7. Because the question asked for only the distinct prime factors, we have to eliminate the numbers that repeat, so we cross out two of the twos. The distinct prime factors of 56 are 2 and 7.

Multiples

Multiples are the results when you multiply your number by any integer. Fifteen is a multiple of five because five times three equals fifteen. Eighteen is a multiple of three, but not a multiple of five. Another way to think about multiples is to consider them "counting by a number."

The first seven positive multiples of 7 are:

$$
\begin{array}{ll}
7 & (7 \times 1) \\
14 & (7 \times 2) \\
21 & (7 \times 3) \\
28 & (7 \times 4) \\
35 & (7 \times 5) \\
42 & (7 \times 6) \\
49 & (7 \times 7)
\end{array}
$$

PRACTICE DRILL 5—FACTORS AND MULTIPLES

1. List the first five multiples of:

    2 _____

    4 _____

    5 _____

    11 _____

2. Is 15 divisible by 3 ?

3. Is 81 divisible by 3 ?

4. Is 77 divisible by 3 ?

5. Is 23 prime?

6. Is 123 divisible by 3 ?

7. Is 123 divisible by 9 ?

8. Is 250 divisible by 2 ?

9. Is 250 divisible by 5 ?

10. Is 250 divisible by 10 ?

11. Is 10 a multiple of 2 ?

12. Is 11 a multiple of 3 ?

13. Is 2 a multiple of 8 ?

14. Is 24 a multiple of 4 ?

15. Is 27 a multiple of 6 ?

16. Is 27 a multiple of 9 ?

17. How many numbers between 1 and 50 are multiples of 6 ?

18. How many even multiples of 3 are there between 1 and 50 ?

19. How many numbers between 1 and 100 are multiples of both 3 and 4 ?

20. What is the greatest multiple of 3 less than 50 ?

When You Are Done

Check your answers in Chapter 3.

Fractions

A fraction really just tells you to divide. For instance, $\frac{5}{8}$ actually means five divided by eight (which equals 0.625 as a decimal).

Another way to think of this is to imagine a pie cut into eight pieces. $\frac{5}{8}$ represents five of those eight pieces of pie.

The parts of a fraction are called the numerator and the denominator. The numerator is the number on top of the fraction. It refers to the portion of the pie, while the denominator is on the bottom of the fraction and tells you how many pieces there are in the entire pie.

$$\frac{numerator}{denominator} = \frac{part}{whole}$$

Reducing Fractions

Imagine a pie cut into two big pieces. You eat one of the pieces. That means that you have eaten $\frac{1}{2}$ of the pie. Now imagine the same pie cut into four pieces; you eat two. That's $\frac{2}{4}$ this time. But look: The two fractions are equivalent!

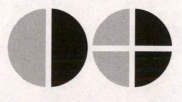

To reduce fractions, simply divide the top number and the bottom number by the same amount. Start out with small numbers like 2, 3, 5, or 10 and reduce again if you need to.

$$\frac{12}{24} \begin{array}{c} \div 2 \\ \div 2 \end{array} = \frac{6}{12} \begin{array}{c} \div 2 \\ \div 2 \end{array} = \frac{3}{6} \begin{array}{c} \div 3 \\ \div 3 \end{array} = \frac{1}{2}$$

In this example, if you happened to see that both 12 and 24 are divisible by 12, then you could have saved two steps. However, don't spend very much time looking for the largest number possible by which to reduce a fraction. Start out with a small number; doing one extra reduction doesn't take very much time and will definitely help prevent careless errors.

Remember!

As the denominator gets smaller, the fraction gets bigger. After all, would you rather have $\frac{1}{4}$ of a cake or $\frac{1}{2}$ of one?

PRACTICE DRILL 6—REDUCING FRACTIONS

1. $\dfrac{6}{8} =$

2. $\dfrac{12}{60} =$

3. $\dfrac{20}{30} =$

4. $\dfrac{36}{96} =$

5. $\dfrac{24}{32} =$

6. $\dfrac{16}{56} =$

7. $\dfrac{1,056}{1,056} =$

8. $\dfrac{154}{126} =$

When You Are Done

Check your answers in Chapter 3.

9. What does it mean when the number on top is larger than the one on the bottom?

Improper Fractions and Mixed Numbers

Changing from Improper Fractions to Mixed Numbers

If you knew the answer to number 9 in the last drill or if you looked it up, you now know that when the number on top is greater than the number on the bottom, the fraction is greater than 1. That makes sense, because we also know that a fraction bar is really just another way of telling us to divide. So, $\frac{10}{2}$ is the same as $10 \div 2$, which equals 5, and which is much greater than 1!

A fraction that has a greater numerator than denominator is called an *improper fraction*. You may be asked to change an improper fraction to a mixed number. A *mixed number* is an improper fraction that has been converted into a whole number and a proper fraction. To do this, let's use $\frac{10}{8}$ as the improper fraction that we are going to convert to a mixed number.

First, divide 10 by 8. This gives us our whole number. 8 goes into 10 once.

Now, take the remainder, 2, and put it over the original fraction's denominator: $\frac{2}{8}$.

So the mixed number is $1\frac{2}{8}$, or $1\frac{1}{4}$.

Elementary Level
You may not see this topic.

Put Away That Calculator!
Remember that a remainder is just the number left over after you do long division; it is not the decimal that a calculator gives you.

PRACTICE DRILL 7—CHANGING IMPROPER FRACTIONS TO MIXED NUMBERS

1. $\dfrac{45}{9}$

2. $\dfrac{72}{42}$

3. $\dfrac{16}{3}$

4. $\dfrac{5}{2}$

5. $\dfrac{8}{3}$

6. $\dfrac{62}{9}$

7. $\dfrac{15}{10}$

8. $\dfrac{22}{11}$

9. $\dfrac{83}{7}$

10. $\dfrac{63}{6}$

When You Are Done
Check your answers in
Chapter 3.

Changing from Mixed Numbers to Improper Fractions

It's important to know how to change a mixed number into an improper fraction because it is easier to add, subtract, multiply, or divide a fraction if there is no whole number in the way. To do this, multiply the denominator by the whole number and then add the result to the numerator. Then put this sum on top of the original denominator. For example:

$$1\frac{1}{2}$$

Multiply the denominator by the whole number: $2 \times 1 = 2$

Add this to the numerator: $2 + 1 = 3$

Put this result over the original denominator: $\frac{3}{2}$

$$1\frac{1}{2} = \frac{3}{2}$$

PRACTICE DRILL 8—CHANGING MIXED NUMBERS TO IMPROPER FRACTIONS

1. $6\dfrac{3}{7}$

2. $2\dfrac{5}{9}$

3. $23\dfrac{2}{3}$

4. $6\dfrac{2}{3}$

5. $7\dfrac{3}{8}$

6. $7\dfrac{2}{5}$

7. $10\dfrac{1}{16}$

8. $5\dfrac{12}{13}$

9. $4\dfrac{5}{9}$

10. $33\dfrac{21}{22}$

When You Are Done
Check your answers in Chapter 3.

Adding and Subtracting Fractions with a Common Denominator

To add or subtract fractions with a common denominator, just add or subtract the top numbers and leave the bottom numbers alone.

$$\frac{5}{7} + \frac{1}{7} = \frac{6}{7}$$

$$\frac{5}{7} - \frac{1}{7} = \frac{4}{7}$$

Adding and Subtracting Fractions When the Denominators Are Different

In the past, you have probably tried to find common denominators so that you could just add or subtract straight across. There is an easier way; it is called the *Bowtie*.

This diagram may make the Bowtie look complicated. It's not. There are three simple steps to adding and subtracting fractions.

Step 1: Multiply diagonally going up.
First **B** × **C**. Write the product next to **C**.
Then **D** × **A**. Write the product next to **A**.

Step 2: Multiply straight across the bottom, **B** × **D**.
Write the product as the denominator in your answer.

Step 3: To add, add the numbers written next to **A** and **C**.
Write the sum as the numerator in your answer.
To subtract, subtract the numbers written next to **A** and **C**. Write the difference as the numerator in your answer.

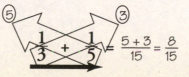

No More "Least Common Denominators"
Using the Bowtie to add and subtract fractions eliminates the need for the least common denominator, but you may need to reduce the result.

PRACTICE DRILL 9—ADDING AND SUBTRACTING FRACTIONS

1. $\dfrac{3}{8} + \dfrac{2}{3} =$

2. $\dfrac{1}{3} + \dfrac{3}{8} =$

3. $\dfrac{4}{7} + \dfrac{2}{7} =$

4. $\dfrac{3}{4} - \dfrac{2}{3} =$

5. $\dfrac{7}{9} + \dfrac{5}{4} =$

6. $\dfrac{2}{5} - \dfrac{3}{4} =$

7. $\dfrac{10}{12} + \dfrac{7}{2} =$

8. $\dfrac{17}{27} - \dfrac{11}{27} =$

9. $\dfrac{3}{20} + \dfrac{2}{3} =$

(Upper Level)

When You Are Done
Check your answers in Chapter 3.

10. $\dfrac{x}{3} + \dfrac{4x}{6} =$

11. $\dfrac{2x}{10} + \dfrac{x}{5} =$

12. $\dfrac{3y}{6} - \dfrac{y}{12} =$

Multiplying Fractions—Middle and Upper Levels only

Multiplying is the easiest thing to do with fractions. All you need to do is multiply straight across the tops and bottoms.

$$\frac{3}{7} \times \frac{4}{5} = \frac{3 \times 4}{7 \times 5} = \frac{12}{35}$$

Dividing Fractions—Middle and Upper Levels only

Dividing fractions is almost as simple as multiplying. You just have to flip the second fraction and then multiply.

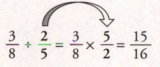

$$\frac{3}{8} \div \frac{2}{5} = \frac{3}{8} \times \frac{5}{2} = \frac{15}{16}$$

Dividing fractions is easy as pie; just flip the second fraction and multiply.

PRACTICE DRILL 10—MULTIPLYING AND DIVIDING FRACTIONS

1. $\dfrac{2}{3} \times \dfrac{1}{2} =$

2. $\dfrac{5}{8} \div \dfrac{1}{2} =$

3. $\dfrac{4}{5} \times \dfrac{3}{10} =$

4. $\dfrac{24}{15} \times \dfrac{10}{16} =$

5. $\dfrac{16}{25} \div \dfrac{4}{5} =$

Remember Reciprocals?

A reciprocal results when you flip a fraction—that is, exchange the numerator and the denominator. So the reciprocal of $\dfrac{2}{3}$ is what? Yep, that's right: $\dfrac{3}{2}$.

When You Are Done

Check your answers in Chapter 3.

Decimals

Remember, decimals and fractions are just two different ways of writing the same thing. To change a fraction into a decimal, you just divide the bottom number into the top number.

Be sure you know the names of all the decimal places. Here's a quick reminder.

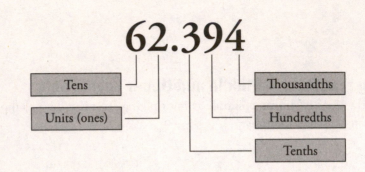

Adding Decimals

To add decimals, just line up the decimal places and add.

$$\begin{array}{r} 48.02 \\ +\underline{19.12} \\ 67.14 \end{array}$$

Subtracting Decimals

To subtract, do the same thing. Line up the decimal places and subtract.

$$\begin{array}{r} 67.14 \\ -\underline{48.02} \\ 19.12 \end{array}$$

Multiplying Decimals—Middle and Upper Levels only

To multiply decimals, first count the number of digits to the right of the decimal point in the numbers you are multiplying. Then, multiply and, on the product, count that same number of spaces from right to left—this is where you put the decimal point.

$$\begin{array}{r} 0.5 \\ \times\underline{4.2} \\ 2.10 \end{array}$$ (two digits to the right of the decimal point)

Dividing Decimals—Middle and Upper Levels only

To divide, move the decimal points in both numbers the same number of spaces to the right until you are working only with integers.

$$12.5 \div 0.25 = 0.25\overline{)12.5}$$

Now move both decimals over two places and solve the problem.

$$25\overline{)1250}^{50}$$

And you're done! Remember: you do not put the decimals back into the problem.

PRACTICE DRILL 11—DECIMALS

1. $1.43 + 17.27 =$

2. $2.49 + 1.7 =$

3. $7 - 2.038 =$

4. $4.25 \times 2.5 =$

5. $0.02 \times 0.90 =$

6. $180 \div 0.03 =$

7. $0.10 \div 0.02 =$

When You Are Done
Check your answers in Chapter 3.

Converting Fractions to Decimals and Back Again

From Fractions to Decimals

As we learned when we introduced fractions a little earlier, a fraction bar is really just a division sign.

$$\frac{10}{2} \text{ is the same as } 10 \div 2 \text{ or } 5$$

In the same sense:

$$\frac{1}{2} = 1 \div 2 \text{ or } 0.5$$

In fact, we can convert any fraction to its decimal equivalent by dividing the top number by the bottom number:

$$\frac{11}{2} = 11 \div 2 = 5.5$$

From Decimals to Fractions

To change a decimal to a fraction, look at the digit furthest to the right. Determine what place that digit is in (e.g., tenths, hundredths, and so on) and then put the decimal (without the decimal point) over that number (e.g., 10, 100, and so on). Let's change 0.5 into a fraction.

5 is in the tenths place so we put it over 10.

$$\frac{5}{10} \text{ reduces to } \frac{1}{2}$$

PRACTICE DRILL 12—FRACTIONS AS DECIMALS

Fill in the table below by converting the fractions to decimals and vice versa. The fractions and decimals in this table are those most often tested on the SSAT and ISEE, so memorize them now and save yourself time later.

Fraction	Decimal
$\frac{1}{2}$	0.5
$\frac{1}{3}$	
$\frac{2}{3}$	
	0.25
	0.75
$\frac{1}{5}$	
	0.4
	0.6
$\frac{4}{5}$	
	0.125

When You Are Done
Check your answers in Chapter 3.

Percents—Middle and Upper Levels only

Percentages are really just an extension of fractions. Let's go back to that pie we were talking about in the section on fractions. Let's say we had a pie that was cut into four equal pieces. If you ate one piece of the pie, then we could say that the *fractional part* of the pie that you have eaten is:

$$\frac{1}{4} \quad \frac{\text{(the number of pieces you ate)}}{\text{(the total number of pieces in the pie)}} \quad \frac{\text{part}}{\text{whole}}$$

Now let's find out what percentage of the pie you have eaten. Percent literally means "out of 100." When we find a percent, we are really trying to see how many times out of 100 something happens. To determine the percent, you simply take the fractional part and multiply it by 100.

$$\frac{1}{4} \times 100 = \frac{100}{4} = 25\%$$

You've probably seen percents as grades on your tests in school. What does it mean to get 100% on a test? It means you got every question correct. Let's say you got 25 questions right out of a total of 25. So we put the number of questions you got right over the total number of questions and multiply by 100.

$$\frac{25}{25} = 1 \quad 100 = 100\%$$

Let's says that your friend didn't do as well on this same test. He answered 20 questions correctly. Let's figure out the percentage of questions he got right.

$$\frac{20}{25} = \frac{4}{5} \quad 100 = 80\%$$

What percentage did he get wrong?

$$\frac{5}{25} = \frac{1}{5} = 20\%$$

Notice that the percentage of questions he got right (80%) plus the percentage of questions he got wrong (20%) equals 100%.

PRACTICE DRILL 13—PERCENTS

1. A bag of candies contains 15 butterscotches, 20 caramels, 5 pepper-
    mints, and 10 toffees.

    The butterscotches make up what percentage of the candies?_____

    The caramels?_____

    The peppermints?_____

    The toffees?_____

2. A student answered 75% of the questions on a test correctly and left
    7% of the questions blank. What percentage of the questions did the
    student answer incorrectly?_____

3. Stephanie's closet contains 40 pairs of shoes. She has 8 pairs of
    sneakers, 12 sets of sandals, 16 pairs of boots, and the rest are high
    heels.

    What percentage of the shoes are sneakers? _____

    Sandals?_____

    Boots?_____

    High heels?_____

    How many high heels does Stephanie own? _____

4. A recipe for fruit punch calls for 4 cups of apple juice, 2 cups of cran-
    berry juice, 3 cups of grape juice, and 1 cup of seltzer. What percent-
    age of the punch is juice?_____

5. Five friends are chipping in for a birthday gift for their teacher. David
    and Jakob each contribute $13. Stephanie, Kate, and Janice each
    contribute $8.

    What percentage of the total did the girls contribute?_____

    The boys?_____

When You Are Done
Check your answers in
Chapter 3.

More Percents—Middle and Upper Levels Only

Another place you may have encountered percents is at the shopping mall. Stores offer special discounts on their merchandise to entice shoppers to buy more stuff. Most of these stores discount their merchandise by a certain percentage. For example, you may see a $16 shirt that is marked 25% off the regular price. What does that mean?

Percents are not "real" numbers. In the above scenario, the shirt was not $25 less than the regular price (then they'd have to pay you money!), but 25% less. So how do we figure out how much that shirt really costs and how much money we are saving?

To find how much a percent really is in "real" numbers, you need to *first take the percent and change it to a fraction.*

Because percent means "out of 100," to change a percent to a fraction, simply put the percent over 100.

$$25\% = \frac{25}{100} = \frac{1}{4}$$

Now let's get back to that shirt. Multiply the regular price of the shirt, $16, by the fraction.

$$\$16 \times \frac{1}{4} = \$4$$

This means 25% of 16 is $4. You get $4 off the original price of the shirt. If you subtract that from the original price, you find that the new sale price is $12.

Guess what percentage the sale price is of the regular price? If you said 75 percent, you'd be right!

Tip: Changing a decimal to a percent is the same as changing a fraction to a percent. Multiply the decimal by 100 (move the decimal two spaces to the right). So 0.25 as a percent is 0.25 × 100 = 25%.

PRACTICE DRILL 14—MORE PERCENTS

Fill in the missing information in the table below.

Fraction	Decimal	Percent
$\dfrac{1}{2}$	0.5	50%
$\dfrac{1}{3}$		
	$0.6\overline{6}$	
		25%
	0.75	
$\dfrac{1}{5}$		
		40%
	0.6	
$\dfrac{4}{5}$		
		12.5%

1. 25% of 84 =

2. $33\dfrac{1}{3}$ % of 27 =

3. 20% of 75 =

Tip:
The word *of* in word problems means multiply!

4. 17% of 300 =

5. 16% of 10% of 500 =

6. A dress is marked down 15% from its regular price. If the regular price is $120, what is the sale price of the dress? The sale price is what percentage of the regular price of the dress?

7. Steve goes to school 80% of the 365 days of the year. How many days does Steve go to school?

8. Jennifer answered all 36 questions on her history test. If she got 25% of the questions wrong, how many questions did she get right?

When You Are Done
Check your answers in
Chapter 3.

9. During a special one-day sale, the price of a television was marked down 20% from its original price of $100. Later that day, the television was marked down an additional 10%. What was the final sale price?

Exponents—Middle and Upper Levels Only

Exponents are just another way to indicate multiplication. For instance, 3^2 simply means to multiply three by itself two times, so $3^2 = 3 \times 3 = 9$. Even higher exponents aren't very complicated. For example:

$$2^5 = 2 \times 2 \times 2 \times 2 \times 2 = 32$$

The questions on the SSAT don't generally use exponents higher than four or five, so this is likely to be as complicated as it gets.

**When in Doubt,
Write It Out!**
Don't try to compute
exponents in your head.
Write them out and
multiply!

The rule for exponents is simple: When in doubt, write it out! Don't try to figure out two times two times two times two times two in your head (just look at how silly it looks written down using words!). Instead, write it as a math problem and just work through it one step at a time.

What would you do if you were asked to solve this problem?

$$Q^3 \times Q^2 =$$

Let's look at this one carefully. Q^3 means $Q \times Q \times Q$ and Q^2 means $Q \times Q$. Put them together and you've got:

$$(Q \times Q \times Q) \times (Q \times Q) =$$

How many Q's is that? Count them. Five! The answer is Q^5. Be careful when multiplying exponents like this so that you don't get confused and multiply the actual exponents, which would give you Q^6. If you are ever unsure, don't spend a second worrying; just write out the exponent and count the number of things you are multiplying.

Square Roots

A square root is just the opposite of squaring a number. $2^2 = 2 \times 2$ or 4, so the square root of 4 is 2.

You will see square roots written this way on a test: $\sqrt{4}$.

PRACTICE DRILL 15—EXPONENTS AND SQUARE ROOTS

1. $2^3 =$

2. $2^4 =$

3. $3^3 =$

4. $4^3 =$

5. $\sqrt{81}$

6. $\sqrt{100}$

7. $\sqrt{49}$

8. $\sqrt{64}$

9. $\sqrt{9}$

When You Are Done
Check your answers in Chapter 3.

More Exponents—Upper Level Only

Multiplying and Dividing Exponents with the Same Base

You can multiply and divide exponents *with the same base* without having to expand out and calculate the value of each exponent. The bottom number, the one you are multiplying, is called the base. (However, note that to multiply $2^3 \times 5^2$ you must calculate the value of each exponent separately and then multiply the results.)

To multiply, add the exponents.

$$2^3 \times 2^4 = 2^7$$

To divide, subtract the exponents.

$$2^8 \div 2^5 = 2^3$$

To take an exponent to another power, multiply the exponents.

$$(2^3)^3 = 2^9$$

For exponents with the same base, remember MADSPM:
When you *Multiply* with exponents, *Add* them. When you *Divide* with exponents, *Subtract*. When you see *Powers* with exponents, *Multiply*.

PRACTICE DRILL 16—MORE EXPONENTS

1. $3^5 \times 3^3 =$

2. $7^2 \times 7^7 =$

3. $5^3 \times 5^4 =$

4. $15^{23} \div 15^{20} =$

5. $4^{13} \div 4^4 =$

6. $10^{10} \div 10^6 =$

7. $(5^3)^6 =$

8. $(8^{12})^3 =$

9. $(9^5)^5 =$

10. $(2^2)^{14} =$

When You Are Done
Check your answers in Chapter 3.

REVIEW DRILL 1—THE BUILDING BLOCKS

1. Is 1 a prime number?

2. How many factors does 100 have?

3. $-10 + (-20) =$

4. $100 + 50 \div 5 \times 4 =$

5. $\dfrac{3}{7} - \dfrac{1}{3} =$

6. $\dfrac{4}{5} \div \dfrac{5}{3} =$

7. $1.2 \times 3.4 =$

8. $\dfrac{x}{100} \times 30 = 6$

9. $1^5 =$

10. $\sqrt{16} =$

11. What are the first 10 perfect squares?

ALGEBRA

An Introduction

If you're a Lower Level, Elementary Level, or Middle Level student you may not yet have begun learning about algebra in school, but don't let that throw you. If you know how to add, subtract, multiply, and divide, you can solve an algebraic equation. Lower and Elementary Level students only need to understand the section below titled "Solving Simple Equations." Middle Level students should complete all of the "Solving Simple Equations" drills and as much of the Upper Level material as possible. Upper Level students need to go through the entire Algebra section carefully to make sure they can solve each of the question types.

Solving Simple Equations

Algebraic equations involve the same basic operations that we've dealt with throughout this chapter, but instead of using only numbers, these equations use a combination of numbers and letters. These letters are called *variables*. Here are some basic rules about working with variables that you need to understand.

- A variable (usually x, y, or z) replaces an unknown number in an algebraic equation.
- It is usually your job to figure out what that unknown number is.
- If a variable appears more than once in an equation, that variable is always replacing the same number.
- When a variable is directly to the right of a number, with no sign in between them, the operation that is holding them together is multiplication (e.g., $3y = 3 \times y$).
- You can add and subtract like variables (e.g., $2z + 5z = 7z$).
- You cannot add or subtract unlike variables (e.g., $2z$ and $3y$ cannot be combined).

To solve simple algebraic equations, you need to think abstractly about the equation. Let's try one.

$$2 + x = 7$$

What does x equal?

Well, what number plus 2 gives you 7? If you said 5, you were right and $x = 5$.

$$2y = 16$$

What does y equal?

Now you need to ask yourself what multiplied by 2 gives you 16. If you said 8, you were right! $y = 8$.

Tip: You can check to see if you found the right number for the variable by replacing the variable with the number you found in the equation. So in the last problem, if we replace y with 8 and rewrite the problem, we get $2 \times 8 = 16$. And that's true, so we got it right!

PRACTICE DRILL 17—SOLVING SIMPLE EQUATIONS

1.   If $35 - x = 23$, then $x =$

2.   If $y + 12 = 27$, then $y =$

3.   If $z - 7 = 21$, then $z =$

4.   If $5x = 25$, then $x =$

5.   If $18 \div x = 6$, then $x =$

6.   If $3x = 33$, then $x =$

7.   If $65 \div y = 13$, then $y =$

8.   If $14 = 17 - z$, then $z =$

9.   If $\frac{1}{2}y = 24$, then $y =$

10.   If $136 + z = 207$, then $z =$

11.   If $7x = 84$, then $x =$

12.   If $y \div 2 = 6$, then $y =$

13.   If $z \div 3 = 15$, then $z =$

14.   If $14 + x = 32$, then $x =$

15.   If $53 - y = 24$, then $y =$

When You Are Done

Check your answers in Chapter 3.

Note:
*   Lower and Elementary Level students should stop here. The next section you will work on is Geometry.
*   All Middle and Upper Level students should continue.

Manipulating an Equation—Middle and Upper Levels Only

To solve an equation, your goal is to isolate the variable, meaning that you want to get the variable on one side of the equation and everything else on the other side.

$$3x + 5 = 17$$

To solve this equation, follow these two steps.

Step 1: Move elements around using addition and subtraction. Get variables on one side and numbers on the other. Simplify.

Step 2: Divide both sides of the equation by the *coefficient*, the number in front of the variable. If that number is a fraction, multiply everything by the denominator.

For example:

$$3x + 5 = 17$$

$$\underline{-5 \quad -5} \qquad \text{Subtract 5 from both sides to get rid of the numbers on the left side.}$$

$$3x \quad = 12$$

$$\div 3 \qquad \div 3 \qquad \text{Divide both sides by 3 to get rid of the 3 on the left side.}$$

$$x \quad = \quad 4$$

Remember: Whatever you do to one side, you must also do to the other.

Equal Rights for Equations!
You can do anything you want to one side of the equation, as long as you make sure to do exactly the same thing to the other side.

PRACTICE DRILL 18—MANIPULATING AN EQUATION

1. If $8 = 11 - x$, then $x =$

2. If $4x = 20$, then $x =$

3. If $5x - 20 = 10$, then $x =$

4. If $4x + 3 = 31$, then $x =$

5. If $m + 5 = 3m - 3$, then $m =$

6. If $2.5x = 20$, then $x =$

7. If $0.2x + 2 = 3.6$, then $x =$

8. If $6 = 8x + 4$, then $x =$

9. If $3(x + y) = 21$, then $x + y =$

10. If $3x + 3y = 21$, then $x + y =$

When You Are Done
Check your answers in
Chapter 3.

11. If $100 - 5y = 65$, then $y =$

Manipulating Inequalities—Middle and Upper Levels Only

Manipulating an inequality is just like manipulating an equation that has an equal sign, except for one rule: If you multiply or divide by a negative number, flip the inequality sign.

Let's try an example.

$$-3x < 6$$

Divide both sides by -3 and then flip the inequality sign.

$$x > -2$$

Helpful Trick
Think of the inequality sign as an alligator, and the alligator always eats the bigger meal.

PRACTICE DRILL 19—MANIPULATING INEQUALITIES

Solve for x.

1. $4x > 16$

2. $13 - x > 15$

3. $15x - 20x < 25$

4. $12 + 2x > 24 - x$

5. $7 < -14 - 3x$

When You Are Done
Check your answers in Chapter 3.

Solving Percent Questions with Algebra—Middle and Upper Levels Only

Percentages

Learn a Foreign Language

"Percent language" is easy to learn because there are only four words you need to remember!

Solving percent problems is easy when you know how to translate them from "percent language" into "math language." Once you've done the translation, you guessed it—just manipulate the equation!

Whenever you see words from the following table, just translate them into math terms and go to work on the equation!

Percent Language	Math Language
% or "percent"	out of 100 ($\frac{x}{100}$)
of	times (as in multiplication) ($\times$)
what	your favorite variable (p)
is, are, were, was, did	equals ($=$)

"What percent" is represented by $\frac{x}{100}$.

For example:

$$24 \text{ is } 60 \text{ percent of what?}$$

$$24 = \frac{60}{100} \times m$$

PRACTICE DRILL 20—TRANSLATING AND SOLVING PERCENT QUESTIONS

1. 30 is what percent of 250 ?

2. What is 12% of 200 ?

3. What is 25% of 10% of 200 ?

4. 75% of 20% of what number is 12 ?

5. 16% of what number is 25% of 80 ?

6. What percent is equal to $\dfrac{3}{5}$?

7. 30 is what percent of 75 ?

8. What is 11% of 24 ?

9. What percent of 24 is equal to 48 ?

10. 60% of what percent of 500 is equal to 6 ?

When You Are Done
Check your answers in
Chapter 3.

GEOMETRY

An Introduction

Just as in the previous Algebra section, this Geometry section contains some material that is above the level tested on the Lower, Elementary, and Middle Level Exams. These students should not work on sections that are indicated for higher levels.

Perimeter

The perimeter is the distance around the outside of any figure. To find the perimeter of a figure, just add up the lengths of all the sides.

What are the perimeters of these figures?

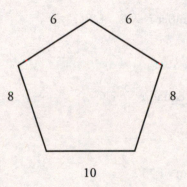

Perimeter = 6 + 6 + 8 + 8 + 10 = 38

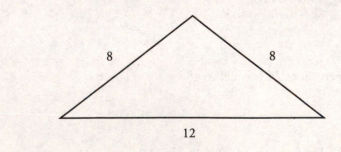

Perimeter = 8 + 8 + 12 = 28

Angles—Middle and Upper Levels Only

Straight Lines

Angles that form a straight line always total 180°.

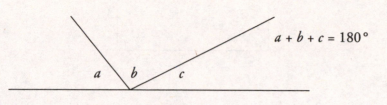

$$a + b + c = 180°$$

Triangles

All of the angles in a triangle add up to 180°.

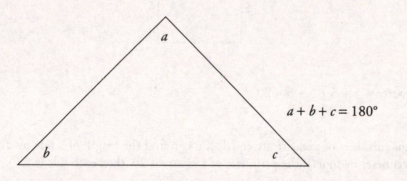

$$a + b + c = 180°$$

The Rule of 180°
There are 180° in a straight line and in a triangle.

Four-Sided Figures

The angles in a square, rectangle, or any other four-sided figure always add up to 360°.

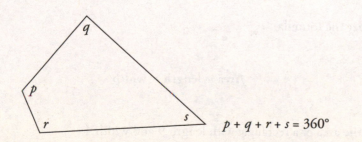

$$p + q + r + s = 360°$$

The Rule of 360°
There are 360° in a four-sided figure and in a circle.

Squares and Rectangles

A *rectangle* is a four-sided figure with four right (90°) angles. Opposite sides are equal in a rectangle. The perimeter is equal to the sum of the sides.

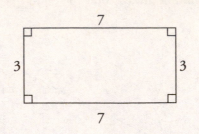

Perimeter
P = side + side + side...until you run out of sides.

Perimeter = 3 + 3 + 7 + 7 = 20

A *square* is a special type of rectangle where all the sides are equal.

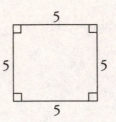

Perimeter = 5 + 5 + 5 + 5 = 20

Because all sides of a square are equal, you can find the length of a side by dividing its perimeter by four. If the perimeter of a square is 20, then each side is 5.

Area

Area is the amount of space taken up by a two-dimensional figure. An easy way to think about area is as the amount of paper that a figure covers. The larger the area, the more paper the figure takes up.

To determine the area of a square or rectangle, multiply the length by the width.

Area of a Rectangle
A = *lw*

Remember the formula:

$$\textbf{Area} = \textbf{length} \times \textbf{width}$$

What is the area of a rectangle with length 9 and width 4 ?

In this case the length is 9 and the width is 4, so 9 × 4 = 36. Now look at another example.

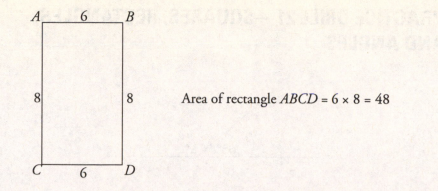

Area of rectangle $ABCD = 6 \times 8 = 48$

The area of squares and rectangles is given in *square feet, square inches,* and so on.

To find the area of a square you multiply two sides, and because the sides are equal, you're really finding the square of the sides. You can find the length of a side of a square by taking the square root of the area. So if a square has an area of 25, one side of the square is 5.

Area of a Square
$A = s^2$

Volume

Volume is very similar to area, except it takes into account a third dimension. To compute the volume of a figure, you simply find the area and multiply by a third dimension.

For instance, to find the volume of a rectangular object, you would multiply the length by the width (a.k.a. the area) by the height (the third dimension). Since a rectangular solid (like a box) is the only kind of figure you are likely to see in a volume question, simply use the formula below.

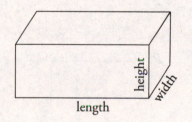

length × width × height = volume

For example:

> What is the volume of a rectangular fish tank with the following specifications?
> length: 6 inches
> height: 6 inches
> width: 10 inches

Volume of a Rectangular Solid
$V = lwh$

There isn't much to it. Just plug the numbers into the formula.

> length × width × height = volume
> $6 \times 10 \times 6 = 360$

PRACTICE DRILL 21—SQUARES, RECTANGLES, AND ANGLES

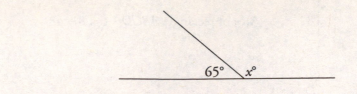

1. What is the value of x ?

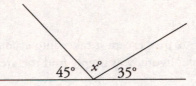

2. What is the value of x ?

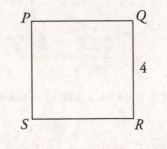

3. *PQRS* is a square. What is its perimeter? Area?

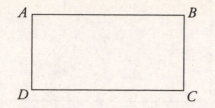

4. *ABCD* is a rectangle with length 7 and width 3. What is its perimeter? Area?

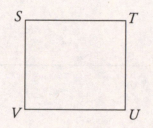

5. *STUV* is a square. Its perimeter is 12. What is its area?

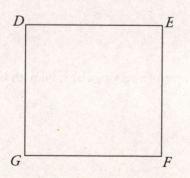

6. *DEFG* is a square. Its area is 81. What is its perimeter?

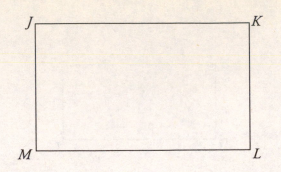

7. *JKLM* is a rectangle. If its width is 4, and its perimeter is 20, what is its area?

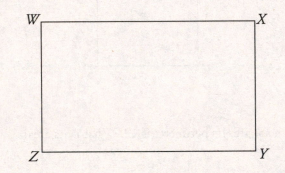

8. *WXYZ* is a rectangle. If its length is 6 and its area is 30, what is its perimeter?

When You Are Done
Check your answers in
Chapter 3.

9. What is the volume of a rectangular solid with height 3, width 4, and length 2 ?

Triangles

Isosceles Triangles

Any triangle with two equal sides is an isosceles triangle.

If two sides of a triangle are equal, the angles opposite those sides are always equal.

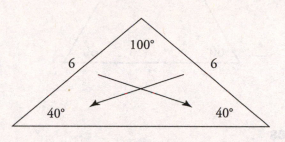

This particular isosceles triangle has two equal sides (of length 6) and therefore two equal angles (40° in this case).

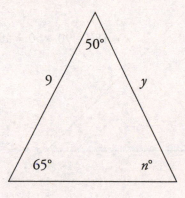

If you already know that the above triangle is isosceles, then you also know that *y* must equal one of the other sides and *n* must equal one of the other angles. If *n* = 65, then *y* must equal 9.

Equilateral Triangles

An equilateral triangle is a triangle with three equal sides. If all the sides are equal, then all the angles must be equal. Each angle in an equilateral triangle is 60°.

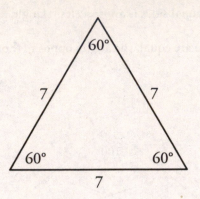

Right Triangles

A right triangle is a triangle with one 90° angle.

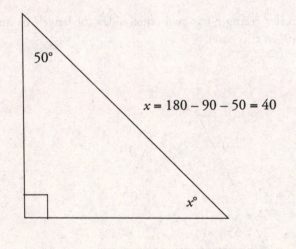

$$x = 180 - 90 - 50 = 40$$

This is a right triangle.
It is also an isosceles triangle.
What does that tell you?

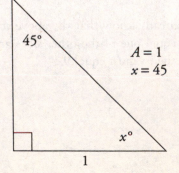

$$A = 1$$
$$x = 45$$

Area

To find the area of a triangle, you multiply $\frac{1}{2}$ times the length of the base times the length of the triangle's height, or $\frac{1}{2}b \times h$.

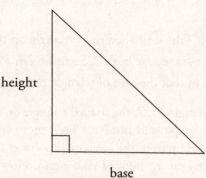

height

base

What is the area of a triangle with base 6 and height 3 ?

(A) 3
(B) 6
(C) 9
(D) 12
(E) 18

Just put the values you are given into the formula and do the math. That's all there is to it!

$$\frac{1}{2}b \times h = \text{area}$$

$$(\frac{1}{2})(6) \times 3 = \text{area}$$

$$3 \times 3 = 9$$

So, (C) is the correct answer.

The only tricky point you may run into when finding the area of a triangle is when the triangle is not a right triangle. In this case, it becomes slightly more difficult to find the height, which is easiest to think of as the distance to the point of the triangle from the base. Here's an illustration to help.

Elementary and Lower Levels
The test writers may give you the formula for area of a triangle, but memorizing it will still save you time!

Don't Forget!
$A = \frac{1}{2}bh$
Remember the base and the height must form a 90-degree angle.

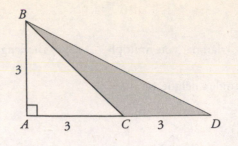

First look at triangle *BAC*, the unshaded right triangle on the left side. Finding its base and height is simple—they are both 3. So using our formula for the area of a triangle, we can figure out that the area of triangle *BAC* is $4\frac{1}{2}$.

Now let's think about triangle *BCD*, the shaded triangle on the right. It isn't a right triangle, so finding the height will involve a little more thought. Remember the question, though: How far up from the base is the point of triangle *BCD*? Think of the shaded triangle sitting on the floor of your room. How far up would its point stick up from the floor? Yes, 3! The height of triangle *BCD* is exactly the same as the height of triangle *BAC*. Don't worry about drawing lines inside the shaded triangle or anything like that, just figure out how high its point is from the ground.

Okay, so just to finish up, to find the base of triangle *BCD* (the shaded one) you will use the same area formula, and just plug in 3 for the base and 3 for the height.

$$\frac{1}{2}b \times h = \text{area}$$

$$(\frac{1}{2})(3) \times 3 = \text{area}$$

And once you do the math, you'll see that the area of triangle *BCD* is $4\frac{1}{2}$.

Not quite convinced? Let's look at the question a little differently. The base of the entire figure (triangle *DAB*) is 6, and the height is 3. Using your trusty area formula, you can determine that the area of triangle *DAB* is 9. You know the area of the unshaded triangle is $4\frac{1}{2}$, so what's left for the shaded part? You guessed it, $4\frac{1}{2}$.

Similar Triangles—Middle and Upper Levels Only

Similar triangles are triangles that have the same angles but sides of different lengths. The ratio of any two corresponding sides will be the same as the ratio of any other two corresponding sides. For example, a triangle with sides 3, 4, and 5 is similar to a triangle with sides of 6, 8, and 10, because the ratio of each of the corresponding sides (3:6, 4:8, and 5:10) can be reduced to 1:2.

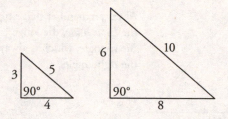

The easiest way to approach similar triangles questions that ask you for a missing side is to set up a ratio or proportion. For example, look at the question below:

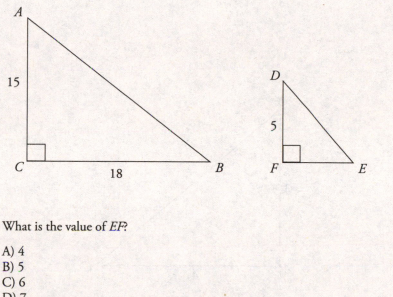

What is the value of *EF*?

A) 4
B) 5
C) 6
D) 7
E) 8

These triangles are similar because they have the same angles. To find side *EF*, you just need to set up a ratio or proportion.

$15/18 = 5/EF$

$15(EF) = 90$

$EF = 6$

Therefore, the answer is (C), 6.

The Pythagorean Theorem—Upper Level Only

For all right triangles, $a^2 + b^2 = c^2$, where a, b, and c are the lengths of the triangle's sides.

Try It!

Test your knowledge of triangles with the problems that follow. If the question describes a figure that isn't shown, make sure you draw the figure yourself!

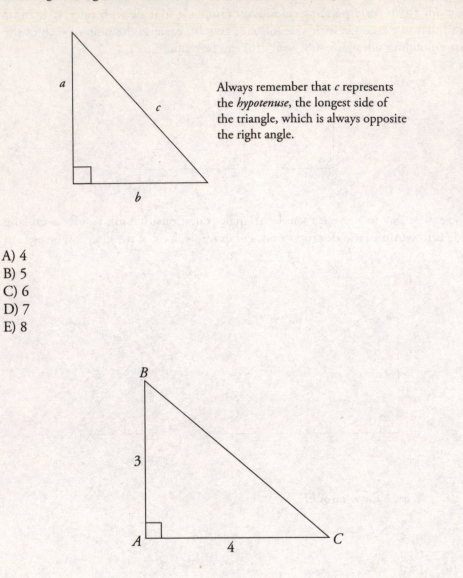

Always remember that c represents the *hypotenuse*, the longest side of the triangle, which is always opposite the right angle.

A) 4
B) 5
C) 6
D) 7
E) 8

1.   What is the length of side BC?

Just put the values you are given into the formula and do the math, remembering that line BC is the hypotenuse:

$a^2 + b^2 = c^2$
$3^2 + 4^2 = c^2$
$9 + 16 = c^2$
$25 = c^2$
$5 = c$

So, (B) is the correct answer.

PRACTICE DRILL 22—TRIANGLES

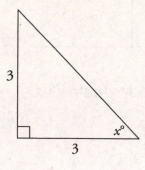

1.   What is the value of x ?

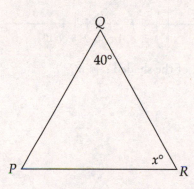

2.   Triangle PQR is an isosceles triangle. $PQ = QR$. What is the value of x ?

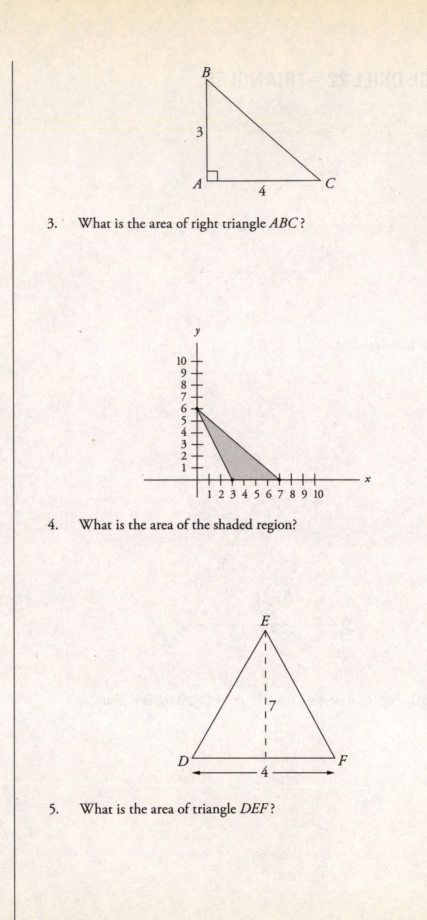

3. What is the area of right triangle *ABC*?

4. What is the area of the shaded region?

5. What is the area of triangle *DEF*?

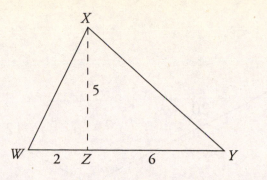

6. What is the area of triangle *WXZ*? Triangle *ZXY*? Triangle *WXY*?

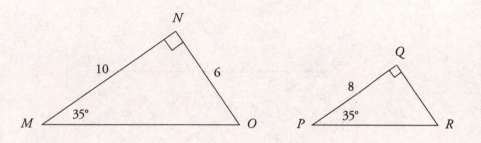

7. What is the length of line *QR*?

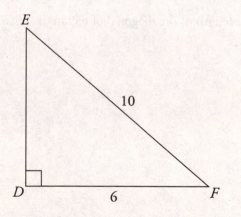

8. What is the length of side *DE*?

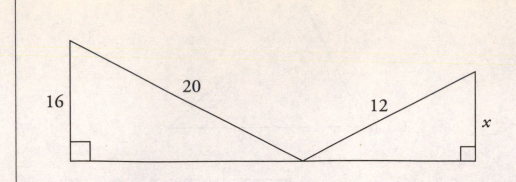

9.   What is the value of *x* ?

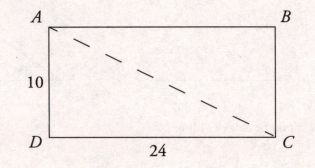

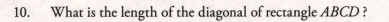

10.   What is the length of the diagonal of rectangle *ABCD* ?

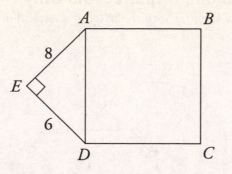

11.   What is the perimeter of square *ABCD* ?

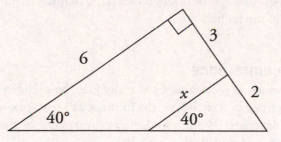

12.   What is the value of *x* ?

Note:
  •   Lower Level students should stop here. The next section you will
       work on is Word Problems.
  •   Middle and Upper Level students should continue.

When You Are Done
Check your answers in
Chapter 3.

Circles—Middle and Upper Levels Only

You are probably already familiar with the parts of a circle, but let's review them anyway.

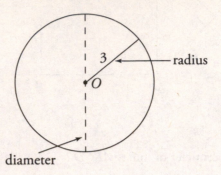

Any line drawn from the origin (the center of the circle) to its edge is called a **radius**.

Any line that passes through the origin is called the **diameter**. The diameter is two times the length of the radius.

Shorthand

Diameter: $d = 2r$

Circumference: $C = \pi d$

Area: $A = \pi r^2$

Area and Circumference

Circumference (which is written as C) is really just the perimeter of a circle. To find the circumference of a circle, use the formula $2\pi r$ (r stands for the radius) or πd (d stands for diameter). We can find the circumference of the circle above by taking its radius, 3, and multiplying it by 2π.

$C = 2\pi r$
$C = 2\pi 3$
$C = 6\pi$

The area of a circle is found by using the formula πr^2.

$A = \pi r^2$
$A = \pi 3^2$
$A = 9\pi$

You can find a circle's radius from its circumference by getting rid of π and dividing the number by 2. Or you can find the radius from a circle's area by getting rid of π and taking the square root of the number.

So if a circle has an area of 81π, its radius is 9. If a circle has a circumference of 16π, its radius is 8.

What's up with π?

The Greek letter π is spelled "pi" and pronounced "pie." It is a symbol used with circles. Written as a number, π is a nonrepeating, nonending decimal (3.1415927…). We use π to determine the true length of circles. However, on the ISEE and SSAT, we simply leave π as the Greek letter. So when figuring out area or circumference, make sure that you include π in your equation at the beginning and include it in every step of your work as you solve. Remember, π represents a number and it must always be included in either the area or circumference formula.

PRACTICE DRILL 23—CIRCLES

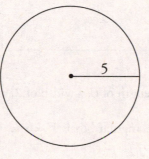

1. What is the circumference of the above circle? What is the area?

2. What is the area of a circle with radius 4 ?

3. What is the area of a circle with diameter 8 ?

4. What is the radius of a circle with area 9π ?

5. What is the diameter of a circle with area 9π ?

6. What is the circumference of a circle with area 25π ?

When You Are Done
Check your answers in Chapter 3.

3-D Shapes – Upper Level Only

Both the SSAT and ISEE Upper Level tests include 3-D shape geometry questions. While these question types tend to be few and far between, it is important you are prepared for them if they do come up.

Boxes

A three-dimensional box has three important lines: length, width, and height.

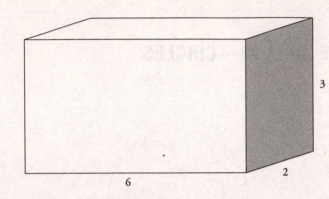

This rectangular box has a length of 6, a width of 2, and a height of 3.

The volume formula of a rectangular box is $V = lwh$.

$V = lwh$
$V = 6(2)(3)$
$V = 36$

Cubes

Cubes are just like rectangular boxes, except that all the sides are equal.

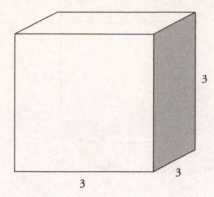

The volume formula for the cube is still just $V = lwh$, but since the length, width and height are all equal it can also be written as $V = s^3$, where s = sides.

$V = s^3$
$V = 3^3$
$V = 9$

Cylinders

Cylinders are like circles with height added. For a cylinder with a radius of r and a height of h, the volume formula is $V = \pi r^2 h$.

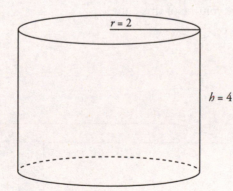

$V = \pi r^2 h$
$V = \pi 2^2 4$
$V = \pi 4(4)$
$V = 16\pi$

PRACTICE DRILL 24—3D SHAPES

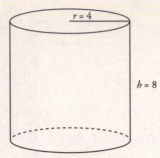

1. What is the volume of this cylinder?

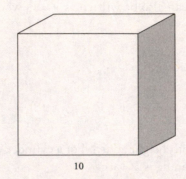

2. What is the volume of this cube?

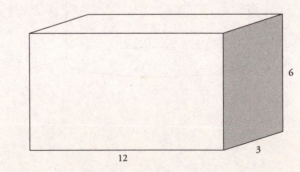

3. What is the volume of this rectangular box?

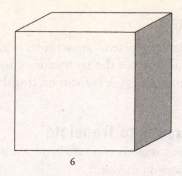

6

4.   A cube with a side length of 6 has 54 gallons poured into it. How many more gallons must be poured into the cube for it to be completely filled?

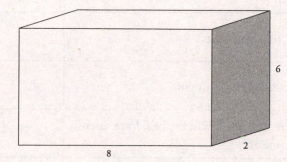

6

8   2

5.   The rectangular box pictured is filled by identical cubes with side lengths of 2. How many cubes does it take to fill the rectangular box?

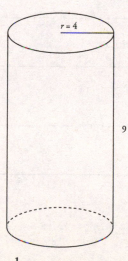

r = 4

9

6.   The cylinder pictured is $\frac{1}{3}$ full of grain. What is the volume of the grain in the cylinder?

When You Are Done
Check your answers in Chapter 3.

WORD PROBLEMS

Many arithmetic and algebra problems are written in paragraph form with many words. The hard part is usually not the arithmetic or the algebra; the hard part is translating the words into math. So let's focus on **translating**.

Key Words and Phrases to Translate

Specific words and phrases show up repeatedly in word problems. You should be familiar with all of the ones on this page.

What You Read in English	What You Do in Math
and, more than, the sum of, plus	+
less than, the difference between, take away from	−
of, the product of, as much as	×
goes into, divided by, the quotient	÷
is, are, was, were, the result will be, has, have, earns, equals, is the same as	=
what, what number, a certain number	variable (x, y, z)
half of a number	$\frac{1}{2}x$
twice as much as, twice as old as	$2x$
% (percent)	$\overline{}\,100$
how many times greater	divide the two numbers

Proportions

Proportions show relationships between two sets of information. For example, if you wanted to make cookies and you had a recipe for a dozen cookies but wanted to make two dozen cookies, you would have to double all of the ingredients. That's a proportion. Here's how we'd look at it in equation form.

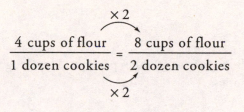

$$\frac{4 \text{ cups of flour}}{1 \text{ dozen cookies}} = \frac{8 \text{ cups of flour}}{2 \text{ dozen cookies}}$$

Whenever a question gives you one set of data and part of another set, it will ask you for the missing part of the second set of data. To find the missing information, set up the information in a fraction like the one shown above. Be careful to put the same information in the same place. In our example, we have flour on top and cookies on the bottom. Make sure both fractions have the flour over the cookies. Once we have our fraction set up, we can see what the relationship is between the two elements (in this case, flour and cookies). Whatever that relationship is, it's the same as the relationship between the other two things.

PRACTICE DRILL 25—WORD PROBLEMS

1. There are 32 ounces in 1 quart. 128 ounces equals how many quarts? How many ounces are there in 7 quarts?

2. A car travels at a rate of 50 miles per hour. How long will it take to travel 300 miles?

3. Betty is twice as old as her daughter Fiona. Fiona is twice as old as her dog Rufus. If Rufus is 11, how old is Betty?

4. A clothing store sold 1,250 pairs of socks this year. Last year, the store sold 250 pairs of socks. This year's sales are how many times greater than last year's sales?

5. There are 500 students at Eisenhower High School. $\frac{2}{5}$ of the total students are freshmen. $\frac{3}{5}$ of all the freshmen are girls. How many freshman girls are there?

When You Are Done
Check your answers in Chapter 3.

REVIEW DRILL 2 —THE BUILDING BLOCKS

1. If one-third of b is 15, then what is b ?

2. If $7x - 7 = 49$, then what is x ?

3. If $4(y - 5) = 20$, then what is y ?

4. $8x + 1 < 65$. Solve for x.

5. 16 is what percent of 10 ?

6. What percent of 32 is 24 ?

7. What is the area of a triangle with base 7 and height 6 ?

(Middle & Upper Levels)

8. What is the diameter of a circle with an area of 9π ?

9. What is the radius of a circle with a circumference 12π ?

10. What is the area of a circle with a diameter of 10 ?

When You Are Done
Check your answers in Chapter 3.

Chapter 3
Answer Key to Fundamental Math Drills

The Building Blocks

Practice Drill 1—Math Vocabulary

1. 6   0, 1, 2, 3, 4, 5

2. 1, 3, 5   Many sets of integers would answer this question correctly.

3. 3   3, 5, and 7

4. 8

5. That number   The smallest positive integer is 1, and any number times 1 is equal to itself.

6. 90 $5 \times 6 \times 3 = 90$

7. 30 $3 + 11 + 16 = 30$

8. 60 $90 - 30 = 60$

9. −2, −4, −6   2, 4, and 6 are consecutive integers and the question wants negative. Other sets of consecutive integers would also answer the question correctly.

10. Yes

11. 22 $5 + 6 + 4 + 7 = 22$

12. 6   13 goes into 58, 4 times. $4 \times 13 = 52$ and $58 - 52 = 6$.

13. 1, 5, 11, 55

14. 12 $5 + 8 + 9 = 22$ and $1 + 2 + 0 + 7 = 10$. $22 - 10 = 12$

15. No   The remainder of $19 \div 5$ is 4. And 21 is not divisible by 4.

16. 2, 2, 3, 13   Draw a factor tree.

17. 16 $3 + 13 = 16$

18. 9 $12 \times 3 = 36$ and $9 \times 4 = 36$.

19. 1, 2, 3, 4, 6, 8, 9, 12, 18, 24, 36, 72

20. There are 9 even factors and 3 odd factors.

Practice Drill 2—Adding and Subtracting Negative Numbers

1. –8
2. –14
3. –4
4. 27
5. 21
6. 4
7. –22
8. –29
9. –6
10. 90
11. 0
12. 29
13. 24
14. –30
15. –14

Practice Drill 3—Multiplying and Dividing Negative Numbers

1. –4
2. –36
3. 65
4. 11
5. 63
6. –13
7. 84
8. –5
9. 9
10. –8
11. –75
12. 72
13. –4
14. 34
15. –11

Practice Drill 4—Order of Operations

1. 9
2. 16
3. 7
4. 50
5. 6
6. 30
7. 24
8. 60
9. 101
10. –200

Practice Drill 5—Factors and Multiples

1. 2, 4, 6, 8, 10
   4, 8, 12, 16, 20
   5, 10, 15, 20, 25
   11, 22, 33, 44, 55
2. Yes
3. Yes
4. No
5. Yes
6. Yes   Use the divisibility rule for 3. 1 + 2 + 3 = 6 and 6 is divisible by 3.
7. No
8. Yes
9. Yes
10. Yes
11. Yes
12. No
13. No   2 is a factor of 8.
14. Yes
15. No
16. Yes
17. 8   6, 12, 18, 24, 30, 36, 42, 48
18. 8   Even multiples of 3 are really just multiples of 6.
19. 8   Multiples of both 3 and 4 are also multiples of 12. 12, 24, 36, 48, 60, 72, 84, 96
20. 48

Practice Drill 6—Reducing Fractions

1. $\dfrac{3}{4}$

2. $\dfrac{1}{5}$

3. $\dfrac{2}{3}$

4. $\dfrac{3}{8}$

5. $\dfrac{3}{4}$

6. $\dfrac{2}{7}$

7. 1

8. $\dfrac{11}{9}$

9. If the number on top is larger than the number on the bottom, the fraction is greater than 1.

Practice Drill 7—Changing Improper Fractions to Mixed Numbers

1. 5

2. $1\dfrac{5}{7}$

3. $5\dfrac{1}{3}$

4. $2\dfrac{1}{2}$

5. $2\dfrac{2}{3}$

6. $6\dfrac{8}{9}$

7. $1\dfrac{1}{2}$

8. 2

9. $11\dfrac{6}{7}$

10. $10\dfrac{1}{2}$

Practice Drill 8—Changing Mixed Numbers to Improper Fractions

1. $\dfrac{45}{7}$

2. $\dfrac{23}{9}$

3. $\dfrac{71}{3}$

4. $\dfrac{20}{3}$

5. $\dfrac{59}{8}$

6. $\dfrac{37}{5}$

7. $\dfrac{161}{16}$

8. $\dfrac{77}{13}$

9. $\dfrac{41}{9}$

10. $\dfrac{747}{22}$

Practice Drill 9—Adding and Subtracting Fractions

1. $1\dfrac{1}{24}$ or $\dfrac{25}{24}$

2. $\dfrac{17}{24}$

3. $\dfrac{6}{7}$ Did you use the Bowtie? You didn't need to because there was already a common denominator there!

4. $\dfrac{1}{12}$

5. $2\dfrac{1}{36}$ or $\dfrac{73}{36}$

6. $\dfrac{7}{20}$

7. $4\dfrac{1}{3}$ or $\dfrac{13}{3}$

8. $\dfrac{2}{9}$

9. $\dfrac{49}{60}$

10. $\dfrac{18x}{18} = x$

11. $\dfrac{20x}{50} = \dfrac{2x}{5}$

12. $\dfrac{30y}{72} = \dfrac{5y}{12}$

Practice Drill 10—Multiplying and Dividing Fractions

1. $\dfrac{1}{3}$

2. $1\dfrac{1}{4}$ or $\dfrac{5}{4}$

3. $\dfrac{6}{25}$

4. 1

5. $\dfrac{4}{5}$

Practice Drill 11—Decimals

1. 18.7
2. 4.19
3. 4.962
4. 10.625
5. 0.018
6. 6,000
7. 5

Practice Drill 12—Fractions as Decimals

Fraction	Decimal
$\dfrac{1}{2}$	0.5
$\dfrac{1}{3}$	$0.3\overline{3}$
$\dfrac{2}{3}$	$0.6\overline{6}$
$\dfrac{1}{4}$	0.25
$\dfrac{3}{4}$	0.75
$\dfrac{1}{5}$	0.2
$\dfrac{2}{5}$	0.4
$\dfrac{3}{5}$	0.6
$\dfrac{4}{5}$	0.8
$\dfrac{1}{8}$	0.125

Practice Drill 13—Percents

1. The butterscotches are 30% of the candy.
   The caramels are 40% of the candy.
   The peppermints are 10% of the candy.
   The toffees are 20% of the candy.

2. 18%   100% = 72% + 8% + percentage
   of questions answered incorrectly

3. The sneakers make up 20% of the shoes.
   The sandals make up 30% of the shoes.
   The boots make up 40% of the shoes.
   The high heels make up 10% of the shoes.
   There are 4 pairs of high heel shoes.

4. 90%   9 out of the 10 cups are juice.

5. The girls contributed 48%, and the boys
   contributed 52%.

Practice Drill 14—More Percents

Fraction	Decimal	Percent
$\frac{1}{2}$	0.5	50%
$\frac{1}{3}$	$0.3\overline{3}$	$33\frac{1}{3}\%$
$\frac{2}{3}$	$0.6\overline{6}$	$66\frac{2}{3}\%$
$\frac{1}{4}$	0.25	25%
$\frac{3}{4}$	0.75	75%
$\frac{1}{5}$	0.2	20%
$\frac{2}{5}$	0.4	40%
$\frac{3}{5}$	0.6	60%
$\frac{4}{5}$	0.8	80%
$\frac{1}{8}$	0.125	12.5%

1. 21
2. 9
3. 15
4. 51
5. 8
6. The sale price is $102 (15% of $120 = $18).
   The sale price is 85% of the regular price.
7. 292
8. 27
9. $72

Practice Drill 15—Exponents and Square Roots

1. 8
2. 16
3. 27
4. 64
5. 9
6. 10
7. 7
8. 8
9. 3

Practice Drill 16—More Exponents

1. 3^8
2. 7^9
3. 5^7
4. 15^3
5. 4^9
6. 10^4
7. 5^{18}
8. 8^{36}
9. 9^{25}
10. 2^{28}

Review Drill 1—The Building Blocks

1. No

2. 9   1, 2, 4, 5, 10, 20, 25, 50, 100

3. −30

4. 140

5. $\dfrac{2}{21}$

6. $\dfrac{12}{25}$

7. 4.08

8. 20 $\dfrac{6}{30} = \dfrac{1}{5} = \dfrac{20}{100}$

9. 1

10. 4

11. 1, 4, 9, 16, 25, 36, 49, 64, 81, 100

Algebra

Practice Drill 17—Solving Simple Equations

1. $x = 12$
2. $y = 15$
3. $z = 28$
4. $x = 5$
5. $x = 3$
6. $x = 11$
7. $y = 5$
8. $z = 3$
9. $y = 48$
10. $z = 71$
11. $x = 12$
12. $y = 12$
13. $z = 45$
14. $x = 18$
15. $y = 29$

Practice Drill 18—Manipulating an Equation

1. 3
2. 5
3. 6
4. 7
5. 4
6. 8
7. 8
8. $\dfrac{1}{4}$
9. 7
10. 7   Numbers 9 and 10 are really the same equation. Did you see it?
11. 7

Practice Drill 19—Manipulating an Inequality

1. $x > 4$
2. $x < -2$
3. $x > -5$
4. $x > 4$
5. $x < -7$

Practice Drill 20—Translating and Solving Percent Questions

1. 12%
2. 24
3. 5
4. 80
5. 125
6. 60%
7. 40%
8. 2.64 or $2\dfrac{16}{25}$ or $\dfrac{66}{25}$
9. 200%
10. 2

Geometry

Practice Drill 21—Squares, Rectangles, and Angles

1. 115°

2. 100°

3. The perimeter of *PQRS* is 16. Its area is also 16.

4. The perimeter of *ABCD* is 20. Its area is 21.

5. The area of *STUV* is 9. One side of the square is 3.

6. The perimeter of *DEFG* is 36. One side of the square is 9.

7. The area of *JKLM* is 24. The other side of the rectangle is 6.

8. The perimeter of *WXYZ* is 22. The other side of the rectangle is 5.

9. 24

Practice Drill 22—Triangles

1. 45°

2. 70°

3. 6

4. 12 — Some questions won't directly label the lengths of the sides, but that's only because that information can be found in a different way. (Every SSAT and ISEE problem, no matter how tricky, is solvable!) In this case, count the height and base of the triangle by counting off the ticks on the coordinate plane. The height is 6 and the base is 4, which means that the area ($A = 1/2bh$) is $A = (1/2)6 * 4 = (1/2)24 = 12$.

5. 14

6. *WXZ* = 5
   ZXY = 15
   WXY = 20

7. 4.8

8. *DE* = 8

9. 9.6

10. 26

11. 40

12. 2.4

Practice Drill 23—Circles

1. Circumference = 10π. Area = 25π.
2. 16π
3. 16π
4. 3
5. 6
6. 10π

Practice Drill 24—3D Shapes

1. 128π
2. 1000
3. 216
4. 162
5. 12
6. 48π

Word Problems

Practice Drill 25—Word Problems

1. 128 ounces = 4 quarts. There are 224 ounces in 7 quarts.
2. 6 hours
3. 44
4. 5
5. 120

Review Drill 2—Building Blocks

1. 45
2. 8
3. 10
4. $x < 8$
5. 160%
6. 75%
7. 21
8. 6
9. 6
10. 25π Be careful not to just fill in a familiar formula with the given numbers. The area formula for a circle is $A = \pi r^2$, but you aren't given r. Instead, you're given the diameter, d, and you must remember to first divide that number (10) by 2, which means that $r = 5$ and $A = 25\pi$.

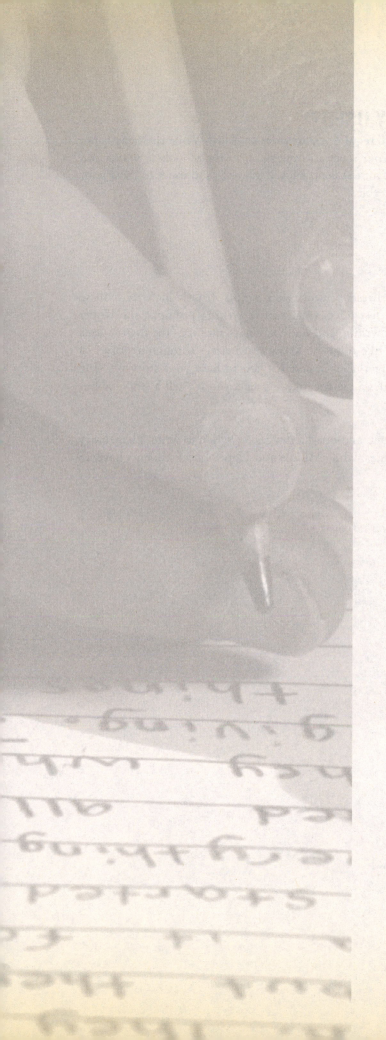

Chapter 4
Writing the Essay

HOW IS THE ESSAY USED?

Both the ISEE and the SSAT require you to write an essay. While the essay is not graded and does not affect your score, a copy is sent to the schools to which you apply. For this reason, you want to take the essay seriously and use it to show yourself to be thoughtful and likeable.

THE SSAT ESSAY

The Middle and Upper Level tests present two prompts, from which you will select one. The Middle Level test offers two creative writing prompts; the Upper Level test offers one creative writing and one essay style prompt. The instructions tell you that schools would like to get to know you better "through a story," so you should select the prompt that is easiest for you to base your story on. The Elementary Level test provides a picture and instructs you to "tell a story" about what happened.

In all cases, you have about one-and-one-half pages on which to write. Elementary Level students have 15 minutes, while Middle and Upper Level students have 25 minutes.

Here are sample prompts.

Elementary Level

Look at the picture and tell a story about what happened. Make sure your story includes a beginning, a middle, and an end.

Middle Level

Ⓐ I picked up the magazine and saw on the cover…

Ⓑ No one else was in the museum.

Upper Level

> (A)   Describe a mistake that you would correct if you could go back in time.

> (B)   Sometimes, the results are quite different from what you would expect.

THE ISEE ESSAY

All three ISEE tests ask you to "write an essay" on an assigned prompt. You have close to two pages on which to write. You have 30 minutes.

Here are sample prompts.

Lower Level

> **Who is your favorite teacher? Why have you chosen this person?**

Middle Level

> **If you could solve one problem in the world today, what would you choose and how would you solve the problem?**

Upper Level

> **Name someone you consider to be a success and describe what it is about that person that makes him or her successful.**

PLANNING AND WRITING YOUR ESSAY

When you read your ISEE prompt or decide upon your SSAT prompt, do not start writing immediately! It is important that you spend a few minutes thinking about what you want to say and how you will organize your thoughts. A planned essay reads much better than a rambling, free-association essay. Also, the time you spend organizing your thoughts will enable you to write your essay more quickly once you get started. You just need to follow your outline and express the ideas you have already developed.

For the SSAT, you are writing a story, which means you must include a beginning, middle, and end. So, your planning time will be used to decide what story you want to tell and how that story progresses. It does not really matter what your story topic is, as long as it responds to the chosen prompt and is delivered in an organized way. Of course, you don't want to be silly; your goal is to make the schools you are applying to like you. On the other hand, you don't have to write a work of creative fiction either. Your story can relate something you have done or seen. If you happen to be a natural storyteller, though, have at it!

For the ISEE, your essay will be a more traditional essay with an introduction, body paragraphs, and a conclusion. Your introduction will summarize the topic and explain your position, and your body paragraphs will include examples or reasons for your position. Thus, you want to spend your planning time deciding how you want to answer the prompt and what examples or reasons you will use to support your point of view. If you are used to using three examples in essays at school, there is no need for that here. You don't have the space or the time. Rather, having one or two well-developed examples or reasons will be fine.

For both tests, be sure to avoid spelling, grammar, and punctuation errors. It is easier to avoid these errors if you have planned your essay in advance. Also, write neatly; again, this is easier if you plan your essay before your write it. Be sure to clearly indent each new paragraph as well. It is a good idea to leave yourself a bit of time at the end to review what you have written, so you can check these issues.

You should write one or two practice essays and show them to a parent, teacher, or other adult who can give you feedback. Tell him or her that your goal is to provide an organized, thoughtful, and likeable reply to the prompt, with a minimum of spelling and grammar errors.

On the two pages that follow, write an essay using the prompt (or one of the two prompts for SSAT) above. Be sure to use the prompt for the test level (and test!) you are taking. After you have received feedback from someone, you can write another essay using the second set of prompts.

(Continued on next page)

Are you ready for another prompt?

Middle Level SSAT

Ⓐ   I heard the strange noise and quickly…

Ⓑ   The train pulled out of the station just as I got there.

Upper Level SSAT

Ⓐ   Give three reasons you admire your best friend.

Ⓑ   I couldn't believe she asked me for a favor.

Lower Level ISEE

> Describe something you wish you could change about the city or town in which you live.

Middle Level ISEE

> If you could spend one week anywhere in the world, where would you go? What would you do there?

Upper Level ISEE

> Describe a book or work of art that had an effect on you. What about it affected you?

_____

_____

_____

_____

_____

_____

_____

_____

_____

_____

_____

_____

_____

_____

_____

(Continued on next page)

Part II
The SSAT

Chapter 5
Everything You Always Wanted to Know About the SSAT

WHAT IS THE SSAT?

The Secondary School Admission Test (SSAT) is a standardized test made up of a writing sample, which is not scored but is sent along with each score report, and a series of multiple-choice questions. There are three different types of sections on the SSAT: Verbal, Reading, and Quantitative (Math). You will receive a score for each of these three section types. In addition, your score report will show an overall score, which is a combination of your verbal, reading, and quantitative scores. You will also receive a percentile score of between 1 percent and 99 percent that compares your test scores with those of other test takers from the previous three years.

What's on the SSAT?

The Verbal section of the SSAT tests your knowledge of vocabulary using two different question types: synonyms and analogies. There are no sentence completions on the SSAT. The Reading section tests your ability to read and understand short passages. These reading passages include both fiction (including poetry and folklore) and nonfiction. The Math sections test your knowledge of general mathematical concepts, including arithmetic, algebra, and geometry. There are no quantitative comparison questions on the Math sections of the SSAT.

Three Levels

There are three different versions of the SSAT. The Upper Level is taken by students applying to ninth grade or above. The Middle Level test (formerly called the Lower Level test) is taken by students applying to the sixth, seventh, or eighth grades. The new Elementary Level test is taken by students applying to the fourth or fifth grade.

For the Middle and Upper Levels, the test lasts about 155 minutes, with five different sections.

Writing Sample (ungraded)	1 essay topic	25 minutes
Quantitative	25 questions	30 minutes
Reading	40 questions	40 minutes
Verbal	60 questions	30 minutes
Quantitative (a second section)	25 questions	30 minutes

The Elementary Level test is about 110 minutes, including a 15-minute break, with four different sections.

Quantitative	30 questions	30 minutes
Verbal	30 questions	20 minutes
Reading	28 questions	30 minutes
Writing Sample (ungraded)	1 prompt	15 minutes

This book will focus mainly on the Upper and Middle Level tests, but look out for sidebars containing information about the Elementary Level test. In addition, a practice Elementary Level test is available online when you register this book. You can reference the "Register Your Book Online!" spread at the start of this book, located after the table of contents, for more detailed instructions on how to access that test.

One difference between the Upper and Middle Level tests is their scale. The Upper Level test gives a student four scaled scores ranging from 500 on the low end to 800 at the top. Scores on the Middle Level test range from 440 to 710 (704 for Quantitative). There are also some small differences in content; for instance, vocabulary on the Middle Level test is less challenging than it is on the Upper Level test. In Math, you will see similar general concepts tested (arithmetic, algebra, geometry, charts, and graphs) on both tests, but naturally, the Middle Level test will ask slightly easier questions than the Upper Level test. However, many of the questions are exactly the same on each level.

The scale on the Elementary Level test is 300–600.

As you work through the chapters and the online drills, you will notice that sets of practice problems do not distinguish between Upper and Middle Level questions. Instead, you will find practice sets that generally increase in difficulty as you move from earlier to later questions. Therefore, if you are taking the Middle Level test, don't worry if you have trouble with questions at the ends of the practice sets. **Students should stop each practice set at the point where they have reached vocabulary or math concepts with which they are unfamiliar.** This point will be different for every student.

Because the Middle Level SSAT tests fifth, sixth, and seventh graders, and the Upper Level SSAT tests eighth, ninth, tenth, and eleventh graders, there is content on the tests that students testing at the lower end of each of the groups will have difficulty answering. Younger students' scaled scores and percentiles will not be harmed by this fact. Both sets of scores take into consideration a student's age and gender. However, younger students may feel intimidated by this. **If you are at the lower end of your test's age group, there will be questions you are not supposed to be able to answer, and that's perfectly all right.**

Likewise, the material in this book follows the content of the two tests without breaking it down further into age groups or grades. Content that will appear only on the Upper Level test has been labeled as Upper Level only. Students taking the Middle Level test do not need to work on the Upper Level content. Additionally, younger students may not yet have seen some of the material included in the Middle Level review. Parents are advised to help these students with their work and to seek a teacher's advice or instruction if necessary.

Chapter 6
SSAT Math

INTRODUCTION

This section will provide you with a review of all the math that you need to know to do well on the SSAT. When you get started, you may feel that the material is too easy. Don't worry. The SSAT measures your basic math skills, so although you may feel a little frustrated reviewing things you have already learned, basic review is the best way to improve your score.

We recommend that you work through these math sections in order, reading each section and then doing each set of online drills. If you have trouble with one section, mark the page so you can come back later to go over it again. Keep in mind that you shouldn't breeze over pages or sections just because they look familiar. Take the time to read over all of the Math sections, so you'll be sure to know all the math you'll need!

Lose Your Calculator!

You will *not* be allowed to use a calculator on the SSAT. If you have developed a habit of reaching for your calculator whenever you need to add or multiply a couple of numbers, follow our advice: Put your calculator away now and take it out again after the test is behind you. Do your math homework assignments without it, and complete the practice sections in this book without it. Trust us, you'll be glad you did.

Write It Down

Do not try to do math in your head. You are allowed to write in your test booklet. You *should* write in your test booklet. Even when you are just adding a few numbers together, write them down and do the work on paper. Writing things down will not only help eliminate careless errors but also give you something to refer to if you need to check over your work.

One Pass, Two Pass

Within any Math section you will find three types of questions:

- Those you can answer easily without spending too much time
- Those that, if you had all the time in the world, you could do
- Some questions that you have absolutely no idea how to tackle

Don't Get Stuck

Make sure you don't spend too much time working on one tough question; there might be easier questions left in the section.

When you work on a Math section, start out with the first question. If you think you can do it without too much trouble, go ahead. If not, save it for later. Move on to the second question and decide whether or not to do that one. In general, the questions in each Math section are in a very rough order of difficulty. This means that earlier questions tend to be somewhat easier than later ones. You will likely find yourself answering more questions toward the beginning of the sections and leaving more questions blank toward the end.

Once you've made it all the way through the section, working slowly and carefully to do all the questions that come easily to you, go back and try some of the ones that you think you can do but will take a little longer. You should pace yourself so that time will run out while you're working on the second pass through the section. By working this way, you'll know that you answered all the questions that were easy for you. Using a two-pass system is a smart test-taking strategy.

Guesstimating

Sometimes accuracy is important. Sometimes it isn't.

Which of the following fractions is less than $\frac{1}{4}$?

(A) $\frac{4}{18}$

(B) $\frac{4}{12}$

(C) $\frac{7}{7}$

(D) $\frac{10}{9}$

(E) $\frac{12}{5}$

Before making any kind of calculation, think about this question. It asks you to find a fraction smaller than $\frac{1}{4}$. Even if you're not sure which one is actually smaller, you can certainly eliminate some wrong answers.

Start simple: $\frac{1}{4}$ is less than 1, right? Are there any fractions in the answer choices that are greater than 1? Get rid of (D) and (E).

Some Things Are Easier Than They Seem
Guesstimating, or finding approximate answers, can help you eliminate wrong answers and save lots of time.

Look at answer choice (C). $\frac{7}{7}$ equals 1. Can it be less than $\frac{1}{4}$? Eliminate (C). Already, without doing any math, you have a 50 percent chance of guessing the right answer.

Here's another good example.

A group of three men buys a one-dollar raffle ticket that wins $400. If the one dollar that they paid for the ticket is subtracted and the remainder of the prize money is divided equally among the men, how much will each man receive?

(A) $62.50
(B) $75.00
(C) $100.00
(D) $133.00
(E) $200.00

This isn't a terribly difficult question. To solve it mathematically, you would take $400, subtract $1, and then divide the remainder by three. But by using a little bit of logic, you don't have to do any of that.

The raffle ticket won $400. If there were four men, each one would have won about $100 (actually slightly less because the problem tells you to subtract the $1 price of the ticket, but you get the idea). So far so good?

However, there weren't four men; there were only three. This means fewer men among whom to divide the winnings, so each one should get more than $100, right? Look at the answer choices. Eliminate (A), (B), and (C).

Two choices left. Answer choice (E) is $200, half of the amount of the winning ticket. If there were three men, could each one get half? Unfortunately not. Eliminate (E). What's left? The right answer!

Guesstimating also works very well with some geometry questions, but just to give you something you can look forward to, we'll save that for the Geometry review.

WORKING WITH ANSWER CHOICES

In Chapter 2, Fundamental Math Skills for the SSAT & ISEE, we reviewed the concepts that will be tested on the SSAT tests. However, the questions in those practice drills were slightly different from the ones that you will see on your exam. Questions on test day are going to give you five answers to choose from. And as you'll soon see, there are many benefits to working with multiple-choice questions.

For one, if you really mess up calculating the question, chances are your answer choice will not be among the ones given. Now you have a chance to go back and try that problem again more carefully. Another benefit is that you may be able to use the information in the answer choices to help you solve the problems (don't worry; we'll tell you how soon).

We are now going to introduce to you the type of multiple-choice questions you will see on the SSAT. Each one of the following questions will test some skill that we covered in the Fundamental Math Skills chapter. If you don't see how to solve the question, take a look back at Chapter 2 for help.

Math Vocabulary

1. Which of the following is the greatest even integer less than 25 ?

    (A) 26
    (B) 24.5
    (C) 22
    (D) 21
    (E) 0

The first and most important thing you need to do on this—and every—problem is to read and understand the question. What important vocabulary words did you see in the question? There is "even" and "integer." You should always underline the important words in the questions. This way you will make sure to pay attention to them and avoid careless errors.

Now that we understand that the question is looking for an even integer, we can eliminate any answers that are not even or an integer. Cross out (B) and (D). We can also eliminate (A) because 26 is greater than 25 and we want a number less than 25. Now all we have to do is ask which is greater—0 or 22. (C) is the right answer.

> **A Tip About Answer Choices**
> Notice that the answer choices are often in numerical order.

Try it again.

Set A = {All multiples of 7}

Set B = {All odd numbers}

2. All of the following are members of both set A and set B above EXCEPT

   (A)   7
   (B) 21
   (C) 49
   (D) 59
   (E) 77

Did you underline the words *multiples of 7* and *odd*? Because all the answer choices are odd, you can't eliminate any that would not be in Set B, but only (D) is not a multiple of 7. So (D) is the right answer.

The Rules of Zero

Remember the Rules of Zero
Zero is even. It's neither positive nor negative, and anything multiplied by 0 = 0.

3. x, y, and z stand for three distinct numbers, where $xy = 0$ and $yz = 15$. Which of the following must be true?

   (A) $y = 0$
   (B) $x = 0$
   (C) $z = 0$
   (D) $xyz = 15$
   (E) It cannot be determined from the information above.

Because x times y is equal to zero, and x, y, and z are different numbers, we know that either x or y is equal to zero. If y was equal to zero, then y times z should also be equal to zero. Because it is not, we know that it must be x that equals zero. Answer choice (B) is correct.

The Multiplication Table

4. Which of the following is equal to $6 \times 5 \times 2$?

   (A) $60 \div 3$

   (B) 14×7

   (C) $2 \times 2 \times 15$

   (D) 12×10

   (E) $3 \times 3 \times 3 \times 9$

$6 \times 5 \times 2 = 60$ and so does $2 \times 2 \times 15$. Answer choice (C) is correct.

Working with Negative Numbers

5. $7 - 9$ is the same as

   (A) $7 - (-9)$

   (B) $9 - 7$

   (C) $7 + (-9)$

   (D) $-7 - 9$

   (E) $-9 - 7$

Remember that subtracting a number is the same as adding its opposite. Answer choice (C) is correct.

Order of Operations

6. $9 + 6 \div 2 \times 3 =$

   (A) 7

   (B) 9

   (C) 10

   (D) 13

   (E) 18

Remember your PEMDAS rules? When a problem has multiplication and division, proceed left to right; in this case division comes first. The correct answer is (E).

Don't Do More Work Than You Have To

When looking at answer choices, start with what's easy; only work through the hard ones when you have eliminated all of the others.

Factors and Multiples

Factors Are Small; Multiples Are Large
The factors of a number are always equal to or less than that number. The multiples of a number are always equal to or greater than that number. Be sure not to confuse the two!

7. What is the sum of the prime factors of 42 ?

  (A) 18
  (B) 13
  (C) 12
  (D) 10
  (E)   7

How do we find the prime factors? The best way is to draw a factor tree. Then we will see that the prime factors of 42 are 2, 3, and 7. Add them up and we get 12, answer choice (C).

Fractions

8. Which of the following is less than $\dfrac{4}{6}$?

  (A) $\dfrac{3}{5}$

  (B) $\dfrac{4}{6}$

  (C) $\dfrac{5}{7}$

  (D) $\dfrac{7}{8}$

  (E) $\dfrac{9}{7}$

When comparing fractions, you have three choices. You can find a common denominator and then compare the fractions (such as when you add or subtract fractions). You can also change the fractions to decimals. If you have memorized the fraction-to-decimal chart in Fundamentals (Chapter 2), you probably found the right answer without too much difficulty. It's answer choice (A). Or, if you remember the Bowtie method, you can compare answers that way too!

Percents

9. Thom's CD collection contains 15 jazz CDs, 45 rap albums, 30 funk CDs, and 60 pop albums. What percent of Thom's CD collection is funk?

   (A) 10%
   (B) 20%
   (C) 25%
   (D) 30%
   (E) 40%

First we need to find the fractional part that represents Thom's funk CDs. He has 30 out of a total of 150. We can reduce $\frac{30}{150}$ to $\frac{1}{5}$. As a percent, $\frac{1}{5}$ is 20%, answer choice (B).

Exponents

10. $2^6 =$

    (A) 2^3
    (B) 3^2
    (C) 4^2
    (D) 4^4
    (E) 8^2

Expand 2^6 out and we can multiply to find that it equals 64. Answer choice (E) is correct.

Square Roots

11. The square root of 75 falls between what two integers?

    (A) 5 and 6
    (B) 6 and 7
    (C) 7 and 8
    (D) 8 and 9
    (E) 9 and 10

If you have trouble with this one, try using the answer choices and work backward. As we discussed in Fundamentals (Chapter 2), a square root is just the opposite of squaring a number. So let's square the answer choices. Then we find that 75 falls between 8^2 (64) and 9^2 (81). Answer choice (D) is correct.

Elementary Level
You shouldn't expect to see exponents or roots on your tests.

Simple Algebraic Equations

12. $11x = 121$. What does $x = ?$

    (A)   2
    (B)   8
    (C)   10
    (D)   11
    (E)   12

Remember, if you get stuck, use the answer choices and work backward. Each one provides you with a possible value for x. Start with the middle answer choice and replace x with it. $11 \times 10 = 110$. That's too small. Now we know that not only is (C) incorrect, but also that (A) and (B) are incorrect because they are smaller than (C). The correct answer choice is (D).

The Case of the Mysteriously Missing Sign
If there is no operation sign between a number and a variable (letter), the operation is multiplication.

Solve for *X*

13. If $3y + 17 = 25 - y$, then $y =$

    (A)   1
    (B)   2
    (C)   3
    (D)   4
    (E)   5

Just as above, if you get stuck, use the answer choices. The correct answer is (B).

Percent Algebra

Percent
Percent means "out of 100," and the word *of* in a word problem tells you to multiply.

14. 25% of 30% of what is equal to 18 ?

    (A)   1
    (B)   36
    (C)   120
    (D)   240
    (E)   540

If you don't remember the math conversion table, look it up in Fundamentals (Chapter 2). You can also use the answer choices and work backward. Start with answer choice (C) and find out what 25% of 30% of 120 is (9). The correct answer is (D).

Geometry

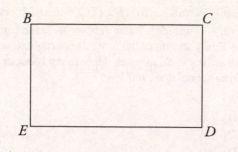

15. *BCDE* is a rectangle with a perimeter of 44. If the length of *BC* is 15, what is the area of *BCDE* ?

(A)   105
(B)   15
(C)   17
(D)   14
(E)   It cannot be determined.

From the perimeter, we can find that the sides of the rectangle are 7 and 15. So the area is 105, answer choice (A).

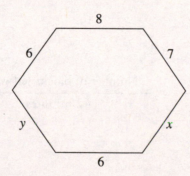

16. If the perimeter of this polygon is 37, what is the value of $x + y$?

(A)   5
(B)   9
(C)   10
(D)   16
(E)   20

The sum of x and y is equal to the perimeter of the polygon minus the lengths of the sides we know. Answer choice (C) is correct.

Word Problems

17. Emily is walking to school at a rate of 3 blocks every 14 minutes. When Jeff walks at the same rate as Emily and takes the most direct route to school, he arrives in 56 minutes. How many blocks away from school does Jeff live?

    (A) 3
    (B) 5
    (C) 6
    (D) 9
    (E) 12

This is a proportion question because we have two sets of data that we are comparing. Set up your fraction.

$$\frac{3 \text{ blocks}}{14 \text{ minutes}} = \frac{\text{Number of blocks Jeff walks}}{56 \text{ minutes}}$$

We know that we must do the same thing to the top and bottom of the first fraction to get the second fraction. Notice that the denominator of the second fraction (56) is 4 times the denominator of the first fraction (14). Therefore, the numerator of the second fraction must be 4 times the numerator of the first fraction (3).

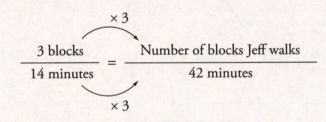

So Jeff walks 12 blocks in 56 minutes. Answer choice (E) is correct.

18. Half of the 30 students in Mrs. Whipple's first-grade class got sick on the bus on the way back from the zoo. Of these students, $\frac{2}{3}$ of them were sick because they ate too much cotton candy. The rest were sick because they sat next to the students who ate too much cotton candy. How many students were sick because they sat next to the wrong student?

    (A) 5
    (B) 10
    (C) 15
    (D) 20
    (E) 25

This is a really gooey fraction problem. Because we've seen the word *of* we know we have to multiply. First we need to multiply $\frac{1}{2}$ by 30, the number of students in the class. This gives us 15, the number of students who got sick. Now we have another *of* so we must multiply the fraction of students who ate too much cotton candy, $\frac{2}{3}$, by the number of students who got sick, 15. This gives us 10. So then the remainder, those who were unlucky in the seating plan, is 15 – 10 or 5, answer choice (A).

19. A piece of rope is 18 inches long. It is cut into 2 unequal pieces. The longer piece is twice as long as the shorter piece. How long, in inches, is the shorter piece?

    (A) 2
    (B) 6
    (C) 9
    (D) 12
    (E) 18

Again, if you are stuck for a place to start, go to the answer choices. Because we are looking for the length of the shorter rope, we can eliminate any answer choice that gives us a piece equal to or longer than half the rope. That gets rid of (C), (D), and (E). Now if we take one of the pieces, we can subtract it from the total length of the rope to get the length of the longer piece. For answer choice (B), if 6 is the length of the shorter piece, we can subtract that from 18 and know that the length of the longer piece must be 12. 12 is double 6, so we have the right answer.

As you're going through this chapter, don't forget about the online drills. As you do a lesson, make sure you do the corresponding drill.

HOW DID YOU DO?

That was a good sample of some of the kinds of questions you'll see on the SSAT. Now there are a few things to check other than your answers. Remember that taking the test involves much more than just getting answers right. It's also about guessing wisely, using your time well, and figuring out where you're likely to make mistakes. Once you've checked to see what you've gotten right and wrong, you should then consider the points that follow to improve your score.

Time and Pacing

How long did it take you to do the 15 questions? 15 minutes? It's okay if you went a minute or two over. However, if you finished very quickly (in fewer than 10 minutes) or slowly (more than 20 minutes), look at any problems that may have affected your speed. Which questions seriously slowed you down? Did you answer some quickly but not correctly? Your answers to these questions will help you plan which and how many questions to answer on the SSAT.

Question Recognition and Selection

Did you use your time wisely? Did you do the questions in an order that worked well for you? Which kinds of questions were the hardest for you? Remember that every question on the SSAT, whether easy or hard, is worth one point, and that you don't have to answer all the questions to get a good score. In fact, because of the guessing penalty, skipping questions can actually raise your score. So depending on your personal speed, you should concentrate most on getting as many easy and medium questions right as possible, and worry about harder problems later. Keep in mind that in Math sections, the questions generally go from easiest to hardest throughout. Getting the easy and medium questions right takes time, but you know you can solve them—so give yourself that time!

POE and Guessing

Did you actively look for wrong answers to eliminate, instead of just looking for the right answer? (You should.) Did you physically cross off wrong answers to keep track of your POE? Was there a pattern to when guessing worked (more often when you could eliminate one wrong answer, and less often when you picked simpler-looking over harder-looking answers)?

Be Careful

Did you work problems out on a separate piece of paper? Did you move too quickly or skip steps on problems you found easier? Did you always double-check what the question was asking? Often students miss questions that they know how to do! Why? It's simple—they work out problems in their heads or don't read carefully. Work out every SSAT math problem on the page. Consider it a double-check because your handwritten notes confirm what you've worked out in your head.

Ratios

A ratio is like a recipe. It tells you how much of each ingredient goes into a mixture.

For example:

To make punch, mix two parts grape juice with three parts orange juice.

This ratio tells you that for every two units of grape juice, you will need to add three units of orange juice. It doesn't matter what the units are; if you were working with ounces, you would mix two ounces of grape juice with three ounces of orange juice to get five ounces of punch. If you were working with gallons, you would mix two gallons of grape juice with three gallons of orange juice. How much punch would you have? Five gallons.

To work through a ratio question, first you need to organize the information you are given. Do this using the Ratio Box.

In a club with 35 members, the ratio of boys to girls is 3:2. To complete your Ratio Box, fill in the ratio at the top and the "real world" at the bottom.

	Boys	**Girls**	**Total**
Ratio	3	+ 2	= 5
Multiplier			
Real Value			35

Then look for a "magic number" that you can multiply by the ratio to get to the real world. In this case, the magic number is 7. That's all there is to it!

	Boys	**Girls**	**Total**
Ratio	3	+ 2	= 5
Multiplier	× 7	× 7	× 7
Real Value	21	14	35

Averages

There are three parts to every average problem: total, number, and average. Most SSAT problems will give you two of the three pieces and ask you to find the third. To help organize the information you are given, use the Average Pie.

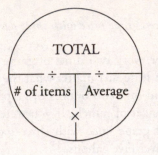

The Average Pie organizes all of your information visually. It is easy to see all of the relationships between the pieces of the pie.

- TOTAL = (*# of items*) × (*Average*)

- # of items = $\dfrac{Total}{Average}$

- Average = $\dfrac{Total}{\# \ of \ items}$

For example, if your friend went bowling and bowled three games, scoring 71, 90, and 100, here's how you would compute her average score using the Average Pie.

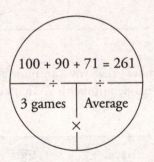

To find the average, you would simply write a fraction that represents $\dfrac{Total}{\# \ of \ items}$, in this case $\dfrac{261}{3}$.

The math becomes simple. 261 ÷ 3 = 87. Your friend bowled an average of 87.

Practice working with the Average Pie by using it to solve the following problems.

Percent Change—Upper Level Only

There is one special kind of percent question that shows up on the SSAT: percent change. This type of question asks you to find what percent something has increased or decreased. Instead of taking the part and dividing it by the whole, you will take the difference between the two numbers and divide it by the original number. Then, to turn the fraction to a percent, divide the numerator by the denominator and multiply by 100.

For example:

> The number of people who watched *Empire* last year was 3,600,000. This year, only 3,000,000 are watching the show. By approximately what percent has the audience decreased?

$$\frac{\text{The difference}}{\text{The original}} = \frac{600,000}{3,600,000} \quad \text{(The difference is } 3,600,000 - 3,000,000.\text{)}$$

The fraction reduces to $\frac{1}{6}$, and $\frac{1}{6}$ as a percent is 16%.

Plugging In

The SSAT will often ask you questions about real-life situations where the numbers have been replaced with variables. One of the easiest ways to tackle these questions is with a powerful technique called *Plugging In*.

> Mark is two inches taller than John, who is four inches shorter than Terry. If t represents Terry's height in inches, then in terms of t, an expression for Mark's height is
>
> (A) $t + 6$
> (B) $t + 4$
> (C) $t + 2$
> (D) t
> (E) $t - 2$

Take the Algebra Away, and Arithmetic Is All That's Left

When you Plug In for variables, you won't need to write equations and won't have to solve algebra problems. Doing simple arithmetic is always easier than doing algebra.

The problem with this question is that we're not used to thinking of people's heights in terms of variables. Have you ever met someone who was t inches tall?

Whenever you see variables used in the question and in the answer choices, just plug in a number to replace the variable.

1. Choose a number for t.
2. Using that number, figure out Mark's and John's heights.
3. Put a box around Mark's height because that's what the question asked you for.
4. Plug your number for t into the answer choices and choose the one that gives you the number you found for Mark's height.

Here's How It Works

Mark is two inches taller than John, who is four inches shorter than Terry. If t represents Terry's height in inches, then ~~in terms of t,~~ an expression for Mark's height is:

(A) $t + 6$
(B) $t + 4$
(C) $t + 2$
(D) t
(E) $t - 2$

> Cross this out! Because you are Plugging In, you don't need to pay any attention to "in terms of" any variable.

For Terry's height, let's pick 60 inches. This means that $r = 60$.

Remember, there is no right or wrong number to pick. 50 would work just as well.

But given that Terry is 60 inches tall, now we can figure out that, because John is four inches shorter than Terry, John's height must be $(60 - 4)$, or 56 inches.

The other piece of information we learn from the problem is that Mark is two inches taller than John. If John's height is 56 inches, that means Mark must be 58 inches tall.

Here's what we've got:

Terry   60 inches = t
John   56 inches
Mark   58 inches

Now, the question asks for Mark's height, which is 58 inches. The last step is to go through the answer choices substituting 60 for *t* and choose the one that equals 58.

(A)	$t + 6$	$60 + 6 = 66$	ELIMINATE
(B)	$t + 4$	$60 + 4 = 64$	ELIMINATE
(C)	$t + 2$	$60 + 2 = 62$	ELIMINATE
(D)	t	60	ELIMINATE
(E)	$t - 2$	$60 - 2 = 58$	PICK THIS ONE!

After reading this explanation, you may be tempted to say that Plugging In takes too long. Don't be fooled. The method itself is often faster and (more importantly) more accurate than regular algebra. Try it out. Practice. As you become more comfortable with Plugging In, you'll get even quicker and better results. You still need to know how to do algebra, but if you do only algebra, you may have difficulty improving your SSAT score. Plugging In gives you a way to break through whenever you are stuck. You'll find that having more than one way to solve SSAT math problems puts you at a real advantage.

Plugging In The Answers (PITA)

Plugging In The Answers is similar to Plugging In. When you have *variables* in the answer choices, you plug in. When you have *numbers* in the answer choices, you should generally plug in the answers. The only time this may get tricky is when you have a question that asks for a percent or fraction of some unknown number.

Plugging In The Answers works because on a multiple-choice test, the right answer is always one of the answer choices. On this type of question, you can't plug in any number you want because only one number will work. Instead, you can plug in numbers from the answer choices, one of which must be correct. Here's an example.

> Nicole baked a batch of cookies. She gave half to her friend Lisa and six to her mother. If she now has eight cookies left, how many did Nicole bake originally?
>
> (A)   8
> (B)   12
> (C)   20
> (D)   28
> (E)   32

See what we mean? It would be hard to just start making up numbers of cookies and hope that eventually you guessed correctly. However, the number of cookies that Nicole baked originally must be either 8, 12, 20, 28, or 32 (the five answer choices). So pick one—always start with (C)—and then work backward to determine whether you have the right choice.

Work on Plugging In The Answers with the online drills you've downloaded!

Let's start with (C): Nicole baked 20 cookies. Now work through the events listed in the question.

She had 20 cookies—from answer choice (C)—and she gave half to Lisa. That leaves Nicole with 10 cookies.

What next? She gives 6 to her mom. Now she's got 4 left.

Keep going. The problem says that Nicole now has 8 cookies left. But if she started with 20—answer choice (C)—she would only have 4 left. So is (C) the right answer? No.

No problem. Choose another answer choice and try again. Be smart about which answer choice you pick. When we used the number in (C), Nicole ended up with fewer cookies than we wanted her to have, didn't she? So the right answer must be a number larger than 20, the number we took from (C).

The good news is that the answer choices in most Plugging In The Answers questions go in order, so it is easy to pick the next larger or smaller number—you just pick either (B) or (D), depending on which direction you've decided to go.

Back to Nicole and her cookies. We need a number larger than 20. So let's go to answer choice (D)—28.

Nicole started out with 28 cookies. The first thing she did was give half, or 14, to Lisa. That left Nicole with 14 cookies.

Then she gave 6 cookies to her mother. 14 − 6 = 8. Nicole has 8 cookies left over. Keep going with the question. It says, "If she now has eight cookies left…" She has eight cookies left and, *voilà*—she's supposed to have 8 cookies left.

What does this mean? It means you've got the right answer! Pick (D) and move on.

If answer choice (D) had not worked, and you were still certain that you needed a number larger than answer choice (C), you also would be finished. Since you started with the middle answer choice (C), which didn't work, and then you tried the next larger choice, (D), which didn't work either, you could pick the only answer bigger than (C) that was left—in this case (E)—and be done.

This diagram helps illustrate the way you should move through the answer choices.

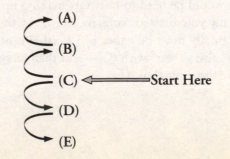

To wrap up, Plugging in the Answers should always go the following way:

1. **Start with answer choice (C).** This number is now what you are working with.
2. **Work the problem.** Go through the problem with that number, using information to help you determine if it is the correct answer.
3. **If (C) doesn't work, try another answer.** Remember to think logically about which answer choice you should check next.
4. **Once you find the correct answer, STOP.**

GEOMETRY

Guesstimating: A Second Look

Guesstimating worked well back in the introduction when we were just using it to estimate or "ballpark" the size of a number, but geometry problems are undoubtedly the best place to guesstimate whenever you can.

Let's try the next problem. Remember, unless a particular question tells you otherwise, you can safely assume that figures *are* drawn to scale.

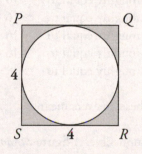

A circle is inscribed in square *PQRS*. What is the area of the shaded region?

(A) $16 - 6\pi$
(B) $16 - 4\pi$
(C) $16 - 3\pi$
(D) $16 - 2\pi$
(E) 16π

Elementary Level
This question is harder than what you will encounter, but it's a good idea to learn how guesstimating can help you!

Wow, a circle inscribed in a square—that sounds tough!

It isn't. Look at the picture. What fraction of the square looks like it is shaded? Half? Three-quarters? Less than half? In fact, about one-quarter of the area of the square is shaded. You've just done most of the work necessary to solve this problem.

Now, let's just do a little math. The length of one side of the square is 4, so the area of the square is 4×4 or 16.

So the area of the square is 16, and we said that the shaded region was about one-fourth of the square. One-fourth of 16 is 4, right? So we're looking for an answer choice that equals about 4. Let's look at the choices.

(A) $16 - 6\pi$
(B) $16 - 4\pi$
(C) $16 - 3\pi$
(D) $16 - 2\pi$
(E) 16π

This becomes a little complicated because the answers include π. For the purposes of guesstimating, and in fact for almost any purpose on the SSAT, you should just remember that π is a little more than 3.

Let's look back at those answers.

(A)	$16 - 6\pi$	is roughly equal to	$16 - (6 \times 3) = -2$
(B)	$16 - 4\pi$	is roughly equal to	$16 - (4 \times 3) = 4$
(C)	$16 - 3\pi$	is roughly equal to	$16 - (3 \times 3) = 7$
(D)	$16 - 2\pi$	is roughly equal to	$16 - (2 \times 3) = 10$
(E)	16π	is roughly equal to	$(16 \times 3) = 48$

Now let's think about what these answers mean.

Choice (A) is geometrically impossible. A figure *cannot* have a negative area. Eliminate it.

Choice (B) means that the shaded region has an area of about 4. Sounds pretty good.

Choice (C) means that the shaded region has an area of about 7. The area of the entire square was 16, so that would mean that the shaded region was almost half the square. Possible, but doubtful.

Choice (D) means that the shaded region has an area of about 10. That's more than half the square and in fact, almost three-quarters of the entire square. No way; cross it out.

Finally, (E) means that the shaded region has an area of about 48. What? The whole square had an area of 16. Is the shaded region three times as big as the square itself? Not a chance. Eliminate (E).

At this point you are left with only (B), which we feel pretty good about, and (C), which seems a little large. What should you do?

Pick (B) and pat yourself on the back because you chose the right answer without doing a lot of unnecessary work. Also, remember how useful it was to guesstimate and make sure you do it whenever you see a geometry problem, unless the problem tells you that the figure is not drawn to scale!

Weird Shapes

Whenever the test presents you with a geometric figure that is not a square, rectangle, circle, or triangle, draw a line or lines to divide that figure into the shapes that you do know. Then you can easily work with shapes you know all about.

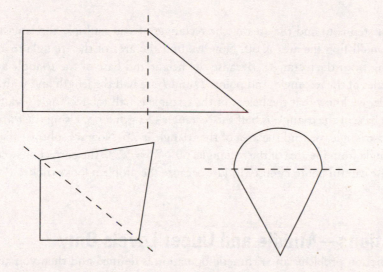

Shaded Regions—Middle and Upper Levels Only

Sometimes geometry questions show you one figure inscribed in another and then ask you to find the area of a shaded region inside the larger figure and outside the smaller figure (like the problem at the beginning of this section). To find the areas of these shaded regions, find the area of the outside figure and then subtract from that the area of the figure inside. The difference is what you need.

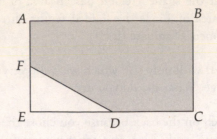

ABCE is a rectangle with a length of 10 and width of 6. Points F and D are the midpoints of AE and EC, respectively. What is the area of the shaded region?

(A) 25.5
(B) 30
(C) 45
(D) 52.5
(E) It cannot be determined from the information given.

The first step is to find the area of the rectangle. If you multiply the length by the width, you'll find the area is 60. Now we find the area of the triangle that we are removing from the rectangle. Because the height and base of the triangle are parts of the sides of the rectangle, and points D and F are half the length and width of the rectangle, we know that the height of the triangle is half the rectangle's width, or 3, and the base of the triangle is half the rectangle's length, or 5. Using the formula for area of a triangle, we find the area of the triangle is 7.5. Now we subtract the area of the triangle from the area of the rectangle. 60 − 7.5 = 52.5. The correct answer choice is (D). Be careful not to choose (E) just because the problem looks tricky!

Functions—Middle and Upper Levels Only

In a function problem, an arithmetic operation is defined and then you are asked to perform it on a number. A function is just a set of instructions written in a strange way.

$$\# x = 3x(x + 1)$$

On the left there is usually a variable with a strange symbol next to or around it.
In the middle is an equal sign.
On the right are the instructions. These tell you what to do with the variable.

$\# x = 3x(x + 1)$ *What does # 5 equal?*

$\# 5 = (3 \times 5)(5 + 1)$ *Just replace each x with a 5!*

Here, the function (indicated by the # sign) simply tells you to substitute a 5 wherever there was an *x* in the original set of instructions. Functions look confusing because of the strange symbols, but once you know what to do with them, they are just like manipulating an equation.

Sometimes more than one question will refer to the same function. The following drill, for example, contains two questions about one function. In cases such as this, the first question tends to be easier than the second.

Charts and Graphs

Charts

Chart questions are simple, but you must be careful. Follow these three steps and you'll be well on the way to mastering any chart question.

1. Read any text that accompanies the chart. It is important to know what the chart is showing and what scale the numbers are on.
2. Read the question.
3. Refer to the chart and find the specific information you need.

If there is more than one question about a single chart, the later questions will tend to be more difficult than the earlier ones. Be careful!

Here is a sample chart.

Don't Be in Too Big of a Hurry
When working with charts and graphs, make sure you take a moment to look at the chart or graph, figure out what it tells you, and then go to the questions.

Club Membership by State, 1995 and 1996		
State	**1995**	**1996**
California	300	500
Florida	225	250
Illinois	200	180
Massachusetts	150	300
Michigan	150	200
New Jersey	200	250
New York	400	600
Texas	50	100

There are many different questions that you can answer based on the information in this chart. For instance:

> What is the difference between the number of members who came from New York in 1995 and the number of members who came from Illinois in 1996?

This question asks you to look up two simple pieces of information and then do a tiny bit of math.

First, the number of members who came from New York in 1995 was 400.

Second, the number of members who came from Illinois in 1996 was 180.

Finally, look back at the question. It asks you to find the difference between these numbers. 400 − 180 = 220. Done.

> The increase in the number of members from New Jersey from 1995 to 1996 was what percent of the total number of members in New Jersey in 1995 ?

You should definitely know how to do this one! Do you remember how to translate percentage questions? If not, go back to Fundamental Math Skills (Chapter 2).

In 1995 there were 200 club members from New Jersey. In 1996 there were 250 members from New Jersey. That represents an increase of 50 members. To determine what percent that is of the total amount in 1995, you will need to ask yourself, "50 (the increase) is what percent of 200 (the number of members in 1995)?"

Translated, this becomes:

$$50 = \frac{g}{100} \times 200$$

With a little bit of simple manipulation, this equation becomes:

$$50 = 2g$$

and

$$25 = g$$

So from 1995 to 1996, there was a 25% increase in the number of members from New Jersey. Good work!

Which state had as many club members in 1996
as a combination of Illinois, Massachusetts, and
Michigan had in 1995 ?

First, take a second to look up the number of members who came from Illinois,
Massachusetts, and Michigan in 1995 and add them together.

$$200 + 150 + 150 = 500$$

Which state had 500 members in 1996? California. That's all there is to it!

Graphs

Some questions will ask you to interpret a graph. You should be familiar with both
pie and bar graphs. These graphs are generally drawn to scale (meaning that the
graphs give an accurate visual impression of the information) so you can always
guess based on the figure if you need to.

The way to approach a graph question is exactly the same as the way to approach a
chart question. Follow the same three steps.

1. Read any text that accompanies the graph. It is important to know
    what the graph is showing and what scale the numbers are on.
2. Read the question.
3. Refer back to the graph and find the specific information you need.

This is how it works.

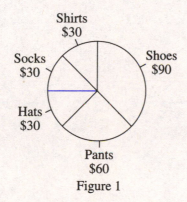

Figure 1

The graph in Figure 1 shows Emily's clothing
expenditures for the month of October. On which
type of clothing did she spend the most money?

(A)   Shoes
(B)   Shirts
(C)   Socks
(D)   Hats
(E)   Pants

This one is easy. You can look at the pieces of the pie and identify the largest, or you can look at the amounts shown in the graph and choose the largest one. Either way, the answer is (A) because Emily spent more money on shoes than on any other clothing items in October.

Emily spent half of her clothing money on which two items?

(A)   Shoes and pants
(B)   Shoes and shirts
(C)   Hats and socks
(D)   Socks and shirts
(E)   Shirts and pants

Again, you can find the answer to this question two different ways. You can look for which two items together make up half the chart, or you can add up the total amount of money Emily spent ($240) and then figure out which two items made up half (or $120) of that amount. Either way is just fine, and either way the right answer is (B), shoes and shirts.

Look over the drills and your answers. How did you do?

Chapter 7
SSAT Verbal

INTRODUCTION

The Verbal section on the SSAT consists of:

- 30 synonym questions (questions 1 to 30)
- 30 analogy questions (questions 31 to 60)

That's 60 questions—but you only have 30 minutes! Should you try to spend 30 seconds on each question to get them all done? NO!

You Mean I Don't Have to Do All the Questions?

Nope. You'll actually improve your score by answering fewer questions, as long as you're still using all of the allotted time.

"Allotted Time"?
If you can't define *allotted*,
make a flash card for it!
Look in Chapter 1 for ideas
on how to use flash cards
to learn new words.

Remember, this test is designed for students in three or four different grade levels. There will be vocabulary in some of these questions that is aimed at students older than you, and almost no one in your grade will get those questions right. On the SSAT score report, you will be compared only with students in your own grade. The younger you are in your test level, the fewer questions you are expected to complete. Fifth graders are expected to do the least number of questions on the Middle Level test. Eighth graders are expected to do the least number of questions on the Upper Level test.

Why rush through the questions you can get right to get to the really tough ones that almost nobody gets? That approach only ensures that you will make hasty, careless errors. Work slowly on the questions that have vocabulary that you know to make sure you get them right. Then try the ones that have some harder words in them.

Which Questions Should I Do?

The questions are arranged in a rough order of difficulty—the harder synonyms tend to come toward the end of the synonym section, and the harder analogies tend to come at the end of the analogy section. However, everyone is different, and some questions are harder for certain people than they are for others. You know some words that your friends don't, and vice versa.

You get as many points for an easy question as you do for a hard one. So here's the plan: Do all the questions that are easy for you first. Easy questions are those where you know the definitions of all the words involved. Then go back through and do the questions with words that sound familiar, even if you are not sure of their dictionary definitions—these are words you sort of know. As you work through these questions, you'll probably be concentrating mostly on the beginning and middle of each section, but don't be afraid to glance ahead—there may be some words you know toward the end. Remember to skip a number on the answer sheet when you skip a question.

Knowing your own vocabulary is the key to quickly deciding if you can answer a question easily.

Bubble Practice
Whenever you do a practice test, use the sample answer sheet so you get used to skipping around when you're filling in bubbles.

Know Yourself

Categorize the words you see in SSAT questions into:

- Words you know
- Words you sort of know
- Words you really don't know

Be honest with yourself when it comes to deciding whether you know a word or not so you can tell which of the techniques you learn in this book works best for each question you tackle. Keep your idea of the word's meaning flexible because the test writers sometimes use the words in ways that you and I do not! (They claim to use dictionary definitions.)

The easiest way to get a verbal question right is by making sure all the words in it fall into the first category—words you know. The best way to do this is by learning new vocabulary *every day.* Check out the Vocabulary chapter (Chapter 1) for the best ways to do this.

You can raise your verbal score moderately just by using the techniques we teach in this chapter. But if you want to see a substantial rise, you need to build up your vocabulary, too.

Eliminate Answer Choices

With math questions, there's always a correct answer; the other answers are simply wrong. With verbal questions, however, things are not that simple. Words are much more slippery than numbers. So verbal questions have *best* answers, not *correct* ones. The other answers aren't necessarily wrong, but the people who score the SSAT think they're not as good as the *best* ones. This means that your goal is to eliminate *worse* answer choices in the Verbal and Reading sections.

Get used to looking for *worse* answers. There are many more of them than there are *best* answers, so *worse* answers are easier to find! When you find them, cross them out in the question booklet to make sure you don't spend any more time looking at them. No matter which other techniques you use to answer a question, eliminate wrong answers first instead of trying to magically pick out the best answer right away.

One thing to remember for the Verbal section: You should not eliminate answer choices that contain words you don't know. If you don't know what a word means, it could be the right answer.

What If I Can't Narrow It Down to One Answer?

Should you guess? Yes. If you can eliminate even one answer choice, you should guess from the remaining choices.

Where Do I Start?

In the Verbal section, do analogies first—they're easier to get right when you don't know all the words in the question.

Take two passes over each section, in the following order:

- analogies with words you know
- analogies with words you sort of know
- analogies with words you really don't know
- synonyms with words you know
- synonyms with words you sort of know

There is no need to ever try to do synonyms with words that you really don't know. You will rarely be able to eliminate answer choices in a synonym question for which you do not know the stem word.

ANALOGIES

What Is an Analogy?

An analogy, on the SSAT, asks you to:

1. Decide how two words are related.
2. Choose another set of words that has the same relationship.

It looks like this:

> A is to B as
>
> (A) C is to D
> (B) C is to D
> (C) C is to D
> (D) C is to D
> (E) C is to D

Or like this:

> A is to B as C is to
>
> (A) D
> (B) D
> (C) D
> (D) D
> (E) D

A, B, C, and D stand for words. We will call any words that are in the question part of the analogy the *stem words*. To figure out the relationship, ignore the "A is to B as C is to D" sentence that they've given you. It doesn't tell you what you need to know. Cross out "is to" and "as."

Next use the techniques that we describe on the next few pages depending on the words in the question. Get your pencil ready because you need to try these strategies out as we go along.

When You Know the Words

Make a Sentence

Here's an analogy for which you'll know all the words.

Kitten is to cat as

- (A) bull is to cow
- (B) snake is to frog
- (C) squirrel is to raccoon
- (D) puppy is to dog
- (E) spider is to fly

You want to be sure you get an easy question like this one right because it's worth just as much as a hard one. Here's how to be sure you don't make a careless mistake.

Picture what the first two words ("A" and "B") stand for and how those two words are related.

Kitten is to cat as   (Cross out "is to" and "as."
                            Just picture a kitten and a cat.)

Make a sentence to describe what you see. (We sometimes call this a "definitional" sentence.) A good sentence will do two things:

- Define one of the words using the other one.

- Stay short and simple.

A kitten _____ cat.
(Make a sentence.)

Now look at the answer choices and eliminate any that cannot have the same relationship as the one you've got in your sentence.

- (A) bull is to cow
- (B) snake is to frog
- (C) squirrel is to raccoon
- (D) puppy is to dog
- (E) spider is to fly

Shop Around
Try every answer choice in a verbal question to be sure you're picking the *best* answer there.

If your sentence was something like "A kitten is a young cat," you can eliminate all but (D). After all, a bull is not a young cow; a snake is not a young frog; a squirrel is not a young raccoon; and a spider is not a young fly. If you had a sentence that did not work, think about how you would define a kitten. Stay away from sentences that use the word *you*, as in "You see kittens with female cats." Also avoid sentences like "A kitten is a cat." These sentences don't give you a definition or description of one of the words. Get specific. Yes, a kitten is a cat, but what *else* do you know about it?

As you go through the answer choices, cross out the choices as you eliminate them. In the kitten analogy, you probably knew that (D) was a good fit for your sentence, but don't stop there! Always check all the answers. On the SSAT, often a so-so answer will appear before the *best* answer in the choices, and you don't want to get sidetracked by it. Try *all* the answers so you can be sure to get all the easy analogies right.

In making your sentence, you can start with either of the first two words. Try to start your sentence by defining the first word, but if that doesn't work, start by defining the second word.

Rev It Up
Use the most specific, descriptive words you can when you make a sentence. You want the sentence to define one of the words.

House is to tent as
> (Cross out "is to" and "as." Picture a house and a tent.)

A house _____ tent.

(Can you make a definitional sentence? Not really.)

A tent _____ house.

(Make a sentence. Now eliminate answer choices.)

House is to tent as bed is to

(A) table
(B) stool
(C) floor
(D) blanket
(E) hammock

Draw an arrow to remind yourself that you started with the second word instead of the first, as we have here. If you reverse the words in your sentence, you need to reverse them when you're trying out the answer choices, too. If you have a sentence like, "A tent is a temporary house," then you can eliminate all but (E).

Write your sentence above the question, between the two words. It's a good idea to do this as you start practicing analogies, and most students find it helpful to write out their sentences all the time. If you have a tendency to change your sentence as you go through the answers, you should always write it down.

Notice that in the house analogy, they've *given* you the first word of the answer pair. Some of the analogies will be like this, but they're really no different from the others. You'll still be using the same techniques for them, and you may find them a little easier.

Make Another Sentence

Why would you ever need to change your sentence? Let's see.

If at First You Don't Succeed…
Then try the other word! You can start your sentence with the first word (A) or the second word (B).

> Motor is to car as
> (Cross out. Picture them. Write a sentence. Eliminate.)
>
> (A) knob is to door
> (B) shovel is to earth
> (C) bulb is to lamp
> (D) sail is to boat
> (E) pond is to ocean

Did you get it down to one? If not, make your sentence more specific. You may have said "A car has a motor," in which case you can only eliminate (B) and (E). The best words to use are active verbs and descriptive adjectives. What does a motor *do* for a car? Make a more specific sentence. (Remember to draw an arrow if you start with the word *car*.)

A motor makes a car move. You could also say that a car is powered by a motor. Either sentence will help you eliminate all but (D). When your sentence eliminates some, but not all, of the choices, make it more specific.

If you have trouble picturing the relationship or making a more specific sentence, ask yourself questions that will help you get at how the two words are related.

Below are some questions to ask yourself that will help you make sentences. ("A" and "B" are the first two words in the analogy. Remember, you can start with either one.) Refer back to these questions if you get stuck when trying to make a sentence.

Help!
These questions will help you come up with a sentence that defines one of the words in an analogy. Refer to them as much as you need to, until you are asking yourself these questions automatically.

- What does A/B do?
- What does A/B mean?
- How does A/B work?
- What does A/B look like?
- How is A/B used?
- Where is A/B found?
- How do A and B compare?
- How are A and B associated?

When You Know Only One of the Words

Working Backward

If you know only one of the words, go straight to the answer choices. Make a sentence with each answer choice. Keep your sentence as definitional as possible. If your sentence uses *can* or *might* or *could*, or if you find yourself really reaching to try to make up a sentence, then the relationship is not a strong definitional one and that answer is probably not right. Eliminate it. Each time you can create a good sentence with an answer choice, you should then try the sentence with the stem words. If you don't know a word in an answer choice, do not eliminate it.

Cygnet is to swan as

(A)	chicken is to egg	a chicken lays eggs—a cygnet lays swans?
~~(B)~~	frog is to snake	a snake can eat a frog—not strong
~~(C)~~	turtle is to raccoon	no sentence—not strong
(D)	puppy is to dog	a puppy is a young dog—a cygnet is a young swan?
~~(E)~~	spider is to fly	some spiders eat flies—not strong

Pick the *best* or most likely relationship for *cygnet* and *swan*. Which relationship is most like a definition?

Cross out (C), because we couldn't make a sentence at all. (B) and (E) are not great because snakes and spiders eat other things, too, and their definitions are not based on what they eat. Eliminate them. Now look at (A) and (D). Try their sentences on the stem words. Could something lay a swan? Probably not! Could something be a young swan? Sure, there could be a word that means *baby swan*. Sure enough, *cygnet* is exactly that.

Try Working Backward with these analogies.

Kinesiology is to motion as

(A)   numerology is to progress   _____

(B)   navigation is to ocean   _____

(C)   astronomy is to weather   _____

(D)   criminology is to perversion   _____

(E)   psychology is to mind   _____

Only (B) and (E) allow you to make strong sentences. Navigation is how you get around on the ocean. Psychology is the study of the mind. So try those sentences: Could kinesiology be how you get around on the motion? No. Could kinesiology be the study of human motion? Yep. We got it down to (E).

Apiary is to bees as

(A)   stable is to horses   _____

(B)   jar is to honey   _____

(C)   florist is to flowers   _____

(D)   dirt is to ants   _____

(E)   leash is to dog   _____

Eliminate (B), (D), and (E) because the word relationships are not strong. A stable is a place where horses are kept. A florist is someone who works with flowers. Now, do you think that an apiary is a place where bees are kept? Possibly. Do you think an apiary is someone who works with bees? Also possible. Take a guess between (A) and (C). Look up *apiary* and make a flash card for it.

When You Sort of Know the Words

Use "Side of the Fence"
If you can't make a definitional sentence because you're not sure what the words mean, but you've got some idea from having seen the words before, determine whether the words are on the same side of the fence or different sides. That is, are they similar enough to be grouped together, or are they different enough that you'd say they're on different sides of a fence? If they are similar in meaning, write "S" next to the pair. If their meanings are more like opposites, write "D." So cat and kitten would get an "S," while black and white would get a "D."

Because the answer pair has to have the same relationship as that of the stem words, you can eliminate any answers that don't match. If your words are similar, you can eliminate any answers that are different. If your words are different, you can eliminate any answers that are similar.

Now we can try a whole analogy.

Lurid is to horror as

(A) comical is to amusement
(B) illegal is to law
(C) cowardly is to fear
(D) ghastly is to serenity
(E) humane is to treatment

Don't try to make a sentence—just decide if *lurid* and *horror* are similar or different. Then make the same decision for all the answer choices. You should wind up with a question that looks as follows:

Lurid is to horror as   S

(A) comical is to amusement   S
(B̶) illegal is to law   D
(C) cowardly is to fear   S
(D̶) ghastly is to serenity   D
(E̶) humane is to treatment   nice phrase, but it's
                                                   not a relationship

Now you can guess from just two answers—you've increased your odds considerably! Remember to mark up your test booklet as you eliminate, and guess even if you've eliminated only one choice. If you're not sure of the definition of *lurid*, or any other word on this page, make a flash card for it!

Work Backward
You can use this technique for words you just sort of know, in addition to using it on analogies where you just know one of the words. Try it on this one. *Patent* is a word we all sort of know.

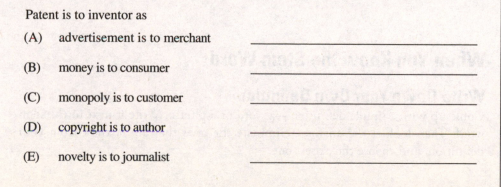

Patent is to inventor as

(A)   advertisement is to merchant   _____

(B)   money is to consumer   _____

(C)   monopoly is to customer   _____

(D)   copyright is to author   _____

(E)   novelty is to journalist   _____

Choices (C) and (E) should be crossed out for sure—the words are not strongly related. You've made sentences with the other answer choices. Which sentence works best with *patent* and *inventor*? (D).

Practice what you've learned about analogies with your online drills!

When You Really Don't Know Either of the Words

If you have never seen the stem words before, you're better off putting a circle around the question number in the test booklet and skipping the question. If you have time to go back to the ones you've circled and skipped, then try this.

Work Backward as Much as You Can

Go straight to the answer choices, and make sentences with them. Now, you can't try the sentences with the stem words because you don't know the stem words, right? So just look at the sentences you have. Which ones are not likely to be correct? The ones that are not like definitions. Eliminate those answer choices—the ones in which the words are not related in such a way that you need one to define the other.

Look at these possible answer choices and decide if they're definitional or if you should eliminate them on a question for which you do not know the stem words. Write a sentence for the answers you'd keep.

SYNONYMS

What Is a Synonym?

On the SSAT, a synonym question asks you to choose the answer choice that comes closest in meaning to the stem word (the word in capitals). Often the best answer won't mean the exact same thing as the stem word, but it will be closer than any of the other choices.

Just like analogies, you need to decide which vocabulary category the synonym stem word falls into for you, so you know which technique to use. First, do all the synonyms for which you know the stem word, and then go back and do the ones with stem words you sort of know.

When You Know the Stem Word

Write Down Your Own Definition

Come up with a simple definition—a word or a phrase. Write it next to the stem word. Then look at the answers, eliminate the ones that are farthest from your definition, and choose the closest one.

It's very simple. Don't let the test writers put words in your mouth. Make sure you're armed with your own definition before you look at their answer choices. They often like to put in a word that is a close second to the best answer, and if you've got your own synonym ready, you'll be able to make the distinction.

If you need to, cover the answers with your hand, so you can think of your definition before looking. Eventually you may not have to write down your definitions, but you should start out that way.

As you compare the choices with your definition, cross out the ones that are definitely not right. Crossing out answer choices is something you should *always* do—it saves you time because you don't go back to choices you've already decided were not the best.

As always, don't eliminate the words you don't know.

Try this one. Write your definition of WITHER before you look at the answer choices.

WITHER: _____ (definition)

(A) play
(B) spoil
(C) greatly improve
(D) wilt
(E) give freely

The stem word means *shrivel* or *dry up*. Which answer is closest? (D). You may have been considering (B), but (D) is closer.

Write Another Definition

Why would you ever need to change your definition? Let's see.

MANEUVER:

(A) avoidance
(B) deviation
(C) find
(D) contrivance
(E) invent

Your definition may be something like *move* or *control* if you know the word from hearing it applied to cars. But that definition isn't in the answer choices. The problem is that you're thinking about *maneuver* as a verb. However, *maneuver* can also be a noun. It means *a plan, scheme,* or *trick*. Now go back and eliminate. The answer is (D).

Parts of Speech?
If you need to, go back and review parts of speech in the "Word Parts" section of Chapter 1.

The SSAT sometimes uses secondary definitions, which can be the same part of speech or a different part of speech from the primary definition. Just stay flexible in your definitions, and you'll be fine.

When You Sort of Know the Stem Word

Why Should You Do Synonyms Last? Why Are They Harder Than Analogies?

Synonyms are harder to beat than analogies because the SSAT gives you no context with which to figure out words that you sort of know. But that doesn't mean you should only do the easy synonyms. You can get the medium ones, too. You just need to create your own context to figure out words you don't know very well.

Keep in mind that your goal is to eliminate the worst answers, to make an educated guess. You'll be able to do this for every synonym that you sort of know, and even if you just eliminate one choice, *guess*. You'll gain points overall.

Make Your Own Context

You can create your own context for the word by figuring out how you've heard it used before. Think of the other words you've heard used with the stem word. Is there a certain phrase that comes to mind? What does that phrase mean?

If you still can't come up with a definition for the stem word, just use the context in which you've heard the word to eliminate answers that wouldn't fit at all in that same context.

How about this stem word:

ABOMINABLE

Where have you heard *abominable*? The Abominable Snowman, of course. Think about it—you know it's a monster-like creature. Which answer choices can you eliminate?

ABOMINABLE:

(A)	enormous	the enormous snowman? maybe
(B)	terrible	the terrible snowman? sure
~~(C)~~	rude	the rude snowman? probably not
~~(D)~~	showy	the showy snowman? nope
~~(E)~~	talkative	the talkative snowman? only Frosty!

You can throw out everything but (A) and (B). Now you can guess, with a much better shot at getting the answer right than guessing from five choices. Or you can think about where else you've heard the stem word. Have you ever heard something called an *abomination*? Was it something terrible or was it something enormous? (B) is the answer.

Try this one. Where have you heard this stem word? Try the answers in that context.

SURROGATE:

(A) friendly
(B) requested
(C) paranoid
(D) numerous
(E) substitute

Have you heard the stem word in *surrogate mother*? If you have, you can definitely eliminate (B), (C), and (D), and (A) isn't great either. A surrogate mother is a substitute mother.

Try one more.

ENDANGER:

(A) rescue
(B) frighten
(C) confuse
(D) threaten
(E) isolate

Everyone's associations are different, but you've probably heard of *endangered species* or *endangered lives*. Use either of those phrases to eliminate answer choices that can't fit into it. Rescued species? Frightened species? Confused species? Threatened species? Isolated species? (D) works best.

Use Word Parts to Piece Together a Definition

Prefixes, roots, and suffixes can help you figure out what a word means. You should use this technique in addition to (not instead of) word association, because not all word parts retain their original meanings.

You may have never seen this stem word before, but if you've been working on your Vocabulary chapter, you know that the root *pac* or *peac* means peace. You can see the same root in *Pacific, pacifier,* and the word *peace* itself. So what's the answer to this synonym?

PACIFIST:

(A) innocent person
(B) person opposed to war
(C) warmonger
(D) wanderer of lands
(E) journeyman

The answer is (B).

In the following stem word, we see *cred*, a word part that means "belief" or "faith." You can see this word part in *incredible, credit,* and *credibility*. The answer is now simple.

CREDIBLE:

(A) obsolete
(B) believable
(C) fabulous
(D) mundane
(E) superficial

Choice (B) again. What are the word parts in the following stem word?

MONOTONOUS:

(A) lively
(B) educational
(C) nutritious
(D) repetitious
(E) helpful

Mono means "one." *Tone* has to do with sound. If something keeps striking one sound, how would you describe it? (D) is the answer.

The only way you'll be able to use word parts is if you know them. Get cracking on the Vocabulary chapter!

Words You Really Don't Know

Don't waste time on words you've never seen if you don't know any of their word parts. Check Chapter 5 to see how many synonyms you need to do.

Practice your newfound synonym knowledge with online drills. Then go outside for a long walk and let everything you've learned settle in!

Chapter 8
SSAT Reading

AN OPEN BOOK TEST

Keep in mind when you approach the Reading Section of the test that *it is an open book test*. Moreover, you can't read the passages in advance of the test to prepare, and you have a limited amount of time to get through the passages and questions. So, what does this all mean? You will be much better served to take a *strategic* approach.

Read with a Purpose

When you read for school you have to read everything—carefully. Not only is there is no time for such an approach on the SSAT, but reading carefully at the outset does not even make sense. Each passage has only a few questions, and all you need to read and process is the information that will provide answers to those questions. As only questions can generate points, your goal is to get to the questions as quickly as possible.

Even so, it does help to have a high-level overview of the passage before you attack the questions. There are two ways to do accomplish this goal.

- If you are a fairly fast reader, get through the passage quickly, ignoring the nitty-gritty and focusing on the overall point of each paragraph.
- If you don't read quickly enough to read the entire passage in a way that will provide you with the overall point of the paragraphs, read the first sentence of each paragraph. For a very short passage, you should read through it quickly, however.

Once you have identified the point of each paragraph, those points will flow into the overall purpose of the passage and also provide a map of where to find detailed information. Once you have established the purpose and map, you should go right to the questions.

Answering Questions

Some questions are about particular parts of a passage, while others are about the passage as a whole. Depending on how well you understood the purpose of the passage, you may be able to answer big picture questions quite easily. Detail questions, on the other hand, will require some work; after all, you didn't get lost in the details when you got through the passage quickly!

For a particular detail question, you will need to go back to the passage with the question in mind and *find the answer in the passage*. Let's repeat that last part: you should *find the answer in the passage*. If you know what the answer should look like, it is much easier to evaluate the answers. True, some questions cannot be answered in advance, such as "Which one of the following questions is answered in the passage?" But the general rule is *find the answer* before you go to the answer choices.

By reading more quickly up front, you have more time to spend on finding the answer to a particular question.

In all cases, you should use effective process of elimination. Correct answers are fully supported by the text of the passage. There is no reading between the lines, connecting the dots, or getting inside the author's head. If you are down to two answers, determine which one is not supported by the text of the passage. It takes only one word to doom an otherwise good answer.

In short, follow this process for detail questions:

- Read and understand the question.
- Go to the passage and *find the answer* (unless the question is too open-ended).
- Use process of elimination, getting rid of any answer that is not consistent with the answer you found and/or is not fully supported by the text of the passage.

We will look at some specific question types shortly, but if you follow the general approach outlined here, you will be able to answer more questions accurately.

Pacing

Let's amend that last statement: You will be able to answer more questions accurately if you have a sound pacing plan. While reading up front more quickly will generate more time for the questions, getting through all the passages and all the questions in the time allotted is difficult for almost all students.

There are up to eight passages on the SSAT, some short and some quite long. Some are fairly easy to read, and some are dense. They cover a broad array of topics, from history to science to fiction and even poetry. You may relate to some passages but not to others. On top of that, if you are rushing through the section to make sure you answer every single question, you are likely making a lot of mistakes. Slow down to increase your accuracy.

Doing fewer passages accurately can generate more points than rushing through more passages.

How many passages should you do? That depends on you. You should attack as many passages as you can while still maintaining a high degree of accuracy. If, for example, dropping to six passages allows you to answer all but one or two questions correctly, while rushing through seven creates a lot of silly mistakes, do six.

Also, pick your passages wisely. You don't get extra credit for answering questions on a hard passage correctly. If you begin a passage and are thinking "Uh, what?" move on to another passage. You might end up coming back to the passage, or you may never look at it again. What is most important is that you nail the easier passages before you hit the harder ones.

STEP ONE: READING THE PASSAGE

Let's put the new reading approach into practice.

Label the Paragraphs

After you read each paragraph, ask yourself what you just read. Put it in your own words—just a couple of words—and label the side of the paragraph with your summary. This way you'll have something to guide you back to the relevant part of the passage when you answer a question. The key to labeling the paragraphs is to practice—you need to do it quickly, coming up with one or two words that accurately remind you of what's in the paragraph.

If the passage has only one paragraph, come up with a single label. Poems do not need to be labeled.

State the Main Idea

After you have read the entire passage, ask yourself the following two questions:

- "What?" What is the passage about?
- "So what?" What's the author's point about this topic?

The answers to these questions will show you the main idea of the passage. Scribble down this main idea in just a few words. The answer to "What?" is the thing that was being talked about—"bees" or "weather forecasting." The answer to "So what?" gives you the rest of the sentence—"Bees do little dances that tell other bees where to go for pollen," or "Weather forecasting is complicated by many problems."

Don't assume you will find the main idea in the first sentence. While often the main idea is in the beginning of the passage, it is not *always* in the first sentence or even the first paragraph. The beginning may just be a lead-in to the main point.

STEP TWO: ANSWERING THE QUESTIONS

Now, we're getting to the important part of the Reading section. This is where you need to spend time in order to avoid careless errors. After reading a passage, you'll have a group of questions that are in no particular order. The first thing you need to decide is whether the question you're answering is general or specific.

General Questions

General questions are about the passage as a whole. They come in a variety of forms but ideally all can be answered based on your initial read.

Main idea
- Which of the following best expresses the main point?
- The passage is primarily about
- The main idea of the passage is
- The best title for this passage would be

Purpose
- The purpose of the passage is
- The author wrote this passage to

Tone/attitude
- The author's tone is
- The attitude of the author is one of

Odd ball
- Where would you be likely to find this passage?
- Which is likely to happen next?
- The author will most likely discuss next

Notice that these questions all require you to know the main idea, but the ones at the beginning of the list don't require anything else, and the ones toward the end require you to use a bit of common sense.

Answering a General Question

Keep your answers to "What?" and "So what?" in mind. The answer to a general question will concern the main idea. If it helps, you can go back to your paragraph labels. The labels will allow you to look at the passage again without getting bogged down in the details.

- For a straight **main idea** question, just ask yourself, "What was the 'What? So what?' for this passage?"
- For a **general purpose** question, ask yourself, "Why did the author write this?"

- For a **tone/attitude** question, ask yourself, "How did the author feel about the subject?" Think about tone as you would a text message. Would you say the author feels ☺ or ☹? These signs can help you with process of elimination.
- For an **oddball** question, use common sense and sound process of elimination.

Answer the question in your own words before looking at the answer choices. Eliminate answers that are not consistent with your predicted answer, as well as those that are too broad or too narrow. They should be "just right."

Specific Questions

Specific questions are about a detail or section of the passage. While the questions can be presented in a number of different ways, they boil down to questions about WHAT the author said, WHY the author said something, and Vocab-in-Context.

What?
- According to the passage/author
- The author states that
- Which of these questions is answered by the passage?
- The author implies in line X
- It can be inferred from paragraph X
- The most likely interpretation of X is

Why?
- The author uses X to
- Why does the author say X?

Vocab-in-Context
- What does the passage mean by X?
- X probably represents/means
- Which word best replaces the word X without changing the meaning?
- As it is used in X, _____ most nearly means

Specific interpretation
- The author would be most likely to agree with which one of the following?
- Which one of the following questions is answered in the passage?

Once you have read and understood the question, go to the passage to find the answer. You should be able to find the answer quickly:

- Use your **paragraph labels** to go straight to the information you need.
- Use the **line or paragraph reference**, if there is one, but be careful. With a line reference ("In line 10…"), be sure to read the whole surrounding paragraph, not just the line. If the question says, "In line 10…," then you need to read lines 5 through 15 to actually find the answer.
- Use words that stand out in the question and passage. Names, places, and long words will be easy to find back in the passage. We call these **lead words** because they lead you back to the right place in the passage.

Once you're in the right area, answer the question in your own words. Then look at the answer choices and eliminate any that aren't like your answer or are not supported by the text of the passage.

For Vocab-in-Context questions, be sure to come up with your own word, based on the surrounding sentences. It does not matter if you do not know the word being tested, as long as you can figure it out from context. Also, even if you do know the word, it may be used in a unusual way. So, always ignore the word and come up with your own before process of elimination.

Questions with Special Formats

I, II, III questions   The questions that have three Roman numerals are confusing and time-consuming. They look like this:

According to the passage, which of the following is true?

> I.   The sky is blue.
>
> II.   Nothing rhymes with "orange."
>
> III.   Smoking cigarettes increases lung capacity.

(A)   I only
(B)   II only
(C)   III only
(D)   I and II only
(E)   I, II, and III

On the SSAT, you will need to look up each of the three statements in the passage. This will always be time-consuming, but you can make them less confusing by making sure you look up just one statement at a time.

For instance, in the question above, say you look back at the passage and see that the passage says statement I is true. Write a big "T" next to it. What can you eliminate now? (B) and (C). Now you check out II and you find that sure enough, the passage says that, too. So II gets a big "T" and you cross off (A). Next, looking in the paragraph you labeled "Smoking is bad," you find that the passage actually says that smoking decreases lung capacity. What can you eliminate? (E).

You may want to skip a I, II, III question because it will be time-consuming, especially if you're on your last passage and there are other questions you can do instead.

EXCEPT/LEAST/NOT questions   This is another confusing type of question. The test writers are reversing what you need to look for, asking you which answer is false.

> All of the following can be inferred from the
> passage EXCEPT

Before you go any further, cross out the "EXCEPT." Now, you have a much more positive question to answer. Of course, as always, you will go through *all* the answer choices, but for this type of question you will put a little "T" or "F" next to the answers as you check them out. Let's say we've checked out these answers:

(A) Americans are patriotic.	**T**
(B) Americans have great ingenuity.	**T**
(C) Americans love war.	**F**
(D) Americans do what they can to help one another.	**T**
(E) Americans are brave in times of war.	**T**

Which one stands out? The one with the "F." That's your answer. You made a confusing question much simpler than the test writers wanted it to be. If you don't go through all the choices and mark them, you run the risk of accidentally picking one of the choices that you know is true because that's what you usually look for on reading questions.

You should skip an EXCEPT/LEAST/NOT question if you're on your last passage and there are other questions you can do instead.

STEP THREE: PROCESS OF ELIMINATION

Before you ever look at an answer choice, you've come up with your own answer, in your own words. What do you do next?

Well, you're looking for the closest answer to yours, but it's a lot easier to eliminate answers than to try to magically zone in on the best one. Work through the answers using Process of Elimination. As soon as you eliminate an answer, cross off the letter in your test booklet so that you no longer think of that choice as a possibility.

How Do I Eliminate Answer Choices?

On a General Question
Eliminate an answer that is:

* Too small. The passage may mention it, but it's only a detail—not a main idea.
* Not mentioned in the passage.
* In contradiction to the passage—it says the opposite of what you read.
* Too big. The answer tries to say that more was discussed than really was.
* Too extreme. An extreme answer is too negative or too positive, or it uses absolute words like *all, every, never,* or *always.* Eliminating extreme answers makes tone/attitude questions especially easy and quick.
* Against common sense. The passage is not likely to back up answers that just don't make sense at all.

On a Specific Question
Eliminate an answer that is:

* Too extreme
* In contradiction to passage details
* Not mentioned in the passage
* Against common sense

If you look back at the questions you did for the Viking passage, you'll see that many of the wrong answer choices fit into the categories above.

On a Tone Question
Eliminate an answer that is:

* Too extreme
* Opposite meaning
* Against common sense. These are answers that make the author seem confused or uninterested, which an SSAT author will never be.

What Kinds of Answers Do I Keep?

Best answers are likely to be:

- Paraphrases of the words in the passage
- Traditional and conservative in their outlook
- Moderate, using words like *may, can,* and *often*

When You've Got It Down to Two

If you've eliminated all but two answers, don't get stuck and waste time. Keep the main idea in the back of your mind and step back.

- Reread the question.
- Look at what makes the two answers different.
- Go back to the passage.
- Which answer is worse? Eliminate it.

Put all of these elements together when you go online to do the practice drills!

Part III
SSAT Practice Tests

If you are taking the new Elementary Level SSAT, turn the page for instructions on how to download your full-length practice test from PrincetonReview.com.

HOW TO TAKE A PRACTICE TEST

Here are some reminders for taking your practice test.

- Find a quiet place to take the test where you won't be interrupted or distracted, and make sure you have enough time to take the entire test.

- Time yourself strictly. Use a timer, watch, or stopwatch that will ring, and do not allow yourself to go over time for any section.

- Take a practice test in one sitting, allowing yourself breaks of no more than two minutes between sections.

- Use the attached answer sheets to bubble in your answer choices.

- Each bubble you choose should be filled in thoroughly, and no other marks should be made in the answer area.

- Make sure to double-check that your bubbles are filled in correctly!

Chapter 9
Upper Level
SSAT Practice Test

Upper Level Practice Test

Be sure each mark *completely* fills the answer space.
Start with number 1 for each new section of the test. You may find more answer spaces than you need.
If so, please leave them blank.

SECTION 1

1 Ⓐ Ⓑ Ⓒ Ⓓ Ⓔ	6 Ⓐ Ⓑ Ⓒ Ⓓ Ⓔ	11 Ⓐ Ⓑ Ⓒ Ⓓ Ⓔ	16 Ⓐ Ⓑ Ⓒ Ⓓ Ⓔ	21 Ⓐ Ⓑ Ⓒ Ⓓ Ⓔ
2 Ⓐ Ⓑ Ⓒ Ⓓ Ⓔ	7 Ⓐ Ⓑ Ⓒ Ⓓ Ⓔ	12 Ⓐ Ⓑ Ⓒ Ⓓ Ⓔ	17 Ⓐ Ⓑ Ⓒ Ⓓ Ⓔ	22 Ⓐ Ⓑ Ⓒ Ⓓ Ⓔ
3 Ⓐ Ⓑ Ⓒ Ⓓ Ⓔ	8 Ⓐ Ⓑ Ⓒ Ⓓ Ⓔ	13 Ⓐ Ⓑ Ⓒ Ⓓ Ⓔ	18 Ⓐ Ⓑ Ⓒ Ⓓ Ⓔ	23 Ⓐ Ⓑ Ⓒ Ⓓ Ⓔ
4 Ⓐ Ⓑ Ⓒ Ⓓ Ⓔ	9 Ⓐ Ⓑ Ⓒ Ⓓ Ⓔ	14 Ⓐ Ⓑ Ⓒ Ⓓ Ⓔ	19 Ⓐ Ⓑ Ⓒ Ⓓ Ⓔ	24 Ⓐ Ⓑ Ⓒ Ⓓ Ⓔ
5 Ⓐ Ⓑ Ⓒ Ⓓ Ⓔ	10 Ⓐ Ⓑ Ⓒ Ⓓ Ⓔ	15 Ⓐ Ⓑ Ⓒ Ⓓ Ⓔ	20 Ⓐ Ⓑ Ⓒ Ⓓ Ⓔ	25 Ⓐ Ⓑ Ⓒ Ⓓ Ⓔ

SECTION 2

1 Ⓐ Ⓑ Ⓒ Ⓓ Ⓔ	9 Ⓐ Ⓑ Ⓒ Ⓓ Ⓔ	17 Ⓐ Ⓑ Ⓒ Ⓓ Ⓔ	25 Ⓐ Ⓑ Ⓒ Ⓓ Ⓔ	33 Ⓐ Ⓑ Ⓒ Ⓓ Ⓔ
2 Ⓐ Ⓑ Ⓒ Ⓓ Ⓔ	10 Ⓐ Ⓑ Ⓒ Ⓓ Ⓔ	18 Ⓐ Ⓑ Ⓒ Ⓓ Ⓔ	26 Ⓐ Ⓑ Ⓒ Ⓓ Ⓔ	34 Ⓐ Ⓑ Ⓒ Ⓓ Ⓔ
3 Ⓐ Ⓑ Ⓒ Ⓓ Ⓔ	11 Ⓐ Ⓑ Ⓒ Ⓓ Ⓔ	19 Ⓐ Ⓑ Ⓒ Ⓓ Ⓔ	27 Ⓐ Ⓑ Ⓒ Ⓓ Ⓔ	35 Ⓐ Ⓑ Ⓒ Ⓓ Ⓔ
4 Ⓐ Ⓑ Ⓒ Ⓓ Ⓔ	12 Ⓐ Ⓑ Ⓒ Ⓓ Ⓔ	20 Ⓐ Ⓑ Ⓒ Ⓓ Ⓔ	28 Ⓐ Ⓑ Ⓒ Ⓓ Ⓔ	36 Ⓐ Ⓑ Ⓒ Ⓓ Ⓔ
5 Ⓐ Ⓑ Ⓒ Ⓓ Ⓔ	13 Ⓐ Ⓑ Ⓒ Ⓓ Ⓔ	21 Ⓐ Ⓑ Ⓒ Ⓓ Ⓔ	29 Ⓐ Ⓑ Ⓒ Ⓓ Ⓔ	37 Ⓐ Ⓑ Ⓒ Ⓓ Ⓔ
6 Ⓐ Ⓑ Ⓒ Ⓓ Ⓔ	14 Ⓐ Ⓑ Ⓒ Ⓓ Ⓔ	22 Ⓐ Ⓑ Ⓒ Ⓓ Ⓔ	30 Ⓐ Ⓑ Ⓒ Ⓓ Ⓔ	38 Ⓐ Ⓑ Ⓒ Ⓓ Ⓔ
7 Ⓐ Ⓑ Ⓒ Ⓓ Ⓔ	15 Ⓐ Ⓑ Ⓒ Ⓓ Ⓔ	23 Ⓐ Ⓑ Ⓒ Ⓓ Ⓔ	31 Ⓐ Ⓑ Ⓒ Ⓓ Ⓔ	39 Ⓐ Ⓑ Ⓒ Ⓓ Ⓔ
8 Ⓐ Ⓑ Ⓒ Ⓓ Ⓔ	16 Ⓐ Ⓑ Ⓒ Ⓓ Ⓔ	24 Ⓐ Ⓑ Ⓒ Ⓓ Ⓔ	32 Ⓐ Ⓑ Ⓒ Ⓓ Ⓔ	40 Ⓐ Ⓑ Ⓒ Ⓓ Ⓔ

SECTION 3

1 Ⓐ Ⓑ Ⓒ Ⓓ Ⓔ	13 Ⓐ Ⓑ Ⓒ Ⓓ Ⓔ	25 Ⓐ Ⓑ Ⓒ Ⓓ Ⓔ	37 Ⓐ Ⓑ Ⓒ Ⓓ Ⓔ	49 Ⓐ Ⓑ Ⓒ Ⓓ Ⓔ
2 Ⓐ Ⓑ Ⓒ Ⓓ Ⓔ	14 Ⓐ Ⓑ Ⓒ Ⓓ Ⓔ	26 Ⓐ Ⓑ Ⓒ Ⓓ Ⓔ	38 Ⓐ Ⓑ Ⓒ Ⓓ Ⓔ	50 Ⓐ Ⓑ Ⓒ Ⓓ Ⓔ
3 Ⓐ Ⓑ Ⓒ Ⓓ Ⓔ	15 Ⓐ Ⓑ Ⓒ Ⓓ Ⓔ	27 Ⓐ Ⓑ Ⓒ Ⓓ Ⓔ	39 Ⓐ Ⓑ Ⓒ Ⓓ Ⓔ	51 Ⓐ Ⓑ Ⓒ Ⓓ Ⓔ
4 Ⓐ Ⓑ Ⓒ Ⓓ Ⓔ	16 Ⓐ Ⓑ Ⓒ Ⓓ Ⓔ	28 Ⓐ Ⓑ Ⓒ Ⓓ Ⓔ	40 Ⓐ Ⓑ Ⓒ Ⓓ Ⓔ	52 Ⓐ Ⓑ Ⓒ Ⓓ Ⓔ
5 Ⓐ Ⓑ Ⓒ Ⓓ Ⓔ	17 Ⓐ Ⓑ Ⓒ Ⓓ Ⓔ	29 Ⓐ Ⓑ Ⓒ Ⓓ Ⓔ	41 Ⓐ Ⓑ Ⓒ Ⓓ Ⓔ	53 Ⓐ Ⓑ Ⓒ Ⓓ Ⓔ
6 Ⓐ Ⓑ Ⓒ Ⓓ Ⓔ	18 Ⓐ Ⓑ Ⓒ Ⓓ Ⓔ	30 Ⓐ Ⓑ Ⓒ Ⓓ Ⓔ	42 Ⓐ Ⓑ Ⓒ Ⓓ Ⓔ	54 Ⓐ Ⓑ Ⓒ Ⓓ Ⓔ
7 Ⓐ Ⓑ Ⓒ Ⓓ Ⓔ	19 Ⓐ Ⓑ Ⓒ Ⓓ Ⓔ	31 Ⓐ Ⓑ Ⓒ Ⓓ Ⓔ	43 Ⓐ Ⓑ Ⓒ Ⓓ Ⓔ	55 Ⓐ Ⓑ Ⓒ Ⓓ Ⓔ
8 Ⓐ Ⓑ Ⓒ Ⓓ Ⓔ	20 Ⓐ Ⓑ Ⓒ Ⓓ Ⓔ	32 Ⓐ Ⓑ Ⓒ Ⓓ Ⓔ	44 Ⓐ Ⓑ Ⓒ Ⓓ Ⓔ	56 Ⓐ Ⓑ Ⓒ Ⓓ Ⓔ
9 Ⓐ Ⓑ Ⓒ Ⓓ Ⓔ	21 Ⓐ Ⓑ Ⓒ Ⓓ Ⓔ	33 Ⓐ Ⓑ Ⓒ Ⓓ Ⓔ	45 Ⓐ Ⓑ Ⓒ Ⓓ Ⓔ	57 Ⓐ Ⓑ Ⓒ Ⓓ Ⓔ
10 Ⓐ Ⓑ Ⓒ Ⓓ Ⓔ	22 Ⓐ Ⓑ Ⓒ Ⓓ Ⓔ	34 Ⓐ Ⓑ Ⓒ Ⓓ Ⓔ	46 Ⓐ Ⓑ Ⓒ Ⓓ Ⓔ	58 Ⓐ Ⓑ Ⓒ Ⓓ Ⓔ
11 Ⓐ Ⓑ Ⓒ Ⓓ Ⓔ	23 Ⓐ Ⓑ Ⓒ Ⓓ Ⓔ	35 Ⓐ Ⓑ Ⓒ Ⓓ Ⓔ	47 Ⓐ Ⓑ Ⓒ Ⓓ Ⓔ	59 Ⓐ Ⓑ Ⓒ Ⓓ Ⓔ
12 Ⓐ Ⓑ Ⓒ Ⓓ Ⓔ	24 Ⓐ Ⓑ Ⓒ Ⓓ Ⓔ	36 Ⓐ Ⓑ Ⓒ Ⓓ Ⓔ	48 Ⓐ Ⓑ Ⓒ Ⓓ Ⓔ	60 Ⓐ Ⓑ Ⓒ Ⓓ Ⓔ

SECTION 4

1 Ⓐ Ⓑ Ⓒ Ⓓ Ⓔ	6 Ⓐ Ⓑ Ⓒ Ⓓ Ⓔ	11 Ⓐ Ⓑ Ⓒ Ⓓ Ⓔ	16 Ⓐ Ⓑ Ⓒ Ⓓ Ⓔ	21 Ⓐ Ⓑ Ⓒ Ⓓ Ⓔ
2 Ⓐ Ⓑ Ⓒ Ⓓ Ⓔ	7 Ⓐ Ⓑ Ⓒ Ⓓ Ⓔ	12 Ⓐ Ⓑ Ⓒ Ⓓ Ⓔ	17 Ⓐ Ⓑ Ⓒ Ⓓ Ⓔ	22 Ⓐ Ⓑ Ⓒ Ⓓ Ⓔ
3 Ⓐ Ⓑ Ⓒ Ⓓ Ⓔ	8 Ⓐ Ⓑ Ⓒ Ⓓ Ⓔ	13 Ⓐ Ⓑ Ⓒ Ⓓ Ⓔ	18 Ⓐ Ⓑ Ⓒ Ⓓ Ⓔ	23 Ⓐ Ⓑ Ⓒ Ⓓ Ⓔ
4 Ⓐ Ⓑ Ⓒ Ⓓ Ⓔ	9 Ⓐ Ⓑ Ⓒ Ⓓ Ⓔ	14 Ⓐ Ⓑ Ⓒ Ⓓ Ⓔ	19 Ⓐ Ⓑ Ⓒ Ⓓ Ⓔ	24 Ⓐ Ⓑ Ⓒ Ⓓ Ⓔ
5 Ⓐ Ⓑ Ⓒ Ⓓ Ⓔ	10 Ⓐ Ⓑ Ⓒ Ⓓ Ⓔ	15 Ⓐ Ⓑ Ⓒ Ⓓ Ⓔ	20 Ⓐ Ⓑ Ⓒ Ⓓ Ⓔ	25 Ⓐ Ⓑ Ⓒ Ⓓ Ⓔ

Upper Level SSAT
Writing Sample
Time - 25 Minutes
1 Topic

Writing Sample

Schools would like to get to know you better through a story you will tell using one of the ideas below. Please choose the idea you find most interesting and write a story using the idea in your first sentence. Please fill in the circle next to the one you choose.

Ⓐ   What did a parent tell you to do that you now wish you had done?

Ⓑ   It was a pleasant surprise.

_____

_____

_____

_____

_____

_____

_____

_____

GO ON TO THE NEXT PAGE.

Upper Level SSAT
Section 1
Time - 30 Minutes
25 Questions

Following each problem in this section, there are five suggested answers. Work each problem in your head or in the blank space provided at the right of the page. Then look at the five suggested answers and decide which one is best.

<u>Note:</u> Figures that accompany problems in this section are drawn as accurately as possible EXCEPT when it is stated in a specific problem that its figure is not drawn to scale.

Sample Problem:

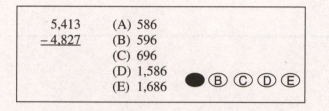

USE THIS SPACE FOR FIGURING.

1. If $h = 2$, and h, i, and j are consecutive even integers and $h < i < j$, what is $h + i + j$?

    (A) 3
    (B) 5
    (C) 9
    (D) 10
    (E) 12

---

2. If $x = \dfrac{1}{2} + \dfrac{1}{3} + \dfrac{1}{4}$ and $y = \dfrac{1}{2} + \dfrac{2}{3} + \dfrac{3}{4}$, then $x + y =$

    (A) 3

    (B) 1

    (C) $\dfrac{2}{3}$

    (D) $\dfrac{1}{24}$

    (E) $\dfrac{1}{3}$

GO ON TO THE NEXT PAGE.

3. If the product of 412.7 and 100 is rounded to the nearest hundred, the answer will be

    (A) 400
    (B) 4,100
    (C) 4,127
    (D) 41,270
    (E) 41,300

USE THIS SPACE FOR FIGURING.

$$\boxed{1}$$

4. If $\frac{4}{5}$ of a number is 28, then $\frac{1}{5}$ of that number is

    (A) 4
    (B) 7
    (C) 21
    (D) 35
    (E) 112

5. $14 + 3 \times 7 + (12 \div 2) =$

    (A) 140

    (B) 125

    (C) $65\frac{1}{2}$

    (D) 41

    (E) 20

6. Maggie wants to mail postcards to 25 of her friends and needs one stamp for each postcard. If she buys 3 stamps at a time, how many sets of stamps must she buy in order to mail all of her postcards?

    (A) 3
    (B) 8
    (C) 9
    (D) 10
    (E) 25

GO ON TO THE NEXT PAGE.

Questions 7 and 8 refer to the following chart.

USE THIS SPACE FOR FIGURING.

Money Raised from Candy Sale

Cost of Candy	$1.00	$5.00	$10.00	$15.00
# Sold	100	25	20	5

Figure 1

7. How much more money was raised by the $10.00 candy than by the $5.00 candy?

(A) $32
(B) $50
(C) $75
(D) $125
(E) $200

8. The money raised by the $15.00 candy is approximately what percent of the total money raised from the candy sale?

(A) 15%
(B) 20%
(C) 30%
(D) 45%
(E) 50%

9. An art gallery has three collections: modern art, sculpture, and photography. If the 24 items that make up the modern art collection represent 25% of the total number of items in the gallery, then the average number of items in each of the other two collections is

(A) 8
(B) 24
(C) 36
(D) 96
(E) 288

GO ON TO THE NEXT PAGE.

10. At Calvin U. Smith Elementary School, the ratio of students to teachers is 9:1. What fractional part of the entire population at the school is teachers?

    (A) $\frac{1}{10}$

    (B) $\frac{1}{9}$

    (C) $\frac{1}{8}$

    (D) $\frac{8}{1}$

    (E) $\frac{9}{1}$

11. The Ace Delivery Company employs two drivers to make deliveries on a certain Saturday. If Driver A makes d deliveries and Driver B makes $d + 2$ deliveries, then in terms of d, the average number of deliveries made by each driver is

    (A) d

    (B) $d + 1$

    (C) $d + 2$

    (D) $\frac{1}{2}d + 2$

    (E) $\frac{3}{2}d$

12. Which of the following is equal to w ?

    (A) $180 - v$
    (B) $180 + v$
    (C) 105
    (D) 115
    (E) $2v$

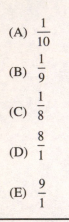

Figure 2

GO ON TO THE NEXT PAGE.

13. Tracy goes to the store and buys only candy bars and cans of soda. She buys 3 times as many candy bars as cans of soda. If she buys a total of 24 items, how many of those items are candy bars?

    (A) 3
    (B) 12
    (C) 18
    (D) 21
    (E) 24

14. $-\left(\dfrac{4}{3}\right)^3 =$

    (A) $\dfrac{64}{27}$

    (B) $\dfrac{12}{9}$

    (C) $-\dfrac{12}{27}$

    (D) $-\dfrac{12}{9}$

    (E) $-\dfrac{64}{27}$

15. Of the following choices, which value for x would satisfy the equation $\dfrac{1}{5} + x > 1$?

    (A) $\dfrac{3}{4}$

    (B) $\dfrac{4}{5}$

    (C) $\dfrac{6}{7}$

    (D) $\dfrac{6}{8}$

    (E) $\dfrac{7}{9}$

GO ON TO THE NEXT PAGE.

16. Given the equations $2x + y = 8$ and $z + y = 8$, find the value of x ?

    (A) −8
    (B) −4
    (C) 4
    (D) 16
    (E) It cannot be determined from the information given.

USE THIS SPACE FOR FIGURING.

17. A, B, and C are squares. The length of one side of square A is 3. The length of one side of square B is twice the length of a side of square A, and the length of one side of square C is twice the length of a side of square B. What is the average area of the three squares?

    (A) 21
    (B) 36
    (C) 63
    (D) 84
    (E) 144

A	*B*	*C*

Figure 3

18. There are 12 homes on a certain street. If 4 homes are painted blue, 3 are painted red, and the remaining homes are green, what fractional part of the homes on the street are green?

    (A) 7

    (B) 5

    (C) $\dfrac{7}{12}$

    (D) $\dfrac{5}{12}$

    (E) $\dfrac{1}{12}$

GO ON TO THE NEXT PAGE.

19. Melissa lives 30 miles from work and Katy lives 40 miles from work. If Melissa and Katy work at the same office, how many miles apart do the girls live from each other?

    (A) 10
    (B) 35
    (C) 50
    (D) 70
    (E) It cannot be determined from the information given.

USE THIS SPACE FOR FIGURING.

20. If, at a fundraising dinner, x guests each donate $200 and y guests each donate $300, in terms of x and y, what is the total number of dollars raised?

    (A) $250(x + y)$

    (B) $200x + 300y$

    (C) $250xy$

    (D) $\dfrac{xy}{250}$

    (E) $500xy$

21. A rectangular fish tank with dimensions 2 feet × 3 feet × 4 feet is being filled by a hose that produces 6 cubic feet of water per minute. At this rate, how many minutes will it take to fill the tank?

    (A) 24
    (B) 6
    (C) 4
    (D) 3
    (E) 2

GO ON TO THE NEXT PAGE.

22. With 4 days left in the Mountain Lake Critter Collection Contest, Mary has caught 15 fewer critters than Natalie. If Mary is to win the contest by collecting more critters than Natalie, at least how many critters per day must Mary catch?

    (A) 4
    (B) 5
    (C) 16
    (D) 30
    (E) 46

USE THIS SPACE FOR FIGURING.

1

23. If $3x - y = 23$ and x is an integer greater than 0, which of the following is NOT a possible value for y ?

    (A) 9
    (B) 7
    (C) 4
    (D) 1
    (E) −2

24. Anna, A, and Bob, B, are avid readers. If Anna and Bob together read an average of 200 pages in a day and Bob reads fewer pages than Anna, which equation must be true?

    (A) $A - 200 = 200 - B$
    (B) $A = 200$ and $B = 200$
    (C) $A - B = 100$
    (D) $A = 200 + B$
    (E) $A + B = 200$

25. $30.00 is taken off the price of a dress. If the new price is now 60% of the original price, what was the original price of the dress?

(A) $75.00
(B) $60.00
(C) $50.00
(D) $45.00
(E) $30.00

STOP

IF YOU FINISH BEFORE TIME IS CALLED,
YOU MAY CHECK YOUR WORK ON THIS SECTION ONLY.
DO NOT TURN TO ANY OTHER SECTION IN THE TEST.

GO ON TO THE NEXT PAGE.

Upper Level SSAT
Section 2
Time - 40 Minutes
40 Questions

Read each passage carefully and then answer the questions about it. For each question, decide on the basis of the passage which one of the choices best answers the question.

The reading passages in this test are brief excerpts or adaptations of excerpts from published material. To make the text suitable for testing purposes, we may have, in some cases, altered the style, contents, or point of view of the original.

Florence Nightingale was a woman ahead of her time. Before the nineteenth century, the profession of nursing was largely untrained. Midwives were the only practitioners who had any training at all. For the most part, sick people were looked after by the women of the house in their own homes.

Florence Nightingale began a school in London, England to set the standards for nursing. She was able to do this because she had already established a reputation for her work with soldiers during the Crimean War. She carried a lamp above her head as she walked among the wounded men, thereby earning the nickname "the lady with the lamp." It was this great lady who lit the way for nursing to become the respected profession it is today.

---

1. The passage is mainly about

   (A) the impact of nursing on the soldiers of the Crimean War
   (B) Florence Nightingale and her influence on the profession of nursing
   (C) the difference between nurses and midwives
   (D) how Florence Nightingale earned the nickname "the lady with the lamp"
   (E) why only females entered the profession of nursing

2. Which of the following was a method most people used to receive care before Florence Nightingale's time?

   (A) They would be cared for only by doctors.
   (B) They would be cared for by their children.
   (C) They were largely left uncared for.
   (D) They were cared for by midwives.
   (E) They were cared for by female relatives.

3. The style of the passage is most like that found in a(n)

   (A) personal letter to a trusted friend
   (B) anthology of short biographies of famous women
   (C) history of nineteenth-century England
   (D) textbook on medicine
   (E) editorial written for a daily paper

4. According to the author, the primary reason that Florence Nightingale was able to open a school for nursing was that

   (A) she was already famous for her work in the war
   (B) her family was willing to finance her work
   (C) she had gained notoriety as a difficult woman to challenge
   (D) she had cared for many wealthy sick people herself
   (E) she worked endless hours every night

5. According to the passage, all of the following could be said of nurses EXCEPT

   (A) prior to Florence Nightingale, only midwives were trained
   (B) Florence Nightingale raised the standards of their profession
   (C) they are well-respected professionals today
   (D) they are exceedingly well paid for their work
   (E) prior to Florence Nightingale, their work was done often by female relatives

GO ON TO THE NEXT PAGE.

2

In England during the mid-1600s, a group of poor English farmers led by Gerrard Winstanley united to form an organization known as the True Levelers. Their stated goal was to change the laws regarding real estate and ownable property so that all willing citizens would be able to support themselves through farming. At the time in England, there was great social unrest and food prices were very high. Most of the land throughout the country was strictly divided and controlled by a small number of the elite ruling class. The True Levelers believed that they could "level" the different classes of society by creating communities in which the farmable private land was owned by all and available for agrarian purposes. To fight the unequal system that only benefited the wealthy landowners, the True Levelers defiantly occupied private and public land and began farming.

Because much of farming involves plowing and planting, these groups of communal farmers became better known by the name Diggers. Their hope was that their act of rebellion would stir the sympathies of the other poor people throughout the country. The Digger philosophy was to unite all the poor and working classes behind the idea that the land should be shared. If thousands of common English folk began to claim reasonable access to the land, the powerful landowners would be unable to stop them. In practice for a brief time, Digger communities flourished as they welcomed anyone who wished to merely grow their own food and live freely.

Sadly, the landowners believed the Diggers were a threat and began to take steps to preserve their control over the farmable land. Many members of the Digger communities were harassed, threatened, and jailed. Planting vegetables was viewed as a rebellious act and dealt with as if it were a crime. The majority of land reverted back into the hands of the landowners. Ultimately, most of the Digger communities that had briefly thrived were disbanded. In their place, other political groups arose and continued to protest the various injustices of the time. The Digger name continues to the present day in some English folk songs as a reminder of their ideals.

6. The word "agrarian" is most similar to which of the following?

   (A) Testing
   (B) Private
   (C) Unequal
   (D) Farming
   (E) Aggressive

7. Which of the following can be inferred about the Diggers as described in the passage?

   (A) They had a different political philosophy than the True Levelers.
   (B) They allowed others to join them in their farming activities.
   (C) They were skilled political speakers.
   (C) They defeated the powerful landowners through military force.
   (E) They were exceptional folk singers.

8. Which of the following was the most significant point of conflict between landowners and Diggers?

   (A) The Diggers had the willingness but not the space on which to grow enough food to support themselves.
   (B) Wealthy landowners in England at the time were usually violent.
   (C) There was no agreement between Diggers and True Levelers.
   (D) The quality of vegetables grown by the Diggers was inferior to that produced on wealthy estates.
   (E) The local government did not have any authority in the dispute.

GO ON TO THE NEXT PAGE.

9. The passage is primarily about

   (A) working hard even in challenging times
   (B) social problems in England in the seventeenth century
   (C) the inhumanity of wealthy English landowners
   (D) Gerrard Winstanley's ideas
   (E) the brief history of an English community organization

10. According to the passage, what is the most significant difference between True Levelers and the Diggers?

   (A) The True Levelers believed in farming private land, while the Diggers believed in farming public land.
   (B) The True Levelers followed Gerrard Winstanley, while the Diggers had other leaders.
   (C) There is no difference between the two groups, as the names refer to the same people.
   (D) The True Levelers were accepted by landowners, while the Diggers were jailed.
   (E) The True Levelers are not remembered in folk songs, while the Diggers are.

GO ON TO THE NEXT PAGE.

Flax has been raised for many thousands of years, for many different reasons. Probably the two most important reasons are for the fabric made from it and the oil produced from it. The woody stem of the flax plant contains the long, strong fibers that are used to make linen. The seeds are rich in an oil important for its industrial uses.

The people of ancient Egypt, Assyria, and Mesopotamia raised flax for cloth; Egyptian mummies were wrapped in linen. Since the discovery of its drying ability, the oil from flaxseed, called linseed oil, has been used as a drying agent in paints and varnishes.

The best fiber and the best seed cannot be obtained from the same kinds of plant. Fiber flax grows tall and has few branches. It needs a short, cool growing season with plenty of rainfall evenly distributed. Otherwise, the plants become woody and the fiber is rough and dry. On the other hand, seed flax grows well in places that are too dry for fiber flax. The plants are lower to the ground and have more branches.

11. Which of the following would be the best title for the passage?

(A) "How Mummies Were Preserved"
(B) "The Many Uses of the Flax Plant"
(C) "The Difference Between Seeds and Fibers"
(D) "The Types of Plant Life Around the World"
(E) "Ancient Sources of Oil and Linen"

12. The author suggests that ancient people raised flax primarily for

(A) its oil, used to preserve wood
(B) its oil, used as a rich source of nutrient
(C) its fabric, used for their clothes
(D) its fabric, used to wrap their dead
(E) its fabric and oil, for industrial uses

13. This passage sounds as if it were an excerpt from

(A) a letter to the Egyptians
(B) a book on plant life
(C) a scientific treatise
(D) a persuasive essay from an ecologist
(E) a friendly reminder to a politician

14. Which of the following questions is answered by the passage?

(A) Can the same plant be grown for the best fabric and the best oil?
(B) How did the Egyptians wrap their mummies?
(C) What temperature is optimal for growing flax?
(D) How is flax harvested?
(E) Is it possible to produce a new type of flax for fabric and oil production?

15. Which of the following is the author most likely to discuss next?

(A) How flax is used around the world today
(B) Other types of useful plants
(C) Other sources of oil
(D) The usefulness of synthetic fabrics
(E) The advantages of pesticides and crop rotation

GO ON TO THE NEXT PAGE.

William, Duke of Normandy, conquered England in 1066. One of the first tasks he undertook as king was the building of a fortress in the city of London. Begun in 1066 and completed several years later by William's son, William Rufus, this structure was called the White Tower.

The Tower of London is not just one building, but an 18-acre complex of buildings. In addition to the White Tower, there are 19 other towers. The Thames River flows by one side of the complex and a large moat, or shallow ditch, surrounds it. Once filled with water, the moat was drained in 1843 and is now covered with grass.

The Tower of London is the city's most popular tourist attraction. A great deal of fascinating history has taken place within its walls. The tower has served as a fortress, royal residence, prison, royal mint, public records office, observatory, military barracks, place of execution, and city zoo.

As recently as 1941, the tower was used as a prison for Adolf Hitler's associate Rudolf Hess. Although it is no longer used as a prison, the tower still houses the crown jewels and a great deal of English history.

16. The primary purpose of this passage is to

(A) discuss the future of the Tower of London
(B) discuss the ramifications of using the Tower as a prison
(C) argue that the Tower is an improper place for crown jewels
(D) describe and discuss the history of the Tower of London
(E) debate the relative merits of the uses of the Tower in the past to the present

17. All of the following were uses for the Tower of London EXCEPT

(A) a place where money was made
(B) a palace for the royals
(C) a place where executions were held
(D) a place of religious pilgrimage
(E) a place where records were stored

18. Which of the following questions is answered by the passage?

(A) What controversy has surrounded the Tower of London?
(B) How much revenue does the Tower generate for England?
(C) In what year did construction on the Tower of London begin?
(D) What is the type of stone used in the Tower of London?
(E) Who was the most famous prisoner in the Tower?

19. When discussing the Tower of London the author's tone could best be described as

(A) bewildered
(B) objective
(C) overly emotional
(D) envious
(E) disdainful

20. Which of the following does the author imply about Rudolf Hess?

(A) He was executed at the Tower of London.
(B) He was one of the last prisoners in the Tower of London.
(C) He died an untimely death.
(D) He was a tourist attraction.
(E) He was respectful of the great Tower of London.

21. The author would most probably agree that

(A) the Tower of London is useful only as a tourist attraction
(B) the Tower of London could never be built today
(C) the Tower of London cannot generate enough revenue to justify its expenses
(D) the Tower of London has a complex history
(E) the prisoners at the Tower were relatively well treated

GO ON TO THE NEXT PAGE.

Most art enthusiasts agree that *Mona Lisa* by Leonardo da Vinci is the most famous painting in the world. It is the portrait of a woman, the wife of Francesco del Giocondo, a wealthy Florentine business man. The name roughly translates from Italian to mean "Madam Lisa" and is a respectful term. Anyone who has ever viewed the painting, seasoned art critic or inexperienced museum visitor, remembers well its greatest feature—Mona Lisa's smile. It is this smile that has captured the imagination of the millions of visitors who have seen the painting over the years.

There is something powerful and alluring contained in Mona Lisa's smile that intrigues all who see it. The reason for her smile has long been the subject of discussion in the art world. But perhaps it is the fact that no one knows why she smiles that makes *Mona Lisa* the most famous of all paintings. There is something so appealing and recognizably human about an unexplained smile to which everyone can relate. Furthermore, if we ever tire of analyzing why

Mona Lisa smiles, we can consider how da Vinci managed to capture the smile. What could he have been thinking while painting? A genuine smile is hard to capture even in a photograph with a modern camera, yet Leonardo da Vinci managed to capture this subtle expression in a painting. It is amazing that da Vinci was able to create for eternity a frozen picture of a smile that in reality lasts less than an instant.

The painting now hangs in the Musee du Louvre in Paris, France. Several different owners have possessed it at various times throughout history, including Louis XIV and Napoleon. It was even temporarily in the possession of a former museum employee who stole it in 1911. He was caught in 1913. It is likely that all who held the painting at one time or another wondered about the Mona Lisa smile, just as today's museum visitors do. Now the painting officially belongs to the French government. In some ways, though, it is really a painting (and a mystery) that belongs to the world.

22. Which of the following best expresses the author's attitude toward the painting?

(A) It should be well protected so that it is not stolen again.
(B) It is difficult to preserve such old masterpieces.
(C) Its greatest appeal is the mystery surrounding it.
(D) There will never be a painter as great as Leonardo da Vinci again.
(E) Everyone should have a chance to own great art.

23. Which of the following is a fact from the passage?

(A) A good smile lasts only a few seconds.
(B) There is tremendous mystery surrounding which painter created *Mona Lisa*.
(C) Napoleon donated *Mona Lisa* to the Musee du Louvre.
(D) There has been some focus on Mona Lisa's smile in artistic communities.
(E) All art historians agree that *Mona Lisa* is the greatest work of art in the world.

24. The author implies which of the following?

(A) A painting can be owned, but the powerful effect of a work of art is available to everyone who sees it.
(B) Leonardo da Vinci was hiding a secret that he wished to reveal through his painting.
(C) *Mona Lisa* has caused much turmoil in the art world due to its peculiar details.
(D) The Musee du Louvre does not have proper equipment in place for capturing modern criminals.
(E) The only detail viewers of *Mona Lisa* can later recall is her smile.

25. The author's tone can best be described as

(A) appreciative
(B) investigative
(C) artistic
(D) confused
(E) indifferent

GO ON TO THE NEXT PAGE.

The first old "horseless carriages" of the 1880s may have been worthy of a snicker or two, but not the cars of today. The progress that has been made over the last one hundred years has been phenomenal. In fact, much progress was made even in the first twenty years—in 1903, cars could travel at 70 miles per hour. The major change from the old cars to today is the expense. Whereas cars were once a luxury that only the very wealthy could afford, today, people of all income levels own cars.

In fact, there are so many cars that if they were to line up end to end, they would touch the moon. Cars are used for everyday transportation for millions of people, for recreation, and for work. Many people's jobs depend on cars—police officers, health care workers, and taxi drivers all rely on automobiles.

One thing that hasn't changed is how cars are powered. The first cars ran on gas and diesel fuel just as the most modern ones do. The newer cars, however, are much more fuel efficient and much research is devoted to saving fuel and finding new sources of energy for cars.

26. The "progress" mentioned in line 2 most likely refers to

(A) the ability of a car to move forward
(B) technological advancement
(C) research
(D) the new types of fuels available
(E) the cost of the car

27. Which of the following is answered by the passage?

(A) What are some ways people use cars?
(B) Why did people laugh at the "horseless carriage"?
(C) Where will the fuels of the future come from?
(D) When will cars become even more efficient?
(E) How much money is spent on cars today?

28. The passage is primarily concerned with

(A) the problem of fuel consumption
(B) the difficulty of driving
(C) the invention of the car
(D) the development of the car from the past to now
(E) the future of automobiles

29. According to the passage, scientists devote much of their research today to

(A) making cars faster
(B) making more cars
(C) making cars more affordable
(D) making cars more fuel efficient
(E) making cars that hold more people

30. When discussing the technological advances of the early car, the author's tone could best be described as

(A) proud
(B) hesitant
(C) informative
(D) pedantic
(E) sarcastic

31. The author would most likely agree that

(A) cars are incredibly useful to many different sorts of people
(B) the problems we face in the future are very important
(C) cars are more trouble than they are worth
(D) early car owners were all snobs
(E) we will never make the same technological advances as we did in the past

GO ON TO THE NEXT PAGE.

> By the rude bridge that arched the flood,
> Their flag to April's breeze unfurled,
> Here once the embattled farmers stood
> And fired the shot heard round the world.
> The foe long since in silence slept;
> Alike the conqueror silent sleeps;
> And Time the ruined bridge has swept
> Down the dark stream which seaward creeps.
> On this green bank, by this soft stream,
> We set to-day a votive stone;
> That memory may their deed redeem,
> When, like our sires, our sons are gone.
> Spirit, that made those heroes dare
> To die, and leave their children free,
> Bid Time and Nature gently spare
>   The shaft we raise to them and thee.
>
> —"Concord Hymn" by Ralph Waldo Emerson

2

32. The statements in lines 3–4 most likely mean

   (A) the narrator is a farmer
   (B) the place described is a battle site
   (C) a crime took place at that site
   (D) the farmers described were all killed
   (E) it is a cold day

33. In the poem, the speaker claims which of the reasons for writing this poem?

   I.   To warn future generations about the horrors of war
   II. To keep the memory of the great deeds of soldiers alive
   III. To gain courage to fight himself

   (A) I only
   (B) II only
   (C) II and III only
   (D) I and III only
   (E) I, II, and III

34. The "votive stone" referred to in line 10 probably refers to

   (A) a candle
   (B) a weapon
   (C) an old stone fence
   (D) a war memorial
   (E) a natural landmark

35. With which statement would the author most strongly agree?

   (A) All war is in vain.
   (B) Farming is a difficult life.
   (C) It is important to remember the brave soldiers.
   (D) How a man fights is as important as how he lives his life.
   (E) A memorial is an insignificant way to remember the past.

GO ON TO THE NEXT PAGE.

Jose Ferrer was known as one of the most successful American film actors of his generation, but he actually began his career in theater. He was born January 8, 1909 in Puerto Rico and moved to the United States when he was six years old. His acting skills were first showcased while he attended Princeton University and performed with the Triangle Club, a student acting group whose alumni also include Jimmy Stewart and F. Scott Fitzgerald.

After graduating, Ferrer continued to perform in theater until he made his Broadway debut in 1935 in the play *Charley's Aunt*. He had many successful roles on Broadway, including a role in 1943 when he played the villain Iago in Shakespeare's play *Othello*. The title role of *Othello* in that production was played by the acclaimed actor Paul Robeson. With these two powerful performers, *Othello* became the longest running play in Broadway history (at the time). Ferrer's greatest role, though, was still to come.

In 1946, Ferrer was cast in the title role of *Cyrano de Bergerac*. He won the prestigious Tony award as Cyrano, the tragic hero who fights men with supreme courage but cowardly hides his love for the beautiful Roxanne. His success in this role led directly to his repeated performances as Cyrano in a film version (for which he won an Oscar) and a television version (for which he won an Emmy). He is the only actor to win all three of those special awards for playing the same role. This feat is all the more remarkable because Cyrano de Bergerac was known as a desirable role, one that had been played very well previously by other talented actors.

Through these roles, Ferrer earned a reputation on Broadway as an extremely flexible actor, talented enough to play many diverse roles. Eight years after his debut in professional theater, he finally started performing in movies. Once he began appearing in films, that skill translated into many great performances and memorable roles. His film career included both acting and directing opportunities and lasted nearly forty years.

36. Which of the following is the primary purpose of the passage?

(A) To discuss the success of Puerto Rican actors on Broadway
(B) To suggest that Jose Ferrer was the best actor ever to play Cyrano de Bergerac
(C) To provide a synopsis of the career of a well-regarded American actor
(D) To contrast the history of theater with the history of television
(E) To compare two great Broadway actors, Paul Robeson and Jose Ferrer

37. The author would most likely agree with which of the following?

(A) Ferrer's career was long because he was able to play many different roles.
(B) Ferrer regretted waiting years before he became a screen actor.
(C) Princeton University's Triangle Club allowed Ferrer to learn from Jimmy Stewart and F. Scott Fitzgerald.
(D) Cyrano de Bergerac is the greatest role ever written for the Broadway stage.
(E) Cyrano de Bergerac was Ferrer's favorite role to perform.

GO ON TO THE NEXT PAGE.

2

38. Which of the following can be inferred from the passage?

    (A) Most members of the Triangle Club have successful acting careers.
    (B) Ferrer was more honored by his Tony award than by his Emmy or Oscar.
    (C) The record-setting run of *Othello* may have been in part due to Paul Robeson.
    (D) Ferrer did not perform again on Broadway after he began performing in movies.
    (E) Ferrer's performance as Cyrano set a record that still stands today.

39. The author would most likely agree with all of the following EXCEPT

    (A) Paul Robeson was seen by some as a very talented actor.
    (B) Ferrer is somewhat responsible for the success of the longest-running Broadway play in history.
    (C) Some actors consider Cyrano de Bergerac a role they would like to perform.
    (D) It is difficult to win prestigious acting awards.
    (E) Ferrer's successful performance in Othello was his first Broadway performance.

40. Which of the following best describes the author's attitude toward Jose Ferrer?

    (A) Indifference
    (B) Envy
    (C) Friendship
    (D) Isolation
    (E) Admiration

STOP

IF YOU FINISH BEFORE TIME IS CALLED, YOU MAY CHECK YOUR WORK ON THIS SECTION ONLY. DO NOT TURN TO ANY OTHER SECTION IN THE TEST.

Upper Level SSAT
Section 3
Time - 30 Minutes
60 Questions

This section consists of two different types of questions. There are directions and a sample question for each type.

Each of the following questions consists of one word followed by five words or phrases. You are to select the one word or phrase whose meaning is closest to the word in capital letters.

Sample Question:

```
CHILLY:
(A)  lazy
(B)  nice
(C)  dry
(D)  cold
(E)  sunny      Ⓐ Ⓑ Ⓒ ● Ⓔ
```

1. CONTORT:
    (A) bend
    (B) deform
    (C) color
    (D) amuse
    (E) occupy

2. GRIM:
    (A) clean
    (B) relaxing
    (C) frown
    (D) harsh
    (E) irresponsible

3. PROHIBIT:
    (A) attempt
    (B) recount
    (C) diminish
    (D) conserve
    (E) forbid

4. VACANT:
    (A) stark
    (B) varied
    (C) dreary
    (D) rented
    (E) huge

5. AUSTERE:
    (A) plentiful
    (B) ornate
    (C) miserly
    (D) severe
    (E) empty

6. QUELL:
    (A) stifle
    (B) dissemble
    (C) articulate
    (D) rock gently
    (E) praise highly

7. FORTIFY:
    (A) emphasize
    (B) strengthen
    (C) revere
    (D) diffuse
    (E) surround

8. PROCLIVITY:
    (A) efficiency
    (B) tend
    (C) authenticity
    (D) propensity
    (E) proprietary

GO ON TO THE NEXT PAGE.

9. FORMIDABLE:
   (A) malleable
   (B) powerful
   (C) talented
   (D) fear
   (E) trainable

10. STYMIE:
    (A) construct
    (B) swindle
    (C) depress
    (D) frustrate
    (E) reason

11. ERRATIC:
    (A) constant
    (B) amiable
    (C) innate
    (D) inconsistent
    (E) caustic

12. CONCILIATE:
    (A) pacify
    (B) replace
    (C) inform
    (D) expose
    (E) surpass

13. REFRACTORY:
    (A) stubborn
    (B) excessive
    (C) ironic
    (D) inhumane
    (E) improper

14. TRUNCATE:
    (A) packed
    (B) shorten
    (C) grow
    (D) remind
    (E) reproach

15. MEAGER:
    (A) gullible
    (B) novel
    (C) sparse
    (D) vulnerable
    (E) providential

16. CREDIBLE:
    (A) obsolete
    (B) plausible
    (C) fabulous
    (D) mundane
    (E) superficial

17. CULPABLE:
    (A) elusive
    (B) unheralded
    (C) esoteric
    (D) worthy of blame
    (E) sanctioned

18. DEPLORE:
    (A) rejoice
    (B) mitigate
    (C) lament
    (D) imply
    (E) prevent

19. ACCLAIM:
    (A) compliment
    (B) feast
    (C) assert
    (D) blame
    (E) compose

20. GUILE:
    (A) vengeance
    (B) fear
    (C) trust
    (D) loathing
    (E) cunning

GO ON TO THE NEXT PAGE.

21. FALLOW:
    (A) prompt
    (B) unused
    (C) deep
    (D) secondary
    (E) recessive

22. CHAMPION:
    (A) deter
    (B) force
    (C) fight
    (D) side with
    (E) change

23. IMBUE:
    (A) renew
    (B) suffuse
    (C) dawdle
    (D) compete
    (E) impress

24. POSTHUMOUS:
    (A) in the future
    (B) post war
    (C) after death
    (D) during the age of
    (E) promptly

25. INAUSPICIOUS:
    (A) colorless
    (B) prudent
    (C) misplaced
    (D) ominous
    (E) raising intelligent questions

26. RENAISSANCE:
    (A) carnival
    (B) fortune
    (C) burial
    (D) revival
    (E) earlier time

27. DECOMPOSITION:
    (A) combustion
    (B) infiltration
    (C) perturbation
    (D) equalization
    (E) disintegration

28. AGGRANDIZEMENT:
    (A) assessment
    (B) leniency
    (C) restitution
    (D) annulment
    (E) glorification

29. GULLIBLE:
    (A) stranded
    (B) easily deceived
    (C) distant
    (D) assailable
    (E) scheduled

30. REFUTATION:
    (A) attraction
    (B) disprove
    (C) legal activity
    (D) deny
    (E) enthusiastic response

GO ON TO THE NEXT PAGE.

The following questions ask you to find relationships between words. For each question, select the answer choice that best completes the meaning of the sentence.

Sample Question:

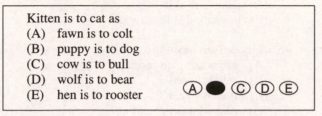

Kitten is to cat as
(A) fawn is to colt
(B) puppy is to dog
(C) cow is to bull
(D) wolf is to bear
(E) hen is to rooster

Choice (B) is the best answer because a kitten is a young cat, just as a puppy is a young dog. Of all the answer choices, (B) states a relationship that is most like the relationship between <u>kitten</u> and <u>cat</u>.

---

31. Composer is to score as
    (A) conductor is to orchestra
    (B) operator is to telephone
    (C) teacher is to classroom
    (D) attorney is to trial
    (E) author is to book

32. Stanza is to poem as
    (A) sonnet is to play
    (B) drama is to theater
    (C) paragraph is to essay
    (D) teacher is to class
    (E) preface is to book

33. Sovereign is to monarchy as principal is to
    (A) school
    (B) administrators
    (C) workers
    (D) crew
    (E) town

34. Cylinder is to can as
    (A) circle is to square
    (B) perimeter is to area
    (C) cube is to dice
    (D) line is to angle
    (E) arc is to sphere

35. Laughter is to joke as
    (A) read is to story
    (B) question is to answer
    (C) wince is to pain
    (D) talk is to conversation
    (E) cramp is to swim

36. Massive is to weight as
    (A) gargantuan is to size
    (B) acute is to hearing
    (C) tender is to feeling
    (D) simple is to thought
    (E) foolish is to idea

37. Pint is to quart as
    (A) cup is to teaspoon
    (B) mile is to road
    (C) measure is to recipe
    (D) week is to year
    (E) temperature is to thermometer

38. Scrawl is to writing as
    (A) decipher is to code
    (B) babble is to speaking
    (C) carve is to stone
    (D) tango is to dancing
    (E) direct is to acting

GO ON TO THE NEXT PAGE.

39. Stoic is to emotion as
    (A) serious is to concern
    (B) soothe is to injury
    (C) amorphous is to shape
    (D) choke is to morsel
    (E) breathe is to life

40. Frugal is to spending as unruly is to
    (A) fractious
    (B) impossible
    (C) obedient
    (D) warmth
    (E) pride

41. Integrity is to honesty as
    (A) comprehension is to instruction
    (B) fame is to happiness
    (C) resolution is to determination
    (D) severity is to compassion
    (E) quotation is to report

42. Lily is to flower as pine is to
    (A) oak
    (B) needle
    (C) forest
    (D) winter
    (E) wood

43. Kitchen is to galley as
    (A) wheel is to car
    (B) fireplace is to heat
    (C) lobby is to apartment
    (D) house is to ship
    (E) exhibit is to museum

44. Blooming is to rose as
    (A) withered is to vine
    (B) prolific is to weed
    (C) fertile is to field
    (D) edible is to corn
    (E) ripe is to tomato

45. Mask is to face as
    (A) coat is to fabric
    (B) shoe is to foot
    (C) belt is to leather
    (D) hem is to skirt
    (E) invitation is to party

46. Agenda is to meeting as
    (A) clipboard is to paper
    (B) rule is to order
    (C) map is to car
    (D) blueprint is to building
    (E) gavel is to podium

47. Pathology is to disease as psychology is to
    (A) mind
    (B) science
    (C) doctor
    (D) anguish
    (E) hospital

48. Autobiography is to author as
    (A) autograph is to signature
    (B) self-sufficiency is to provision
    (C) automation is to worker
    (D) self-portrait is to artist
    (E) autopsy is to doctor

49. Bird is to migration as
    (A) parrot is to imitation
    (B) ranger is to conservation
    (C) bear is to hibernation
    (D) lawyer is to accusation
    (E) traveler is to location

50. Border is to country as
    (A) perimeter is to object
    (B) land is to owner
    (C) road is to street
    (D) area is to volume
    (E) capital is to state

GO ON TO THE NEXT PAGE.

51. Patter is to rain as
    (A) rainbow is to storm
    (B) call is to telephone
    (C) clank is to chain
    (D) volume is to radio
    (E) eruption is to volcano

52. Brazen is to tact as
    (A) lethargic is to energy
    (B) agile is to strength
    (C) humongous is to size
    (D) ancient is to time
    (E) fallen is to grace

53. Taciturn is to words as
    (A) thrifty is to money
    (B) petty is to concern
    (C) silly is to extras
    (D) startled is to surprise
    (E) trusting is to care

54. Scalpel is to razor as surgeon is to
    (A) barber
    (B) gardener
    (C) chef
    (D) patient
    (E) engineer

55. Storyteller is to listener as
    (A) accompanist is to composer
    (B) critique is to commentator
    (C) banter is to humorist
    (D) anthologist is to editor
    (E) pantomime is to viewer

56. Gully is to erosion as
    (A) drought is to precipitation
    (B) mine is to excavation
    (C) clot is to dispersion
    (D) forest is to cultivation
    (E) water is to inundation

57. Drip is to deluge as
    (A) shine is to polish
    (B) warm is to heat
    (C) yearn is to wish
    (D) smolder is to blaze
    (E) bend is to straight

58. Lax is to resolution as
    (A) hapless is to circumstance
    (B) detrimental is to destruction
    (C) deceitful is to sincerity
    (D) vulnerable is to wound
    (E) accessible is to rewarded

59. Hammer is to pound as
    (A) vase is to flowers
    (B) briefcase is to papers
    (C) nail is to wood
    (D) screwdriver is to tool
    (E) jack is to raise

60. Lexicon is to words as anthology is to
    (A) reading
    (B) library
    (C) books
    (D) works
    (E) pages

STOP

IF YOU FINISH BEFORE TIME IS CALLED,
YOU MAY CHECK YOUR WORK ON THIS SECTION ONLY.
DO NOT TURN TO ANY OTHER SECTION IN THE TEST.

Upper Level SSAT
Section 4
Time - 30 Minutes
25 Questions

Following each problem in this section, there are five suggested answers. Work each problem in your head or in the blank space provided at the right of the page. Then look at the five suggested answers and decide which one is best.

<u>Note:</u> Figures that accompany problems in this section are drawn as accurately as possible EXCEPT when it is stated in a specific problem that its figure is not drawn to scale.

Sample Problem:

5,413 $- 4,827$	(A) 586 (B) 596 (C) 696 (D) 1,586 (E) 1,686

● Ⓑ Ⓒ Ⓓ Ⓔ

---

1. $2^4 =$

   (A) 24
   (B) 16
   (C) 8
   (D) 6
   (E) 4

USE THIS SPACE FOR FIGURING.

---

2. $x =$

   (A) 30
   (B) 60
   (C) 90
   (D) 120
   (E) 300

$x°$ / 60°

Figure 1

---

3. If $-4 < x < 2$, how many possible integer values for x are there?

   (A) 6
   (B) 5
   (C) 4
   (D) 3
   (E) 2

GO ON TO THE NEXT PAGE.

Questions 4-6 refer to the following graph.

Ken's Savings Account Balance, 2011–2014

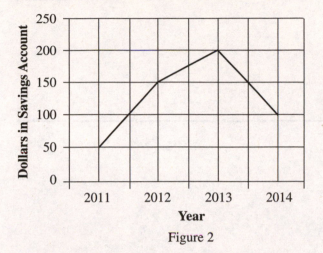

Figure 2

4. By how many dollars did Ken's savings account balance grow from 2011 to 2012?

    (A) $25.00
    (B) $50.00
    (C) $75.00
    (D) $100.00
    (E) $150.00

5. The decrease in Ken's account balance from 2013 to 2014 equals what percent of Ken's account balance at the start of 2012?

    (A) 100%

    (B) 75%

    (C) $66\frac{2}{3}$ %

    (D) 50%

    (E) 25%

6. If during 2014, Ken withdrew from his account one-half the amount he withdrew in 2013, how many dollars would be left in his account at the end of 2014?

    (A) $50
    (B) $75
    (C) $100
    (D) $150
    (E) $200

GO ON TO THE NEXT PAGE.

7. A large square box is made up of smaller square boxes. Each of these smaller boxes has a side length of 3 inches. How many of these smaller boxes are used to create the larger box if the larger box's base has a perimeter of 36 inches?

    (A) 9
    (B) 27
    (C) 36
    (D) 64
    (E) 108

USE THIS SPACE FOR FIGURING.

4

8. Calculate $10x - y^2$ when $x = 4$ and $y = 5$.

    (A) 4
    (B) 7
    (C) 15
    (D) 25
    (E) 30

9. Which of the following fractions is greatest?

    (A) $\dfrac{3}{4}$

    (B) $\dfrac{5}{8}$

    (C) $\dfrac{1}{2}$

    (D) $\dfrac{3}{7}$

    (E) $\dfrac{5}{9}$

10. If $x + y = z$, then $z =$

    (A) 180
    (B) 90
    (C) 60
    (D) 45
    (E) 30

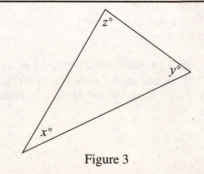

Figure 3

GO ON TO THE NEXT PAGE.

11. Anita bowled a 100, a 120, and an 88 on her first three games. What must her score be on the fourth game to raise her average for the day to a 130 ?

(A) 80

(B) 95

(C) $102\frac{2}{3}$

(D) 145

(E) 212

USE THIS SPACE FOR FIGURING.

12. There are 35 girls and 24 boys in a club. One quarter of the boys are wearing red shirts. Forty percent of the girls are wearing yellow shirts. How many more club members are wearing yellow shirts than red shirts?

(A) 1
(B) 3
(C) 8
(D) 9
(E) 12

13. 36 is 16 percent of

(A) 25
(B) 52
(C) 112
(D) 125
(E) 225

14. Mr. Patterson pays $1,200 each month for a storage warehouse that measures 75 feet by 200 feet. What is the monthly cost per square foot?

(A) $0.08
(B) $0.75
(C) $0.80
(D) $8.00
(E) $450.00

GO ON TO THE NEXT PAGE.

15. The ratio of rhubarb plants to tomato plants in Jim's garden is 4 to 5. If there is a total of 45 rhubarb and tomato plants all together, how many of these plants are rhubarb plants?

    (A) 4
    (B) 5
    (C) 9
    (D) 20
    (E) 25

16. If m is a positive integer, and if $3 + 16 \div m$ is an integer less than 19, which of the following must be true of m ?

    (A) $m = 19$
    (B) m is even
    (C) $m = 16$
    (D) m is a prime number
    (E) m is a multiple of four

17. If an item that is discounted by 20% still costs more than $28.00, the original price of the item must be

    (A) less than $3.50
    (B) less than $7.00
    (C) less than $35.00
    (D) equal to $35.00
    (E) more than $35.00

18. What is the perimeter of triangle *MNO* ?

    (A) 3
    (B) 9
    (C) 18
    (D) 27
    (E) It cannot be determined from the information given.

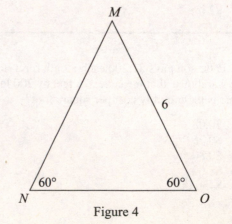

Figure 4

GO ON TO THE NEXT PAGE.

19. It takes Alice between 2 and $2\frac{1}{2}$ hours to drive home from college. If the trip is 100 miles, her average speed, in miles per hour, must always be between

    (A) 10 and 20
    (B) 25 and 30
    (C) 30 and 35
    (D) 40 and 50
    (E) 50 and 60

USE THIS SPACE FOR FIGURING.

20. What is the value of the underlined digit? 470.1<u>8</u>

    (A) 8 hundredths
    (B) 8 tenths
    (C) 8 ones
    (D) 8 tens
    (E) 8 hundreds

GO ON TO THE NEXT PAGE.

Questions 21 and 22 refer to the following chart.

Number of Patients Seen by Four Doctors During a Certain Week

	Monday	Tuesday	Wednesday	Thursday	Friday	Total
Dr. Adams	6	12	10	0	0	28
Dr. Chou	8	8	0	8	8	32
Dr. Davis	4	0	5	3	4	16
Dr. Rosenthal	0	8	10	6	0	24
Total	18	28	25	1	12	100

Figure 5

21. The number of patients that Dr. Davis saw on Friday represents what percent of the total number of patients she saw during the entire week?

    (A) $33\frac{1}{3}$%

    (B) 25%

    (C) 10%

    (D) 4%

    (E) It cannot be determined from the information given.

22. Over the entire week, Dr. Adams and Dr. Davis together saw what percent of the total number of patients seen by all four doctors?

    (A) 16%
    (B) 28%
    (C) 44%
    (D) 50%
    (E) 88%

USE THIS SPACE FOR FIGURING.

GO ON TO THE NEXT PAGE.

23. A store sells mints for 50¢ each or $4.80 for a case of 12 mints. The cost per mint is what percent greater when the mints are purchased separately than when purchased in a case?

    (A) 10%
    (B) 20%
    (C) 22%
    (D) 25%
    (E) 30%

USE THIS SPACE FOR FIGURING.

24. Michael sells chocolate covered bananas. On average, he sells 130 chocolate covered bananas each day. Michael is looking to expand business and runs a special on bananas purchased after 4 P.M. Customers will only pay $3.00 rather than $4.00 for a chocolate covered banana. In order to maintain his current revenue, what is the minimum number of customers needed to buy $3.00 bananas if Michael has 40 customers buying $4.00 bananas each day?

    (A) 90
    (B) 120
    (C) 130
    (D) 170
    (E) 360

25. If the length of one of the legs of a right triangle is decreased by 10%, and the length of the other leg is increased by 20%, then what is the approximate percent change in the area of the triangle?

    (A) 2%
    (B) 8%
    (C) 10%
    (D) 15%
    (E) 18%

STOP

IF YOU FINISH BEFORE TIME IS CALLED,
YOU MAY CHECK YOUR WORK ON THIS SECTION ONLY.
DO NOT TURN TO ANY OTHER SECTION IN THE TEST.

Chapter 10
Upper Level SSAT
Practice Test:
Answers and
Explanations

ANSWER KEY

SSAT UL Math 1

1.	E	4.	B	7.	C	10.	A	13.	C	16.	E	19.	E	22.	A	25.	A
2.	A	5.	D	8.	A	11.	B	14.	E	17.	C	20.	B	23.	A		
3.	E	6.	C	9.	C	12.	D	15.	C	18.	D	21.	C	24.	A		

SSAT UL Reading 2

1.	B	5.	D	9.	E	13.	B	17.	D	21.	D	25.	A	29.	D	33.	B	37.	A
2.	E	6.	D	10.	C	14.	A	18.	C	22.	C	26.	B	30.	C	34.	D	38.	C
3.	B	7.	B	11.	B	15.	A	19.	B	23.	D	27.	A	31.	A	35.	C	39.	E
4.	A	8.	A	12.	D	16.	D	20.	B	24.	A	28.	D	32.	B	36.	C	40.	E

SSAT UL Verbal 3

1.	A	7.	B	13.	A	19.	A	25.	D	31.	E	37.	D	43.	D	49.	C	55.	E
2.	D	8.	D	14.	B	20.	E	26.	D	32.	C	38.	B	44.	E	50.	A	56.	B
3.	E	9.	B	15.	C	21.	B	27.	E	33.	A	39.	C	45.	B	51.	C	57.	D
4.	A	10.	D	16.	B	22.	D	28.	E	34.	C	40.	C	46.	D	52.	A	58.	C
5.	D	11.	D	17.	D	23.	B	29.	B	35.	C	41.	C	47.	A	53.	A	59.	E
6.	A	12.	A	18.	C	24.	C	30.	B	36.	A	42.	E	48.	D	54.	A	60.	D

SSAT UL Math 4

1.	B	4.	D	7.	B	10.	B	13.	E	16.	B	19.	D	22.	C	25.	B
2.	D	5.	C	8.	C	11.	E	14.	A	17.	E	20.	A	23.	D		
3.	B	6.	A	9.	A	12.	C	15.	D	18.	C	21.	B	24.	B		

EXPLANATIONS

Section 1 Math

1. **E** The value of h is given, so $i = 4$ and $j = 6$ since the 3 numbers are consecutive, even integers with h as the smallest, i as the middle number, and j as the largest. Therefore, $h + i + j = 2 + 4 + 6 = 12$, so the correct answer is (E).

2. **A** Rather than calculating the values for x and y before adding them together, notice that fractions with like denominators can be added together to equal 1: $\frac{1}{2} + \frac{1}{2} = 1$, $\frac{1}{3} + \frac{2}{3} = 1$, and $\frac{1}{4} + \frac{3}{4} = 1$. Thus, $x + y = 1 + 1 + 1 = 3$. The correct answer is (A).

3. **E** If 412.7 is multiplied by 100, then the decimal will move 2 places to the right, which would equal 41,270. Be careful! Choice (D) is a trap answer. The question asks for the product to be rounded to the nearest hundred. 300 is the nearest hundred to 270. Therefore, the rounded value is 41,300, which is answer (E).

4. **B** Translate the English words to their math equivalents. $\frac{4}{5}$ of a number is 28 means $\frac{4}{5}(n) = 28$. To cancel the fraction, multiply both sides by the reciprocal $\left(\frac{5}{4}\right)$ to get $n = 35$. For the second part of the question, $\frac{1}{5}$ of that number means $\frac{1}{5}(35)$, which is equal to 7. Therefore, the correct answer is (B).

5. **D** Remember order of operations (PEMDAS). Start inside the parentheses first: $14 + 3 \times 7 + (12 \div 2)$ $= 14 + 3 \times 7 + (6)$. Next multiply: $14 + 3 \times 7 + (6) = 14 + 21 + 6$. Then add to get $14 + 21 + 6 + 41$. Therefore, the correct answer is (D).

6. **C** Since the answer choices represent the number of sets of stamps she must buy, plug in (PITA). Start in the middle with (C). If she buys 9 sets and 3 stamps come in each set, then she has 27 stamps total ($3 \times 9 = 27$). Eliminate (D) and (E) since they will be too big. To see if she could buy fewer stamps, test (B). If she bought 8 sets of stamps, then she has a total of 24 stamps ($3 \times 8 = 24$). With 8 sets, she would be 1 stamp short. Therefore, in order to have enough stamps to mail all 25 post-cards, she will need 9 sets of stamps. The correct answer is (C).

7. **C** Use the chart to find the amount of money raised for each type of candy. There were 20 of the $10 candy sold, so the total amount raised was $200 ($20 \times 10 = 200$). There were 25 of the $5 candy sold, so the total amount raised was $125 ($25 \times 5 = 125$). To find out how much more money was raised by selling the $10 candy, subtract: $200 - 125 = 75$. Therefore, the correct answer is (C). Note that (D) is the total amount raised from the $5 candy and (E) is the total amount raised from the $10 candy.

8. **A** Use the chart to find the amount of money raised. There were 5 of the $15 candy sold, so the total amount raised was $75 (5 × 15 = 75). To find the total money raised from all the candy, add the individual totals: (100 × 1) + 125 + 200 + 75 = 500. Then find what percent 75 is out of 500: $\frac{75}{100} = \frac{x}{100}$. Cross-multiply to get 500x = 7,500, and then divide to get x = 15. The correct answer is (A).

9. **C** If 24 items make up 25% of the total, then $\frac{24}{x} = \frac{25}{100}$. $\frac{25}{100}$ reduces to $\frac{1}{4}$. Cross-multiply $\frac{24}{x} = \frac{1}{4}$ to get x = 96. If there are 96 total items in the art gallery's collections, then a total of 72 items make up the other 2 collections (96 − 24 = 72). To find the average number of items in each of the other 2 collections, use an average pie.

The total will be 72, and the number of items will be 2. Divide to find the average: $\frac{72}{2}$ = 36. Thus, the correct answer is (C).

10. **A** Use a ratio box. The numbers for the ratio row are provided. Remember to add the 2 numbers to get the total.

	Students	Teachers	Total
Ratio	9	1	10

Since the question asks what fraction the teachers make up the total, only the first row of the ratio box is needed to set up the fraction: $\frac{\text{teachers}}{\text{total}} = \frac{1}{10}$. Therefore, the correct answer is (A).

11. **B** Since there are variables in the question and answers, plug in a value for d (the number of deliveries Driver A makes). If d = 3, then Driver B makes 5 deliveries since d + 2 = 3 + 2 = 5. To find the average number of deliveries made, use an average pie.

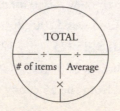

Find the total by adding the number of deliveries each driver makes: $3 + 5 = 8$. There are 2 drivers, so the number of items is 2. Divide to find the average: $\frac{8}{2} = 4$. The correct answer will be the one that equals 4. Plug 3 in for d and check each answer choice. Choice (A) equals 3. Choice (B) equals $3 + 1 = 4$. Choice (C) equals $3 + 2 = 5$. Choice (D) equals $\frac{1}{2}(3) + 2 = 3.5$. Choice (E) equals $\frac{3}{2}(3) = 4.5$. Since it is the only one that matches the target value, (B) is the correct answer.

12. **D** Use the figure provided. The two angles 105° and v must equal 180° since they make up a straight line. Therefore, $v = 75$. The two angles v and $w - 10°$ must also equal 180° since they form a straight line too. Thus, $75 + (w - 10) = 180$, so $w - 10 = 105$ and $w = 115$. The correct answer will be the one that equals 115. Choice (A) equals $180 - 75 = 105$. Choice (B) equals $180 + 75 = 255$. Choice (C) is not equal to 115. Choice (D) works. Choice (E) equals $2(75) = 150$. Since it is the only one that equals 115, (D) is the correct answer.

13. **C** Since the answer choices represent the number of candy bars, plug in (PITA). Start in the middle with (C). If she buys 18 candy bars, then she buys 6 cans of soda since $\frac{18}{3} = 6$. Thus, she bought a total of 24 items since $18 + 6 = 24$, which is true. Therefore, the correct answer is (C).

14. **E** When in doubt with exponents, expand them out. $\left(-\frac{4}{3}\right)^3 = \left(-\frac{4}{3}\right) \times \left(-\frac{4}{3}\right) \times \left(-\frac{4}{3}\right)$. The final result will be negative since $(-) \times (-) \times (-) = (-)$. Eliminate (A) and (B) since they are both positive. Multiply all the numerators together and multiply all the denominators together: $\frac{4 \times 4 \times 4}{3 \times 3 \times 3} = \frac{64}{27}$. Thus, $\left(-\frac{4}{3}\right)^3 = -\frac{64}{17}$. The correct answer is (E).

15. **C** Since the answer choices represent possible values of x, plug in (PITA). Start in the middle with (C). If $x = \frac{6}{7}$, then find $\frac{1}{5} + \frac{6}{7}$. To add fractions with unlike denominators, convert to decimals or use the Bowtie method. If you use the Bowtie method, $\frac{1}{5} + \frac{6}{7} \Rightarrow \frac{7}{35} + \frac{30}{35} = \frac{37}{35}$, which is greater than 1. Since this answer satisfies the inequality, (C) is the correct answer. Note: if you started with a different answer choice, determine whether x needs to be bigger or smaller. Keep checking until you find a value of x that works.

16. **E** Since the answer choices represent possible values of x, plug in (PITA). Start in the middle with (C). If $x = 4$, then the first equation is $2(4) + y = 8 \rightarrow 8 + y = 8$ and $y = 0$. Plug $y = 0$ into the second equation to get $z + 0 = 8$ and $z = 8$. So is (C) the answer? Be careful! What if you had tried (A) first? If $x = -8$, then the first equation is $2(-8) + y = 8 \rightarrow -16 + y = 8$ and $y = 24$. Plug $y = 24$ into the second equation to get $z + 24 = 8$, so $z = -16$. This seems to work too. There can't be multiple

correct answers, so since there is not enough information provided about the values of x, y, and z, the correct answer is (D). Note: normally you don't need to check all the answers when you use PITA. This one is a tricky question! If you noticed that $2z = x$ since both are added to y to yield 8, then you will see that either x or z must be given into order to determine the value of the other variables.

17.   C   Use the figures provided and annotate them with the information provided in the problem. All sides of square A should be labeled as 3 since all sides of a square are equal. If the sides of square B are twice the length of square A, then all the sides of square B should be labeled as 6. If the sides of square C are twice the length of square B, then all the sides of square C should be labeled as 12. To find the area of each square, use the formula $A = s^2$. The area of square A is $A = s^2 = 3^2 = 9$. The area of square B is $A = s^2 = 6^2 = 36$. The area of square C is $A = s^2 = 23^2 = 144$. Finally, to find the average area of the 3 squares, use an average pie.

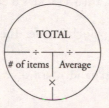

The total will be all the sum of the areas: $9 + 36 + 144 = 189$. The number of items is three since there are 3 squares. Divide to find the average: $\frac{189}{3} = 63$. The correct answer is (C).

18.   D   If there are 12 homes total, subtract out the homes painted blue and red to find the number of homes painted green: $12 - 4 - 3 = 5$. Since 5 homes are painted green, $\frac{green}{total} = \frac{5}{12}$. The correct answer is (D).

19.   E   If Melissa's home and Katy's home are in the same direction from their office, then their homes would be 10 miles apart since $40 - 30 = 10$. However, if Melissa lives 30 miles west of the office and Katy lives 40 miles east of the office, then their homes are 70 miles apart since $30 + 40 = 70$. There are other possibilities as well, so without knowing in which direction they both live, there is not enough information to determine the distance between their homes. The correct answer is (E).

20.   B   Since there are variables in the question, plug in values for x and y. If $x = 2$ and $y = 3$, then the x donors gave $400 since $2(200) = 400$ and the y donors gave $900 since $3(300) = 900$. The total donations raised were $1,300 since $400 + 900 = 1,300$. The correct answer will be the one that equals 1,300. Plug 2 in for x and 3 in for y and check each answer choice. Choice (A) equals

250(2 + 3) = 250(5) = 1,250. Choice (B) equals 200(2) + 300(3) = 400 + 900 = 1,300. Choice (C) equals 250(2)(3) = 500(3) = 1,500. Choice (D) equals $\frac{2 \times 3}{250} = \frac{6}{250}$. Choice (E) equals 500(2)(3) = 1,000(3) = 3,000. Since it is the only one that matches the target value, (B) is the correct answer.

21. **C** First, find the volume of the box, using the formula $V = l \times w \times h$. Plug the given dimensions into the formula: $V = 2$ ft $\times$ 3 ft $\times$ 4 ft $= 24$ ft^3. If the hose produces 6 ft^3 in 1 minute, then set up a proportion to find the time in minutes it will take the hose to produce 24 ft^3: $\frac{1 \text{ min}}{6 \text{ ft}^3} = \frac{x}{24 \text{ ft}^3}$. Cross-multiply to get $6x = 24$ and divide both sides by 6 to get $x = 4$. Therefore, the correct answer is (C). Note: since the answer choices represent possible values for the minutes, you can plug in (PITA).

22. **A** Since the answer choices represent possible values for the least number of critters Mary must catch, plug in (PITA). Start with (A) since it has the smallest number and the question asks for the *least* number of critters. If Mary were to catch 4 critters per day over the next 4 days remaining in the contest, she would catch 16 critters ($4 \times 4 = 16$). Currently Mary has 15 fewer critters than Natalie, but if Mary catches 16 critters, then she will be ahead by 1 critter by the end of the 4 days. The problem proposes that Mary will win the contest; therefore, if Natalie does not catch any more critters, Mary only has to collect 4 critters per day to win. Since there is no answer choice that is smaller, (A) is the correct answer.

23. **A** Pay careful attention to the word *NOT*. Use the answer choices (PITA) for possible values of y (note: all will work but one). In (A), if $y = 9$, then $3x - 9 = 23$. Add 9 to both sides to get $3x = 32$, and divide both sides by 3 to get $x = \frac{32}{3}$. However, x must be an integer. Therefore, (A) is NOT a possible value of x and is the correct answer. Note that if y equaled any of the remaining values, x would have an integer value greater than 0.

24. **A** If Anna and Bob read an average of 200 pages, then use an average pie to find the total.

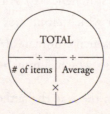

The average (200) and the number of items (2 people) are given, so multiply to find the total: $2 \times 200 = 400$. Therefore, together Anna and Bill read 400 pages. Since there are variables in the question and answers, plug in values for A and B. If Bob reads fewer books then Anna, then B could equal 199 and A could equal 201 since $199 + 201 = 400$. Plug in 201 for A and 199 for B

and check each answer choice. The correct answer will be the one that contains a true statement. Choice (A) is $201 - 200 = 200 - 199$, or $1 = 1$, which is true. Choice (B) cannot be true since $B < A$. Choice (C) is $201 - 199 = 2$, which is not equal to 100. In (D), $201 \neq 200 + 199$ because 201 does not equal 400. In (E), $201 + 199 \neq 200$, since 400 does not equal 200. The only answer choice that contains a true statement is (A), which is the correct answer.

25. A Since the answer choices represent possible values for the original price of the dress, plug them in (PITA). Start in the middle with (C). If the original price was $50, then 60% of 50 is $30 since $\frac{60}{100}(50) = \frac{3,000}{100} = 30$. Since the discount was $30, the new price cannot be $30, since the original price minus the new price does not equal 30: $50 - 30 = 20$. Eliminate (C), (D), and (E) since a larger original price is needed. If the original price was $60, then 60% of 60 is $36 since $\frac{60}{100}(60) = \frac{3,600}{100} = 36$. The discount was $30. The new price cannot be $36 since $60 - 36 = 24$. Eliminate (B). The correct answer should be (A). If the original price was $75, then 60% of 75 is $45 since $\frac{60}{100}(75) = \frac{4,500}{100} = 45$. The discount was $30, so $75 - 45$ must equal 30. It does, so (A) is the correct answer.

Section 2 Reading

1. B On main idea questions ask yourself the "So what?" of the passage. This passage is focused on the influence of Florence Nightingale on the nursing profession. This best matches (B). Although the Crimean War, midwives, and Florence Nightingale's nickname are all mentioned in the passage, these are too specific to be the main idea, which eliminates (A), (C), and (D). Choice (E) contains extreme language; the passage never states that only females become nurses, so it should be eliminated as well. Choice (B) is the correct answer.

2. E This is a specific question, so make sure to go back and find the answer in the passage. At the end of the first paragraph the passage states that in earlier days many people would receive care from women in their own home. This best matches (E). Although midwives are mentioned, the passage does not say whom they cared for which eliminates (D). Neither doctors nor children are mentioned in this part of the passage, which eliminates (A) and (B). The passage does state they were cared for by the women of the house, which eliminates (C). Choice (E) is the correct answer.

3. B For style questions pay attention to the way the author writes. This is a very informative passage focused on a historical figure. This best matches (B). The focus is not on medicine or England in general, but on Florence Nightingale, which eliminates (C) and (D). Since there are not personal opinions included in the story, (A) and (E) can also be eliminated. Choice (B) is the correct answer.

4.   A   This is a specific question, so make sure to go back and find the answer in the passage. The passage states in the second paragraph that she was able to open a school as she was already famous for her nursing work in the Crimean War. This only supports (A). Her family is never mentioned, which eliminates (B). She is never described as difficult or caring for the wealthy, eliminating (C) and (D). Choice (E) contains the extreme language "every night," which is not supported in the passage. Choice (A) is the correct answer.

5.   D   On Except/Not/Least questions cross check each answer choice and write a "T" for true and an "F" for false for each answer choice, based on the passage. The false answer will be the correct choice. This question asks about what could be said of nurses. Choice (A) is supported by the second sentence of the passage, so it is true. Choices (B) and (C) are supported by the last sentence of the passage, so they are true. Choice (E) is supported by the last line of the first paragraph, so it is true as well. The only choice that is not supported by the passage is (D), making it the false answer choice. Choice (D) is correct.

6.   D   This is a specific question, so make sure to go back and find the answer in the passage. The word "agrarian" is found at the end of the first paragraph, where the passage is focusing on the discussion of using private, farmable land, for public farming. This best supports the meaning of "farming" for agrarian, (D). Since the group wanted to take the land out of private hands, (B) can be eliminated. The group wanted the land to be used in an equal manner, which eliminates (C). The other choices do not match the context or subject matter of this paragraph. The best answer is (D).

7.   B   This is a very open-ended question, so check each answer choice with the information provided in the passage and use process of elimination as you go. The True Levelers came to be known as the Diggers; they were not a separate group. Eliminate (A). The passage does state that the goal of the Diggers was to unite many people, which supports (B). There is no mention of the Diggers being skilled speakers or folk singers, which eliminates (C) and (E). And the passage states the opposite of (D); it was the Diggers who were defeated by being jailed not the Diggers who used military force. The correct answer is (B).

8.   A   This is a specific question, so make sure to go back and find the answer in the passage. The Diggers wanted to grow food but did not have the land, since most of the land that could be farmed was held privately. This best supports (A). The passage does not say that landowners were usually violent, which eliminates (B). The Diggers and the True Levelers are the same people, which eliminates (C). Choice (D) is incorrect as there is no mention of how good the vegetables grown by different groups were. Choice (E) is incorrect as it the passage indicates that the local government became involved through the jailing of the Diggers. Choice (A) is the correct answer.

9.   E   On primary purpose questions, ask yourself "Why did the author write this passage? What is the main takeaway for this passage?" This passage is focused on the efforts of poor farmers to create a more equitable use of land for farming. This best supports (E). The times themselves were not the focus of the story, which eliminates (A). Choices (B) and (D) are much too specific to be the primary purpose of the passage, and (C) is too extreme. Choice (E) is the correct answer.

10. **C** This is a specific question, so make sure to go back and find the answer in the passage. As was stated at the beginning of the second paragraph, Diggers was another name for the True Levelers; they are the same group. Therefore (C) is the only possible answer supported by the passage.

11. **B** This question is a "main idea" question in disguise. Ask yourself the "so what?" of the passage. This passage is about the two main uses for the flax plant. This best supports (B). Although mummies and ancient times were mentioned, those topics are much too specific which make (A) and (E) incorrect. Both (C) and (D) are much too vague and general for this specific passage. Only (B) can be correct.

12. **D** This is a specific question, so make sure to go back and find the answer in the passage. Ancient people are discussed at the beginning of the second paragraph, where it states that they raised flax for its cloth, as they wrapped mummies in it. This supports (D). Choices (A), (B), and (E) can be eliminated as they all say that it was oil, not cloth, ancient people raised flax for. Choice (C) is close as it says cloth, but gives the wrong use of the cloth. Choice (D) is the correct answer.

13. **B** For style questions pay attention to the way the author writes. This is a very informative passage focused on a specific plant. This best matches (B). The passage discusses the Egyptians but is not written to the Egyptians, eliminating (A). The passage is not highly scientific or persuasive, eliminating (C) and (D). Choice (E) does not connect to the topic at all, leaving (B) as the correct answer.

14. **A** This is a very open-ended question, so check each answer choice with the information provided in the passage and use process of elimination as you go. The passage does answer the question posed in (A) in the first line of the third paragraph. Since none of the other answer choices are questions that are answered by the passage, (A) is the correct answer.

15. **A** This question is a "main idea" question in disguise. Look at each paragraph and see how they all connect to one another. The first paragraph introduces the flax plant and its two uses. The second paragraph discusses how flax was used in ancient times. The third paragraph is focused on the different types of flax plants that are grown for different purposes. There is no indication that the author would switch to an entirely new subject that isn't about flax, which eliminates (B), (C), (D), and (E), as none of those are focused on flax. The correct answer is (A).

16. **D** On primary purpose questions, ask yourself "Why did the author write this passage? What is the main takeaway for this passage?" This passage is focused on the history of the Tower of London. This best matches (D). The passage does not discuss the future of the tower, eliminating (A), nor the ramifications of using the tower as a prison, eliminating (B). The passage also doesn't argue that the tower is an improper storage site for the crown jewels nor is there a debate over the tower's various uses, eliminating (C) and (E). Choice (D) is the correct answer.

17. **D** On Except/Not/Least questions cross check each answer choice and write a "T" for true and an "F" for false for each answer choice, based on the passage. The false answer will be the correct choice. In the third paragraph the passage states that the tower has been used as a fortress, royal residence,

prison, royal mint, public records office, and a place of execution, all of which make (A), (B), (C), and (E) true. The only thing the passage doesn't say the tower has served as is a place of religious pilgrimage. This makes (D) false and, therefore, the correct answer.

18.　C　This is a very open-ended question, so check each answer choice with the information provided in the passage and use process of elimination as you go. The first paragraph of the passage answers the question posed in (C): Construction began on the tower in 1066. This makes (C) the correct answer.

19.　B　On tone questions, eliminate answer choices that are too extreme or don't make sense based on the passage. This passage is very informative and historical. This eliminates extreme choices such as (A), (C), (D), and (E). The only choice that works with the passage is just (B).

20.　B　This is a specific question, so make sure to go back and find the answer in the passage. The author says that Rudolf Hess was held in the tower as a prisoner as recently as 1941. The author then goes on to say that the tower is no longer used as a prison. This best supports (B), that Hess was one of the last prisoners in the tower. As there is no other information provided about Hess in the passage, none of the other answers are supported. Choice (B) is the correct answer.

21.　D　This is a very open-ended question, so check each answer choice with the information provided in the passage and use process of elimination as you go. Choices (A) and (B) both contain extreme language, only and never, that is not supported by the passage. The passage doesn't mention the cost of the tower, nor how well the prisoners in it were treated, so eliminate (C) and (E). The information in the passage as a whole does support answer (D); the tower does have a complex history as we have read. Choice (D) is the correct answer.

22.　C　On attitude questions, eliminate answer choices that are too extreme or don't make sense based on the passage. The author is focused most clearly on the *Mona Lisa*'s smile and how intriguing it is. This best supports (C). The author does not seem to be afraid of its being stolen again, eliminating (A). The author never mentions how difficult it is to preserve old paintings, eliminating (B). Choice (E) is also never indicated, and (D) contains extreme language. Eliminate them both. Only (C) can be the correct answer.

23.　D　This is a very open-ended question, so check each answer choice with the information provided in the passage and use process of elimination as you go. The passage is focused on how intriguing the world finds the *Mona Lisa*'s smile, which strongly supports (D). The author never states how long a good smile lasts, eliminating (A). The author clearly states who painted the *Mona Lisa*, eliminating (B). The passage does not say that the painting was donated, let alone by Napoleon, eliminating (C). The passage can't possibly know what all art historians think, as that is extreme, eliminating (E). Choice (D) is the correct answer.

24.　A　This is a very open-ended question, so check each answer choice with the information provided in the passage and use process of elimination as you go. Choice (A) is well supported by the passage, especially the last line which says the painting really belongs to us all. There is no mention that

Da Vinci was the one with a secret, eliminating (B). Choice (C) is far too negative considering the tone of the passage; eliminate it as well. Answer (D) is far beyond what is discussed in passage, and (E) is much too extreme by using the word "only." The correct answer is (A).

25. **A** On tone questions, eliminate answer choices that are too extreme or don't make sense based on the passage. The author is positive throughout the passage, which eliminates (B), (D), and (E). Although the passage is focused on art the tone is not artistic, merely positive. This leaves (A) as the correct answer.

26. **B** This is a specific question, so make sure to go back and find the answer in the passage. "Progress" as used in the second sentence refers to the "advances" that were made; this best supports (B). Although the passage does mention expense and fuel, these are not what is referred to in this line, eliminating (D) and (E). Neither (A) nor (C) is mentioned in the passage. Choice (B) is the correct answer.

27. **A** This is a very open-ended question, so check each answer choice with the information provided in the passage and use process of elimination as you go. The second paragraph answers the question posed in (A); it discusses the various uses and jobs that cars are used for. Although laughing at the horseless carriages is mentioned in the first line, the passage doesn't say why that is. Eliminate (B). Although fuel, efficiency, and cost are mentioned in the passage, the questions posed in (C), (D), and (E) are not answered. The correct answer is (A).

28. **D** On main idea questions ask yourself the "So what?" of the passage. This passage is focused on the technological advances of cars. This best matches (D). Although fuel consumption is mentioned, it is not what the passage is primarily concerned with. Eliminate (A). The invention of the car is not discussed, nor is the future of the car or the difficulty of driving one, eliminating (B), (C), and (E). The correct answer is (D).

29. **D** This is a specific question, so make sure to go back and find the answer in the passage. Research is mentioned in the last line of the passage, where it states that much research is devoted to saving fuel and finding new sources of energy. This best supports (D). None of the other answer choices are mentioned in relation to research in the passage. Choice (D) is the correct answer.

30. **C** On tone questions, eliminate answer choices that are too extreme or don't make sense based on the passage. The author's tone regarding the technological advances discussed in the passage is positive and well informed. This best matches (C). The author is not negative, which eliminates (B), (D), and (E). Since the author is not responsible for these advances, (A) does not work. The correct answer is (C).

31. **A** This is a very open-ended question, so check each answer choice with the information provided in the passage and use process of elimination as you go. The second paragraph supports (A), as it lists the many uses people have found for cars. Choices (D) and (E) both contain extreme language that

is not supported by the passage. The author also never addresses how important future problems are nor does he or she state that cars are more trouble than they are worth. Choice (A) is the correct answer.

32. **B** This is a specific question, so make sure to go back and find the answer in the passage. The third and fourth lines refer to the embattled farmers, who fired a shot heard round the world. The use of the words embattled and shot best support (B). The narrator is not referring to himself, eliminating (A). Weather is not mentioned in these lines, eliminating (E). Choices (C) and (D) contain language that is seen in the passage but neither is exactly what the passage states in these lines. The correct answer is (B).

33. **B** This is a specific question, so make sure to go back and find the answer in the passage. The author only gives one reason for writing this poem, to set down the memory of those who fought. This only matches number 2 in the list provided, making (B) the correct answer.

34. **D** This is a specific question, so make sure to go back and find the answer in the passage. The votive stone is what the author refers to as marking the memory of those who fought. This best matches (D), a war memorial. None of the other choices aligns with any information in the passage. Choice (D) is the correct answer.

35. **C** This is a very open-ended question, so check each answer choice with the information provided in the passage and use process of elimination as you go. The author says that we should remember those who have died in battle, not that war is in vain, which eliminates (A). The poem is not about farming, which eliminates (B). Choice (E) is the opposite of what the passage states; eliminate it. Choice (C) is what the passage states; remembering those who are fallen in battle is very important. Choice (D) is not mentioned in the passage, so it cannot be correct. The best answer is (C).

36. **C** On primary purpose questions, ask yourself "Why did the author write this passage? What is the main takeaway for this passage?" This passage is focused on the actor Jose Ferrer and the great roles he played. This best matches (C). Choices (A) and (D) are much too broad in their scope to be the primary purpose of this passage. Choice (B) is extreme; there is no indication that Ferrer was the best actor to play a role. Choice (D) is too narrow in its scope, as it is not focused on these two actors. The correct answer is (C).

37. **A** This is a very open-ended question, so check each answer choice with the information provided in the passage and use process of elimination as you go. Choice (A) is supported by the last paragraph of the passage. Regret is not mentioned in the passage, so eliminate (B). The passage does state that Ferrer, Stewart, and Fitzgerald were all in the Triangle Club but not that they learned from each other, eliminating (C). Both (D) and (E) are extreme and not supported by the passage. Choice (A) is the correct answer.

38. **C**   This is a very open-ended question, so check each answer choice with the information provided in the passage and use process of elimination as you go. Choice (A) is too extreme based on the word "most"; only three actors are mentioned who were in the Triangle Club. Choice (B) is also too extreme based on the word "more"; eliminate it. Choice (C) is supported by the passage, as both actors of Othello are noted as being acclaimed and that with these two powerful performers the show was a hit. Choice (D) can be eliminated as there is no mention of whether or not Ferrer returned to Broadway. It was the Othello role that set a record, eliminating (E). Choice (C) is the correct answer.

39. **E**   On Except/Not/Least questions cross check each answer choice and write a "T" for true and an "F" for false for each answer choice, based on the passage. The false answer will be the correct choice. Choices (A) and (B) are supported by the second paragraph, so they are true. Choices (C) and (D) are supported by the third paragraph, so they are true. Only (E) is not supported by the passage, making it false. The correct answer is (E).

40. **E**   On attitude questions, eliminate answer choices that are too extreme or don't make sense based on the passage. The author is very positive about Jose Ferrer. This means any negative or neutral choices can be eliminated, such as (A), (B), and (D). Since there is no indication the author knows Ferrer, friendship in (C) does not make sense. The best choice is admiration, (E).

Section 3 Verbal

1. **A**   To contort means to twist or distort. A word or phrase you might be familiar with is a contortionist, someone who twists his or her body into unusual shapes. This meaning best matches (A), bend.

2. **D**   Grim means foreboding, serious, or dour. A word or phrase you might be familiar with is "the grim reaper," a fictional portrayal of death. All answer choices with positive connotations can be eliminated, which includes (A) and (B). Although (C) and (E) have negative connotations, neither match the meaning of grim as well as (D), harsh.

3. **E**   To prohibit means to block or hamper. A word or phrase you might be familiar with is prohibition, the period of time in American history during which alcohol consumption was illegal. This meaning best matches (E), forbid.

4. **A**   Vacant means empty or available. A word or phrase you might be familiar with is vacancy or vacant lot. This meaning best matches (A), stark.

5. **D**   Austere means serious or grim. This meaning best matches (D), severe.

6. **A**   To quell means to quiet or put out. This meaning best matches (A), stifle.

7. **B**   To fortify means to reinforce or bolster. Think of other words that begin with the word fort: fort, fortification, fortitude. This meaning best matches (B), strengthen.

8.   **D**   A proclivity is a preference or liking. This meaning best matches (D), propensity.

9.   **B**   Formidable means challenging or difficult to overcome. A word or phrase you might be familiar with is a formidable task or a formidable opponent. This best matches (B), powerful.

10. **D**   To stymie means to upset or thwart. A word or phrase you might be familiar with is to stymie the flow of progress, which would be to upset the flow of progress. This meaning best matches (D), frustrate.

11. **D**   Erratic most nearly means unpredictable or irregular. A word or phrase you might be familiar with is erratic behavior, which would be irregular or unpredictable behavior. This meaning best matches (D), inconsistent.

12. **A**   To conciliate means to console or appease. You may have heard the phrase a conciliation round in sports or competition. This meaning best matches (A), pacify.

13. **A**   Refractory means to be headstrong or obstinate. This meaning best matches (A), stubborn.

14. **B**   To truncate means to abbreviate. This meaning best matches (B), shorten.

15. **C**   Meager means small or lacking in quantity. A word or phrase you might be familiar with is a meager portion, which would be a small portion. This best matches (C), sparse.

16. **B**   Credible means trustworthy or believable. A word or phrase you might be familiar with is a credible source, which would be a trustworthy source. This best matches (B), plausible.

17. **D**   Culpable means guilty of something or responsible for something. A word or phrase you might be familiar with is the accused was found to be culpable for the crimes. This best matches (D), worthy of blame.

18. **C**   To deplore means to regret or rue. A word or phrase you might be familiar with is a deplorable situation, which would be a regretful or distasteful situation. This best matches (C), lament.

19. **A**   Acclaim most nearly means praise or approval. You might be familiar with the phrase "the movie was well acclaimed." This best matches (A), compliment.

20. **E**   Guile means craftiness or cleverness. This best matches (E), cunning.

21. **B**   Fallow means unplanted or unseeded. This best matches (B), unused.

22. **D**   To champion means to support or defend. A word or phrase you might be familiar with is that Martin Luther King Jr. championed the Civil Rights Movement. This best matches (D), side with.

23. **B**   To imbue means to infuse or instill. This meaning best matches (B), suffuse.

24. **C**   Posthumous means after death, which becomes clearer if you break the word down into its two roots: post, meaning after, and humous coming from homo, meaning man. A word or phrase you

may be familiar with is he received the award posthumously, which would mean he received the award after his death. This best matches (C), after death.

25.   D   Inauspicious means unpromising or discouraging. This best matches (D), ominous.

26.   D   Renaissance means rebirth. A word or phrase you may be familiar with is the Renaissance, the time in Europe in which a reawakening of classical study and art occurred in Europe. This meaning best matches (D), revival.

27.   E   Decomposition means decay. A word or phrase you may be familiar with is the decomposition, or the decay of a body. This meaning best matches (E), disintegration.

28.   E   An aggrandizement is an enlargement. One clue is the root word "grand," which means large or impressive. This meaning best matches (E), glorification.

29.   B   To be gullible means to be overly trusting or naïve. This meaning best matches (B), easily deceived.

30.   B   A refutation is a refusal or a denial. A word or phrase you may be familiar with is to refute the evidence, which would be to deny the evidence. This meaning best matches (B), disprove.

31.   E   Remember to make a sentence with the words in the analogy, and try to find the answer choice that matches the same sentence. For this question one sentence could be "a composer writes a score." The only answer choice that also works with this sentence is (E), an author writes a book.

32.   C   Remember to make a sentence with the words in the analogy, and try to find the answer choice that matches the same sentence. For this question one sentence could be "A poem is made up of several stanzas." The only answer choice that also works with this sentence is (C), an essay is made up of several paragraphs.

33.   A   Don't worry if the format changes from two words to one word in the answer choices! Remember to make a sentence with the first two words in the analogy, and try to find the answer choice that matches the same sentence. For this question one sentence could be "A sovereign is the head of a monarchy." The only answer choice that also works with this sentence is (A), a principal is the head of a school.

34.   C   Remember to make a sentence with the words in the analogy, and try to find the answer choice that matches the same sentence. For this question one sentence could be "a can is a cylinder." The only answer choice that also works with this sentence is (C), a dice is a cube.

35.   C   Remember to make a sentence with the words in the analogy, and try to find the answer choice that matches the same sentence. For this question one sentence could be "laughter is the result of a joke." The only answer choice that also works with this sentence is (C), wince is the result of pain.

36.   A   Remember to make a sentence with the words in the analogy, and try to find the answer choice that matches the same sentence. For this question one sentence could be "massive is a description

of large weight." The only answer choice that also works with this sentence is (A), gargantuan is a description of large size.

37. **D** Remember to make a sentence with the words in the analogy, and try to find the answer choice that matches the same sentence. For this question one sentence could be "a pint is smaller than a quart." The only answer choice that also works with this sentence is (D), a week is smaller than a year.

38. **B** Remember to make a sentence with the words in the analogy, and try to find the answer choice that matches the same sentence. For this question one sentence could be "scrawl is a form of writing." The answer choices that also works with this sentence are (B), babble is a form of speaking, and (D), tango is a form of dancing. Since two answer choices work with the sentence, try to make the sentence a little more specific. An example would be "scrawl is a quick/sloppy/messy form of writing." Do these words match the relationship between babble and speaking or tango and dancing? Babble and speaking. Choice (B) is the best answer.

39. **C** Remember to make a sentence with the words in the analogy, and try to find the answer choice that matches the same sentence. For this question one sentence could be "stoic is a type of emotion." The only answer choices that matches this sentence is (C), amorphous is a type of shape.

40. **C** Don't worry if the format changes from two words to one word in the answer choices! Remember to make a sentence with the words in the analogy, and try to find the answer choice that matches the same sentence. For this question, one sentence could be "frugal is the opposite of spending." The only answer choice that matches this sentence is (C), unruly is the opposite of obedient.

41. **C** Remember to make a sentence with the words in the analogy, and try to find the answer choice that matches the same sentence. For this question, one sentence could be "integrity is similar to honesty." The only answer choice that matches this sentence is (C), resolution is similar to determination.

42. **E** Don't worry if the format changes from two words to one word in the answer choices! Remember to make a sentence with the words in the analogy, and try to find the answer choice that matches the same sentence. For this question, one sentence could be "a lily is a type of flower." The only answer choice that matches this sentence is (E), pine is a type of wood.

43. **D** Remember to make a sentence with the words in the analogy, and try to find the answer choice that matches the same sentence. If you run into trouble, it may be easier to try to make a sentence with the first word in the question and the answer choices, and then check to see if the same sentence works for the second words. For example, does the word kitchen have a relationship to the word wheel in (A)? No. What about fireplace? Maybe "a kitchen can have a fireplace." What about "lobby"? No. What about house? Maybe "a kitchen is found in a house." What about exhibit? No. Between (B) and (D), which choice has the same relationship between the second words? Choice (D): a galley is found on a ship. Choice (D) is the best answer!

44. **E**   Remember to make a sentence with the words in the analogy, and try to find the answer choice that matches the same sentence. For this question, one sentence could be "a rose is blooming." The only answer choice that matches this sentence is (E), a tomato is ripening. Although (A) might seem like it works, since a vine can be withering, keep in mind that "blooming" is something that happens in a rose's prime, just like ripening for a tomato. This makes (E) the best answer.

45. **B**   Remember to make a sentence with the words in the analogy, and try to find the answer choice that matches the same sentence. For this question, one sentence could be "you wear a mask on your face." The only answer choice that matches this sentence is (B), you wear a shoe on your foot.

46. **D**   Remember to make a sentence with the words in the analogy, and try to find the answer choice that matches the same sentence. For this question one sentence could be "a meeting follows an agenda." The only answer choice that matches this sentence is (D), a building follows a blueprint.

47. **A**   Don't worry if the format changes from two words to one word in the answer choices! Remember to make a sentence with the words in the analogy, and try to find the answer choice that matches the same sentence. For this question, one sentence could be "pathology is the study of diseases." The only answer choice that matches this sentence is (A), "psychology is the study of minds."

48. **D**   Remember to make a sentence with the words in the analogy, and try to find the answer choice that matches the same sentence. For this question, one sentence could be "an author creates an autobiography." The only answer choice that matches this sentence is (D), an artist creates a self-portrait.

49. **C**   Remember to make a sentence with the words in the analogy, and try to find the answer choice that matches the same sentence. For this question, one sentence could be "migration is something birds do in the winter." The only answer choice that matches this sentence is (C), hibernation is something bears do in the winter.

50. **A**   Remember to make a sentence with the words in the analogy, and try to find the answer choice that matches the same sentence. For this question, one sentence could be "a border surrounds a country." The only answer choice that matches this sentence is (A), a perimeter surrounds an object.

51. **C**   Remember to make a sentence with the words in the analogy, and try to find the answer choice that matches the same sentence. For this question, one sentence could be "patter is the sound rain makes." The only answer choice that matches this sentence is (C), clank is the sound a chain makes.

52. **A**   Remember to make a sentence with the words in the analogy, and try to find the answer choice that matches the same sentence. For this question, one sentence could be "brazen is the opposite of tact." The only answer choice that matches this sentence is (A), lethargic is the opposite of energy.

53. **A**   Remember to make a sentence with the words in the analogy, and try to find the answer choice that matches the same sentence. For this question, one sentence could be "taciturn people don't use

many words." The only answer choice that matches this sentence is (A), thrifty people don't use much money.

54. **A** Remember to make a sentence with the words in the analogy, and try to find the answer choice that matches the same sentence. If you run into trouble it may be easier to try to make a sentence with the first words in each set and the second words in each set. For example, in this question the first words in each set are "scalpel" and "surgeon." A sentence you could use is "a surgeon uses a scalpel." Now find the same relationship with the second words in each set, "razor" and the answer choices. Does a barber use a razor? Yes! Choice (A) is the correct answer.

55. **E** Remember to make a sentence with the words in the analogy, and try to find the answer choice that matches the same sentence. For this question, one sentence could be "a storyteller entertains a listener." The only answer choice that matches this sentence is (E), a pantomime entertains a viewer.

56. **B** Remember to make a sentence with the words in the analogy, and try to find the answer choice that matches the same sentence. For this question, one sentence could be "erosion creates a gully." The only answer choice that matches this sentence is (B), excavation creates a mine.

57. **D** Remember to make a sentence with the words in the analogy, and try to find the answer choice that matches the same sentence. For this question, one sentence could be "a drip is small and slow whereas a deluge is big and fast." The only answer choice that matches this sentence is (D), smolder is small and slow whereas a blaze is big and fast.

58. **C** Remember to make a sentence with the words in the analogy, and try to find the answer choice that matches the same sentence. For this question, one sentence could be "lax is the opposite of resolution." The only answer choice that matches this sentence is (C), deceitful is the opposite of sincerity.

59. **E** Remember to make a sentence with the words in the analogy, and try to find the answer choice that matches the same sentence. For this question, one sentence could be "you pound things with a hammer." The only answer choice that matches this sentence is (E), you raise things with a jack.

60. **D** Don't worry if the format changes from two words to one word in the answer choices! Remember to make a sentence with the first two words in the analogy, and try to find the answer choice that matches the same sentence. For this question, one sentence could be "a lexicon is a collection of words." The only answer choice that matches this sentence is (D), an anthology is a collection of works.

Section 4 Math

1. **B** When in doubt with exponents, expand them out. $2^4 = 2 \times 2 \times 2 \times 2 = 16$. The correct answer is (B).

2. **D** Use the figure provided to determine the measure of angle x. Since the two angles make up a straight line, $x + 60 = 180$. Therefore, $x = 120(180 - 60 = 120)$, and the correct answer is (D). Note: Ballparking works well too—the measure of x is definitely greater than $90°$, so eliminate (A), (B), and (C). The two angles form a straight line, not a circle, so $300°$ is much too large. Eliminate (E), and only (D) remains.

3. **B** Pay attention to the inequality signs: x is between -4 and 2 but doesn't equal those values. If x is an integer between -4 and 2, then x could equal $-3, -2, -1, 0$, or 1. Don't forget about 0! Therefore, there are 5 possible integer values for x. The correct answer is (B).

4. **D** Use the graph provided to find the requested amounts. According to the graph, he had $50 in his savings account at the beginning of 2011. At the beginning of 2012, he had $150 in his savings account. Thus, his savings account balance grew $100 since $150 - 50 = 100$. The correct answer is (D).

5. **C** Use the graph provided to find the requested amounts. According to the graph, he had $200 at the beginning of 2013 but only $100 at the beginning of 2014. Thus, his account balance decreased by $100 ($200 - $100 = $100). His account balance at the start of 2012 was $150. Therefore, the question is now asking 100 is what percent of 150. To find the percentage, translate the English words to their math equivalents $\left(100 = \dfrac{x}{100}(150) \right)$ or set up a proportion $\left(\dfrac{100}{150} = \dfrac{x}{100} \right)$ and solve for x. Since $\dfrac{100}{150}$ reduces to $\dfrac{2}{3}$, $x = 66.6\overline{6}$. Therefore, the correct answer is (C). Note: Remember that Ballparking can help eliminate obviously wrong answers. Choice (A) is incorrect since 150 would be 100% of 150, and (D) and (E) are wrong since both are too small—75 would be 50% of 150.

6. **A** Use the graph provided to find the requested amounts. According to the graph, his account balance decreased by $100 during 2013: ($ in 2013) − ($ in 2014) → $200 − $100 = $100. One-half of that amount would be $50 since $\dfrac{1}{2}(100) = \dfrac{100}{2} = 50$. Therefore, if he withdrew $50 from his savings account at the end of 2014, he would have $50 left: ($ in 2014) − ($50) → $100 − $50 = $50.

The correct answer is (A). Note: Since he is withdrawing money at the end of 2014, the amount remaining must be less than the starting amount ($100); therefore, eliminate (C), (D), and (E) since those amounts are too large to be his account balance after withdrawing money.

7. **B** Draw a picture since one is not provided. If the perimeter of the box's base is 36, each side of the base will be 9 inches since $\frac{36}{4} = 9$. The side measure of each of the smaller square boxes is given (3 inches), so 3 smaller square boxes make up each side of the larger box's base $\left(\frac{9}{3} = 3 \right)$. Since the box is square, it is a cube, and all sides of a cube are equal. If there are 3 smaller boxes making up each side of the base (length and width), then 3 smaller boxes will stack to make the height. Thus, there are 3 rows of 3 boxes each, stacked 3 rows high, to form the larger box. $3 \times 3 \times 3 = 27$, so the correct answer is (B).

8. **C** The values of x and y are given, so plug those values into the equation to solve. Remember order of operations (PEMDAS). In this case, start with exponents, then multiply, then subtract: $10x - y^2 = 10(4) - 5^2 = 10(4) - 25 = 40 - 25 = 15$. The correct answer is (C).

9. **A** There are several ways to solve this problem (e.g. using the Bowtie method or finding a common denominator for the fractions). Another option would be to convert the fractions to decimal form. Choice (A) equals 0.75, (B) equals 0.625, (C) equals 0.5, (D) is about 0.429, and (E) is $0.5\overline{5}$. The answer that has the greatest value is (A), so it is the correct answer.

10. **B** Use the figure provided. Since the answer choices represent possible values of z, plug in (PITA). Start in the middle with (C). If $z = 60$, then $x + y = 60$ since $x + y = z$. Thus, $60 + 60 = 120$. Since there are a total of 180° in a triangle, this is incorrect and a larger value for z is needed (eliminate choices C, D, and E). If $z = 90$, then $x + y = 90$ since $x + y = z$. Thus, $90 + 90 = 180$. This equals the total measure of the angles in a triangle, so (B) is the correct answer. Note: Solving by substitution also works. If $x + y = z$, then $(x + y) + z = 180$ or $z + z = 180$. Combine like terms to get $2z = 180$ and divide by 2 on both sides to get $z = 90$.

11. **E** Use an average pie.

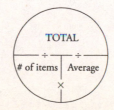

For this problem, draw 2 average pies. The first average pie will represent her first 3 games. The total will be the sum of the points for all 3 games: $100 + 120 + 88 = 308$. The number of items will be 3 since she played 3 games. The second average pie will represent all 4 games. The average (130) and the number of items (4 games) are given. Multiply to find the total number of points scored in all 4 games: $130 \times 4 = 520$. To find the number of points she must score in the 4th game to achieve this average score, subtract the two totals: 4 game total − 3 game total = $520 − 308 = 212$. Therefore, the correct answer is (E). Note: (C) represents the average score for the first 3 games.

12. **C** Break word problems into bite-sized pieces. If one quarter, or $\frac{1}{4}$, of the boys are wearing red shirts, then 6 boys are wearing red shirts since $\frac{1}{4} \times 24 = \frac{24}{4} = 6$. If 40% of the girls are wearing yellow shirts, then 14 girls are wearing yellow ($0.4 \times 35 = 14$). To find how many more club members are wearing yellow shirts than red shirts, subtract: yellow − red = $14 − 6 = 8$. Therefore, the correct answer is (C).

13. **E** Translate the English words into their math equivalents. Thus, *36 is 16 percent of* is the same as $36 = \frac{16}{100}(x)$, where x represents the values in the answer choices. Solve for x or plug in (PITA) for x. To solve for x, cancel the fraction on the right by multiplying both sides by the reciprocal: $36 = \frac{16}{100}(x) \rightarrow \left(\frac{100}{16}\right)(36) = x$. Divide $\frac{3{,}600}{16} = x$ to get $x = 225$. Therefore, the correct answer is (E).

14. **A** There is a total of 15,000 ft² in the warehouse since $75 \times 200 = 15{,}000$. To find the monthly cost per square foot, divide the total monthly cost by the total square feet: $\frac{\text{monthly cost}}{\text{ft}^2} = \frac{1{,}200}{15{,}000}$. Thus, $15{,}000 \overline{)1{,}200.00}^{\,0.08}$, and the correct answer is (A).

15. **D** Use a ratio box. The numbers for the ratio row are provided. Remember to add the 2 numbers to get the total. The total number of plants is also given, so add that value to the ratio box.

	Rhubarb	Tomato	Total
Ratio	4	5	9
Multiplier			
Real Value			45

What number does 9 need to be multiplied by to get 45? 5. Therefore, 5 goes in all the cells for the multiplier row.

	Rhubarb	Tomato	Total
Ratio	4	5	9
Multiplier	5	5	5
Real Value	20		45

The question asks for the total number of rhubarb plants. Since $4 \times 5 = 20$, the correct answer is (D). Note: (A), (B), and (C) are the values in the ratio row. Choice (E) is the total number of tomato plants.

16. **B** The question is looking for what *must be* true of the integer m given that $3 + 16 \div m < 19$ and

$3 + 16 \div m$ is an integer. Since the answer choices represent statements about m, plug in (PITA). If $m = 19$, then $3 + 16 \div m$ will not be an integer: $3 + 16 \div 19 = 3 + \dfrac{16}{19}$. Eliminate (A). If $m = 16$, then $3 + 16 \div 16 = 3 + 1 = 4$. 4 is an integer less than 19, so m could be 16. 16 is even and a multiple of 4, so keep (B), (C), and (E). Choice (D) can be eliminated since 16 is not a prime number. Try another value for m. If $m = 2$, then $3 + 16 \div 2 = 3 + 8 = 11$. 11 is an integer less than 19. Therefore, since 2 also works as a value of m, eliminate (C) since 16 isn't the only value of m that works. Also eliminate (E) since 2 is not a multiple of 4 (it's a factor). The correct answer is (B).

17. **E** Use the answer choices to plug in a value for the original price of the item. If the item were $35 originally, then a 20% discount would be $7 ($0.2 \times \$35 = \$7$). The item would cost $28 after the discount ($\$35 - \$7 = \$28$). Since the item still costs more than $28, then original price must be greater than $35. Therefore, the correct answer is (E).

18. **C** Use the figure provided. Since the 2 angles given are 60° and there are a total of 180° in a triangle, then angle M is 60° (180 – 60 – 60 = 60). Therefore, it is an equilateral triangle. To find the perimeter of a shape, add up all the sides. In an equilateral triangle, all sides are equal, so if one side is 6, all three sides are equal to 6. Thus, the correct answer is (C) since $6 + 6 + 6 = 18$.

19. **D** Use the formula $d = r \times t$ (distance = rate × time). The distance and a range for the time are given, so plug those values into the formula to find the range for her average speed. If it takes her 2 hours, then $100 = r \times 2$ and $r = \dfrac{100}{2} = 50$. Eliminate (A), (B), and (C) since they do not include 50 in the speed range. If it takes her 2.5 hours, then $100 = r \times 2.5$ and $r = \dfrac{100}{2.5} = 40$. Therefore, her speed will be between 40 and 50 mph, so the correct answer is (D).

20. **A** Since the digit 8 in the given number is two places to the right of the decimal, it is in the hundredths place and would be equivalent to eight hundredths. The correct answer is (A). Choice (B) is equal to 0.8, which would need to be one place to the right of the decimal. Choice (C) is equal to 8 and would be one place to the left of the decimal. Choice (D) is equal to 80; the 8 would need to be two places to the left of the decimal. Finally, (E) is equal to 800, and the 8 would need to be three places to the left of the decimal.

21. **B** Use the chart provided to find the requested values. According to the chart, Dr. Davis saw 4 patients on Friday and a total of 16 patients that week. Therefore, the question is asking 4 is what percent of 16. Translate the English words into their math equivalents $\left(4 = \dfrac{x}{100}(16)\right)$ or set up a proportion $\left(\dfrac{4}{16} = \dfrac{x}{100}\right)$ and solve for x. Since 4 is $\dfrac{1}{4}$ of 16, then the patients she saw on Friday represent one-quarter or 25% of the patients she saw during the entire week. The correct answer is (B).

22. **C** Use the chart provided to find the requested values. According to the chart, Dr. Adams saw a total of 28 patients during the entire week and Dr. Davis saw a total of 16 patients that week. Together, they saw 44 patients (28 + 16 = 44). According to the chart, all 4 doctors saw a total of 100 patients that week, so the question is asking 44 is what percent of 100. Translate the English words into their math equivalents $\left(44 = \dfrac{x}{100}(100)\right)$ or set up a proportion $\left(\dfrac{44}{100} = \dfrac{x}{100}\right)$ and solve for x. Since $x = 44$, the correct answer is (C).

23. **D** If 12 mints were purchased separately, the total cost would be $6 since 0.5 × 12 = 6. The cost per mint when purchased in a case is $0.40 since $\dfrac{4.8}{12} = 0.4$. To determine percent change, use the formula: % change $= \dfrac{\text{difference}}{\text{original}} \times 100$. The difference between the two prices is $0.10 since 0.5 − 0.4 = 0.1. The original amount will be the smaller amount ($0.40). Note that if the question says *percent greater*, the *original* will be the smaller number. $\dfrac{\text{difference}}{\text{original}} \times 100 = \dfrac{0.5 - 0.4}{0.4} \times 100 = \dfrac{0.1}{0.4} \times 100 = \dfrac{10}{0.4} = 25$. Therefore, the correct answer is (D).

24. **B** To determine his current revenue, multiply the number of bananas he sells each day (130) by the cost per banana ($4): 130 × 4 = 520. He will still have 40 customers buying bananas for $4 each, so he knows he will make $160 (40 × 4 = 160). To match his current revenue, he needs to make $360 (520 − 160 = 360). Divide that total by the cost per banana ($3) to find how many $3

bananas he must sell to maintain his current revenue: $\frac{360}{3} = 120$. Thus, the correct answer is (B). Note: Another option is to use the answer choices (PITA) as possible values for the number of $3 bananas he needs to sell to match his current revenue. Since the question asks for the minimum number, start with (A). And remember, there is always money in the banana stand.

25. **B** Since the base and height of the right triangle are not provided, plug in values. Let $b = 10$ and $h = 10$. If the length of one side (let's say the base) is decreased by 10%, then the new base is 9 since $0.1 \times 10 = 1$ and $10 - 1 = 9$. If the length of the other side (let's say the height) is increased by 20%, then the new height is 12 since $0.2 \times 10 = 2$ and $10 + 2 = 12$. To find the area of a triangle, use the formula $A = \left(\frac{1}{2}\right)bh$. The area of the original triangle is $\left(\frac{1}{2}\right)(10)(10) = 50$, and the area of the new triangle is $\left(\frac{1}{2}\right)(9)(12) = 54$. Next, to determine percent change, use the formula:

% change $= \frac{\text{difference}}{\text{original}} \times 100$. The difference of the areas is 4 since $54 - 50 = 4$, and the original

area is 50. Thus, $\frac{54 - 50}{50} \times 100 = \frac{4}{50} \times 100 = \frac{400}{50} = 8$. Therefore, the correct answer is (B).

Chapter 11
Middle Level
SSAT Practice Test

Middle Level Practice Test

Be sure each mark *completely* fills the answer space.
Start with number 1 for each new section of the test. You may find more answer spaces than you need.
If so, please leave them blank.

SECTION 1

1 Ⓐ Ⓑ Ⓒ Ⓓ Ⓔ	6 Ⓐ Ⓑ Ⓒ Ⓓ Ⓔ	11 Ⓐ Ⓑ Ⓒ Ⓓ Ⓔ	16 Ⓐ Ⓑ Ⓒ Ⓓ Ⓔ	21 Ⓐ Ⓑ Ⓒ Ⓓ Ⓔ
2 Ⓐ Ⓑ Ⓒ Ⓓ Ⓔ	7 Ⓐ Ⓑ Ⓒ Ⓓ Ⓔ	12 Ⓐ Ⓑ Ⓒ Ⓓ Ⓔ	17 Ⓐ Ⓑ Ⓒ Ⓓ Ⓔ	22 Ⓐ Ⓑ Ⓒ Ⓓ Ⓔ
3 Ⓐ Ⓑ Ⓒ Ⓓ Ⓔ	8 Ⓐ Ⓑ Ⓒ Ⓓ Ⓔ	13 Ⓐ Ⓑ Ⓒ Ⓓ Ⓔ	18 Ⓐ Ⓑ Ⓒ Ⓓ Ⓔ	23 Ⓐ Ⓑ Ⓒ Ⓓ Ⓔ
4 Ⓐ Ⓑ Ⓒ Ⓓ Ⓔ	9 Ⓐ Ⓑ Ⓒ Ⓓ Ⓔ	14 Ⓐ Ⓑ Ⓒ Ⓓ Ⓔ	19 Ⓐ Ⓑ Ⓒ Ⓓ Ⓔ	24 Ⓐ Ⓑ Ⓒ Ⓓ Ⓔ
5 Ⓐ Ⓑ Ⓒ Ⓓ Ⓔ	10 Ⓐ Ⓑ Ⓒ Ⓓ Ⓔ	15 Ⓐ Ⓑ Ⓒ Ⓓ Ⓔ	20 Ⓐ Ⓑ Ⓒ Ⓓ Ⓔ	25 Ⓐ Ⓑ Ⓒ Ⓓ Ⓔ

SECTION 2

1 Ⓐ Ⓑ Ⓒ Ⓓ Ⓔ	9 Ⓐ Ⓑ Ⓒ Ⓓ Ⓔ	17 Ⓐ Ⓑ Ⓒ Ⓓ Ⓔ	25 Ⓐ Ⓑ Ⓒ Ⓓ Ⓔ	33 Ⓐ Ⓑ Ⓒ Ⓓ Ⓔ
2 Ⓐ Ⓑ Ⓒ Ⓓ Ⓔ	10 Ⓐ Ⓑ Ⓒ Ⓓ Ⓔ	18 Ⓐ Ⓑ Ⓒ Ⓓ Ⓔ	26 Ⓐ Ⓑ Ⓒ Ⓓ Ⓔ	34 Ⓐ Ⓑ Ⓒ Ⓓ Ⓔ
3 Ⓐ Ⓑ Ⓒ Ⓓ Ⓔ	11 Ⓐ Ⓑ Ⓒ Ⓓ Ⓔ	19 Ⓐ Ⓑ Ⓒ Ⓓ Ⓔ	27 Ⓐ Ⓑ Ⓒ Ⓓ Ⓔ	35 Ⓐ Ⓑ Ⓒ Ⓓ Ⓔ
4 Ⓐ Ⓑ Ⓒ Ⓓ Ⓔ	12 Ⓐ Ⓑ Ⓒ Ⓓ Ⓔ	20 Ⓐ Ⓑ Ⓒ Ⓓ Ⓔ	28 Ⓐ Ⓑ Ⓒ Ⓓ Ⓔ	36 Ⓐ Ⓑ Ⓒ Ⓓ Ⓔ
5 Ⓐ Ⓑ Ⓒ Ⓓ Ⓔ	13 Ⓐ Ⓑ Ⓒ Ⓓ Ⓔ	21 Ⓐ Ⓑ Ⓒ Ⓓ Ⓔ	29 Ⓐ Ⓑ Ⓒ Ⓓ Ⓔ	37 Ⓐ Ⓑ Ⓒ Ⓓ Ⓔ
6 Ⓐ Ⓑ Ⓒ Ⓓ Ⓔ	14 Ⓐ Ⓑ Ⓒ Ⓓ Ⓔ	22 Ⓐ Ⓑ Ⓒ Ⓓ Ⓔ	30 Ⓐ Ⓑ Ⓒ Ⓓ Ⓔ	38 Ⓐ Ⓑ Ⓒ Ⓓ Ⓔ
7 Ⓐ Ⓑ Ⓒ Ⓓ Ⓔ	15 Ⓐ Ⓑ Ⓒ Ⓓ Ⓔ	23 Ⓐ Ⓑ Ⓒ Ⓓ Ⓔ	31 Ⓐ Ⓑ Ⓒ Ⓓ Ⓔ	39 Ⓐ Ⓑ Ⓒ Ⓓ Ⓔ
8 Ⓐ Ⓑ Ⓒ Ⓓ Ⓔ	16 Ⓐ Ⓑ Ⓒ Ⓓ Ⓔ	24 Ⓐ Ⓑ Ⓒ Ⓓ Ⓔ	32 Ⓐ Ⓑ Ⓒ Ⓓ Ⓔ	40 Ⓐ Ⓑ Ⓒ Ⓓ Ⓔ

SECTION 3

1 Ⓐ Ⓑ Ⓒ Ⓓ Ⓔ	13 Ⓐ Ⓑ Ⓒ Ⓓ Ⓔ	25 Ⓐ Ⓑ Ⓒ Ⓓ Ⓔ	37 Ⓐ Ⓑ Ⓒ Ⓓ Ⓔ	49 Ⓐ Ⓑ Ⓒ Ⓓ Ⓔ
2 Ⓐ Ⓑ Ⓒ Ⓓ Ⓔ	14 Ⓐ Ⓑ Ⓒ Ⓓ Ⓔ	26 Ⓐ Ⓑ Ⓒ Ⓓ Ⓔ	38 Ⓐ Ⓑ Ⓒ Ⓓ Ⓔ	50 Ⓐ Ⓑ Ⓒ Ⓓ Ⓔ
3 Ⓐ Ⓑ Ⓒ Ⓓ Ⓔ	15 Ⓐ Ⓑ Ⓒ Ⓓ Ⓔ	27 Ⓐ Ⓑ Ⓒ Ⓓ Ⓔ	39 Ⓐ Ⓑ Ⓒ Ⓓ Ⓔ	51 Ⓐ Ⓑ Ⓒ Ⓓ Ⓔ
4 Ⓐ Ⓑ Ⓒ Ⓓ Ⓔ	16 Ⓐ Ⓑ Ⓒ Ⓓ Ⓔ	28 Ⓐ Ⓑ Ⓒ Ⓓ Ⓔ	40 Ⓐ Ⓑ Ⓒ Ⓓ Ⓔ	52 Ⓐ Ⓑ Ⓒ Ⓓ Ⓔ
5 Ⓐ Ⓑ Ⓒ Ⓓ Ⓔ	17 Ⓐ Ⓑ Ⓒ Ⓓ Ⓔ	29 Ⓐ Ⓑ Ⓒ Ⓓ Ⓔ	41 Ⓐ Ⓑ Ⓒ Ⓓ Ⓔ	53 Ⓐ Ⓑ Ⓒ Ⓓ Ⓔ
6 Ⓐ Ⓑ Ⓒ Ⓓ Ⓔ	18 Ⓐ Ⓑ Ⓒ Ⓓ Ⓔ	30 Ⓐ Ⓑ Ⓒ Ⓓ Ⓔ	42 Ⓐ Ⓑ Ⓒ Ⓓ Ⓔ	54 Ⓐ Ⓑ Ⓒ Ⓓ Ⓔ
7 Ⓐ Ⓑ Ⓒ Ⓓ Ⓔ	19 Ⓐ Ⓑ Ⓒ Ⓓ Ⓔ	31 Ⓐ Ⓑ Ⓒ Ⓓ Ⓔ	43 Ⓐ Ⓑ Ⓒ Ⓓ Ⓔ	55 Ⓐ Ⓑ Ⓒ Ⓓ Ⓔ
8 Ⓐ Ⓑ Ⓒ Ⓓ Ⓔ	20 Ⓐ Ⓑ Ⓒ Ⓓ Ⓔ	32 Ⓐ Ⓑ Ⓒ Ⓓ Ⓔ	44 Ⓐ Ⓑ Ⓒ Ⓓ Ⓔ	56 Ⓐ Ⓑ Ⓒ Ⓓ Ⓔ
9 Ⓐ Ⓑ Ⓒ Ⓓ Ⓔ	21 Ⓐ Ⓑ Ⓒ Ⓓ Ⓔ	33 Ⓐ Ⓑ Ⓒ Ⓓ Ⓔ	45 Ⓐ Ⓑ Ⓒ Ⓓ Ⓔ	57 Ⓐ Ⓑ Ⓒ Ⓓ Ⓔ
10 Ⓐ Ⓑ Ⓒ Ⓓ Ⓔ	22 Ⓐ Ⓑ Ⓒ Ⓓ Ⓔ	34 Ⓐ Ⓑ Ⓒ Ⓓ Ⓔ	46 Ⓐ Ⓑ Ⓒ Ⓓ Ⓔ	58 Ⓐ Ⓑ Ⓒ Ⓓ Ⓔ
11 Ⓐ Ⓑ Ⓒ Ⓓ Ⓔ	23 Ⓐ Ⓑ Ⓒ Ⓓ Ⓔ	35 Ⓐ Ⓑ Ⓒ Ⓓ Ⓔ	47 Ⓐ Ⓑ Ⓒ Ⓓ Ⓔ	59 Ⓐ Ⓑ Ⓒ Ⓓ Ⓔ
12 Ⓐ Ⓑ Ⓒ Ⓓ Ⓔ	24 Ⓐ Ⓑ Ⓒ Ⓓ Ⓔ	36 Ⓐ Ⓑ Ⓒ Ⓓ Ⓔ	48 Ⓐ Ⓑ Ⓒ Ⓓ Ⓔ	60 Ⓐ Ⓑ Ⓒ Ⓓ Ⓔ

SECTION 4

1 Ⓐ Ⓑ Ⓒ Ⓓ Ⓔ	6 Ⓐ Ⓑ Ⓒ Ⓓ Ⓔ	11 Ⓐ Ⓑ Ⓒ Ⓓ Ⓔ	16 Ⓐ Ⓑ Ⓒ Ⓓ Ⓔ	21 Ⓐ Ⓑ Ⓒ Ⓓ Ⓔ
2 Ⓐ Ⓑ Ⓒ Ⓓ Ⓔ	7 Ⓐ Ⓑ Ⓒ Ⓓ Ⓔ	12 Ⓐ Ⓑ Ⓒ Ⓓ Ⓔ	17 Ⓐ Ⓑ Ⓒ Ⓓ Ⓔ	22 Ⓐ Ⓑ Ⓒ Ⓓ Ⓔ
3 Ⓐ Ⓑ Ⓒ Ⓓ Ⓔ	8 Ⓐ Ⓑ Ⓒ Ⓓ Ⓔ	13 Ⓐ Ⓑ Ⓒ Ⓓ Ⓔ	18 Ⓐ Ⓑ Ⓒ Ⓓ Ⓔ	23 Ⓐ Ⓑ Ⓒ Ⓓ Ⓔ
4 Ⓐ Ⓑ Ⓒ Ⓓ Ⓔ	9 Ⓐ Ⓑ Ⓒ Ⓓ Ⓔ	14 Ⓐ Ⓑ Ⓒ Ⓓ Ⓔ	19 Ⓐ Ⓑ Ⓒ Ⓓ Ⓔ	24 Ⓐ Ⓑ Ⓒ Ⓓ Ⓔ
5 Ⓐ Ⓑ Ⓒ Ⓓ Ⓔ	10 Ⓐ Ⓑ Ⓒ Ⓓ Ⓔ	15 Ⓐ Ⓑ Ⓒ Ⓓ Ⓔ	20 Ⓐ Ⓑ Ⓒ Ⓓ Ⓔ	25 Ⓐ Ⓑ Ⓒ Ⓓ Ⓔ

Middle Level SSAT
Writing Sample

Time - 25 Minutes
1 Topic

<u>Writing Sample</u>

Schools would like to get to know you better through a story you tell using one of the ideas below. Please choose the idea you find most interesting and write a story using the use as your first sentence. Please fill in the circle next to the one you choose.

(A)   What I noticed across the street caused me to...

(B)   The room was surprisingly cold.

_____

_____

_____

_____

_____

_____

_____

_____

_____

GO ON TO THE NEXT PAGE.

Middle Level SSAT
Section 1
Time - 30 Minutes
25 Questions

Following each problem in this section, there are five suggested answers. Work each problem in your head or in the blank space provided at the right of the page. Then look at the five suggested answers and decide which one is best.

Note: Figures that accompany problems in this section are drawn as accurately as possible EXCEPT when it is stated in a specific problem that its figure is not drawn to scale.

Sample Problem:

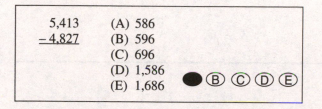

5,413	(A) 586
−4,827	(B) 596
	(C) 696
	(D) 1,586
	(E) 1,686

1. Which fraction equals $\frac{2}{3}$?

    (A) $\frac{3}{2}$

    (B) $\frac{3}{6}$

    (C) $\frac{9}{12}$

    (D) $\frac{8}{12}$

    (E) $\frac{5}{6}$

USE THIS SPACE FOR FIGURING.

2. Which of the following is an even positive integer that lies between 22 and 27 ?

    (A) 25
    (B) 24
    (C) 22
    (D) 21
    (E) 20

GO ON TO THE NEXT PAGE.

3. In the number 281, the sum of the digits is how much less than the product of the digits?

   (A) 16
   (B) 11
   (C) 10
   (D) 5
   (E) 4

4. $(109 - 102) \times 3 - 4^2 =$

   (A) 5
   (B) 0
   (C) −5
   (D) −7
   (E) −336

5. A concert is held at a stadium that has 25,000 seats. If exactly $\frac{3}{4}$ of the seats were filled, to the nearest thousand, how many people attended the concert?

   (A) 10,000
   (B) 14,000
   (C) 15,000
   (D) 19,000
   (E) 21,000

6. The perimeter of a square with an area of 81 is

   (A) 81
   (B) 54
   (C) 36
   (D) 18
   (E) 9

7. If the sum of three consecutive positive integers is 9, what is the middle integer?

   (A) 1
   (B) 2
   (C) 3
   (D) 4
   (E) 5

GO ON TO THE NEXT PAGE.

8. A number greater than 2 that is a factor of both 20 and 16 is also a factor of which number?

   (A) 10
   (B) 14
   (C) 18
   (D) 24
   (E) 30

USE THIS SPACE FOR FIGURING.

1

9. $(2^3)^2 =$

   (A) 2
   (B) 2^5
   (C) 2^6
   (D) 4^5
   (E) 4^6

10. If $\dfrac{1}{2}$ is greater than $\dfrac{M}{16}$, then M could be

    (A) 7
    (B) 8
    (C) 9
    (D) 10
    (E) 32

11. The sum of the lengths of two sides of an equilateral triangle is 4. What is the perimeter of the triangle?

    (A) 2
    (B) 4
    (C) 6
    (D) 8
    (E) 12

GO ON TO THE NEXT PAGE.

Questions 12–14 refer to the following chart.

USE THIS SPACE FOR FIGURING.

Stacey's Weekly Mileage

Day	Miles Driven
MONDAY	35
TUESDAY	70
WEDNESDAY	50
THURSDAY	105
FRIDAY	35
SATURDAY	35
SUNDAY	20
Total	**350**

Figure 1

12. What percentage of her total weekly mileage did Stacey drive on Monday?

    (A) 10%
    (B) 20%
    (C) 35%
    (D) 60%
    (E) 90%

13. The number of miles Stacey drove on Thursday is equal to the sum of the miles she drove on which days?

    (A) Monday and Wednesday
    (B) Saturday and Sunday
    (C) Tuesday, Wednesday, and Friday
    (D) Friday, Saturday, and Sunday
    (E) Monday, Friday, and Saturday

14. The number of miles Stacey drove on Sunday is equal to what percent of the number of miles she drove on Wednesday?

    (A) 10%
    (B) 20%
    (C) 40%
    (D) 50%
    (E) 80%

GO ON TO THE NEXT PAGE.

15. If $x = 5$, which of the following is equal to $\frac{1}{x}$?

    (A) 10%
    (B) 20%
    (C) 40%
    (D) 2
    (E) 3

USE THIS SPACE FOR FIGURING.

16. What is 20% of 25% of 80 ?

    (A) 4
    (B) 5
    (C) 10
    (D) 16
    (E) 20

17. During one week, Roy worked 3 hours on Monday, 5 hours on Tuesday, and 8 hours each day on Saturday and Sunday. The following week Roy worked a total of 40 hours. What was the average number of hours Roy worked each week?

    (A) 32
    (B) 28
    (C) 24
    (D) 12
    (E) 6

18. A box with dimensions $4 \times 8 \times 10$ is equal in volume to a box with dimensions $16 \times g \times 2$. What does g equal?

    (A) 2
    (B) 4
    (C) 8
    (D) 10
    (E) 16

GO ON TO THE NEXT PAGE.

19. Otto wants to buy two tapes that regularly sell for *b* dollars each. The store is having a sale in which the second tape costs half price. If he buys the tapes at this store, what is the overall percent he will save on the price of the two tapes?

(A) 10%

(B) 25%

(C) $33\frac{1}{3}\%$

(D) 50%

(E) 75%

USE THIS SPACE FOR FIGURING.

20. In a certain month Ben eats 8 dinners at Italian restaurants, 4 dinners at Chinese restaurants, and 6 dinners at steakhouses. If these dinners account for all Ben's restaurant visits during the month, what percent of Ben's restaurant meals were at steakhouses?

(A) 75%

(B) $66\frac{1}{2}\%$

(C) 50%

(D) $33\frac{1}{3}\%$

(E) 10%

21. What is the area of the shaded region?

(A) 48
(B) 36
(C) 24
(D) 12
(E) It cannot be determined from the information given.

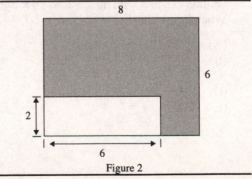

Figure 2

22. In the equation $(2 + \_ + 3)(2) = 16$, what does the _ stand for?

(A) 3
(B) 8
(C) 9
(D) 10
(E) 12

GO ON TO THE NEXT PAGE.

23. At Skytop Farm, the ratio of cows to pigs is 16 to 1. Which of the following could be the total number of cows and pigs at the farm?

    (A) 15
    (B) 16
    (C) 32
    (D) 68
    (E) 74

USE THIS SPACE FOR FIGURING.

24. Sibyl has seen four more films than Linda has seen. Linda has seen twice as many films as Joel has seen. If Sibyl has seen *s* films, then in terms of *s*, which of the following is an expression for the number of films Joel has seen?

    (A) $\dfrac{s}{2} - 2$

    (B) $\dfrac{s}{2} - 4$

    (C) $s - 2$

    (D) $s - 4$

    (E) $\dfrac{8}{s} \cdot 2$

Question 25 refers to the following definition.

For all integers *x*, @ *x* = 2*x*

25. @3 – @2 =

    (A) @4
    (B) @2
    (C) @1
    (D) @–2
    (E) @–3

STOP

IF YOU FINISH BEFORE TIME IS CALLED,
YOU MAY CHECK YOUR WORK ON THIS SECTION ONLY.
DO NOT TURN TO ANY OTHER SECTION IN THE TEST.

Middle Level SSAT
Section 2
Time - 40 Minutes
40 Questions

Read each passage carefully and then answer the questions about it. For each question, decide on the basis of the passage which one of the choices best answers the questions.

The native inhabitants of the Americas arrived from Asia more than 20,000 years ago. They belonged to numerous tribes and many were skilled hunters, farmers, and fishers. Some of the most famous of the tribes of Native Americans are the Sioux, the Cheyenne, the Iroquois, and the Apache.

These tribes settled and developed organized societies. The settlers to North America from Europe fought the Native Americans for land. Geronimo was the last great Native American chief to organize rebellions against the settlers. He led raids across the southwest and into Mexico. Although he eventually was captured, he later became a celebrity.

After a long battle, the United States government moved the Native Americans onto reservations—special sections of land set aside for them—where many still reside today.

1. The main purpose of this passage is to

   (A) report on the current status of Native Americans
   (B) offer a solution to the problems of Native Americans
   (C) give a brief history of Native Americans
   (D) discuss ways Native Americans are able to work on reservations
   (E) give a history of different Native American tribes

2. According to the passage, the fate of Geronimo was

   (A) to live out his life in disgrace
   (B) to become a great war hero with no defeats
   (C) to become famous throughout the country
   (D) to die penniless and alone
   (E) to commit suicide

3. The author's tone in regard to the fate of Native Americans is

   (A) passionate
   (B) objective
   (C) disappointed
   (D) ambivalent
   (E) envious

4. Which of the following is the author most likely to discuss next?

   (A) Possible causes of Native American resentment
   (B) The life of the Native American in modern society
   (C) The battle that defeated Geronimo
   (D) The differences among tribes
   (E) A detailed history of the Sioux

5. The passage names all the following as skills possessed by Native Americans EXCEPT:

   (A) farming
   (B) hunting
   (C) fishing
   (D) gathering
   (E) fighting

GO ON TO THE NEXT PAGE.

2

Twenty percent of all the land on Earth consists of deserts. When most people think of deserts, they think of searing heat, big sand dunes, and camels. But not all deserts are huge sand piles—many are strewn with rocks and some, like those at high altitudes, may actually be quite cold.

Desert life is interesting and varied as well. Though the desert is a punishing place—it is difficult to find food and water in the desert—many animals live there. Because there is so little water, desert animals have adapted. Camels can survive for days without drinking. Other animals get their water from the insects and plants they eat.

The extreme temperatures of the desert can make life difficult as well. Many of the mammals there have thick fur to keep out the heat and the cold. Some desert animals are nocturnal, sleeping by day and hunting by night when the air is cooler. It may seem that all deserts are the same, but they are as different as the animals that inhabit them.

6. The passage is primarily about

   (A) deserts and desert wildlife
   (B) nocturnal animals
   (C) plant life of the desert
   (D) sources of water in the desert
   (E) average desert temperatures

7. Which of the following can be inferred as an example of an adaptation to desert life?

   (A) The large claws of the lizard
   (B) The heavy outer shell of the beetle
   (C) The long ears of the hedgehog that give off heat to cool the animal
   (D) The large hood of the cobra that scares off predators
   (E) The quick speed of the mongoose so that it may catch its prey

8. The style of the passage is most like that found in a(n)

   (A) scientific thesis
   (B) general book on desert life
   (C) advanced text on animal adaptations
   (D) diary of a naturalist
   (E) biography of a desert researcher

9. According to the passage, camels are well adapted to desert life because

   (A) they have long legs
   (B) they have thick fur that keeps them cool
   (C) they have large hooded eyes
   (D) they are capable of hunting at night
   (E) they can store water for many days

10. According to the passage, some deserts

   (A) are filled with lush vegetation
   (B) are home to large bodies of water
   (C) actually get a good deal of rainfall
   (D) can be in a cold climate
   (E) are home to large, thriving cities

11. The word "punishing" in line 5 most closely means

   (A) beating
   (B) harsh
   (C) unhappy
   (D) deadly
   (E) fantastic

GO ON TO THE NEXT PAGE.

The original Olympic Games started in Greece more than 2,000 years ago. These games were a religious festival, and, at their height, lasted for five days. Only men could compete, and the sports included running, wrestling, and chariot racing.

Today's Olympic Games are quite a bit different. First, there are two varieties: Winter Olympics and Summer Olympics. They each boast many men and women competing in a multitude of sports, from skiing to gymnastics. They are each held every four years, but not during the same year. They alternate so that there are Olympic Games every two years. The Olympics are no longer held only in one country. They are hosted by different cities around the world. The opening ceremony is a spectacular display, usually incorporating the traditional dances and culture of the host city.

The highlight of the opening ceremony is the lighting of the Olympic flame. Teams of runners carry the torch from Olympia, the site of the ancient Greek games. Although the games have changed greatly throughout the centuries, the spirit of competition is still alive. The flame represents that spirit.

12. The passage is primarily concerned with

(A) justifying the existence of the Olympic Games
(B) explaining all about the games in Ancient Greece
(C) discussing the differences between Winter Olympics and Summer Olympics
(D) comparing the modern Olympic Games to those in Ancient Greece
(E) explaining the process for choosing a host country

13. The author mentions "traditional dances and culture of the host city" in order to

(A) give an example of how the opening ceremony is so spectacular
(B) explain the differences among the different host cities
(C) show that Ancient Greek games were quite boring by contrast
(D) make an analogy to the life of the Ancient Greeks
(E) illustrate the complexity of the modern games

14. The author's tone in the passage can best be described as

(A) disinterested
(B) upbeat
(C) gloating
(D) depressing
(E) fatalistic

15. The lighting of the torch is meant to symbolize

(A) the destruction caused in Ancient Greece
(B) the spirit of Ancient Greek competition
(C) the rousing nature of the games
(D) the heat generated in competition
(E) an eternal flame so that the games will continue forever

16. Which of the following can be inferred from the passage?

(A) Women in ancient Greece did not want to compete in the Olympics.
(B) The Olympics were held every year.
(C) The Olympics used to be held in just one country.
(D) Ice skating is a winter event.
(E) Opening ceremonies today are more spectacular than ones in ancient Greece.

GO ON TO THE NEXT PAGE.

Like snakes, lizards, and crocodiles, turtles are reptiles. The earliest fossils recognized as turtles are about 200 million years old and date from the time when dinosaurs roamed Earth. Unbelievably, turtles have changed little in appearance since that time.

There are many different types of turtles in many different climates around the world. In contrast to other reptiles, whose populations are confined largely to the tropics, turtles are most abundant in southeastern North America and southeastern Asia. They live in lakes, ponds, salt marshes, rivers, forests, and even deserts. The sizes of turtles vary. Bog or mud turtles grow no larger than about 4 inches (10 centimeters) long. At the other end of the spectrum is the sea-roving leatherback turtle, which may be more than 6.5 feet (2 meters) in length and weigh more than 1,100 pounds (500 kilograms).

Turtles live longer than most other animals, but reports of turtles living more than a century are questionable. Several kinds, however, have lived more than 50 years in captivity. Even in natural environments, box turtles and slider turtles can reach ages of 20 to 30 years. The ages of some turtles can be estimated by counting the growth rings that form each year on the external bony plates of the shell.

17. The author mentions dinosaurs in the first paragraph to

(A) illustrate the age of the turtle fossils
(B) uncover the mystery of turtle origins
(C) show that turtles may become extinct
(D) give an example of the type of predator that turtles once faced
(E) bring the life of the turtle into focus

18. Turtles are different from other reptiles because they

(A) date back to dinosaur times
(B) have not adapted to their environment
(C) live in different climates
(D) are desert dwellers
(E) are good pets

19. When the author discusses the theory that turtles may live to be more than 100, the tone can best be described as

(A) respectful
(B) ridiculing
(C) horrified
(D) interested
(E) skeptical

20. One of the ways to verify the age of a turtle is to

(A) measure the turtle
(B) count the rings on its shell
(C) examine the physical deterioration of its shell
(D) weigh the turtle
(E) subtract its weight from its length

21. The author would most probably agree that

(A) turtles are more interesting than other reptiles
(B) there is a lot to be learned about turtles
(C) turtles live longer than any other animal
(D) turtles can be very dangerous
(E) there are no bad turtles

GO ON TO THE NEXT PAGE.

The summer holidays! Those magic words! The mere mention of them used to send shivers of joy rippling over my skin. All my summer holidays, from when I was four years old to when I was seventeen (1920 to 1932), were idyllic. This, I am certain, was because we always went to the same idyllic place, and that place was Norway.

Except for my ancient half-sister and my not-quite-so-ancient half-brother, the rest of us were all pure Norwegian by blood. We all spoke Norwegian and all our relations lived over there. So in a way, going to Norway every summer was like going home.

Even the journey was an event. Do not forget that there were no commercial aeroplanes in those times, so it took us four whole days to complete the trip out and another four days to get home again.

22. The author's goal in writing was to express

   (A) his affection for Norway
   (B) his dislike of his half-sister and half-brother
   (C) dismay at the drudgery of the journey
   (D) how different life was back then
   (E) his realization that the trip was so long

23. The author uses the word "idyllic" in the first paragraph to mean

   (A) scary
   (B) pleasant
   (C) religious
   (D) cold
   (E) boring

24. The author uses the analogy that "going to Norway every summer was like going home" to illustrate

   (A) how much he dreaded the journey
   (B) how frequently they went to Norway
   (C) why his half-sister and half-brother were going along
   (D) how long they stayed in Norway
   (E) how happy and comfortable he was there

25. The author mentions the length of the trip in order to

   (A) make the reader sympathetic to his plight
   (B) make the reader understand why the trip was an adventure
   (C) help the reader visualize the boredom that he faced
   (D) give the reader some sympathy for the half-sister and half-brother
   (E) help the reader visualize Norway

GO ON TO THE NEXT PAGE.

You may love to walk along the seashore and collect beautiful shells, but do you ever think about whose home that shell was before you found it? That's right, seashells are the home of a whole group of creatures known as shellfish. Some of the most common types of shellfish are the mussel, the clam, and the scallop.

It may surprise you to learn that the shellfish themselves make the shells. They manage to draw calcium carbonate, a mineral, from the water. They use that mineral to build the shell up layer by layer. The shell can grow larger and larger as the shellfish grows in size.

There are two main types of shells. There are those that are a single unit, like a conch's shell, and those that are in two pieces, like a clam's shell. The two-piece shell is called a bivalve, and the two pieces are hinged together, like a door, so that the shell can open and close for feeding.

26. The "home" mentioned in line 2 most likely refers to

(A) the sea
(B) the planet
(C) the places shellfish can be found
(D) the shell
(E) a shelter for fish

27. Which of the following questions is answered by the passage?

(A) How do shellfish reproduce?
(B) How much does the average shellfish weigh?
(C) What is the average life span of a shellfish?
(D) What do shellfish feed on?
(E) How do shellfish make their shells?

28. This passage is primarily concerned with

(A) how shellfish differ from other fish
(B) the life span of shellfish
(C) shellfish and their habitats
(D) a general discussion of shells
(E) the origin of shells

29. The author uses the comparison of the bivalves' hinge to a door in order to

(A) illustrate how the shell opens and closes
(B) explain why the shell is so fragile
(C) give a reason for the shells that are found open
(D) explain the mechanism for how the shells are made
(E) illustrate that shellfish are not so different from other fish

30. What is the best title of the selection?

(A) "A Conch by Any Other Name Would Shell as Sweet"
(B) "Going to the Beach"
(C) "I Can Grow My Own Home!"
(D) "The Prettiest Aquatic Life"
(E) "How to Find Shells"

31. According to the passage, the primary difference between the conch's shell and the clam's shell is that

(A) the conch shell is more valuable than the clam's shell
(B) the conch shell protects better than the clam's shell
(C) the conch shell is more beautiful than the clam's shell
(D) the clam's shell is more difficult for the clam to manufacture than the conch shell is for the conch to manufacture
(E) the conch shell has fewer pieces than the clam shell

GO ON TO THE NEXT PAGE.

By day the bat is cousin to the mouse;

He likes the attic of an aging house.

His fingers make a hat about his head.

His pulse-beat is so slow we think him dead.

He loops in crazy figures half the night

Among the trees that face the corner light.

But when he brushes up against a screen,

We are afraid of what our eyes have seen:

For something is amiss or out of place

When mice with wings can wear a human face.

—Theodore Roethke

32. The "hat" referred to in line 3 is meant to refer to

(A) the attic of the house
(B) the bat's head
(C) the bat's wings
(D) the death of the bat
(E) the mouse

33. The passage uses which of the following to describe the bat?

   I. The image of a winged mouse
  II. The image of a vampire
 III. The way he flies

(A) I only
(B) I and II only
(C) II and III only
(D) I and III only
(E) I, II, and III

34. The author mentions the "crazy figures" in line 5 to refer to

(A) the comic notion of a mouse with wings
(B) the pattern of the bat's flight
(C) the shape of the house
(D) the reason the bat appears dead
(E) the trees in the yard

35. The author would most probably agree with which of the following statements?

(A) Bats are useful animals.
(B) Bats are related to mice.
(C) Bats are feared by many.
(D) Most people have bats in their attic.
(E) Bats are an uninteresting phenomenon.

GO ON TO THE NEXT PAGE.

Did you ever watch a sport and admire the players' uniforms? Perhaps you play in a sport and know the thrill of putting on your team's uniform. Uniforms are important for many different reasons, whether you are playing a sport or watching one.

If you are playing a sport, you have many reasons to appreciate your uniform. You may notice how different uniforms are for different sports. That's because they are designed to make participation both safe and easy. If you participate in track and field, your uniform is designed to help you run faster and move more easily. If you participate in a sport like boxing or football, your uniform will protect you as well. You may wear special shoes, like sneakers or cleats, to help you run faster or keep you from slipping.

If you watch sports, you can appreciate uniforms as well. Imagine how difficult it would be to tell the players on a field apart without their uniforms. And of course, as sports fans all over the world do, you can show support for the team you favor by wearing the colors of the team's uniform.

36. The primary purpose of the passage is to

    (A) discuss the importance of team spirit
    (B) explain why uniforms are important for safety
    (C) give a general history of uniforms
    (D) help shed light on the controversy surrounding uniforms
    (E) give some reasons why uniforms are useful

37. The "support" mentioned in line 12 most probably means

    (A) nourishment
    (B) salary
    (C) endorsement
    (D) brace
    (E) relief

38. Which of the following best describes the author's attitude toward uniforms?

    (A) Most of them are basically the same.
    (B) They have many different purposes.
    (C) They're most useful as protection against injury.
    (D) They are fun to wear.
    (E) They don't serve any real purpose.

39. According to the passage, people need special uniforms for track and field sports to

    (A) help spectators cheer on the team
    (B) distinguish them from other athletes
    (C) protect against injury
    (D) give them freedom of movement
    (E) prevent them from losing

40. According to the passage, the primary reason that spectators like uniforms is that

    (A) they help them to distinguish teams
    (B) they have such vibrant colors
    (C) they make great souvenirs
    (D) they are collectible
    (E) they are not too expensive

STOP

**IF YOU FINISH BEFORE TIME IS CALLED,
YOU MAY CHECK YOUR WORK ON THIS SECTION ONLY.
DO NOT TURN TO ANY OTHER SECTION IN THE TEST.**

Middle Level SSAT
Section 3
Time - 30 Minutes
60 Questions

This section consists of two different types of questions. There are directions and a sample question for each type.

Each of the following questions consists of one word followed by five words or phrases. You are to select the one word or phrase whose meaning is closest to the word in capital letters.

Sample Question:

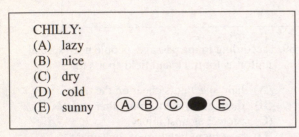

CHILLY:
(A) lazy
(B) nice
(C) dry
(D) cold
(E) sunny

Ⓐ Ⓑ Ⓒ ● Ⓔ

---

1. OBEDIENT:
   (A) amenable
   (B) excessive
   (C) ironic
   (D) inhumane
   (E) improper

2. CONTAMINATE:
   (A) deodorize
   (B) decongest
   (C) deter
   (D) taint
   (E) defoliate

3. WOEFUL:
   (A) wretched
   (B) bloated
   (C) dim
   (D) animated
   (E) reasonable

4. PRACTICAL:
   (A) difficult to learn
   (B) inferior in quality
   (C) providing great support
   (D) having great usefulness
   (E) feeling great regret

5. SCRUTINIZE:
   (A) examine carefully
   (B) announce publicly
   (C) infer correctly
   (D) decide promptly
   (E) warn swiftly

6. CONFIDE:
   (A) judge
   (B) entrust
   (C) secret
   (D) profess
   (E) confuse

7. INITIATE:
   (A) bring to an end
   (B) sign
   (C) commence
   (D) hinder
   (E) guide

8. FORTUNATE:
   (A) lucky
   (B) wealthy
   (C) intelligent
   (D) poor
   (E) downtrodden

GO ON TO THE NEXT PAGE.

9. CRUMBLE:
   (A) eat
   (B) stumble
   (C) dry out
   (D) small
   (E) deteriorate

10. DESPERATE:
   (A) hungry
   (B) frantic
   (C) delicate
   (D) adaptable
   (E) contaminated

11. FRET:
   (A) listen
   (B) provide
   (C) worry
   (D) require
   (E) stash

12. DISGUISE:
   (A) mystery
   (B) convict
   (C) present
   (D) false front
   (E) pressure

13. ASSIST:
   (A) support
   (B) bring
   (C) distrust
   (D) yearn
   (E) destroy

14. REPRIMAND:
   (A) praise
   (B) insure
   (C) liberate
   (D) chide
   (E) forgive

15. EVADE:
   (A) take from
   (B) blind
   (C) help
   (D) sidestep
   (E) successful

16. FATIGUE:
   (A) grow weary
   (B) become fluid
   (C) increase in height
   (D) recede from view
   (E) improve

17. ANTIDOTE:
   (A) foundation
   (B) vacation
   (C) poison
   (D) learning experience
   (E) antitoxin

18. PROPOSE:
   (A) speak up
   (B) marriage
   (C) fall away
   (D) suggest
   (E) lease

19. INCREDIBLE:
   (A) mundane
   (B) uncivilized
   (C) sophisticated
   (D) believable
   (E) extraordinary

20. VIGILANT:
   (A) observant
   (B) sleepy
   (C) overly anxious
   (D) brutal
   (E) moving

GO ON TO THE NEXT PAGE.

21. TATTERED:
    (A) unkempt
    (B) neat
    (C) exuberant
    (D) unruly
    (E) pressed

22. PRECEDE:
    (A) stand alongside
    (B) move toward
    (C) come before
    (D) hurl
    (E) beg

23. LAMENT:
    (A) relish
    (B) drench
    (C) moan
    (D) invent
    (E) incline

24. ENGAGE:
    (A) date
    (B) employ
    (C) train
    (D) dismiss
    (E) fear

25. COMPETENT:
    (A) disastrous
    (B) fast
    (C) cautious
    (D) able
    (E) inanimate

26. SINCERE:
    (A) new
    (B) passionate
    (C) expensive
    (D) genuine
    (E) untold

27. RICKETY:
    (A) strong
    (B) wooden
    (C) antique
    (D) beautiful
    (E) feeble

28. CONSPICUOUS:
    (A) plain as day
    (B) identity
    (C) camouflaged
    (D) shiny
    (E) cramped

29. VERSATILE:
    (A) peaceful
    (B) disruptive
    (C) adaptable
    (D) truthful
    (E) charming

30. CORROBORATION:
    (A) attraction
    (B) confirmation
    (C) legal activity
    (D) unfulfilled expectation
    (E) enthusiastic response

GO ON TO THE NEXT PAGE.

The following questions ask you to find relationships between words. For each question, select the answer choice that best completes the meaning of the sentence.

Sample Question:

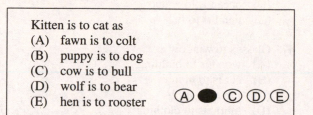

Kitten is to cat as
(A) fawn is to colt
(B) puppy is to dog
(C) cow is to bull
(D) wolf is to bear
(E) hen is to rooster

Choice (B) is the best answer because a kitten is a young cat, just as a puppy is a young dog.
Of all the answer choices, (B) states a relationship that is most like the relationship between <u>kitten</u> and <u>cat</u>.

31. Fish is to water as
    (A) bird is to egg
    (B) roe is to pouch
    (C) lion is to land
    (D) flower is to pollen
    (E) bee is to honey

32. Sick is to healthy as jailed is to
    (A) convicted
    (B) free
    (C) guilty
    (D) trapped
    (E) hurt

33. Dancer is to feet as
    (A) surgeon is to heart
    (B) juggler is to hands
    (C) drummer is to drums
    (D) conductor is to voice
    (E) musician is to eyes

34. Bystander is to event as
    (A) juror is to verdict
    (B) culprit is to crime
    (C) tourist is to journey
    (D) spectator is to game
    (E) model is to portrait

35. Baker is to bread as
    (A) shop is to goods
    (B) butcher is to livestock
    (C) politician is to votes
    (D) sculptor is to statue
    (E) family is to confidence

36. Igneous is to rock as
    (A) stratum is to dig
    (B) fossil is to dinosaur
    (C) computer is to calculator
    (D) watercolor is to painting
    (E) calendar is to date

37. Delicious is to taste as melodious is to
    (A) sound
    (B) movie
    (C) ears
    (D) eyes
    (E) sight

38. Clog is to shoe as
    (A) sneaker is to run
    (B) lace is to tie
    (C) beret is to hat
    (D) shirt is to torso
    (E) sock is to foot

GO ON TO THE NEXT PAGE.

39. Cube is to square as
    (A) box is to cardboard
    (B) circle is to street
    (C) cylinder is to pen
    (D) line is to angle
    (E) sphere is to circle

40. Jam is to fruit as
    (A) bread is to toast
    (B) butter is to milk
    (C) crayon is to color
    (D) height is to stone
    (E) write is to pencil

41. Mile is to quart as
    (A) sky is to height
    (B) coffee is to drink
    (C) pot is to stew
    (D) floor is to ground
    (E) length is to volume

42. Biologist is to scientist as surgeon is to
    (A) doctor
    (B) scar
    (C) cut
    (D) heart
    (E) scalpel

43. Clay is to potter as
    (A) sea is to captain
    (B) magazine is to reader
    (C) marble is to sculptor
    (D) word is to teacher
    (E) bubble is to child

44. Clip is to movie as
    (A) buckle is to shoe
    (B) excerpt is to novel
    (C) jar is to liquid
    (D) room is to house
    (E) filling is to pie

45. Ruthless is to mercy as naive is to
    (A) thoughtfulness
    (B) illness
    (C) worldliness
    (D) contempt
    (E) purity

46. Glacier is to ice as
    (A) rain is to snow
    (B) bay is to sea
    (C) cloud is to storm
    (D) ocean is to water
    (E) pond is to fish

47. Glass is to window as
    (A) wood is to building
    (B) car is to motor
    (C) job is to skills
    (D) fabric is to clothing
    (E) loan is to interest

48. Buttress is to support as scissor is to
    (A) press
    (B) store
    (C) create
    (D) cool
    (E) cut

49. Sneer is to disdain as cringe is to
    (A) loneliness
    (B) bravery
    (C) intelligence
    (D) distrust
    (E) fear

50. Library is to book as
    (A) bank is to money
    (B) museum is to patron
    (C) opera is to audience
    (D) restaurant is to waiter
    (E) concert is to music

51. Famine is to food as
    (A) drought is to water
    (B) paper is to print
    (C) legend is to fantasy
    (D) debate is to issue
    (E) clause is to contract

52. Teacher is to student as
    (A) coach is to player
    (B) assistant is to executive
    (C) nurse is to doctor
    (D) patient is to dentist
    (E) theory is to technician

GO ON TO THE NEXT PAGE.

53. Muffle is to noise as
    (A) engine is to bicycle
    (B) wind is to vane
    (C) dam is to flood
    (D) aroma is to fetid
    (E) nibble is to eat

54. Rest is to exhaustion as
    (A) pack is to vacation
    (B) water is to thirst
    (C) audit is to forms
    (D) jury is to trial
    (E) tide is to ocean

55. Playwright is to script as
    (A) choreographer is to dance
    (B) mathematician is to science
    (C) philosopher is to insight
    (D) enemy is to strategy
    (E) athlete is to prowess

56. Gluttony is to food as
    (A) sheer is to wall
    (B) avarice is to money
    (C) enterprise is to earning
    (D) curiosity is to danger
    (E) mystery is to solution

57. Facile is to effort as
    (A) deception is to trick
    (B) helpful is to friend
    (C) inconsiderate is to thought
    (D) pious is to religion
    (E) incompetent is to task

58. Single-handed is to assistance as anonymous is to
    (A) praise
    (B) authorship
    (C) recognition
    (D) sincerity
    (E) ideas

59. Stable is to horse as kennel is to
    (A) farm
    (B) storage
    (C) dog
    (D) groomer
    (E) boarding

60. Tree is to knee as
    (A) pot is to cot
    (B) bam is to lamb
    (C) forest is to body
    (D) bob is to cob
    (E) seek is to leek

STOP

IF YOU FINISH BEFORE TIME IS CALLED,
YOU MAY CHECK YOUR WORK ON THIS SECTION ONLY.
DO NOT TURN TO ANY OTHER SECTION IN THE TEST.

Middle Level SSAT
Section 4
Time - 30 Minutes
25 Questions

Following each problem in this section, there are five suggested answers. Work each problem in your head or in the blank space provided at the right of the page. Then look at the five suggested answers and decide which one is best.

Note: Figures that accompany problems in this section are drawn as accurately as possible EXCEPT when it is stated in a specific problem that its figure is not drawn to scale.

Sample Problem:

5,413	(A) 586
− 4,827	(B) 596
	(C) 696
	(D) 1,586
	(E) 1,686 ● Ⓑ Ⓒ Ⓓ Ⓔ

1. Which of the following fractions is greatest?   **USE THIS SPACE FOR FIGURING.**

   (A) $\dfrac{3}{4}$

   (B) $\dfrac{5}{8}$

   (C) $\dfrac{1}{2}$

   (D) $\dfrac{3}{7}$

   (E) $\dfrac{5}{9}$

2. The sum of the factors of 12 is

   (A) 28
   (B) 21
   (C) 20
   (D) 16
   (E) 15

GO ON TO THE NEXT PAGE.

3. $16 + 2 \times 3 + 2 =$

    (A) 90
    (B) 56
    (C) 24
    (D) 23
    (E) 18

USE THIS SPACE FOR FIGURING.

4

4. $D + E + F + G =$

    (A) 45
    (B) 90
    (C) 180
    (D) 270
    (E) 360

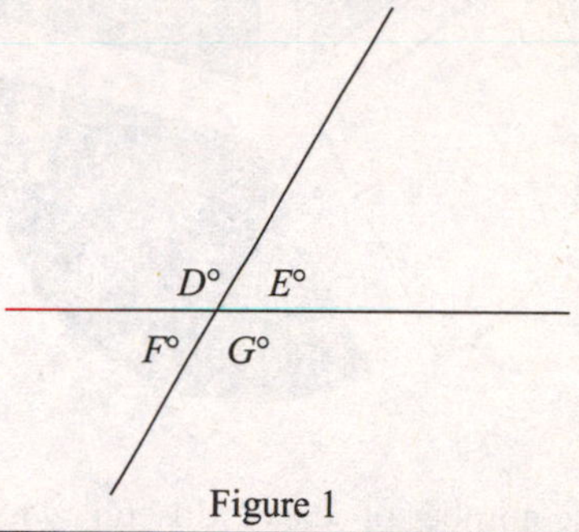

$D°$ $E°$
$F°$ $G°$

Figure 1

5. What are two different prime factors of 48 ?

    (A) 2 and 3
    (B) 3 and 4
    (C) 4 and 6
    (D) 4 and 12
    (E) 6 and 8

6. The difference between 12 and the product of 4 and 6 is

    (A) 12
    (B) 10
    (C) 2
    (D) 1
    (E) 0

7. The sum of the number of degrees in a straight line and the number of degrees in a triangle equals

    (A) 720
    (B) 540
    (C) 360
    (D) 180
    (E) 90

GO ON TO THE NEXT PAGE.

Questions 8–10 refer to the following graph.

USE THIS SPACE FOR FIGURING.

Joseph's Winter Clothing

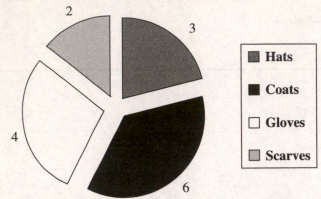

- Hats
- Coats
- Gloves
- Scarves

8. The number of scarves Joseph owns plus the number of coats he owns equals

    (A) 5
    (B) 7
    (C) 8
    (D) 9
    (E) 10

9. Hats represent what percentage of the total number of garments accounted for in the graph?

    (A) 10%
    (B) 20%
    (C) 30%
    (D) 50%
    (E) 80%

10. Which types of garments represent one-third of the total number of garments accounted for in the graph?

    (A) Hats and coats
    (B) Gloves and scarves
    (C) Hats and scarves
    (D) Gloves and coats
    (E) Hats, gloves, and scarves

GO ON TO THE NEXT PAGE.

11. George bought five slices of pizza for $10. At this rate, how many slices of pizza could he buy with $32 ?

    (A) 16
    (B) 15
    (C) 14
    (D) 12
    (E) 10

USE THIS SPACE FOR FIGURING.

12. On a certain English test, the 10 students in Mrs. Bennett's class score an average of 85. On the same test, 15 students in Mrs. Grover's class score an average of 70. What is the combined average score for all the students in Mrs. Bennett's and Mrs. Grover's classes?

    (A) 80
    (B) 77.5
    (C) 76
    (D) 75
    (E) 72

13. If Mary bought e pencils, Jane bought 5 times as many pencils as Mary, and Peggy bought 2 pencils fewer than Mary, then in terms of e, how many pencils did the three girls buy all together?

    (A) $5e - 2$
    (B) 7
    (C) $7e - 2$
    (D) $8e$
    (E) $8e - 2$

14. $\dfrac{4}{1,000} + \dfrac{3}{10} + 3 =$
    (A) 4,033
    (B) 433
    (C) 334
    (D) 3.34
    (E) 3.304

GO ON TO THE NEXT PAGE.

Questions 15 and 16 refer to the following definition.

USE THIS SPACE FOR FIGURING.

$$\boxed{4}$$

For all real numbers f, $\boxed{f} = -2f$

15. $\boxed{0} =$

(A) 4
(B) 2
(C) 0
(D) −2
(E) −4

16. $\boxed{2} \times \boxed{3} =$

(A) $\boxed{24}$
(B) $\boxed{2}$
(C) $\boxed{3}$
(D) $\boxed{-3}$
(E) $\boxed{-12}$

17. $2\dfrac{1}{4}\% =$

(A) 0.0025
(B) 0.0225
(C) 0.225
(D) 2.025
(E) 2.25

18. The area of triangle *UVW* is

(A) $2h^2$
(B) h^2
(C) h
(D) 3
(E) 2

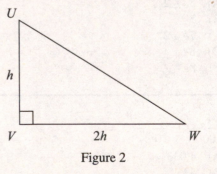

Figure 2

GO ON TO THE NEXT PAGE.

19. 9^4 is equal to which of the following?

(A) $(3) \times (3) \times (3) \times (3)$
(B) $(9) \times (3) \times (9) \times (3)$
(C) $(9) \times (4)$
(D) $(3) \times (3) \times (3) \times (3) \times (3) \times (3) \times (3) \times (3)$
(E) $(9) \times (9) + (9) \times (9)$

USE THIS SPACE FOR FIGURING.

20. It costs h cents to make 12 handkerchiefs. At the same rate, how many cents will it cost to make 30 handkerchiefs?

(A) $30h$

(B) $\dfrac{5h}{2}$

(C) $\dfrac{2h}{5}$

(D) $\dfrac{2}{5h}$

(E) $5h$

21. A girl collects rocks. If her collection consists of 12 pieces of halite, 16 pieces of sandstone, 8 pieces of mica, and 8 pieces of galaxite, then the average number of pieces of each type of rock in her collection is

(A) 8
(B) 11
(C) 12
(D) 16
(E) 44

22. A recipe calls for 24 ounces of water for every two ounces of sugar. If 12 ounces of sugar are used, how much water should be added?

(A) 6
(B) 12
(C) 24
(D) 36
(E) 144

GO ON TO THE NEXT PAGE.

23. The number of people now employed by a certain company is 240, which is 60% of the number employed five years ago. How many more employees did the company have five years ago than it has now?

    (A) 160
    (B) 360
    (C) 400
    (D) 720
    (E) 960

USE THIS SPACE FOR FIGURING.

4

$$
\begin{array}{r}
1B5 \\
\times\ 15 \\
\hline
2{,}025
\end{array}
$$

24. In the multiplication problem above, B represents which digit?

    (A) 1
    (B) 2
    (C) 3
    (D) 5
    (E) 7

25. If the area of each of the smaller squares that make up rectangle *ABCD* is 4, what is the perimeter of rectangle *ABCD* ?

    (A) 220
    (B) 64
    (C) 55
    (D) 32
    (E) 4

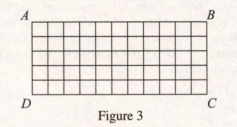

Figure 3

STOP

IF YOU FINISH BEFORE TIME IS CALLED,
YOU MAY CHECK YOUR WORK ON THIS SECTION ONLY.
DO NOT TURN TO ANY OTHER SECTION IN THE TEST.

Chapter 12
Middle Level SSAT
Practice Test:
Answers and
Explanations

ANSWER KEY

SSAT ML Math 1

1. D	4. A	7. C	10. A	13. E	16. A	19. B	22. A	25. C
2. B	5. D	8. D	11. C	14. C	17. A	20. D	23. D	
3. D	6. C	9. C	12. A	15. B	18. D	21. B	24. A	

SSAT ML Reading 2

1. C	6. A	11. B	16. C	21. B	26. D	31. E	36. E
2. C	7. C	12. D	17. A	22. A	27. E	32. C	37. C
3. B	8. B	13. A	18. C	23. B	28. D	33. D	38. B
4. B	9. E	14. B	19. E	24. E	29. A	34. B	39. D
5. D	10. D	15. B	20. B	25. B	30. C	35. C	40. A

SSAT ML Verbal 3

1. A	7. C	13. A	19. E	25. D	31. C	37. A	43. C	49. E	55. A
2. D	8. A	14. D	20. A	26. D	32. B	38. C	44. B	50. A	56. B
3. A	9. E	15. D	21. A	27. E	33. B	39. E	45. C	51. A	57. C
4. D	10. B	16. A	22. C	28. A	34. D	40. B	46. D	52. A	58. C
5. A	11. C	17. E	23. C	29. C	35. D	41. E	47. D	53. C	59. C
6. B	12. D	18. D	24. B	30. B	36. D	42. A	48. E	54. B	60. C

SSAT ML Math 4

1. A	4. E	7. C	10. C	13. C	16. E	19. D	22. E	25. B
2. A	5. A	8. C	11. A	14. E	17. B	20. B	23. A	
3. C	6. A	9. B	12. C	15. C	18. B	21. B	24. C	

EXPLANATIONS

Section 1 Math

1. **D** There are several ways to solve this problem (e.g. using the Bowtie method or finding a common denominator for the fractions). Another option would be to convert the fractions to decimal form. $\frac{2}{3} = 0.6\overline{6}$. Choice (A) equals 1.5, (B) equals 0.5, (C) equals 0.75, (D) equals $0.6\overline{6}$, and (E) equals $0.8\overline{3}$. The only answer that is equal to $\frac{2}{3}$ or $0.6\overline{6}$ is (D). Note: if you found that $\frac{8}{12}$ reduces to $\frac{2}{3}$, you can pick that answer since there will not be two correct answers.

2. **B** Read the question carefully. The question is asking for an *even* number, so eliminate (A) and (D) since both contain odd integers. The question also asks for the number to be *between* 22 and 27; therefore, it must be greater than 22 but less than 27. The only possible answers are 24 and 26. Thus, the correct answer is (B) since (C) and (E) are not greater than 22.

3. **D** The sum of the digits in 281 is 11 since $2 + 8 + 1 = 11$. The product of the digits is 16 since $2 \times 8 \times 1 = 16 \times 1 = 16$. To find out how much less 11 is than 16, subtract: $16 - 11 = 5$. Therefore, the correct answer is (D).

4. **A** Remember to use order of operations (PEMDAS). Start inside the parentheses first: $(109 - 102) \times 3 - 4^2 = (7) \times 3 - 4^2$. Then simplify any exponents: $(7) \times 3 - 4^2 = 7 \times 3 - 16$. Next, multiply to get $21 - 16$, which equals 5. Therefore, the correct answer is (A).

5. **D** If $\frac{3}{4}$ of the seats in the stadium are filled, then to find the number of people who attended the concert, multiply $\frac{3}{4}$ (or 0.75) by the stadium capacity (25,000): $\frac{3}{4}(25,000) = \frac{75,000}{4} = 18,750$. Rounded to the nearest thousand, the number of attendees is 19,000, or (D), which is the correct answer. Note that you can use estimation to solve this problem. $\frac{3}{4}$ of 24 is 18, so the number of attendees should start with or be a little larger than 18. Choice (D) is the closest option.

6. **C** If the area of the square is 81, then use the area formula to find the length of one side of the square: $A = s^2$. If $81 = s^2$, then $\sqrt{81} = s$. Thus, $s = 9$. Since all four sides of a square are equal, each side equals 9. To find the perimeter of a shape, add up of all the sides: $9 + 9 + 9 + 9 = 36$. The correct answer is (C).

7. **C** Use the answers (PITA) to find the middle integer. Start with (C). If the middle integer were 3, then the smallest integer would be 1 and the largest integer would be 5 since the 3 numbers are consecutive. Find the sum of the 3 numbers to see if the result is 9: $1 + 3 + 5 = 9$. These numbers work, so the middle integer is 3, and the correct answer is (C).

8. **D** The first number greater than 2 that is a factor of both 20 and 16 is 4 since $\frac{20}{4} = 5$ and $\frac{16}{4} = 4$.

Check the answer choices to see which one is also divisible by 4, because this would mean that 4 is also a factor of that number. Choices (A), (B), and (C) are not divisible by 4. Choice (D) works: $\frac{24}{4} = 6$. Therefore, the correct answer is (D). Note that (E) 30 is not divisible by 4 either.

9. **C** When in doubt with exponents, expand them out. $(2^3)^2 = (2 \times 2 \times 2)^2 = (2 \times 2 \times 2) \times (2 \times 2 \times 2)$. There is a total of 6 sixes, so the correct answer is (C), or 2^6. Note: using exponent rules works too. Remember MADPSM. Since there is an exponent being raised to another power, multiply: $(2^3)^2 = 2^{3 \times 2} = 26$.

10. **A** Since the answer choices represent possible values of M, plug in (PITA). The problem indicates that $\frac{1}{2}$ is greater than $\frac{M}{16}$. Notice that if you start with (C), $\frac{9}{16}$ will be greater than $\frac{1}{2}$ since $\frac{1}{2} = \frac{8}{16}$. Therefore, (B), (C), (D), and (E) are all too big, and (A) is the correct answer since $\frac{8}{16} > \frac{7}{16}$.

11. **C** In an equilateral triangle, all sides are equal. If the sum of two sides is equal to 4, then each of the two sides is 2 since $\frac{4}{2} = 2$. To find the perimeter of a shape, add up all the sides. If each side is equal to 2, then the perimeter will be $2 + 2 + 2 = 6$. Thus, the correct answer is (C).

12. **A** Use the chart provided to find her total mileage and the miles she drove on Monday. Her total mileage was 350, and she drove 35 miles on Monday. To find what percent 35 is out of 350, set up a proportion: $\frac{35}{350} = \frac{x}{100}$. Cross-multiply to get $350x = 3,500$, and divide to find $x = 10$. Therefore, the correct answer is (A).

13. **E** Use the chart provided to find the miles she drove on Thursday (105 miles). Since the answer choices provide possibilities for the miles she drove on other days, plug in (PITA) to find each sum. In (A), the sum of the mileage is $35 + 50 = 85$. For (B), the result is $35 + 20 = 55$. For (C), the result is $70 + 50 + 35 = 155$. For (D), the result is $35 + 35 + 20 = 90$. Finally, for (E), the result is $35 + 35 + 35 = 105$. Choice (E) is the only option that equals the total miles driven on Thursday and is the correct answer.

14. **C** Use the chart provided to find the miles she drove on Sunday (20) and Wednesday (50). The question now reads 20 is what percent of 50. Translate the English words into their math equivalents: $20 = \frac{x}{100}(50)$. Solve for x. $20 = \frac{50x}{100}$ reduces to $20 = \frac{x}{2}$. Multiply both sides by 2 to get $x = 40$.

20 is 40% of 50, so the correct answer is (C). Note: you can also solve by setting up a proportion: $\frac{20}{50} = \frac{x}{100}$.

15. **B** The value of x is given, so plug 5 in for x: $\frac{1}{x}$ $\frac{1}{5}$. Eliminate (D) and (E) since both are greater than 1 and, therefore, too large. 20% is equivalent to $\frac{20}{100}$, which reduces to $\frac{1}{5}$. Therefore, the correct answer is (B). Note: (A) equals $\frac{1}{10}$ and (C) equals $\frac{2}{5}$.

16. **A** Translate the English words into their math equivalents. Remember that *of* means to multiply. 20% of 25% of 80 is $\frac{20}{100} \times \frac{25}{100} \times 80$. Reduce the fractions to get $\frac{1}{5} \times \frac{2}{4} \times 80$. Multiply the numerators and denominators together: $\frac{1}{5} \times \frac{1}{4} \times \frac{80}{1} = \frac{1 \times 1 \times 80}{5 \times 4 \times 1} = \frac{80}{20} = 4$. The correct answer is (A).

17. **A** To find the average, use an average pie.

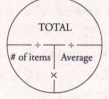

The total will be the sum of all the hours he worked over the 2 weeks: 3 + 5 + 8 + 8 + 40 = 64. The number of items will be 2 since he worked 2 weeks. Divide to find the average: $\frac{64}{2} = 32$. Thus, the correct answer is (A). Note that (C) is only the total number of hours he worked during the first week.

18. **D** To find the volume of a box, use the formula $V = l \times w \times h$. Plug the given dimensions into the formula: $V = 4 \times 8 \times 10 = 32 \times 10 = 320$. If this box is equal in volume to a box with dimensions $16 \times g \times 2$, then $16 \times g \times 2 = 320$. To find g, multiply to get $32 \times g = 320$. Then divide both sides by 32 to get $g = 10$. Therefore, the correct answer is (D). Note: another option is to use the answer choices (PITA). Choice (D) is the only option for g that makes the equation equal to 320.

19. **B** Since there is a variable in the question, plug in a value for b. If $b = 10$, then two tapes cost $20. During the sale, two tapes will cost $15 since $\frac{1}{2}(10) = 5$ and 10 + 5 = 15. Thus, during the sale, he will save $5. To find the overall percent he will save means $5 is what percent of $20. Translate the English words to their math equivalents: $5 = \frac{x}{100} \times 20$. Solve for x. $5 = \frac{20x}{100}$ reduces to $5 = \frac{x}{5}$.

Multiply both sides by 5 to get $x = 25$, so the correct answer is (B). Note: you can also solve by setting up a proportion: $\frac{5}{20} = \frac{x}{100}$.

20. **D** Ben ate 6 dinners at steakhouses and visited 18 restaurants overall since $8 + 4 + 6 = 18$, so convert $\frac{6}{18}$ into a percentage: $\frac{6}{18} = \frac{x}{100}$. $\frac{6}{18}$ reduces to $\frac{1}{3}$. Solve $\frac{1}{3} = \frac{x}{100}$ for x. Cross-multiply to get $3x = 100$. Divide both sides by 3 to get $x = 33.\overline{3}$. Therefore, the correct answer is (D).

21. **B** Use the figure provided to determine the area of the shaded region. One method to solve this problem is to find the total area and subtract out the unshaded area, or Total = shaded + unshaded. To find the area of a rectangle, use the formula $A = l \times w$. The area of the entire shape is $A = 8 \times 6 = 48$. The area of the unshaded region is $A = 6 \times 2 = 12$. Thus, to find the area of the shaded region, plug the areas into the equation: Total = shaded + unshaded $\rightarrow$ 48 = s + 12. Subtract 12 from both sides to get $s = 36$, and the correct answer is (B). Note that (A) is too large since that is the area of the entire shape. Choice (C) would be half the area of the entire shape, which doesn't make sense since the shaded area is greater than half of the entire area. Finally, (D) is the area of the unshaded portion.

22. **A** Since the answer choices represent possible values for ___, plug in (PITA). If ___ equals 9, as in (C), then $(2 + \_\_\_ + 3)(2) = 16 \rightarrow (2 + 9 + 3)(2) = 16$. Simplify the left side of the equation: $(2 + 9 + 3)(2) = (14)(2) = 28$. 28 is not equal to 16, so eliminate (C), (D), and (E) since they are too big. If ___ equals 8, as in (B), then $(2 + \_\_\_ + 3)(2) = 16 \rightarrow (2 + 8 + 3)(2) = 16$. Simplify the left side of the equation: $(2 + 8 + 3)(2) = (13)(2) = 26$. 26 is not equal to 16, so eliminate (B). Therefore, the correct answer is (A). Note that if ___ equals 3, then $(2 + 3 + 3)(2) = (8)(2) = 16$.

23. **D** Use a ratio box. The numbers for the ratio row are provided. Remember to add the 2 numbers to get the total.

	Cows	Pigs	Total
Ratio	16	1	17
Multiplier			
Real Value			

Since the answer choices represent possible values for the total real value (i.e. the total number of cows and pigs on the farm), the total real value needs to be divisible by 17. Eliminate (A) and (B) since those values are too small to be the total real value. Of the remaining answer choices, see which value is divisible by 17. Only (D) is, since $17 \times 4 = 68$. Therefore, the correct answer is (D).

24. **A** Since there are variables in the question and answers, plug in a value for s (the number of films Sibyl has seen). If $s = 10$, then Linda has seen 6 films $(10 - 4 = 6)$. If Linda has seen twice as many films than Joel, then Joel has seen 3 films $\left(\frac{6}{2} = 3 \right)$. Since the question asks for the number of films Joel

has seen, the correct answer will be the one that equals 3. Plug 10 in for s and check each answer choice. Choice (A) equals $\frac{10}{2} - 2 = 5 - 2 = 3$. Choice (B) equals $\frac{10}{2} - 4 = 5 - 4 = 1$. Choice (C) equals $10 - 2 = 8$. Choice (D) equals $10 - 4 = 6$. Choice (E) equals $\frac{8}{10 - 2} = \frac{8}{8} = 1$. Since it is the only one that matches the target value, (A) is the correct answer.

25. **C** Don't be intimidated by weird symbols! Use the definitions provided and plug in the given values for x. For the first part of the equation, @3 means $x = 3$. Plug 3 in for x into the definition. Thus, $@x = 2x \rightarrow @3 = 2(3)$, and $2 \times 3 = 6$. For the second part of the equation, @2 means $x = 2$. Plug 2 in for x. Thus, $@x = 2x \rightarrow @2 = 2(2) \rightarrow 4$. Now the equation looks like $6 - 4 = 2$. The correct answer will be the one that is equal to 2. Eliminate (A) since @4 will not equal 2; it will be greater than @3, which was equal to 6. Also, eliminate (B) since @2 = 4, which is also bigger than 2. In (C), @1 means $x = 1$, so $@x = 2x \rightarrow @1 = 2(1) \rightarrow 2$. This matches the value of the original equation, so the correct answer is (C).

Section 2 Reading

1. **C** On main purpose questions, ask yourself "Why did the author write this passage? What is the main takeaway for this passage?" This passage is focused on the history of Native American tribes: their origins, their formation, etc. This best matches (C). Although the current status of Native Americans is mentioned, it is only briefly touched on in the last sentence of the passage, so (A) cannot be the "main purpose." Choices (B) and (D) are not mentioned in the passage, so they are incorrect. Although the passage mentioned various tribes, it does not provide the history of different tribes but Native Americans in general, eliminating (E). Choice (C) is the correct answer.

2. **C** This is a specific question, so make sure to go back and find the answer in the passage. Geronimo is mentioned in the second paragraph, where it states that he became a famous historical figure after his capture. This best matches (C). There is no mention of disgrace, money, or suicide, all of which eliminates choices (A), (D), and (E). Since the passage clearly states that Geronimo was captured, we cannot assume he had no defeats, which eliminates (B). Choice (C) is the best answer.

3. **B** On tone questions, eliminate answer choices that are too extreme or don't make sense based on the passage. This passage is very informative and history-focused. This best supports (B), objective. Since the author does not express any strong feelings one way or another regarding this topic, (A), (C), and (E) can be eliminated. The author does not appear to be torn between two sides, he or she is just providing factual information, which eliminates (D) as well. Choice (B) is the correct answer.

4. **B** This question is a "main idea" question in disguise. Look at each paragraph and see how they all connect to one another. The first paragraph introduces the origin of Native Americans. The second paragraph discusses the history of Native Americans in America. The third paragraph touches on

where Native Americans live today for the most part. The most logical topic for the next paragraph will be on modern Native Americans, as that is what the author began to discuss at the end of the last paragraph. This best supports (B). Choice (A) is very strong, and does not connect directly back to any previous statement in the passage. Choices (C), (D), and (E) all contain information that is mentioned in the passage, but those topics have already been mentioned and moved on from in the passage. It would not make sense to bring them up again, paragraphs later. The correct answer is (B).

5. **D**   On Except/Not/Least questions cross check each answer choice and write a "T" for true and an "F" for false for each answer choice, based on the passage. The false answer will be the correct choice. This question asks about skills possessed by Native Americans. The first paragraph mentions hunting, farming, and fishing as skills the Native Americans had, making (A), (B), and (C) all true. The second paragraph discusses the Native Americans rebellions, which makes (E) true as well. The only skill that is not mentioned in the passage is gathering, (D). This makes (D) false, and therefore the correct answer.

6. **A**   On main idea questions ask yourself the "So what?" of the passage. This passage is focused on a variety of ecological factors connected to deserts, such as the landscape, temperatures, and animals. This best matches (A). Although the topics in (B), (C), and (D) are all mentioned in the passage, these answers are too specific to be the main idea of the passage. Since average temperatures are not mentioned, (E) is also incorrect. The correct answer is (A).

7. **C**   This is a very open-ended question, so check each answer choice with the information provided in the passage and eliminate as you go. Keep in mind that the examples you have of animal adaptation to the desert include ways to deal with lack of water and extreme temperature. The only answer choice that touches on either of these topics is (C), which relates to an adaptation to manage temperature. Although all of the other choices mention helpful adaptations, they don't relate to the specific challenges related to the desert. Choice (C) is the correct answer.

8. **B**   For style questions pay attention to the way the author writes. This is a very generally informative passage focused on desert environments. This best supports (B). There is nothing personal included in this story, which eliminates (D) and (E). Choice (A) is much too general, while (C) is much too specific. Choice (B) is the correct answer.

9. **E**   This is a specific question, so make sure to go back and find the answer in the passage. Camels are mentioned in the second paragraph as an example of adaptation to desert environments as they can go days without water. This best supports (E), as it is the only choice that mentions water. Although camels may exhibit the other adaptations listed in the other choices, there is no mention of these in the passage about camels. Choice (E) is the correct answer.

10. **D**   This is a very open-ended question, so check each answer choice with the information provided in the passage and eliminate as you go. The passage does not state that deserts can be filled with lush vegetation, it states the opposite in fact. Eliminate (A). There is no indication that deserts have

large bodies of water or receive large amounts of rainfall, also eliminating (B) and (C). There is no mention of urban areas or cities in the passage, which eliminates (E). The passage does state in the first paragraph that deserts can be located in cold climates, which supports (D), making it the correct answer choice.

11. **B** When answering a Vocabulary in Context question, focus on what the word means in the sentence. In line 5 "punishing" is used to mean "brutal" or "hard," since it says such an environment makes basic aspects of life difficult. This best matches (B), harsh. Choices (A) and (D) are too extreme and literal. Choice (C) is not strong enough in this context, and (E) is the opposite of what the author is saying. Choice (B) is the correct answer.

12. **D** On main idea questions ask yourself the "So what?" of the passage. This passage is focused on the modern Olympics and how the games have changed since they began in ancient times. This best supports (D). Since the focus is on both modern and ancient Olympic games, (B) can be eliminated. Since the author neither justifies the existence of the game nor mentions the process for choosing a host city, (A) and (E) can be eliminated. Although the passage does mention both the Winter and Summer Olympics, the difference between those is not the main focus of the passage which eliminates (C). The best answer is (D).

13. **A** This is a specific question, so make sure to go back and find the answer in the passage. The author mentions the traditional dances and culture of the host city as support for the earlier assertion that the opening ceremony is a spectacular event. This best supports (A). The author never mentions specific host cities or their differences, which eliminates (B). This information is focused on the modern games, not the ancient games, which eliminates (C) and (D). Although (E) may seem correct, remember that this information is about the opening ceremony and not the games themselves. The correct answer is (A).

14. **B** On tone questions, eliminate answer choices that are too extreme or don't make sense based on the passage. This passage is very informative and positive about the Olympic games, which best matches (B). Since the author is positive about the games, eliminate (A), (D), and (E). Although the author is positive, (C) is a little too extreme to fit the tone of this passage. Choice (B) is the correct answer.

15. **B** This is a specific question, so make sure to go back and find the answer in the passage. The torch lighting is discussed in the last paragraph, in which it clearly states that the flame represents the spirit of the competition from the original games. This best matches (B). There is no mention of destruction, heat, or eternity mentioned in the last paragraph, eliminating (A), (D), and (E). Choice (C) is simply not supported by the passage; the games are not described as rousing in relation to the torch lighting. The correct answer is (B).

16. **C** This is a very open-ended question, so check each answer choice with the information provided in the passage and eliminate as you go. The passage does not say whether or not women wanted to compete in the ancient games, it simply states that only men could compete. Eliminate (A). The

passage only tells us how often the modern Olympic games are held, so the passage does not support (B). The passage does say that the ancient games were held in Greece only, which does support (C). The passage does not mention ice skating, eliminating (D). And there is no mention of an opening ceremony during the ancient games, eliminating (E). Choice (C) is the correct answer.

17.   **A**   This is a specific question, so make sure to go back and find the answer in the passage. The author mentions dinosaurs in the first paragraph to stress how old turtles are, as the dinosaurs lived a very long time ago. This best matches (A). The mention of dinosaurs does not provide any information related to turtles other than time and longevity, which eliminates all the other answer choices. The correct answer is (A).

18.   **C**   This is a specific question, so make sure to go back and find the answer in the passage. At the beginning of the second paragraph, the author compares turtles to other reptiles by saying that other reptiles generally live in the tropics, while turtles live in a variety of environments. This best supports (C). The author does not say if other reptiles lived in the time of the dinosaurs, which eliminates (A). Turtles can live in a variety of climates, which eliminates (D). Choice (B) is the opposite of what the passage is saying, and (E) is never mentioned in the passage. Choice (C) is the best answer.

19.   **E**   On tone questions, eliminate answer choices that are too extreme or don't make sense based on the passage. The author does not fully agree with reports that turtles live longer than a century, as he refers to such claims as "questionable" in the third paragraph. This best supports (E), skeptical. Choices (B) and (C) are much too extreme, and (A) and (D) do not match "questionable." The correct answer is (E).

20.   **B**   This is a specific question, so make sure to go back and find the answer in the passage. At the end of the passage the author states that one way to tell the age of a turtle may be to count the growth rings that form on the shell. This best matches (B). Measurement, deterioration, and weight are never mentioned in regards to turtle age, eliminating (A), (C), (D), and (E). Choice (B) is the correct answer.

21.   **B**   This is a very open-ended question, so check each answer choice with the information provided in the passage and eliminate as you go. Although the author is very interested in turtles, he does not say other reptiles aren't as interesting so eliminate (A). The author does not address how long other animals live, eliminating (C). The author does not discuss whether or not turtles are "bad" or "dangerous," eliminating (D) and (E). The only answer choice supported by the passage is (B), as the author does include a great deal of information in the passage about turtles.

22.   **A**   This question is a "main idea" question in disguise. Ask yourself the "so what?" of the passage. This passage is about the author's excitement over visiting Norway and his connection to that country. This best supports (A). Although the journey is mentioned, it is not the main focus of the passage. Eliminate (C) and (E). The author does not state that he dislikes his siblings, eliminating (B). The author does not state whether or not life has changed at all, only that he has fond memories of his summer holidays. Eliminate (D). The correct answer is (A).

23. **B** When asked a vocabulary in context question, focus on what the word means in the sentence. In lines 4 and 5 the word "idyllic" is meant to convey the very positive experience the author had during his time in Norway. This means you can eliminate (A), (D), and (E) as they are negative words. There is no reference to religion in the passage, eliminating (C). The only positive word provided that could be the answer is (B), pleasant.

24. **E** This is a specific question, so make sure to go back and find the answer in the passage. Before using this line the author stresses that he is fully Norwegian and has a great deal of family there. The author then stresses that going back to Norway was like going home. This best matches (E), as people are generally happy and comfortable the most when they are home. Since the author is very positive about Norway, eliminate (A). The author does not say why his half-siblings go to Norway nor how long he stayed in Norway, eliminating (C) and (D). Although the author does say he goes to Norway every summer, this is not connected to his discussion of why he felt he was going home when he went to Norway. Eliminate (B). The correct answer is (E).

25. **B** This is a specific question, so make sure to go back and find the answer in the passage. The author mentions the length of time it took to travel to stress how just getting to Norway was "an event." This best supports (B). Since the author was positive about the journey to Norway, (A) and (C) are not supported by the passage. The author does not mention his half-siblings when discussing the journey, eliminating (D). The author also does not describe Norway when discussing the journey, eliminating (E). The correct answer is (B).

26. **D** This is a specific question, so make sure to go back and find the answer in the passage. After the author uses the word home, he or she states that shells are the homes of shellfish. This best supports (D), the shells are the homes. Choices (C) and (E) are too vague compared to (D), so they should be eliminated. Choices (A) and (B) are not supported by the passage. The correct answer is (D).

27. **E** This is a very open-ended question, so check each answer choice with the information provided in the passage and eliminate as you go. The only question that is answered in the passage is (E); in the second paragraph the passage describes how some shellfish make their shells. None of the other questions listed in the answer choices are addressed in the passage. Choice (E) is the answer.

28. **D** This question is a "main idea" question in disguise. Ask yourself the "so what?" of the passage. This passage is about various information regarding shells. This best supports (D), a general discussion of shells. The passage is not focused on the fish that live in shells, which eliminates (A), (B), and (C). The author does discuss how shells are formed, but that is only one piece of the passage so (E) is too specific. The correct answer is (D).

29. **A** This is a specific question, so make sure to go back and find the answer in the passage. The author makes the comparison between the bivalve's hinge and a door in order to explain to the reader how the bivalve shell is structured and how it works. This best supports (A). There is no mention of fragility, eliminating (B). The author is not discussing fish or how the shell is formed in this part of

the passage, eliminating (D) and (E). There is also no mention of how these shells are found, only what they do, eliminating (C). Choice (A) is the correct answer.

30. C   This question is a "main idea" question in disguise. Ask yourself the "so what?" of the passage. This passage is about various information regarding shells: how they are formed, what purpose they serve, what kinds there are. The best match for this information is (C), since a large part of the passage is focused on how fish grow their own shells. Going to the beach and finding shells is mentioned but not the main focus of the story, eliminating (B) and (E). The passage mentions that shells can be beautiful, but this is also not the main point of the passage. Conch shells are mentioned, but (A) is much too specific to be the main idea of the passage. The correct answer is (C).

31. E   This is a specific question, so make sure to go back and find the answer in the passage. In the last paragraph, the conch is described as being a single unit shell while others can be two units. This best supports (E). There is no other information provided about the conch shell, which eliminates all the other answer choices. Choice (E) is the correct answer.

32. C   This is a specific question, so make sure to go back and find the answer in the passage. The "hat" the author refers to is created by the bat's fingers, which are attached to its wings. This best supports (C). The hat is formed by the bat itself, so you can eliminate (A), (D), and (E). The hat the bat forms is above its head, which eliminates (B). Choice (C) is the correct answer.

33. D   This is a specific question, so make sure to go back and check each choice with the information in the passage. In the first and last lines the bat is compared to a mouse, so choice I is correct. The flying pattern of the bat is described in lines five and six, which supports choice III. A vampire is never mentioned in the story, so choice II is incorrect. The only correct answer is (D).

34. B   This is a specific question, so make sure to go back and find the answer in the passage. In line 5, the author is describing how the bat flies. This best supports (B). The author is discussing the bat which eliminates (A), (C), and (E). The author refers to the bat seeming dead in the previous lines, not this line. Eliminate (D). The correct answer is (B).

35. C   This is a very open-ended question, so check each answer choice with the information provided in the passage and eliminate as you go. The passage is highly descriptive of the bat, and that description is not very positive. The author discusses how we can be afraid of the bat and how it looks. This best supports (C). We are not offered a great deal of factual information about the bat, which eliminates the other answer choices. Choice (C) is the correct answer.

36. E   On primary purpose questions, ask yourself "Why did the author write this passage? What is the main takeaway for this passage?" This passage is focused on sports uniforms and their beneficial aspects. This best supports (E). Although team spirit and safety are both mentioned as positive aspects of sports uniforms, these topics are much too specific to be the primary purpose of the passage. Eliminate (A) and (B). There is no history of uniforms provided, which eliminates (C). There is no controversy mentioned, eliminating (D). Choice (E) is the correct answer.

37. **C** When asked a vocabulary in context question, focus on what the word means in the sentence. In line 12, support most nearly means to cheer for, since that's what people do for their teams. This best supports (C). All the other choices are too literal for the context of this story.

38. **B** On attitude questions, eliminate answer choices that are too extreme or don't make sense based on the passage. The author is very positive about uniforms in this passage, and thinks they serve several purposes. This eliminates (A) and (E). The author does not say what they are most useful for, which eliminates (C). The passage does not discuss whether or not uniforms are fun to wear, which eliminates (D). Only (B) is supported by the passage.

39. **D** This is a specific question, so make sure to go back and find the answer in the passage. The uniforms for track and field are discussed in the second paragraph. According to this part of the passage, these uniforms are designed to help runners go faster. This best supports (D), since it is the only choice focused on their physical performance for the sport they are engaged in. Although the author does discuss safety and uniforms, it is in regards to other sports, which eliminates (C). Only (D) is supported by the passage.

40. **A** This is a specific question, so make sure to go back and find the answer in the passage. The author discusses spectators in the final paragraph; spectators are able to tell who is on the team they are rooting for and can show their support by wearing similar colors. This best supports (A). Although the other choices may be true, they are not supported by the text of the passage and so cannot be correct. Choice (A) is the correct answer.

Section 3 Verbal

1. **A** Obedient means to follow directions. A word or phrase you might be familiar with is obey, as in to obey a command. This meaning best matches (A), amenable.

2. **D** To contaminate means to dirty. You might be familiar with the phrase "the water is contaminated," meaning the water is dirty or could cause you harm if you were to drink it. This meaning best matches (D), taint.

3. **A** Woeful means sorrowful; it comes from the word woe, which means misfortune or grief. This meaning best matches (A), wretched.

4. **D** Practical most nearly means useful or rational. A word or phrase you might be familiar with is a practical solution, which would be a useful or effective solution. This meaning best matches (D), having great usefulness.

5. **A** To scrutinize means to examine or inspect. A word or phrase you might be familiar with is to scrutinize every last detail. This meaning best matches (A), examine carefully.

6. **B** To confide means to tell or reveal. You might be familiar with the phrase "to confide a secret." This meaning best matches (B), entrust.

7. **C** To initiate means to begin or to start. This meaning best matches (C), commence.

8. **A** Fortunate most nearly means lucky; it comes from the word fortune, which has a positive connotation. This meaning best matches (A), lucky.

9. **E** Crumble means to break down or break apart. A word or phrase you might be familiar with is to crumble under pressure. This meaning best matches (E), deteriorate.

10. **B** Desperate means distressed. You might be familiar with the phrase "desperate times call for desperate measures." This meaning best matches (B), frantic.

11. **C** To fret means to worry or fuss over. You might be familiar with the phrase "no need to fret," which means no need to worry. This meaning best matches (C), worry.

12. **D** To disguise means to camouflage or masquerade. You might be familiar with the phrase "to disguise the truth," which means to hide or conceal the truth. This meaning best matches (D), false front.

13. **A** To assist means to help or aid. You might be familiar with the phrase "to provide assistance," which means to provide help. This meaning best matches (A), support.

14. **D** To reprimand means to warn or scold. You might be familiar with the phrase "to give a sharp reprimand." This meaning best matches (D), chide.

15. **D** To evade means to avoid or elude. You might be familiar with the phrase "to evade the question," which means to avoid or elude the question. This meaning best matches (D), sidestep.

16. **A** Fatigue means tiredness or exhaustion. You might be familiar with the phrase "to be overcome by fatigue," which means to be overcome by exhaustion. This meaning best matches (A), grow weary.

17. **E** An antidote is a cure or remedy. You might be familiar with the phrase "the antidote for a snake bite." The best match for this meaning is (E), antitoxin.

18. **D** To propose means to suggest or offer. You may be familiar with the word "proposal;" there are marriage proposals and business proposals, for instance. This meaning best matches (D), suggest. Don't be fooled by (B), a marriage proposal is not an actual marriage, only the suggestion or offer of marriage.

19. **E** Incredible means too good to be true or wonderful. This meaning best matches (E), extraordinary.

20. **A** To be vigilant means to be watchful or attentive. You might be familiar with the phrase "vigilante justice," which would be justice that is served when one sees a crime committed. A person is a vigilante because they are vigilant, or watchful. This meaning best matches (A), observant.

21. **A** Tattered means worn, torn, or ragged. This meaning best matches (A), unkempt.

22. **C** To precede means to come directly before. It includes the prefix "pre," which means to come before (just like the word prefix!) This meaning best matches (C), come before.

23. **C** To lament means to cry over or mourn. This meaning best matches (C), moan.

24. **B** To engage means to involve or take part in. You might be familiar with the phrase "to be engaged in extracurricular activities," which would mean to be involved in extracurricular activities. This meaning best matches (B), employ.

25. **D** Competent means capable or well informed. This meaning best matches (D), able.

26. **D** Sincere means honest or truthful. You might be familiar with the phrase "to sign a letter sincerely," which means to sign off in a genuine way. This meaning best matches (D), genuine.

27. **E** Rickety means unstable. This meaning best matches (E), feeble.

28. **A** Conspicuous means obvious or clear. This meaning best matches (A), plain as day.

29. **C** Versatile means easily changeable or flexible. This meaning best matches (C), adaptable.

30. **B** Corroboration means agreement. You might be familiar with the phrase "to corroborate evidence or testimony in a trial." That would mean to agree with or confirm evidence or testimony. This meaning best matches (B), confirmation.

31. **C** Remember to make a sentence with the words in the analogy, and try to find the answer choice that matches the same sentence. For this question, one example sentence could be "a fish lives in water." The only choice that works with this sentence is (C), a lion lives on land.

32. **B** Don't worry if the format changes from two words to one word in the answer choices! Remember to make a sentence with the first two words in the analogy, and try to find the answer choice that matches the same sentence. For this question, one example sentence could be "sick is the opposite of healthy." The only choice that works with this sentence is (B), jailed is the opposite of free.

33. **B** Remember to make a sentence with the words in the analogy, and try to find the answer choice that matches the same sentence. For this question, one example sentence could be "a dancer uses his/her feet to perform." The only choice that works with this sentence is (B), a juggler uses his/her hands to perform. Although (E) may seem to work as well, it is not as strong an answer as (B) as a musician could perform music from memory, therefore not using his or her eyes. A juggler must use his/her hands to juggle, making (B) the stronger answer.

34. **D** Remember to make a sentence with the words in the analogy, and try to find the answer choice that matches the same sentence. For this question, one example sentence could be "a bystander watches an event." The only choice that works with this sentence is (D), a spectator watches a game.

35. **D** Remember to make a sentence with the words in the analogy, and try to find the answer choice that matches the same sentence. For this question, one example sentence could be "a baker makes bread." The only choice that works with this sentence is (D), a sculptor makes a statue.

36. **D** Remember to make a sentence with the words in the analogy, and try to find the answer choice that matches the same sentence. For this question, one example sentence could be "igneous is a type of rock." The only choice that works with this sentence is (D), watercolor is a type of painting.

37. **A** Don't worry if the format changes from two words to one word in the answer choices! Remember to make a sentence with the first two words in the analogy, and try to find the answer choice that matches the same sentence. For this question, one example sentence could be "delicious is a good description of taste." The only choice that works with this sentence is (A), melodious is a good description of sound.

38. **C** Remember to make a sentence with the words in the analogy, and try to find the answer choice that matches the same sentence. For this question, one example sentence could be "a clog is a type of shoe." The only choice that works with this sentence is (C), a beret is a type of hat.

39. **E** Remember to make a sentence with the words in the analogy, and try to find the answer choice that matches the same sentence. For this question, one example sentence could be "a cube is a three-dimensional square." The only choice that works with this sentence is (E), a sphere is a three-dimensional circle.

40. **B** Remember to make a sentence with the words in the analogy, and try to find the answer choice that matches the same sentence. For this question, one example sentence could be "jam is made from fruit." The only choice that works with this sentence is (B), butter is made from milk.

41. **E** Remember to make a sentence with the words in the analogy, and try to find the answer choice that matches the same sentence. If you run into trouble it may be easier to try to make a sentence with the first words in each set and the second words in each set. For example, in this question the first word in the question is "mile." Which answer choice contains a first word that has a relationship to mile? Only (E), length. A mile is a measurement of length. The second word in the question is "quart." Check that word with the second word in (E) to see if they have the same relationship. Is a quart a measurement of volume? Yes! Choice (E) is the correct answer.

42. **A** Don't worry if the format changes from two words to one word in the answer choices! Remember to make a sentence with the first two words in the analogy, and try to find the answer choice that matches the same sentence. For this question, one example sentence could be "a biologist is a type of scientist." The only choice that works with this sentence is (A), a surgeon is a type of doctor.

43. **C** Remember to make a sentence with the words in the analogy, and try to find the answer choice that matches the same sentence. For this question, one example sentence could be "a potter works with clay." The only choice that works with this sentence is (C), a sculptor works with marble.

44. **B** Remember to make a sentence with the words in the analogy, and try to find the answer choice that matches the same sentence. For this question, one example sentence could be "a clip is a small part of a movie." The only choice that works with this sentence is (B), an excerpt is a small part of a novel.

45. **C** Don't worry if the format changes from two words to one word in the answer choices! Remember to make a sentence with the first two words in the analogy, and try to find the answer choice that matches the same sentence. For this question, one example sentence could be "ruthless is the opposite of mercy." The only choice that works with this sentence is (C), naïve is the opposite of worldliness.

46. **D** Remember to make a sentence with the words in the analogy, and try to find the answer choice that matches the same sentence. For this question, one example sentence could be "a glacier is made out of ice." The only choice that works with this sentence is (D), an ocean is made out of water.

47. **D** Remember to make a sentence with the words in the analogy, and try to find the answer choice that matches the same sentence. For this question, one example sentence could be "a window is made out of glass." The only choice that works with this sentence is (D), clothing is made out of fabric.

48. **E** Don't worry if the format changes from two words to one word in the answer choices! Remember to make a sentence with the first two words in the analogy, and try to find the answer choice that matches the same sentence. For this question, one example sentence could be "a buttress supports something." The only choice that works with this sentence is (E), scissors cut something.

49. **E** Don't worry if the format changes from two words to one word in the answer choices! Remember to make a sentence with the first two words in the analogy, and try to find the answer choice that matches the same sentence. For this question one example sentence could be "a sneer is an expression of disdain." The only choice that works with this sentence is (E), cringe is an expression of fear.

50. **A** Remember to make a sentence with the words in the analogy, and try to find the answer choice that matches the same sentence. For this question, one example sentence could be "a library houses books." The only choice that works with this sentence is (A), a bank houses money.

51. **A** Remember to make a sentence with the words in the analogy, and try to find the answer choice that matches the same sentence. For this question, one example sentence could be "a famine is the absence of food." The only choice that works with this sentence is (A), a drought is the absence of water.

52. **A** Remember to make a sentence with the words in the analogy, and try to find the answer choice that matches the same sentence. For this question, one example sentence could be "a teacher instructs a student." The only choice that works with this sentence is (A), a coach instructs a player.

53. **C** Remember to make a sentence with the words in the analogy, and try to find the answer choice that matches the same sentence. For this question, one example sentence could be "to muffle is to stop noise." The only choice that works with this sentence is (C), to build a dam is to stop a flood.

54. **B** Remember to make a sentence with the words in the analogy, and try to find the answer choice that matches the same sentence. For this question, one example sentence could be "exhaustion is the lack of rest." The only choice that works with this sentence is (B), thirst is the lack of water.

55. **A** Remember to make a sentence with the words in the analogy, and try to find the answer choice that matches the same sentence. For this question, one example sentence could be "a playwright creates a script." The only choice that works with this sentence is (A), a choreographer creates a dance.

56. **B** Remember to make a sentence with the words in the analogy, and try to find the answer choice that matches the same sentence. For this question, one example sentence could be "gluttony is the love of food." The only choice that works with this sentence is (B), avarice is the love of money.

57. **C** Remember to make a sentence with the words in the analogy, and try to find the answer choice that matches the same sentence. For this question, one example sentence could be "facile is the lack of effort." The only choice that works with this sentence is (C), inconsiderate is the lack of thought.

58. **C** Don't worry if the format changes from two words to one word in the answer choices! Remember to make a sentence with the first two words in the analogy, and try to find the answer choice that matches the same sentence. For this question, one example sentence could be "single-handed is the opposite of assistance." The only choice that works with this sentence is (C), anonymous is the opposite of recognition.

59. **C** Don't worry if the format changes from two words to one word in the answer choices! Remember to make a sentence with the first two words in the analogy, and try to find the answer choice that matches the same sentence. For this question, one example sentence could be "a horse stays in a stable." The only choice that works with this sentence is (C), a dog stays in a kennel.

60. **C** Remember to make a sentence with the words in the analogy, and try to find the answer choice that matches the same sentence. If you run into trouble, it may be easier to try to make a sentence with the first words in each set and the second words in each set. For example, in this question the first word in the question is "tree." Which answer choice contains a first word that has a relationship to tree? Only (C), forest. A tree is located in a forest. The second word in the question is "knee." Check that word with the second word in (C) to see if they have the same relationship. Is a knee located on a body? Yes! Choice (C) is the correct answer.

Section 4 Math

1. **A** There are several ways to solve this problem (e.g. using the Bowtie method or finding a common denominator for the fractions). Another option would be to convert the fractions to decimal form. Choice (A) equals 0.75, (B) equals 0.625, (C) equals 0.5, (D) is about 0.429, and (E) is $0.5\bar{5}$. The answer that has the greatest value is (A), so it is the correct answer.

2. **A** First find the factors of 12, which are all the numbers that multiply together to equal 12: 1 and 12, 2 and 6, and 3 and 4. To find the sum, add up all the factors: $1 + 2 + 3 + 4 + 6 + 12 = 28$. Therefore, the correct answer is (A).

3. **C** Remember order of operations (PEMDAS). Multiply first; then add: $16 + 2 \times 3 + 2 = 16 + 6 + 2 = 24$. The correct answer is (C).

4. **E** Use the figure provided to find the relationship among the variables. In the figure, angles D and E are on the same line, so their angles total to 180°. The same is true for angles F and G; since they are on the same line, their angles will total to 180°. Therefore, $D + E + F + G = 180° + 180° = 360°$. The correct answer is (E).

5. **A** Draw a factor tree of 48.

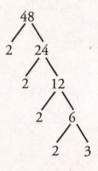

The prime factorization of 48 is $2 \times 2 \times 2 \times 2 \times 3$ or $2^4 \times 3$. Thus, the 2 different prime factors of 48 are 2 and 3, so the correct answer is (A). Note that (B), (C), (D), and (E) contain numbers that are not prime (4, 6, 8, and 12).

6. **A** The product of 4 and 6 is 24 since $4 \times 6 = 24$. To find the difference between two numbers, subtract. Therefore, $24 - 12 = 12$, so the correct answer is (A).

7. **C** There are 180° in a straight line, and there are a total of 180° in a triangle. Thus, the question is asking for the sum of 180° and 180°, which is 360° ($180° + 180° = 360°$). The correct answer is (C).

8. **C** Use the graph provided to find the requested values. The key indicates that the light gray shaded portion represents scarves, so he owns 2 scarves. The black shaded portion represents coats, so he owns 6 coats. Therefore, the total number of scarves and coats that he owns is 8 since $2 + 6 = 8$. The correct answer is (C).

9. **B** Use the graph provided to find the total number of hats and garments he owns. The medium gray shaded portion represents hats, so he owns 3 hats. The total number of garments is the sum of all the portions in the graph: $4 + 2 + 3 + 6 = 15$. Therefore, the question is asking 3 is what percentage of 15. Set up a proportion to solve: $\frac{3}{15} = \frac{x}{100}$. $\frac{3}{15}$ reduces to $\frac{1}{5}$. Cross multiply $\frac{1}{5} = \frac{x}{100}$ to get $5x = 100$. Divide both sides by 5 to get $x = 20$. The correct answer is (B).

10. **C** Use the graph provided to find the needed values. The total number of garments is the sum of all the portions in the graph: $4 + 2 + 3 + 6 = 15$. $\frac{1}{3}$ of 15 is 5 since $\frac{1}{3}(15) = \frac{15}{3} = 5$. The correct answer will be the one that equals 5. Since the answer choices provide possibilities for the types of garments, plug in (PITA) to find each sum. In (A), the sum is $3 + 6 = 9$. For (B), the sum is $4 + 2 = 6$. For (C), the sum is $3 + 2 = 5$. For (D), the sum is $4 + 6 = 10$. Finally, for (E), the sum is $4 + 2 + 3 = 9$. Choice (C) is the only option that equals 5 and is the correct answer.

11. **A** If five slices of pizza cost $10, then one slice of pizza costs $2 since $\frac{10}{5} = 2$. If he has $32, then he could buy 16 slices of pizza since $\frac{32}{2} = 16$. The correct answer is (A).

12. **C** To find the average, use an average pie.

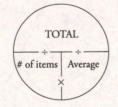

For this problem, draw 3 average pies. The first average pie will represent Mrs. Bennett's class. The average (85) and the number of items (10 students) are given. Multiply to find the total number of points scored on the test: $85 \times 10 = 850$. The second average pie will represent Mrs. Grover's class. The average (70) and the number of items (15 students) are given. Multiply to find the total number of points scored on the test: $70 \times 15 = 1,050$. Finally, the third average pie will represent the average score for both classes. To find the total, add the total points scored from both classes to get $850 + 1,050 = 1,900$. To find the number of items, pay attention to the question. It asks for the average score for all the students in the 2 classes. There are 10 students in one class and 15 students in the other, so there is a total of 25 students. The number of items is 25. Divide the total and the number of items to find the average: $\frac{1,900}{25} = 76$. Therefore, the correct answer is (C).

13.   C   Since there are variables in the question and answers, plug in a value for e (the number of pencils Mary bought). If $e = 10$, then Jane bought 50 pencils since $5 \times 10 = 50$. If Mary bought 10 pencils, then Peggy bought 8 pencils since $10 - 2 = 8$. The question asks for the total number of pencils bought, so add the 3 values to get the target value: $10 + 50 + 8 = 68$. The correct answer will be the one that equals 68. Plug 10 in for e and check each answer choice. Choice (A) equals $5(10) - 2 = 50 - 2 = 48$. Eliminate (B) since $7 \neq 68$. Choice (C) equals $7(10) - 2 = 70 - 2 = 68$. Choice (D) equals $8(10) = 80$. Choice (E) equals $8(10) - 2 = 80 - 2 = 78$. Since it is the only one that matches the target value, (C) is the correct answer.

14.   E   Eliminate (A), (B), (C), and (D) since $\dfrac{4}{1,000} = 0.004$. Therefore, the correct answer is (E). Note that $\dfrac{3}{10} = 0.3$, and 3 should be the units digit (the first spot to the left of the decimal).

15.   C   Don't be intimidated by weird symbols! Use the definitions provided and plug in the given values for f. $\boxed{0}$ means $f = 0$. Plug 0 in for f into the definition. Thus, $\boxed{f} = -2f \rightarrow \boxed{0} = -2(0)$, and $-2 \times 0 = 0$. Therefore, the correct answer is (C).

16.   E   Don't be intimidated by weird symbols! Use the definitions provided and plug in the given values for f. For the first part of the equation, $\boxed{2}$ means $f = 2$. Plug 2 in for f into the definition. Thus, $\boxed{f} = -2f \rightarrow \boxed{2} = -2(2)$, and $-2 \times 2 = -4$. For the second part of the equation, $\boxed{3}$ means $f = 3$. Plug 3 in for f. Thus, $\boxed{f} = -2f \rightarrow \boxed{3} -2(3) \rightarrow -6$. Now the equation looks like $-4 \times -6 = 24$. The correct answer will be the one that is equal to 24. Eliminate (B) and (C), since the values of $\boxed{2}$ and $\boxed{3}$ have already been determined and neither equals 24. Try one of the remaining answer choices. In (E), $\boxed{-12}$ means $f = -12$, so $\boxed{f} = -2f \rightarrow \boxed{-12} = -2(-12) \rightarrow 24$. This matches the value of the original equation, so the correct answer is (E).

17.   B   Convert $2\dfrac{1}{4}$ to a decimal: 2.25. Remember that % means out of 100, so $2.25\% = \dfrac{2.25}{100}$. Divide or move the decimal to the left 2 places to get 0.0225. Thus, the correct answer is (B).

18.   B   To find the area of a triangle, use the formula $A = \dfrac{1}{2}(b)(h)$. Based on the figure provided, the base is $2h$ and the height is h. Since there are variables in the figure and the answer choices, plug in a value for h. If $h = 2$, then the height is 2 and the base is 4. Plug these values into the area formula: $\dfrac{1}{2}(b)(h) = \dfrac{1}{2}(4)(2) = 2 \times 2 = 4$. The correct answer will be the one that equals 4. Plug 2 in for h and check each answer choice. Choice (A) equals $2(2)^2 = 2 \times 4 = 8$. Choice (B) equals $(2)^2 = 4$. Choice (C) equals 2. Choices (D) and (E) do not equal 4. Since it is the only one that matches the target value, (B) is the correct answer.

19.   **D**   When in doubt with exponents, expand them out. $9^4 = 9 \times 9 \times 9 \times 9$. Be careful! Choice (E) is a trap answer (notice the addition symbol). Since each 9 can be written as 3×3, $9 \times 9 \times 9 \times 9 = 3 \times 3 \times 3 \times 3 \times 3 \times 3 \times 3 \times 3$. The correct answer is (D). Note: using exponent rules works too. 9 can be written as 3^2, so $9^4 = (3^2)^4$. Remember MADPSM. Since there is an exponent being raised to another power, multiply: $(3^2)^4 = 3^{2 \times 4} = 3^8$. There are eight 3s being multiplied in (D), so it is the correct answer.

20.   **B**   Since there are variables in the question and answers, plug in a value for h (the cost to make 12 handkerchiefs). If $h = 12$, then it costs 1 cent to make 1 handkerchief. Therefore, the cost to make 30 handkerchiefs will be 30 cents since $30 \times 1 = 30$. The correct answer will be the one that equals 30. Plug 12 in for h and check each answer choice. Choice (A) equals $30(12) = 360$. Choice (B) equals $\frac{5(12)}{2} = \frac{60}{2} = 30$. Choice (C) equals $\frac{2(12)}{5} = \frac{24}{5}$, which is less than 5. Choice (D) equals $\frac{2}{5(12)} = \frac{2}{60}$, which is less than 1. Choice (E) equals $5(12) = 60$. Since it is the only one that matches the target value, (B) is the correct answer.

21.   **B**   To find the average, use an average pie.

The total will be the sum of all the rocks in her collection: $12 + 16 + 8 + 8 = 44$. The number of items will be 4 since there are 4 types of rock in her collection: halite, sandstone, mica, and galaxite. Divide to find the average: $\frac{44}{4} = 11$. Thus, the correct answer is (B). Note that (E) is the total number of rocks in her collection, and (A), (C), and (D) represent the number of rocks in each type.

22.   **E**   Set up a proportion to find the amount of water needed. If $\frac{water}{sugar} = \frac{24}{2} = \frac{x}{12}$, then cross-multiply to get $2x = 288$. Divide both sides by 2 to get $x = 144$. Therefore, the correct answer is (E).

23. **A** 240 is 60% of the number employed 5 years ago. Therefore, 5 years ago, there were 400 employees

because $\dfrac{240}{x} = \dfrac{60}{100} \rightarrow 24{,}000 = 60x \rightarrow 400 = x$. Eliminate (C) because it is a trap answer. The

question is not asking for how many people were employed 5 years ago. The question is asking for

how many more employees the company had 5 years ago than the number they have now. Thus,

$400 - 240 = 160$, so (A) is the correct answer.

24. **C** The answer choices represent possible values of b, so plug in (PITA). Start in the middle with (C).
If B = 3, then the equation is $135 \times 15 = 2{,}025$, which is true. Therefore, the correct answer is (C).
Note: if you started with a different answer choice, determine whether B needs to be bigger or
smaller. Keep checking until you find the value of B that works.

25. **B** If the area of each smaller square is 4, then use the area formula to find the length of one side of the
square: $A = s^2$. If $4 = s^2$, then $\sqrt{4} = s$. Thus, $s = 2$. Since all 4 sides of a square are equal, each side
equals 2. There are 5 small squares (each with a side measure of 2) that make up the width of the
rectangle, so the width of the rectangle is 10 since $2 \times 5 = 10$. There are 11 small squares (each with
a side measure of 2) that make up the length of the rectangle, so the length of the rectangle is 22
since $2 \times 11 = 22$. To find the perimeter of a shape, add up of all the sides. Since opposite sides of a
rectangle are equal, the sides are 10, 22, 10, 22. Therefore, the perimeter is 64 since $10 + 22 + 10 +$
$22 = 64$. The correct answer is (B). Note that (A) is the area of the rectangle since $A = l \times w$.

Part IV
The ISEE

Chapter 13
Everything You Always Wanted to Know About the ISEE

WHAT IS THE ISEE?

The Independent School Entrance Examination (ISEE) is a standardized test made up of a series of multiple-choice questions and a writing sample. The entire test lasts a little less than three hours, during which you will work on five different sections.

Plan Ahead
Early registration will not only give you one less thing to worry about as the test approaches, but it will also get you your first-choice test center.

Lower Level

Verbal Reasoning	34 questions	20 minutes
Quantitative Reasoning	38 questions	35 minutes
Reading Comprehension	25 questions	25 minutes
Mathematics Achievement	30 questions	30 minutes
Essay (ungraded)	1 essay topic	30 minutes

Middle Level

Verbal Reasoning	40 questions	20 minutes
Quantitative Reasoning	37 questions	35 minutes
Reading Comprehension	36 questions	35 minutes
Mathematics Achievement	47 questions	40 minutes
Essay (ungraded)	1 essay topic	30 minutes

Prepare Wisely
Print or order "What to Expect on the ISEE" from the ERB at www.erblearn.org.

Upper Level

Verbal Reasoning	40 questions	20 minutes
Quantitative Reasoning	37 questions	35 minutes
Reading Comprehension	36 questions	35 minutes
Mathematics Achievement	47 questions	40 minutes
Essay (ungraded)	1 essay topic	30 minutes

What's on the ISEE?

The Verbal section of the ISEE tests your knowledge of vocabulary using two different question types: synonyms and sentence completions. There are no analogies on the ISEE. The Reading Comprehension section tests your ability to read and understand short passages. These reading passages include both fiction (including poetry and folklore) and nonfiction. The Math sections test your knowledge of general mathematical concepts through two different question types: problem-solving questions and quantitative comparison questions. The quantitative comparison questions ask you to compare two columns of data. There are no quantitative comparison questions on the Lower Level ISEE.

Upper Versus Middle Versus Lower Levels

There are, in effect, three different versions of the ISEE. The Lower Level test is taken by students who are, at the time of testing, in the fourth and fifth grades. Students who are in the sixth and seventh grades take the Middle Level test. Students who are in the eighth, ninth, tenth, and eleventh grades take the Upper Level test.

There are few major differences between the Lower, Middle, and Upper Level tests. There are some differences in content, however; for instance, vocabulary on the Middle Level test is less challenging than it is on the Upper Level test. The Middle and Upper Level tests cover the same general math concepts (arithmetic, algebra, geometry, charts, and graphs), but naturally, the Middle Level test will ask slightly easier questions than the Upper Level test. There are no quantitative comparison questions on the Lower Level test. The Lower Level test is 20 minutes shorter than the others.

Because the Lower Level ISEE tests both fourth and fifth graders, the Middle Level tests both sixth and seventh graders, and the Upper Level tests eighth, ninth, tenth, and eleventh graders, there are questions on the tests that students testing at the lower end of each of those groups will have difficulty answering. Younger students' scaled scores and percentiles will not be harmed by this fact. Both sets of scores take into consideration a student's age. However, younger students may feel intimidated by this. If you are at the lower end of your test's age group, there will be questions you are not supposed to be able to answer and that's perfectly all right.

Likewise, the material in this book follows the content of the two tests without breaking it down further into age groups or grades. Content that will appear only on the Upper Level test has been labeled as "Upper Level only." Students taking the Lower and Middle Level tests do not need to work on the Upper Level content. Nevertheless, younger students may not have yet seen some of the material included in the Lower and Middle Level review. Parents are advised to help younger students with their work in this book and seek teachers' advice or instruction if necessary.

Chapter 14
ISEE Math

INTRODUCTION

This section will provide you with a review of all the math that you need to do well on the ISEE. When you get started, you may feel that the material is too easy. Don't worry. This test measures your basic math skills, so although you may feel a little frustrated reviewing things you have already learned, this type of basic review is undoubtedly the best way to improve your score.

Lose Your Calculator!

You will not be allowed to use a calculator on the ISEE. If you have developed a habit of reaching for your calculator whenever you need to add or multiply a couple of numbers, follow our advice: Put your calculator away now, and don't take it out again until the test is behind you. Do your homework assignments without it, and complete the practice sections of this book without it. Trust us, you'll be glad you did.

Write It Down

Do not try to do math in your head. You are allowed to write in your test booklet. You should write in your test booklet. Even when you are just adding a few numbers together, write them down and do the work on paper. Writing things down will not only help eliminate careless errors but it will also give you something to refer back to if you need to check over your work.

One Pass, Two Pass

Within any math section, you will find three types of questions:

- Those you can answer easily in a short period of time
- Those that, given enough time, you can do
- Some questions that you have absolutely no idea how to tackle

When you work on a math section, start out with the first question. If it is one of the first type and you think you can do it without too much trouble, go ahead. If not, mark it and save it for later. Move on to the second question and decide whether or not to do that one.

Once you've made it all the way through the section, working slowly and carefully to do all the questions that come easily to you, then go back and try some of those that you think you can do but will take you a little longer. You should pace yourself so that time will run out while you're working on the second pass through the section. Make sure you save the last minute to bubble in an answer for any question you didn't get to. Working this way, you'll know that you answered all the questions that were easy for you. Using a two-pass system is good, smart test-taking.

Guesstimating

Sometimes accuracy is important. Sometimes it isn't.

Which of the following fractions is less than $\frac{1}{4}$?

(A) $\frac{4}{18}$

(B) $\frac{4}{12}$

(C) $\frac{7}{7}$

(D) $\frac{12}{5}$

Without doing a bit of calculation, think about this question. It asks you to find a fraction smaller than $\frac{1}{4}$. Even if you're not sure which one is actually smaller, you can certainly eliminate some wrong answers.

Start simple: $\frac{1}{4}$ is less than 1, right? Are there any fractions in the answer choices that are greater than 1? Get rid of (D).

Look at answer choice (C). $\frac{7}{7}$ equals 1. Can it be less than $\frac{1}{4}$? Eliminate (C). Already, without doing any math, you have a 50 percent chance of guessing the right answer.

Here's another good example.

A group of three men buys a one-dollar raffle ticket that wins $400. If the one dollar that they paid for the ticket is subtracted and the remainder of the prize money is divided equally among the men, how much will each man receive?

(A) $62.50
(B) $75.00
(C) $100.00
(D) $133.00

Some Things Are Easier Than They Seem
Guesstimating, or finding approximate answers, can help you eliminate wrong answers and save lots of time.

This isn't a terribly difficult question. To solve it mathematically, you would take $400, subtract $1, and then divide the remainder by three. But by using a little logic, you don't have to do any of that.

The raffle ticket won $400. If there were four men, each one would have won about $100 (actually slightly less because the problem tells you to subtract the $1 price of the ticket, but you get the idea). So far so good? However, there weren't four men; there were only three. This means fewer men among whom to divide the winnings, so each one should get more than $100, right?

Look at the answer choices. Eliminate (A), (B), and (C). What's left? The right answer!

Guesstimating Geometry

Don't Forget to Guesstimate!

Guesstimating works best on geometry questions. Make sure you use your common sense, combined with POE, to save time and energy.

Now that you've seen a couple examples that used guesstimating in arithmetic and word problems, you will see how we can also guesstimate geometry problems.

Let's try the problem below. Remember that unless a particular question tells you that a figure is not drawn to scale, you can safely assume that the figure is drawn to scale.

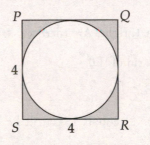

A circle is inscribed in square *PQRS*. What is the area of the shaded region?

(A) $16 - 6\pi$
(B) $16 - 4\pi$
(C) $16 - 3\pi$
(D) 16π

Wow, a circle inscribed in a square—that sounds tough!

Try These Values When Guesstimating:
$\pi \approx 3^{+}$
$\sqrt{2} = 1.4$
$\sqrt{3} = 1.7$

It isn't. Look at the picture. What fraction of the square looks like it is shaded? Half? Three-quarters? Less than half? In fact, about one-quarter of the area of the square is shaded. You've nearly guesstimated the answer!

Now, let's do a tiny bit of math. The length of one side of the square is 4, so the area of the square is 4 × 4 or 16.

So the area of the square is 16 and we said that the shaded region was about one-fourth of the square. One-fourth of 16 is 4, right? So we're looking for an answer choice that equals about 4. Let's look at the choices.

(A) $16 - 6\pi$

(B) $16 - 4\pi$

(C) $16 - 3\pi$

(D) 16π

This could get a little complicated since the answers include π. However, since you're guesstimating, you should just remember that π is just a little more than 3.

Let's look back at those answers.

(A) $16 - 6\pi$ is roughly equal to $16 - (6 \times 3) = -2$

(B) $16 - 4\pi$ is roughly equal to $16 - (4 \times 3) = 4$

(C) $16 - 3\pi$ is roughly equal to $16 - (3 \times 3) = 7$

(D) 16π is roughly equal to $(16 \times 3) = 48$

Now, let's think about what these answers mean.

Therefore, since we guesstimated that the shaded region's area is roughly 4, answer choice (B) must be correct...and it is! Pat yourself on the back because you chose the right answer without doing a lot of unnecessary work. Unless the problem tells you that the figure is not drawn to scale, remember how useful guesstimating on geometry problems can be!

Working with Answer Choices

In Chapter 2, Fundamental Math Skills for the SSAT & ISEE, we reviewed the concepts that the ISEE will be testing on the Lower, Middle, and Upper Level tests. However, the questions in the practice drills were slightly different from those that you will see on your exam. The ones on the exam are going to give you four answers from which to choose, not five.

There are many benefits to working with multiple-choice questions. For one, if you really mess up calculating the question, chances are your answer choice will not be among those given. Now you have a chance to go back and try that problem again more carefully. Another benefit, which this chapter will explore in more depth, is that you may be able to use the information in the answer choices to help you solve the problems.

We are now going to introduce you to the type of multiple-choice questions you will see on the ISEE. Each one of the questions on the pages that follow will test some skill that we covered in the Fundamental Math Skills chapter. If you don't see how to solve the question, take a look back at Chapter 2 for help.

Keep the learning going! Don't forget to tackle the online practice drills!

Math Vocabulary

Notice that the answer choices are often in numerical order.

1. Which of the following is the greatest even integer less than 25 ?

   (A) 26
   (B) 24.5
   (C) 22
   (D) 21

The first and most important thing you need to do on this and every problem is to read and understand the question. What important vocabulary words did you see in the question? There is "even" and "integer." You should always underline the important words in the questions. This way, you will make sure to pay attention to them and avoid careless errors.

Now that we understand that the question is looking for an even integer, we can eliminate any answers that are not even or an integer. Cross out (B) and (D). We can also eliminate (A) because 26 is greater than 25 and we want a number less than 25. So (C) is the right answer.

Try it again.

$$\text{Set A} = \{\text{All multiples of 7}\}$$

$$\text{Set B} = \{\text{All odd numbers}\}$$

2. Which of the following is NOT a member of both set A and set B above?

   (A)   7
   (B) 21
   (C) 49
   (D) 59

Remember the Rules of Zero
Zero is even. It's neither + nor –, and anything multiplied by 0 = 0.

Did you underline the words multiples of 7 and odd? Because all the answer choices are odd, you can't eliminate any that would not be in Set B, but only (D) is not a multiple of 7. So (D) is the right answer.

The Rules of Zero

3. x, y, and z stand for three distinct numbers, where $xy = 0$ and $yz = 15$. Which of the following must be true?

   (A) $y = 0$
   (B) $x = 0$
   (C) $z = 0$
   (D) $xyz = 15$

Because x times y is equal to zero, and x, y, and z are different numbers, we know that either x or y is equal to zero. If y was equal to zero, then y times z should also be equal to zero. Because it is not, we know that it must be x that equals zero. Answer choice (B) is correct.

The Multiplication Table

4. Which of the following is equal to $6 \times 5 \times 2$?

   (A) $60 \div 3$
   (B) 14×7
   (C) $2 \times 2 \times 15$
   (D) 12×10

$6 \times 5 \times 2 = 60$ and so does $2 \times 2 \times 15$. Answer choice (C) is correct.

Working with Negative Numbers

5. $7 - 9$ is the same as

   (A) $7 - (-9)$
   (B) $9 - 7$
   (C) $7 + (-9)$
   (D) $-7 - 9$

Remember that subtracting a number is the same as adding its opposite. Answer choice (C) is correct.

Order of Operations

6. $9 + 6 \times 2 \div 3 =$

   (A) 7
   (B) 9
   (C) 10
   (D) 13

Remember your PEMDAS rules? The multiplication comes first. The correct answer is (D).

The Case of the Mysteriously Missing Sign
If there is no operation sign between a number and a variable (letter), the operation is multiplication.

Don't Do More Work Than You Have To
When looking at answer choices, start with what's easy; only work through the hard ones when you have eliminated all of the others.

Factors and Multiples

Remember!
1 is NOT a prime number.

7. What is the sum of the prime factors of 42 ?

    (A) 18
    (B) 13
    (C) 12
    (D) 10

How do we find the prime factors? The best way is to draw a factor tree. Then we see that the prime factors of 42 are 2, 3, and 7. Add them up and we get 12, answer choice (C).

Fractions

8. Which of the following is less than $\frac{4}{6}$?

    (A) $\frac{3}{5}$

    (B) $\frac{2}{3}$

    (C) $\frac{5}{7}$

    (D) $\frac{7}{8}$

When comparing fractions, you have two choices. You can find a common denominator and then compare the fractions (such as when you add or subtract them). You can also change the fractions to decimals. If you have completed and memorized the fraction-to-decimal charts in the Fundamentals chapter (pages 55 and 59), you probably found the right answer without too much difficulty. It's answer choice (A).

Percents

9. Thom's CD collection contains 15 jazz CDs, 45 rap albums, 30 funk CDs, and 60 pop albums. What percent of Thom's CD collection is funk?

    (A) 10%
    (B) 20%
    (C) 25%
    (D) 30%

First, we need to find the fractional part that represents Thom's funk CDs. He has 30 out of a total of 150. We can reduce $\frac{30}{150}$ to $\frac{1}{5}$; $\frac{1}{5}$ as a percent is 20%, answer choice (B).

Exponents

10. $2^6 =$

    (A) 2^3

    (B) 4^2

    (C) 3^2

    (D) 8^2

Expand 2^6 out and we can multiply to find that it equals 64. Answer choice (D) is correct.

Square Roots

11. The square root of 75 falls between what two integers?

    (A) 5 and 6

    (B) 6 and 7

    (C) 7 and 8

    (D) 8 and 9

If you have trouble with this one, use the answer choices and work backward. As we discussed in the Fundamentals chapter, a square root is just the opposite of squaring a number. So let's square the answer choices. Then we find that 75 falls between 8^2 (64) and 9^2 (81). Answer choice (D) is correct.

Basic Algebraic Equations

12. $11x = 121$. What does $x = $?

    (A)   2

    (B)   8

    (C) 10

    (D) 11

Remember, if you get stuck, use the answer choices and work backward. Each one provides you with a possible value for x. Start with a middle answer choice and replace x with it. $11 \times 10 = 110$. That's too small. Now we know not only that (C) is the incorrect answer, but also that (A) and (B) are incorrect because they are smaller than (C). The correct answer choice is (D).

Solve for *X*—Upper Level Only

13. $3y + 17 = 25 - y$. What does $y = $?

    (A) 1
    (B) 2
    (C) 3
    (D) 4

Just as on the previous question, if you get stuck, use the answer choices. The correct answer is (B).

Percent Algebra—Upper Level Only

Percent means *out of 100,* and the word *of* in a word problem tells you to multiply.

14. 25% of 30% of what is equal to 18 ?

    (A) 1
    (B) 36
    (C) 120
    (D) 240

If you don't remember the math conversion table, look it up in Fundamentals (Chapter 2). You can also use the answer choices and work backward. Start with answer choice (C), and find out what 25% of 30% of 120 is (9). The correct answer is (D).

Geometry

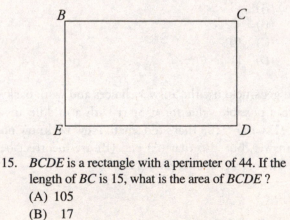

15. *BCDE* is a rectangle with a perimeter of 44. If the length of *BC* is 15, what is the area of *BCDE* ?
    (A) 105
    (B) 17
    (C) 15
    (D) 14

From the perimeter, we can find that the sides of the rectangle are 7 and 15. So the area is 105, (A).

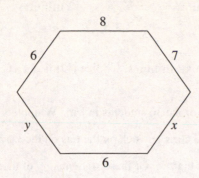

16. If the perimeter of this polygon is 37, what is the value of $x + y$?

(A) 5
(B) 9
(C) 10
(D) 16

$x + y$ is equal to the perimeter of the polygon minus the lengths of the sides we know. Choice (C) is correct.

Word Problems

17. Emily is walking to school at a rate of 3 blocks every 14 minutes. When Jeff walks at the same rate as Emily, and takes the most direct route to school, he arrives in 42 minutes. How many blocks away from school does Jeff live?

(A) 3
(B) 5
(C) 6
(D) 9

This is a proportion question because we have two sets of data we are comparing. Set up your fraction.

$$\frac{3 \text{ blocks}}{14 \text{ minutes}} = \frac{\text{Number of blocks Jeff walks}}{42 \text{ minutes}}$$

Because we know that we must do the same thing to the top and the bottom of the first fraction to get the second fraction, and because $14 \times 3 = 42$, we must multiply 3×3 to get 9.

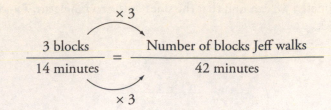

So Jeff walks 9 blocks in 42 minutes. Choice (D) is correct.

18. Half of the 30 students in Mrs. Whipple's first-grade class got sick on the bus on the way back from the zoo. Of these students, $\frac{2}{3}$ of them were sick because they ate too much cotton candy. The rest were sick because they sat next to the students who ate too much cotton candy. How many students were sick because they sat next to the wrong student?

(A)   5
(B)   10
(C)   15
(D)   20

This is a really gooey fraction problem. Because we've seen the word of, we know we have to multiply. First, we need to multiply $\frac{1}{2}$ by 30, the number of students in the class. This gives us 15, the number of students who got sick. Now we have another of, so we must multiply the fraction of students who ate too much cotton candy, $\frac{2}{3}$, by the number of students who got sick, 15. This gives us 10. So then the remainder—those who were unlucky in the seating plan—is 15 – 10, or 5, (A).

19. A piece of rope is 18 inches long. It is cut into 2 unequal pieces. The longer piece is twice as long as the shorter piece. How long is the shorter piece?

(A)   2
(B)   6
(C)   9
(D)   12

Again, if you are stuck for a place to start, go to the answer choices. Because we are looking for the length of the shorter rope, we can eliminate any answer choice that gives us a piece equal to or longer than half the rope. That gets rid of (C) and (D). Now, if we take one of the pieces, we can subtract it from the total length of the rope to get the length of the longer piece. In answer choice (B), if 6 is the length of the shorter piece, we can subtract it from 18 and now we know the length of the longer piece is 12. And 12 is twice the length of 6, so we have the right answer.

How Did You Do?

That was a good sample of the kinds of questions you'll see on the ISEE. There are a few things to check other than your answers. Remember that taking the test involves much more than just getting answers right. It's also about guessing wisely, using your time well, and figuring out where you're likely to make mistakes. Once you've checked to see what you've gotten right and wrong, you should then consider the following to improve your score.

Time and Pacing

How long did it take you to do the 15 questions? 15 minutes? It's okay if you went a minute or two over. However, if you finished very quickly (in fewer than 10 minutes) or slowly (more than 20 minutes), your pacing is off. Take a look at any problems that may have affected your speed. Were there any questions that seriously slowed you down? Did you answer some quickly but not correctly? In general, don't just look to see what you got right, but rather how you got it right.

Question Recognition and Selection

Did you use your time wisely? Did you do the questions in an order that worked well for you? Did you get stuck on one problem and spend too much time on it? Which kinds of questions were hardest for you? Remember that on the ISEE you must answer every question, but you don't have to work on every problem. Every question on the ISEE, whether easy or hard, is worth one point, and there is no penalty for wrong answers. You should concentrate most on getting all easy and medium questions right, and worry about doing harder problems later. Keep in mind that questions generally go from easiest to hardest throughout the section. Getting the easy and medium questions right takes time, but you know you can do it, so give yourself that time! If you don't have time for a question or can't guess wisely, pick a "letter of the day" (the same letter for every problem you can't do), fill it in, and move on. Because there is no penalty for wrong answers, guessing can only help your score.

Practice on your own with online practice drills.

POE and Guessing

Did you actively look for wrong answers to eliminate, rather than looking for the right answer? (You should.) Did you physically cross off wrong answers to keep track of your POE? Was there a pattern to when guessing worked (more often when you could eliminate one wrong answer and less often when you picked simpler-looking over harder-looking numbers)?

Write It Down

Did you work out the online practice questions? Did you move too quickly or skip steps on problems you found easier? Did you always double-check what the question was asking? Students frequently miss questions that they know how to do! Why? It's simple—they work out problems in their heads or don't read carefully. Work out every ISEE math problem on a piece of paper. Consider it a double-check because your handwritten notes confirm what you've worked out in your head.

Ratios

A ratio is like a recipe. It tells you how much of each ingredient goes into a mixture.

For example:

To make punch, mix two parts grape juice with three parts orange juice.

This ratio tells you that for every two units of grape juice, you will need to add three units of orange juice. It doesn't matter what the units are; if you were working with ounces, you would mix two ounces of grape juice with three ounces of orange juice to get five ounces of punch. If you were working with gallons, you would mix two gallons of grape juice with three gallons of orange juice. How much punch would you have? Five gallons.

To work through a ratio question, first you need to organize the information you are given. Do this using the Ratio Box.

In a club with 35 members, the ratio of boys to girls is 3:2. To complete your Ratio Box, fill in the ratio at the top and the "real value" at the bottom.

	BOYS	GIRLS	TOTAL
Ratio	3	2	5
Multiplier			
Real Value			35

Then look for a "magic number" that you can multiply by the ratio to get to the real value. In this case, the magic number is 7. That's all there is to it!

	BOYS	GIRLS	TOTAL
Ratio	3	+ 2	= 5
Multiplier	×7	×7	×7
Real Value	21	14	35

Averages

There are three parts to every average problem: total, number, and average. Most ISEE problems will give you two of the three pieces and ask you to find the third. To help organize the information you are given, use the Average Pie.

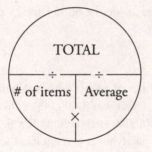

The Average Pie organizes all of your information visually. It is easy to see all of the relationships between pieces of the pie.

- TOTAL = (# of items) × (Average)

- # of items = $\dfrac{Total}{Average}$

- Average = $\dfrac{Total}{\text{# of items}}$

For example, if your friend went bowling and bowled three games, scoring 71, 90, and 100, here's how you would compute her average score using the Average Pie.

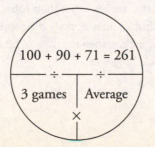

To find the average, you would simply write a fraction that represents $\dfrac{Total}{\text{\# of items}}$, in this case $\dfrac{261}{3}$.

The math becomes simple. $261 \div 3 = 87$. Your friend bowled an average of 87.

Get used to working with the Average Pie by using it to solve the following problems.

Percent Change—Upper Level Only

There is one special kind of percent question that shows up on the ISEE: percent change. This type of question asks you to find by what percent something has increased or decreased. Instead of taking the part and dividing it by the whole, you will take the difference between the two numbers and divide it by the original number. Then, to turn the fraction to a percent, divide the numerator by the denominator and multiply by 100.

For example:

> The number of people who watched *The Voice* last year was 3,600,000. This year, only 3,000,000 are watching the show. By approximately what percent has the audience decreased?

$\dfrac{\text{The difference}}{\text{The original}} = \dfrac{600,000}{3,600,000}$ (The difference is 3,600,000 – 3,000,000.)

The fraction reduces to $\dfrac{1}{6}$, and $\dfrac{1}{6}$ as a percent is 16%.

Plugging In

The ISEE will often ask you questions about real-life situations where the numbers have been replaced with variables. One of the easiest ways to tackle these questions is with a powerful technique called Plugging In.

> Mark is two inches taller than John, who is four inches shorter than Bernal. If b represents Bernal's height in inches, then in terms of b, an expression for Mark's height is
>
> (A) $b + 6$
> (B) $b + 4$
> (C) $b + 2$
> (D) $b - 2$

The problem with this question is that we're not used to thinking of people's heights in terms of variables. Have you ever met someone who was e inches tall?

Whenever you see variables used in the question and in the answer choices, just plug in a number to replace the variable.

1. Choose a number for e.
2. Using that number, figure out Mark's and John's heights.
3. Put a box around Mark's height, because that's what the question asked you for.
4. Plug your number for e into the answer choices and choose the one that gives you the number you found for Mark's height.

Here's How It Works

Mark is two inches taller than John, who is four inches shorter than Evan. If e represents Evan's height in inches, then ~~in terms of e,~~ an expression for Mark's height is

(A) $e + 6$
(B) $e + 4$
(C) $e + 2$
(D) $e - 2$

> *Cross this out! Because you are Plugging In, you don't need to pay any attention to "in terms of" any variable.*

For Evan's height, let's pick 60 inches. This means that $e = 60$. Remember, there is no right or wrong number to pick. 50 would work just as well.

But given that Evan is 60 inches tall, now we can figure out that, because John is four inches shorter than Evan, John's height must be $(60 - 4)$, or 56 inches.

The other piece of information we learn from the problem is that Mark is two inches taller than John. If John's height is 56 inches, that means Mark must be 58 inches tall.

So here's what we've got.

Evan   60 inches = e
John   56 inches
Mark $\boxed{58}$ inches

Now, the question asks for Mark's height, which is 58 inches. The last step is to go through the answer choices substituting 60 for e, and choose the one that equals 58.

(A) $e + 6$ $60 + 6 = 66$ ELIMINATE
(B) $e + 4$ $60 + 4 = 64$ ELIMINATE
(C) $e + 2$ $60 + 2 = 62$ ELIMINATE
(D) $e - 2$ $60 - 2 = 58$ PICK THIS ONE!

After reading this explanation, you may be tempted to say that Plugging In takes too long. Don't be fooled. The method itself is often faster and more accurate than regular algebra. Try it out. Practice. As you become more comfortable with Plugging In, you'll get even quicker and better results. You still need to know how to do algebra, but if you do only algebra, you may have difficulty improving your ISEE score. Plugging In gives you a way to break through whenever you are stuck. You'll find that having more than one way to solve ISEE math problems puts you at a real advantage.

Plugging In The Answers (PITA)

Plugging In The Answers is similar to Plugging In. When *variables* are in the answer choices, plug in. When *numbers* are in the answer choices, plug in the answers.

Plugging In The Answers works because on a multiple-choice test, the right answer is always one of the answer choices. On this type of question, you can't plug in any number you want because only one number will work. Instead, you can plug in numbers from the answer choices, one of which must be correct. Here's an example.

> Nicole baked a batch of cookies. She gave half to her friend Lisa and six to her mother. If she now has eight cookies left, how many did Nicole bake originally?
>
> (A)   8
> (B)   12
> (C)   20
> (D)   28

See what we mean? It would be hard to just start making up numbers of cookies and hope that eventually you guessed correctly. However, the number of cookies that Nicole baked originally must be either 8, 12, 20, or 28 (the four answer choices). So pick one—start with either (B) or (C)—and then work backward to determine whether you have the right choice.

Let's start with (C): Nicole baked 20 cookies. Now work through the events listed in the question. She had 20 cookies and she gave half to Lisa. That leaves Nicole with 10 cookies. Then, she gave 6 to her mom. Now she's got 4 left.

Keep going. The problem says that Nicole now has 8 cookies left. But if she started with 20—answer choice (C)—she would only have 4 left. So is (C) right? No.

No problem. Choose another answer choice and try again. Be smart about which answer choice you pick. When we used the number in (C), Nicole ended up with fewer cookies than we wanted her to have, didn't she? So the right answer must be a number larger than 20, the number we took from (C).

The good news is that the answer choices in most Plugging In The Answers questions go in order, so it is easy to pick the next larger or smaller number, depending on which direction you've decided to go. We need a number larger than 20. So let's go to answer choice (D)—28.

Nicole started out with 28 cookies. The first thing she did was give half, or 14, to Lisa. That left Nicole with 14 cookies. Then she gave 6 cookies to her mother. 14 − 6 = 8. Nicole has 8 cookies left over. Keep going with the question. It says, "If she now has eight cookies left…." She has eight cookies left and, *voilà*—she's supposed to have 8 cookies left.

What does this mean? It means you've got the right answer!

GEOMETRY

Weird Shapes

Whenever the test presents you with a geometric figure that is not a square, rectangle, circle, or triangle, draw a line or lines to divide that figure into the shapes that you do know. Then you can easily work with shapes you know all about.

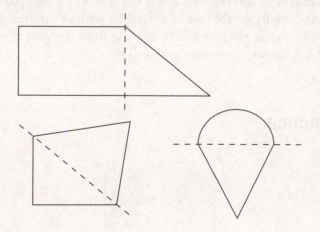

Shaded Regions—Middle and Upper Levels Only

Sometimes geometry questions show you one figure inscribed in another and ask you to find the area of a shaded region inside the larger figure and outside the smaller figure (like the problem at the beginning of this section). To find the areas of these shaded regions, find the area of the outside figure and then subtract the area of the figure inside. The difference is what you need.

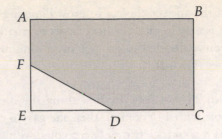

ABCE is a rectangle with a length of 10 and width of 6. Points F and D are the midpoints of AE and EC, respectively. What is the area of the shaded region?

(A) 25.5
(B) 30
(C) 45
(D) 52.5

The first step is to find the area of the rectangle. Multiply the length by the width and find that the area of the rectangle is 60. Now we find the area of the triangle that we are removing from the rectangle. Because the height and base of the triangle are parts of the sides of the rectangle, and points D and F are half the length and width of the rectangle, we know that the height of the triangle is half the rectangle's width, or 3, and the base of the triangle is half the rectangle's length, or 5. Using the formula for the area of a triangle, we find that the area of the triangle is 7.5. Now we subtract the area of the triangle from the area of the rectangle. 60 − 7.5 = 52.5. The correct answer choice is (D).

Extra Practice

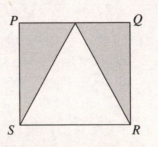

1. PQRS is a square with an area of 144. What is the area of the shaded region?

(A) 50
(B) 72
(C) 100
(D) 120

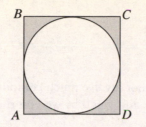

2. In the figure above, the length of side *AB* of square *ABCD* is equal to 4 and the circle has a radius of 2. What is the area of the shaded region?

(A) $4 - \pi$

(B) $16 - 4\pi$

(C) $8 + 4\pi$

(D) 4π

Functions

In a function problem, an arithmetic operation is defined, and then you are asked to perform it on a number. A function is just a set of instructions written in a strange way.

$$\# x = 3x(x + 1)$$

On the left there is usually a variable with a strange symbol next to or around it.

In the middle is an equal sign.

On the right are the instructions. These tell you what to do with the variable.

$\# x = 3x(x + 1)$ *What does # 5 equal?*

$\# 5 = (3 \times 5)(5 + 1)$ Just replace each *x* with a 5!

Here, the function (indicated by the # sign) simply tells you to substitute a 5 wherever there was an *x* in the original set of instructions. Functions look confusing because of the strange symbols, but once you know what to do with them, they are just like manipulating an equation.

Sometimes, more than one question will refer to the same function. The following drill, for example, contains two questions about one function. In cases such as this, the first question tends to be easier than the second.

Charts and Graphs

Charts

Chart questions usually do not involve much computation, but you must be careful. Follow these three steps and you'll be well on the way to mastering any chart question.

Don't Be in Too Big a Hurry

When working with charts and graphs, make sure you take a moment to look at the chart or graph, figure out what it tells you, and then go to the questions.

1.   Read any text that accompanies the chart. It is important to know what the chart is showing and what scale the numbers are on.
2.   Read the question.
3.   Refer to the chart and find the specific information you need.

If there is more than one question about a single chart, the later questions will tend to be more difficult than the earlier ones. Be careful!

Here is a sample chart.

Club Membership by State, 2012 and 2013

State	2012	2013
California	300	500
Florida	225	250
Illinois	200	180
Massachusetts	150	300
Michigan	150	200
New Jersey	200	250
New York	400	600
Texas	50	100

There are many different questions that you can answer based on the information in this chart. For instance:

> What is the difference between the number of members who came from New York in 2012 and the number of members who came from Illinois in 2013?

This question asks you to look up two simple pieces of information and then do a tiny bit of math.

First, the number of members who came from New York in 2012 was 400.

Second, the number of members who came from Illinois in 2013 was 180.

Finally, look back at the question. It asks you to find the difference between these numbers. 400 − 180 = 220. Done.

> The increase in the number of members from New Jersey from 2012 to 2013 was what percent of the total number of members in New Jersey in 2012?

You should definitely know how to do this one! Do you remember how to translate percentage questions? If not, go back to Chapter 2.

In 2012, there were 200 club members from New Jersey. In 2013, there were 250 members from New Jersey. That represents an increase of 50 members. To determine what percent that is of the total amount in 2012, you need to ask yourself, "50 (the increase) is what percent of 200 (the number of members in 2012)?"

Translated, this becomes:

$$50 = \frac{g}{100} \times 200$$

With a little bit of simple manipulation, this equation becomes:

$$50 = 2g$$

and

$$25 = g$$

So from 2012 to 2013, there was a 25% increase in the number of members from New Jersey. Good work!

> Which state had as many club members in 2013 as a combination of Illinois, Massachusetts, and Michigan had in 2012?

First, take a second to look up the number of members who came from Illinois, Massachusetts, and Michigan in 2012 and add them together.

$$200 + 150 + 150 = 500$$

Which state had 500 members in 2013? California. That's all there is to it!

Graphs

Some questions will ask you to interpret a graph. You should be familiar with both pie and bar graphs. These graphs are generally drawn to scale (meaning that the graphs give an accurate visual impression of the information) so you can always guess based on the figure if you need to.

Get in some extra math practice with online drills.

The way to approach a graph question is exactly the same as the way to approach a chart question. Follow the same three steps.

1. Read any text that accompanies the graph. It is important to know what the graph is showing and what scale the numbers are on.
2. Read the question.
3. Refer back to the graph and find the specific information you need.

This is how it works.

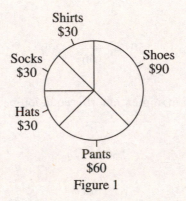

Figure 1

The graph in Figure 1 shows Emily's clothing expenditures for the month of October. On which type of clothing did she spend the most money?

(A) Shoes
(B) Shirts
(C) Socks
(D) Hats

This one is easy. You can look at the pieces of the pie and identify the largest, or you can look at the amounts shown in the graph and choose the largest one. Either way, the answer is (A) because Emily spent more money on shoes than on any other clothing items in October.

Emily spent half of her clothing money on which two items?

(A) Shoes and pants
(B) Shoes and shirts
(C) Hats and socks
(D) Socks and shirts

Again, you can find the answer to this question two different ways. You can look for which two items together make up half the chart, or you can add up the total amount of money Emily spent ($240) and then figure out which two items made up half (or $120) of that amount. Either way is just fine, and, either way, the right answer is (B), shoes and shirts.

QUANTITATIVE COMPARISON—MIDDLE AND UPPER LEVELS ONLY

Quant Comp: Same Book, Different Cover

Quantitative comparison is a type of question—one slightly different from the traditional multiple-choice questions you've seen so far—that tests exactly the same math concepts you have learned so far in this book. There is no new math for you to learn here, just a different approach for this type of question.

You will see a total of 17 quant comp questions in one of your ISEE Math sections.

The Rules of the Game

In answering a quant comp question, your goal is very simple: Determine which column is larger and choose the appropriate answer choice. There are four possible answers.

(A)   means that Column A is always greater
(B)   means that Column B is always greater
(C)   means that Column A is always equal to Column B
(D)   means that A, B, or C are not always true

So that you can use POE in quant comp, where there are no answer choices written out for you, we suggest that you write "A B C D" next to each question. Then when you eliminate an answer, you can cross it off.

Lower Level Test Takers
The ISEE's Lower Level test does not include quantitative comparison questions, so you can skip this section.

They Look Different, but
the Math Is the Same

This section will introduce
you to quantitative
comparison, a different
type of question from the
"regular" multiple-choice
questions you've seen so
far. Don't worry—these
questions test your
knowledge of exactly
the same math skills you
have already learned
in this chapter.

Don't Do Too Much Work

Quant comp is a strange, new question type for most students. Don't let it intimidate you, however. Always keep your goal in mind: to figure out which column is larger. Do you care how much larger one column is? We hope not.

Here's a good example.

Column A	Column B
$2 \times 4 \times 6 \times 8$	$3 \times 5 \times 7 \times 9$

Test takers who don't appreciate the beauty of quant comp look at this one and immediately start multiplying. Look carefully, however, and compare the numbers in both columns.

Which is larger, 2 or 3 ?

Which is larger, 4 or 5 ?

Which is larger, 6 or 7 ?

Which is larger, 8 or 9 ?

In each case, column B contains larger numbers. Now, when you multiply larger numbers together, what happens? You guessed it—even larger numbers!

Which column is larger? Without doing a single bit of multiplication you know that (B) is the right answer. Good work!

(D) Means Different

Answer choice (D) is useful when the relationship between the columns can change. You may have to choose (D) when you have variables in a quant comp problem. For example:

Column A	Column B
$g + 12$	$h - 7$

Which column is larger here depends entirely on what g and h equal, and the problem doesn't give you that information. This is a perfect time to choose (D).

But be careful and don't be too quick to choose (D) when you see a variable.

Column A	Column B
$g + 12$	$g - 7$

With one small change, the answer is no longer (D). Because the variables are the same here, you can determine that no matter what number is represented by g, column A will always be larger. So in this case the answer is (A).

One valuable thing to remember is that when a quant comp question contains no variables and no unknown quantities, the answer cannot be (D).

Column A	Column B
$6 \times 3 \times 4$	$4 \times 6 \times 3$

Even if you somehow forget how to multiply (don't worry, you won't forget), someone somewhere knows how to multiply, so you can get rid of (D).

By the way, look quickly at the last example. First, you eliminate (D) because there are no variables. Do you need to multiply? Nope! The columns contain exactly the same numbers, just written in a different order. What's the answer? You got it: (C)!

Quant Comp Plugging In

Think back to the Algebra section. Plugging In helped you deal with variables, right? The same technique works on quant comp questions. There are some special rules you'll need to follow to make sure you can reap all the benefits that Plugging In has to offer you in the Quantitative Comparison section.

Column A	Column B
x	x^2

Follow these three simple steps, and you won't go wrong.

Step 1: Write "A B C D" next to the problem.
Step 2: Plug In an "easy" number for x. By easy number, we mean a nice simple integer, like 3. When you Plug In 3 for x in the above example, column A is 3 and column B is 9, right? Think about the answer choices and what they mean. Column B is larger, so can the correct answer be (A)? No, eliminate it. Can the correct answer be (C)? No, you can get rid of that one, too!

Weird Numbers
For your second Plug In, try something weird:
Zero
One
Negative
Extreme
Fraction

Step 3: Plug In a "weird" number for x. A weird number is a little harder to define, but it is something that most test takers won't think of—for instance, zero, one, a fraction, or a negative number. In this case, try plugging in 1. Column A is 1 and column B is also 1. So the columns *can* be equal. Now look at the answer choices you have left. Answer choice (B) means that column B is always greater. Is it? No. Cross off (B) and pick (D).

Remember, if you get one result from Plugging In a number and you get a different result by Plugging In another number, you have to pick answer choice (D). But don't think too much about these questions, or you'll end up spending a lifetime looking for the perfect "weird" number. Just remember that you always have to Plug In **twice** on quant comp questions.

Don't worry. There is plenty of Quantitative Comparison practice online!

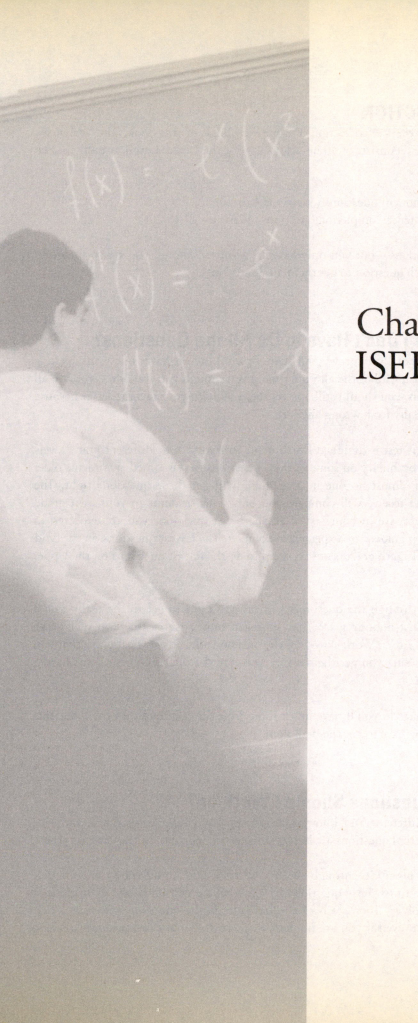

Chapter 15
ISEE Verbal

INTRODUCTION

Take a look at the Verbal section of a practice ISEE in this book. The Verbal section on the ISEE consists of 40 questions (34 for the Lower Level), usually broken into:

- 20 synonym questions (questions 1 to 20)
- 20 sentence completion questions (questions 21 to 40)

That's 40 questions—but you only have 20 minutes! Should you try to spend 30 seconds on each question to get them all done? **No!**

You Mean I Don't Have to Do All the Questions?

Nope. You'll actually improve your score by working on fewer questions, as long as you're still using all of the allotted time. Even though you shouldn't work on all of the questions, you should still answer them all with your favorite letter because there is no penalty for a wrong answer!

"Allotted Time"?
If you can't define *allotted*, make a flash card for it! Look in Chapter 1 for ideas on how to use flash cards to learn new words.

Remember, this test is designed for students in two to four different grade levels. There will be vocabulary on some of these questions that is aimed at students older than you, and almost no one in your grade will get those questions right. The ISEE score you receive will compare you only with students in your own grade. The younger you are in your test level, the fewer questions you are expected to complete. Sixth graders are expected to complete the fewest questions on the Middle Level test. Eighth graders are expected to do the fewest questions on the Upper Level test.

So, why rush through the questions you can get right to get to the really tough ones that almost nobody gets? That approach only ensures that you will make hasty, careless errors. Work slowly on the questions that have vocabulary that you know to make sure you get them right. Then try the ones that have some harder words in them.

If you pace yourself, you'll have much more time for each question than students who think they have to get them all done.

Which Questions Should I Work on?

Everybody's different. You know some words that your friends don't, and vice versa. Some verbal questions are harder for certain people than they are for others.

Guess?
Yes. Fill in an answer even for the questions you don't read. Why? Because there is no penalty for a wrong answer on the ISEE, so you've got nothing to lose (and plenty to gain when you happen to be right!).

So, here's the plan: Go through the first section, and do all the synonyms that are easy for you first. Easy questions are those where you know the definitions of the words involved. Then, go back through and do the questions with words that sound familiar, even if you are not sure of their dictionary definition—these are words you sort of know. Then, move on to sentence completions, leaving yourself more than half the time in the section. Remember to skip a number on the answer sheet when you skip a question—but do fill it in at some point!

Knowing your own vocabulary is the key to deciding if you can answer a question easily.

Know Yourself

Categorize the words you see in ISEE questions into:

- Words you know
- Words you sort of know
- Words you really don't know

Be honest with yourself when it comes to deciding if you know a word or not, so you apply the techniques that are best for the questions on which you are working. Keep your idea of the word's meaning flexible, because the test writers sometimes use the words in ways that you and I do not! (They claim to use dictionary definitions.)

Of course, the easiest way to get a verbal question right is by making sure all the words in it fall into the first category—words you know. The best way to do this is by learning new vocabulary words *every day*. Check out the Vocabulary chapter (Chapter 1) for the best ways to do this.

You can raise your verbal score moderately just by using the techniques we teach in this chapter. But if you want to see a substantial rise in your score, you need to build up your vocabulary, too.

Eliminate Answer Choices

With math questions, there's always one *correct* answer. The other answers are simply wrong. In a verbal question, however, things are not that simple. Words are much more slippery than numbers. So verbal questions have *best* answers, not *correct* answers. The other answers aren't necessarily wrong, but the people who score the ISEE think they're not as good as the *best* one. This means that—even more so than on the Quantitative sections—in the Verbal and Reading sections you should always try to eliminate answer choices.

Get used to looking for *worse* answers. There are many more of them than there are *best* answers, so *worse* answers are easier to find!

When you find them, cross them out in the question booklet to make sure you don't spend any more time looking at them. No matter which other techniques you use to answer a question, first eliminate wrong answers, instead of trying to magically pick out the best answer right away.

Cross Out the Bad Ones
Even when none of the answers looks particularly right, you can usually eliminate at least one.

Shop Around
Try every answer choice in a verbal question to be sure you're picking the *best* answer there.

Don't Rule It Out
Don't eliminate answers
with words you don't
know.

One thing to remember for the Verbal section: You should not eliminate answer choices that contain words you don't know. It doesn't matter that *you* don't know what a word means—it could still be the answer.

What If I Can't Narrow It Down to One Answer?

Should you guess? Yes. Even if you can't eliminate any choices, you should still guess. We mentioned before that you should leave a minute or two at the end of the section to fill in an answer for any questions you did not get to. Why? *Because there's no guessing penalty on the ISEE.* Nothing is subtracted from your score for a wrong answer, and because there are four answer choices, you'll get approximately 25 percent correct of the questions on which you guess randomly.

That means that you should *never* leave a question blank. Pick a letter (A, B, C, or D) to fill in for your random guesses. It doesn't matter which letter you use, but stick with one letter-of-the-day so you don't have to think about it.

Of course, the number of questions you get right will increase if you can eliminate some answer choices before you guess, so we'll teach you techniques to do this.

Where Do I Start?

Bubble Practice
Whenever you do a
practice test, use the
sample answer sheet so
you get used to skipping
around and making sure
you're always on the same
number on the test booklet
and answer sheet.

Do synonyms first in the Verbal section, right where you find them. Get them done in less than ten minutes so you have a little more than half the time in the section for sentence completions. Sentence completions take longer to read and work through, but they have more context to help you get the question right, even if you don't know all the words involved. If you get stuck on a sentence completion, simply fill in the letter-of-the-day and move on. Don't save it for a second pass. Similarly, if you realize you simply don't know the stem word or a synonym, just fill in your guess and keep going.

You'll be doing the questions in the following order:

- Synonyms with words you know
- Synonyms with words you sort of know
- Sentence completions

SYNONYMS

What Is a Synonym?

On the ISEE, a synonym question asks you to choose the answer choice that comes closest in meaning to the stem word (the word in capital letters). Often, the best answer won't mean the exact same thing as the stem word, but it will be closer than any of the other choices.

You need to decide which vocabulary category the synonym stem word falls into for you, so you know which technique to use. First, do all the synonyms for which you know the stem word, and then go back and do the ones with stem words you sort of know.

When You Know the Stem Word

Write Down Your Own Definition

Come up with a simple definition—a word or a phrase. Write it next to the stem word. Then look at the answers, eliminate the ones that are furthest from your definition, and choose the closest one.

Don't Waste Time
Make sure you cross out answers you've eliminated, so you don't look at them again.

It's very simple. Don't let the test writers put words in your mouth. Make sure you're armed with your own definition before you look at their answer choices. They often like to put in a word that is a close second to the best answer; if you've got your own synonym ready, you'll be able to make the distinction.

If you need to, cover the answers with your hand so you can think of your definition before looking. Eventually, you may not have to write down your definitions, but you should start out that way so that you are not influenced by the choices they give you.

As you compare the choices with your definition, cross out the wrong ones with your pencil. Crossing out answer choices is something you should *always* do—it saves you time because you don't go back to choices you've already decided were not the best.

As always, don't eliminate words you don't know. Try this one. Write your definition of WITHER before you look at the answer choices.

    WITHER: _____

      (A)   play
      (B)   spoil
      (C)   greatly improve
      (D)   wilt

The stem word means "shrivel" or "dry up." Which answer is closest? (D). You may have been considering (B), but (D) is closer.

Write Another Definition

Why would you ever need to change your definition? Let's see.

> MANEUVER:
>
> (A) avoidance
> (B) deviation
> (C) find
> (D) contrivance

Parts of Speech?
If you need to, go back and review parts of speech in the Word Parts section of Chapter 1.

Your definition may be something like *move* or *control* if you know the word from hearing it applied to cars. But that definition isn't in the answer choices. The problem is that you're thinking about *maneuver* as a verb. However, *maneuver* can also be a noun. It means "a plan, scheme, or trick." Now go back and eliminate. The answer is (D).

The ISEE sometimes uses secondary definitions, which can be the same part of speech or a different part of speech from the primary definition. Just stay flexible in your definitions, and you'll be fine.

When You Sort of Know the Stem Word

Why should you do synonyms quickly? Why are they harder than sentence completions, even though you should do them faster?

Synonyms can be harder to beat than sentence completions because the ISEE gives you no context with which to figure out words that you sort of know. But that doesn't mean you're done after the easy synonyms. You can get the medium ones, too. You just need to create your own context to figure out words you don't know very well.

Also, keep in mind that your goal is to eliminate the worst answers and make educated guesses. You'll be able to do this for every synonym that you sort of know. Even if you eliminate just one choice, you've increased your chances of guessing correctly. You'll gain points overall.

Make Your Own Context

You can create your own context for the word by figuring out how you've heard it used before. Think of the other words you've heard used with the stem word. Is there a certain phrase that comes to mind? What does that phrase mean?

If you still can't come up with a definition for the stem word, just use the context in which you've heard the word to eliminate answers that wouldn't fit at all in that same context.

How about this stem word?

ABOMINABLE:

Where have you heard *abominable*? The Abominable Snowman, of course. Think about it—you know it's a monster-like creature. Which answer choices can you eliminate?

ABOMINABLE:

(A)	enormous	the enormous snowman? maybe
(B)	terrible	the terrible snowman? sure
(C̶)	rude	the rude snowman? probably not
(D̶)	talkative	the talkative snowman? only Frosty!

You can throw out everything except (A) and (B). Now you can guess, with a much better shot at getting the answer right than guessing from four choices. Or you can think about where else you've heard the stem word. Have you ever heard something called an *abomination*? Was it something terrible or was it something enormous? (B) is the answer.

Try this one. Where have you heard this stem word? Try the answers in that context.

SURROGATE:

(A) requested
(B) paranoid
(C) numerous
(D) substitute

Have you heard the stem word in *surrogate mother*? If you have, you can definitely eliminate (A), (B), and (C). A surrogate mother is a substitute mother.

Try one more.

ENDANGER:

(A) rescue
(B) frighten
(C) confuse
(D) threaten

Everyone's associations are different, but you've probably heard of *endangered species* or *endangered lives*. Use either of those phrases to eliminate answer choices that can't fit into it. Rescued species? Frightened species? Confused species? Threatened species? (D) works best.

Use Word Parts to Piece Together a Definition

Prefixes, roots, and suffixes can help you figure out what a word means. You should use this technique in addition to word association, because not all word parts retain their original meanings.

You may never have seen this stem word before, but if you've been working on your Vocabulary chapter, you know that the root *pac* or *peac* means peace. You can see the same root in *Pacific*, *pacifier*, and the word *peace* itself. So which answer matches this synonym?

PACIFIST:

(A) innocent person
(B) person opposed to war
(C) warmonger
(D) wanderer of lands

It's (B). In the following stem word, we see *cred*, a word part that means "belief" or "faith." You can see this word part in *incredible*, *credit*, and *credibility*. The answer is now simple.

CREDIBLE:

(A) obsolete
(B) believable
(C) fabulous
(D) mundane

(B) again. What are the word parts in the following stem word?

MONOTONOUS:

(A) lively
(B) educational
(C) nutritious
(D) repetitious

Mono means "one." *Tone* has to do with sound. If something keeps striking one sound, how would you describe it? (D) is the answer.

The only way you'll be able to use word parts is if you know them. Get cracking on the Vocabulary chapter!

Words You Really Don't Know

Don't spend time on a synonym with a stem word you've never seen if you don't know any of its word parts. Simply make sure you fill in your letter-of-the-day for that question.

Practice your synonyms with some online drills!

SENTENCE COMPLETIONS

What Is a Sentence Completion?

On an ISEE sentence completion, you need to pick the answer that best fills the blank in the sentence they've given you. Just like with synonym problems, you have to choose the best word from the answer choices, and sometimes it's not a perfect fit. On the Upper Level test, some questions will have two blanks.

Often, however, you'll actually find more than one choice that could fit in the blank. How do you decide which is best to choose?

Just like on the synonym questions, you need to make sure the ISEE test writers don't get to put words in your mouth. That's how they confuse you, especially on the medium and hard questions. You need to have your own answer ready before you look at theirs.

Come Up with Your Own Word

The easiest way to make sure you don't get caught up in the ISEE's tricky answers is to cover them with your hand until you've thought of your own word for the blank. Why waste your time plugging all their answers into the sentence, anyway? Let's look at one.

> Quite ------- conditions continue to exist in many mountain towns in America where houses do not have running water or electricity.

What word would you put in the blank? Something like *basic* or *old-fashioned* or *harsh*? Write down any words that occur to you. Which part of the sentence lets you know which words could fit? "Where houses do not have running water or electricity" gives you the clue.

Just Use the Sentence
Don't try to use outside knowledge to fill in the blank. Use only what the sentence tells you.

When you've come up with one or two words you would put in the blank, write them down. (You may not always have to write them, but during practice you should, so you can compare your answers with the answers in this book.) Then, uncover the answers.

(A)   common
(B)   primitive
(C)   orderly
(D)   lively

Which looks most like your words? (B). Any of the other words could appear in this sentence in real life, right? However, because the only context you have is the sentence itself, you have to use what the sentence gives you to get the *best* answer for the ISEE.

Use the Clue

Try this one.

Museums are good places for students of ------.

What word did you come up with? Art? History? Science? Those words are all different! Don't worry, you will not get a sentence completion like this because there's not enough information to go on—any answer choice could be defended! There will always be a clue to tell you what can go in the blank.

Museums that house paintings and sculptures are good places for students of -------.

What's your word? Something like "art." What told you it was art, and not history or science? Underline the part of the sentence that gave you the clue. The clue is the most important part of the sentence—the part that tells you what to put in the blank.

Try another one. Underline the clue and fill in the blank.

The businessman was ------- because sales were down and costs were up, and his demeanor showed his unhappiness.

Recycle
Often you can use the very same word(s) you see in the clue— or something close!

Don't be afraid to just reuse the clue in the blank—the clue is *unhappiness* and the word *unhappy* would go well in the blank! When it fits, use the clue itself. Now eliminate answers.

(A)   despondent
(B)   persuasive
(C)   indifferent
(D)   unresponsive

Even if you're not sure what *despondent* means, do the other words mean *unhappy*? No. (A) must be the answer.

Cover the answers, underline the clue, and fill in the blank before looking at the choices.

> To join the soccer team, a student absolutely had
> to be able to practice two hours a day; however,
> buying the uniform was -------.
>
> (A) obligatory
> (B) universal
> (C) natural
> (D) optional

Your word was probably something like "not required" or "unnecessary." (Don't worry if you're using a short phrase instead of a word—anything that expresses the meaning of what should go in the blank is fine.) But the clue was "absolutely had to," and your words are the opposite of that. What's going on?

Up until now, all the sentences we've seen have had a clue that was pretty much the same as the word in the blank. But sometimes the word in the blank is actually different from the clue—in fact, an opposite. How can you tell when this is true? Well, which word in the sentence told you? *However*. *However* lets you know that the word in the blank would be the opposite of the clue (the clue was "absolutely had to").

There are many little words that can tell you if the blank is the same as the clue or different.

Use Direction Words

Direction words tell you if the blank continues in the same direction as the clue or if it changes direction.

Which of these responses do you want to hear when you've just asked someone to the prom?

> I really like you, *but* _____.
>
> I really like you, *and* _____.

Why is the first one so awful to hear? *But* lets you know that the sentence is going to suddenly change direction and not be about liking you anymore. Why is the second one so much better? *And* lets you know that the sentence is going to continue in the same direction and continue to be all about liking you. Some other direction words are below. If you can think of any others, add them here.

Different Direction	Same Direction
but	and
however	thus
although	therefore
rather	so
instead	because
despite	in addition
yet	consequently

Now, cover the answers, underline the clue, circle the direction words, and fill in your own word.

Going Thataway
Be careful when you see a direction word—make sure you know which way you need to go. Try plugging in opposites as a test.

When people first began investigating the human brain they were unscientific in their methods, but eventually they began to develop methods that were -------.

(A) objective
(B) inconclusive
(C) lucrative
(D) widespread

Which choice is closest to yours? If you underlined *unscientific* and circled *but*, then you could have written *scientific* in the blank. (A) is closest.

Use "Positive/Negative"

Sometimes you'll have trouble coming up with a word of your own. Don't sweat it; you can still eliminate answers.

Gregor was a gifted violinist who was ------- about practicing, showing a dedication to his art that even surpassed his talent.

If you can't come up with an exact word, decide if it's good or bad. In the sentence above, is Gregor good about practicing or is he bad about practicing? Underline the clue that tells you, and put a little "+" sign if the word is good, and a "−" sign if the word is bad. (You can put an "n" if it's neither.) Gregor is good about practicing, so which of the following answer choices can you eliminate? We've marked whether they're positive or negative, so cross out the ones you know are wrong.

(A)	diligent	+
(B)	ornery	−
(C)	practical	+
(D)	ambivalent	n

(B) and (D) cannot fit because they don't match what we know about the word in the blank (it's positive). So between (A) and (C), which best expresses the same thing as the clue? (A). If you're not sure what *diligent* means, make a flash card for it. (And if you're not sure what to do with the flash card, get cracking on the Vocabulary chapter!)

Two-Blank Sentences—Upper Level Only

Two-blank sentences are usually longer than one-blanks. Does that mean they're harder? Nope. Actually, if you take two-blank sentences slowly, one blank at a time, they can be easier to get right! Check it out.

> Since Europe has been polluting its rivers, the
> ------- of many species of fish has been severely
> -------.

Cover your answers, and look for the clues and direction words. Which blank do you do first? Whichever is easier for you or whichever you have more information for, in the form of clues and direction words. For this example, let's go with the second blank, because we know something bad has been happening to the fish. How do we know? The clues are *polluting its rivers* and *severely*, and the direction word is *Since*, which keeps everything moving in the same direction. We can at least put a "−" sign next to the second blank. Now, when you uncover the answers to check them, only uncover the words for the blank you're working on. Don't even look at the words for the first blank here! You're only going to eliminate answers based on what cannot fit in the second blank.

> (A) XXXX .. augmented
> (B) XXXX .. observed
> (C) XXXX .. approached
> (D) XXXX .. threatened

You can eliminate (B) and (C), because they're not negative enough. Cross them out so you don't look at them again. Do you know what (A) means? If not, you can't eliminate it. Never eliminate words you don't know.

Take It Easy
As long as you do two-blank sentence completions the way we've shown you, they'll be easier because you won't need to know all the vocabulary.

Now look back at the sentence and fill in a word or two for the first blank. What is it that can be negatively affected by pollution? Once you've got a word or two, look at the choices that are left for the first blank.

(A)   acceptance . . augmented
(B)   ~~audacity . . observed~~
(C)   ~~equanimity . . approached~~
(D)   habitat . . threatened

Which sounds better? You may have had a word like *environment* or *survival* filled in. (D) definitely fits better than (A). Notice that if you didn't know what *augmented*, *audacity*, or *equanimity* meant, you could still get this question right. That's because on two-blank sentence completions, as soon as you eliminate an answer choice based on one of its words, the whole thing is gone—you never have to look at it again, and it doesn't matter what the other word in it is. (However, if *augmented*, *audacity*, or *equanimity* comes up in a one-blank sentence, you do need to know it to eliminate it—so make some flash cards for those words.)

Think of all the time you'd waste if you tried plugging the words for each answer choice into the sentence. You'd be reading the sentence four or five times! Plus, you'd find more than one answer choice that sounded okay, and you'd have nothing with which to compare them.

Two-blank sentence completions are your friends on the ISEE. Treat your friends right—do them one blank at a time, coming up with your own words.

Text Complete Sentences—Lower Level Only

For text completions, you need to finish a sentence. This might seem hard, but it's not if you use common sense. The correct answer will follow the correct direction (same/opposite) and make sense in context. Let's try one:

Even though Peter's mom said he wouldn't have dessert if he didn't clean his room, _____.

(A)   he was unable to fall asleep that night
(B)   she decided it was time to go on a diet
(C)   he continued playing with his toys until dinner time
(D)   she prepared a delicious and healthy salad

Which answer makes sense? Choice (C) does. The "even though" tells us that Peter didn't do what he was supposed to do. While choices (B) and (D) relate to food, they have nothing to do with dessert or Peter's room. Choice (A) is just weird.

Time to put it all together and show off what you learned with the online practice questions!

Guess Aggressively When You've Worked on a Sentence

When you've narrowed a sentence completion down to two or three answers, it's probably because you don't know the vocabulary in some of those answers. Just take a guess and move on—you're not going to be able to divine the meanings of the words (and trust us, the proctor will not let you pull out a dictionary). You've increased your chances of getting the question right by eliminating one or two choices, and there's no guessing penalty, so fill in a bubble and move on.

When to Take a Guess

What if you come across a sentence that is so confusing that you can't even decide if the blank(s) should be positive or negative, much less come up with a word of your own? Don't waste your time on it. Just make sure you fill in your letter-of-the-day and move on.

If you only have a minute left, and you're not yet done, make sure you fill in your letter-of-the-day on all remaining questions.

Which Letter Should I Use?
No matter what you may have heard, it doesn't matter which letter you use to fill in answers for questions you don't work on. ERB tries to use letters in equal amounts.

Chapter 16
ISEE Reading

AN OPEN BOOK TEST

Keep in mind when you approach the Reading Section of the ISEE that *it is an open book test*. Moreover, you can't read the passages in advance of the test to prepare, and you have a limited amount of time to get through the passages and questions. What does this all mean? You will be much better served to take a *strategic* approach.

Read with a Purpose

When you read for school you have to read everything—carefully. Not only is there no time for such an approach on the ISEE but reading carefully at the outset does not even make sense. Each passage has only six questions (five for Lower Level), and all you need to read and process is the information that will provide answers to those questions. As only questions can generate points, your goal is to get to the questions as quickly as possible.

Even so, it does help to have a high-level overview of the passage before you attack the questions. There are two ways to do accomplish this goal.

- If you are a fairly fast reader, get through the passage quickly, ignoring the nitty-gritty and focusing on the overall point of each paragraph.
- If you don't read quickly enough to read the entire passage in a way that will provide you with the overall point of the paragraphs, read the first sentence of each paragraph.

Once you have identified the point of each paragraph, those points will flow into the overall purpose of the passage and also provide a map of where to find detailed information. Once you have established the purpose and map, you should go right to the questions.

Answering Questions

Some questions are about particular parts of a passage, while others are about the passage as a whole. Depending on how well you understood the purpose of the passage, you may be able to answer big picture questions quite easily. Detail questions, on the other hand, will require some work; after all, you didn't get lost in the details when you got through the passage quickly!

By reading more quickly up front, you have more time to spend on finding the answer to a particular question.

For a particular detail question, you will need to go back to the passage with the question in mind and *find the answer in the passage*. Let's repeat that last part: you should *find the answer in the passage*. If you know what the answer should look like, it is much easier to evaluate the answer choices. True, some questions cannot be answered in advance, such as "Which one of the following questions is answered in the passage?" But the general rule is *find the answer* before you go to the answer choices.

In all cases, you should use effective process of elimination. Correct answers are fully supported by the text of the passage. There is no reading between the lines, connecting the dots, or getting inside the author's head. If you are down to two answers, determine which one is not supported by the text of the passage. It takes only one word to doom an otherwise good answer.

In short, follow this process for detail questions:

- Read and understand the question.
- Go to the passage and *find the answer* (unless the question is too open-ended).
- Use process of elimination, getting rid of any answer that is not consistent with the answer you found and/or is not fully supported by the text of the passage.

We will look at some specific question types shortly, but if you follow the general approach outlined here, you will be able to answer more questions accurately.

Pacing

Let's amend that last statement: You will be able to answer more questions accurately if you have a sound pacing plan. While reading up front more quickly will generate more time for the questions, getting through all the passages and all the questions in the time allotted is difficult for almost all students.

There are six passages on the ISEE (five for Lower Level), some short and some quite long. Some are fairly easy to read, and some are dense. They cover a broad array of topics, from history to science to fiction. You may relate to some passages but not to others. On top of that, if you are rushing through the section to make sure you answer every single question, you are likely making a lot of mistakes. Slow down to increase your accuracy.

How many passages should you do? That depends on you. You should attack as many passages as you can while still maintaining a high degree of accuracy. If, for example, dropping to five passages allows you to answer all but one or two questions correctly, while rushing through six creates a lot of silly mistakes, do five.

Always pick your passages wisely. You don't get extra credit for answering questions on a hard passage correctly. If you begin a passage and are thinking "Uh, what?" move on to another passage. You might end up coming back to the passage or you may never look at it again. What is most important is that you nail the easier passages before you hit the harder ones.

Doing fewer passages accurately can generate more points than rushing through more passages.

STEP ONE: READING THE PASSAGE

Let's put the new reading approach into practice.

Label the Paragraphs

After you read each paragraph, ask yourself what you just read. Put it in your own words—just a couple of words—and label the side of the paragraph with your summary. This way you'll have something to guide you back to the relevant part of the passage when you answer a question. The key to labeling the paragraphs is practice—you need to do it quickly, coming up with one or two words that accurately remind you of what's in the paragraph.

If the passage has only one paragraph, come up with a single label. Poems do not need to be labeled.

State the Main Idea

After you have read the entire passage, ask yourself two questions.

- **"What?"** What is the passage about?

- **"So what?"** What's the author's point about this topic?

The answers to these questions will show you the main idea of the passage. Scribble down this main idea in just a few words. The answer to "What?" is the thing that was being talked about: "bees" or "weather forecasting." The answer to "So what?" gives you the rest of the sentence: "Bees do little dances that tell other bees where to go for pollen" or "Weather forecasting is complicated by many problems."

Don't assume you will find the main idea in the first sentence. While often the main idea is in the beginning of the passage, it is not always in the first sentence. The beginning may just be a lead-in to the main point.

STEP TWO: ANSWERING THE QUESTIONS

Now, we're getting to the important part of the Reading Comprehension section. This is where you need to spend time to avoid careless errors. After reading a passage, you'll have a group of questions that are in no particular order. The first thing you need to decide is whether the question you're answering is general or specific.

General Questions

General questions are about the passage as a whole. They come in a variety of forms but ideally all can be answered based on your initial read.

Main idea

- Which of the following best expresses the main point?
- The passage is primarily about
- The main idea of the passage is
- The best title for this passage would be

Purpose

- The purpose of the passage is
- The author wrote this passage to

Tone/attitude

- The author's tone is
- The attitude of the author is one of

Organization and Structure

- Which one of the following best describes the organization of the passage as a whole?
- Which one of the following best describes the organization of the second paragraph?

Notice that these questions all require you to know the main idea, but the ones at the beginning of the list don't require anything else, and the ones toward the end require you to use your map.

Answering a General Question

Keep your answers to "What? So what?" in mind. The answer to a general question will concern the main idea. If it helps, you can go back to your paragraph labels. The labels will allow you to look at the passage again without getting bogged down in the details.

- For a straight **main idea** question, just ask yourself, "What was the 'What? So what?' for this passage?"

- For a **general purpose** question, ask yourself, "Why did the author write this?"

- For a **tone/attitude question**, ask yourself, "How did the author feel about the subject?"

- For an **organization and structure question**, use your map for questions about the entire passage, and use process of elimination for questions about a paragraph.

Answer the question in your own words before looking at the answer choices. Eliminate answers that are not consistent with your predicted answer, as well as those that are too broad or too narrow. They should be "just right."

Specific Questions

Specific questions are about a detail or section of the passage. While the questions can be presented in a number of different ways, they boil down to questions about WHAT the author said, WHY the author said something, and Vocab-in-Context.

What?
- According to the passage/author
- The author states that
- Which of these questions is answered by the passage?
- The author implies in line X
- It can be inferred from paragraph X
- The most likely interpretation of X is

Why?
- The author uses X to
- Why does the author say X?

Vocab-in-Context

- What does the passage mean by *X*?
- *X* probably represents/means
- Which word best replaces the word *X* without changing the meaning?
- As it is used in *X*, _____ most nearly means

Specific interpretation

- The author would be most likely to agree with which one of the following?
- Which one of the following questions is answered in the passage?

Once you have read and understood the question, go to the passage to find the answer. You should be able to find the answer quickly:

- Use your **paragraph labels** to go straight to the information you need.
- Use the **line or paragraph reference**, if there is one, but be careful. With a line reference ("In line 10…"), be sure to read the whole surrounding paragraph, not just the line. If the question says, "In line 10…," then you need to read lines 5 through 15 to actually find the answer.
- Use words that stand out in the question and passage. Names, places, and long words will be easy to find back in the passage. We call these **lead words** because they lead you back to the right place in the passage.

Once you're in the right area, answer the question in your own words. Then look at the answer choices and eliminate any that aren't like your answer or are not supported by the text of the passage.

For Vocab-in-Context questions, be sure to come up with your own word based on the surrounding sentences. It does not matter if you do not know the word being tested, as long as you can figure it out from context. Even if you do know the word, it may be used in a unusual way. So, always ignore the word and come up with your own before using process of elimination.

Questions with Special Formats

I, II, III questions   The questions that have three Roman numerals are confusing and time consuming. They look like this.

> According to the passage, which of the following
> is true?
>   I.   The sky is blue.
>   II.   Nothing rhymes with "orange."
>   III.   Smoking cigarettes increases lung capacity.
>
> (A) I only
> (B) II only
> (C) I and II only
> (D) I, II, and III

Which answer is closest to what the author said overall?

On the ISEE, you will need to look up each of the three statements in the passage. This will always be time-consuming, but you can make them less confusing by making sure you look up just one statement at a time.

Look at the question at the bottom of the previous page for instance. You might look back at the passage and see that the passage says I is true. Write a big "T" next to it. What can you eliminate now? (B). Now, you check out II, and you find that sure enough, the passage says that too. II gets a big "T" and you cross off (A). Next, looking in the paragraph that you labeled "smoking is bad," you find that the passage actually says that smoking decreases lung capacity. What can you eliminate? (D).

Why did the author write this passage? Think about the main idea.

You may want to skip a I, II, III question because it will be time-consuming, especially if you're on your last passage and there are other questions you can do instead. If you skip it, remember to fill in your letter-of-the-day.

EXCEPT/LEAST/NOT Questions   This is another confusing type of question. The test writers are reversing what you need to look for, asking you which answer is false.

> All of the following can be inferred from the
> passage EXCEPT

Before you go any further, cross out "EXCEPT." Now, you have a much more positive question to answer. Of course, as always, you will go through all the answer choices, but for this type of question you will put a little "T" or "F" next to the answers as you check them out. Let's say we've checked out these answers.

> (A) Americans are patriotic.   T
> (B) Americans have great ingenuity.   T
> (C) Americans love war.   F
> (D) Americans do what they can to help one another.   T

Which one stands out? The one with the "F." That's your answer. You made a confusing question much simpler than the test writers wanted it to be. If you don't go through all the choices and mark them, you run the risk of accidentally picking one of the choices that you know is true because that's what you usually look for on reading comp questions.

You should skip an EXCEPT/LEAST/NOT question if you're on your last passage and there are other questions you can do instead—just fill in your letter-of-the-day on your answer sheet.

STEP THREE: PROCESS OF ELIMINATION

Before you ever look at an answer choice, you've come up with your own answer, in your own words. What do you do next?

Well, you're looking for the closest answer to yours, but it's much easier to eliminate answers than to try to magically zoom in on the best one. Work through the answers using Process of Elimination. As soon as you eliminate an answer, cross off the letter in your test booklet so that you no longer think of that choice as a possibility.

How Do I Eliminate Answer Choices?

On a General Question
Eliminate an answer that is:

- Too small. The passage may mention it, but it's only a detail—not a main idea.
- Not mentioned in the passage.
- In contradiction to the passage—it says the opposite of what you read.
- Too big. The answer tries to say that more was discussed than really was.
- Too extreme. An extreme answer is one that is too negative or too positive, or uses absolute words like *all*, *every*, *never*, or *always*. Eliminating extreme answers makes tone/attitude questions especially easy and quick.
- Going against common sense. The passage is not likely to back up answers that just don't make sense at all.

On a Specific Question
Eliminate an answer that is:

- Too extreme
- In contradiction to passage details
- Not mentioned in the passage
- Against common sense

If you look back at the questions you did for the Viking passage, you'll see that many of the wrong answer choices fit into the categories above.

On a Tone Question
Eliminate an answer choice that is:

- Too extreme
- Opposite meaning
- Against common sense. These are answers that make the author seem confused or uninterested—an ISEE author won't be either.

What Kinds of Answers Do I Keep?
Best answers are likely to be:

- Paraphrases of the words in the passage
- Traditional and conservative in their outlook
- Moderate, using words like *may*, *can*, and *often*

When You've Got It Down to Two
If you've eliminated all but two answers, don't get stuck and waste time. Keep the main idea in the back of your mind and step back.

- Reread the question.

- Look at what makes the two answers different.

- Go back to the passage.

- Which answer is worse? Eliminate it.

Put it all together and do the practice drills online.

Part V
ISEE Practice Tests

HOW TO TAKE A PRACTICE TEST

Here are some reminders for taking your practice test.

- Find a quiet place to take the test where you won't be interrupted or distracted, and make sure you have enough time to take the entire test.

- Time yourself strictly. Use a timer, watch, or stopwatch that will ring, and do not allow yourself to go over time for any section.

- Take a practice test in one sitting, allowing yourself breaks of no more than two minutes between sections.

- Use the attached answer sheets to bubble in your answer choices.

- Each bubble you choose should be filled in thoroughly, and no other marks should be made in the answer area.

- Make sure to double check that your bubbles are filled in correctly!

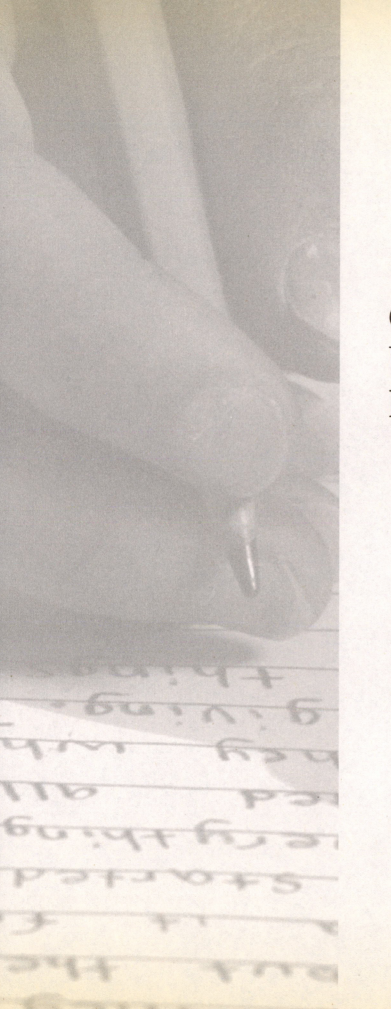

Chapter 17
Upper Level ISEE
Practice Test

Upper Level Practice Test

Be sure each mark *completely* fills the answer space.

SECTION 1

1 Ⓐ Ⓑ Ⓒ Ⓓ	9 Ⓐ Ⓑ Ⓒ Ⓓ	17 Ⓐ Ⓑ Ⓒ Ⓓ	25 Ⓐ Ⓑ Ⓒ Ⓓ	33 Ⓐ Ⓑ Ⓒ Ⓓ
2 Ⓐ Ⓑ Ⓒ Ⓓ	10 Ⓐ Ⓑ Ⓒ Ⓓ	18 Ⓐ Ⓑ Ⓒ Ⓓ	26 Ⓐ Ⓑ Ⓒ Ⓓ	34 Ⓐ Ⓑ Ⓒ Ⓓ
3 Ⓐ Ⓑ Ⓒ Ⓓ	11 Ⓐ Ⓑ Ⓒ Ⓓ	19 Ⓐ Ⓑ Ⓒ Ⓓ	27 Ⓐ Ⓑ Ⓒ Ⓓ	35 Ⓐ Ⓑ Ⓒ Ⓓ
4 Ⓐ Ⓑ Ⓒ Ⓓ	12 Ⓐ Ⓑ Ⓒ Ⓓ	20 Ⓐ Ⓑ Ⓒ Ⓓ	28 Ⓐ Ⓑ Ⓒ Ⓓ	36 Ⓐ Ⓑ Ⓒ Ⓓ
5 Ⓐ Ⓑ Ⓒ Ⓓ	13 Ⓐ Ⓑ Ⓒ Ⓓ	21 Ⓐ Ⓑ Ⓒ Ⓓ	29 Ⓐ Ⓑ Ⓒ Ⓓ	37 Ⓐ Ⓑ Ⓒ Ⓓ
6 Ⓐ Ⓑ Ⓒ Ⓓ	14 Ⓐ Ⓑ Ⓒ Ⓓ	22 Ⓐ Ⓑ Ⓒ Ⓓ	30 Ⓐ Ⓑ Ⓒ Ⓓ	38 Ⓐ Ⓑ Ⓒ Ⓓ
7 Ⓐ Ⓑ Ⓒ Ⓓ	15 Ⓐ Ⓑ Ⓒ Ⓓ	23 Ⓐ Ⓑ Ⓒ Ⓓ	31 Ⓐ Ⓑ Ⓒ Ⓓ	39 Ⓐ Ⓑ Ⓒ Ⓓ
8 Ⓐ Ⓑ Ⓒ Ⓓ	16 Ⓐ Ⓑ Ⓒ Ⓓ	24 Ⓐ Ⓑ Ⓒ Ⓓ	32 Ⓐ Ⓑ Ⓒ Ⓓ	40 Ⓐ Ⓑ Ⓒ Ⓓ

SECTION 2

1 Ⓐ Ⓑ Ⓒ Ⓓ	9 Ⓐ Ⓑ Ⓒ Ⓓ	17 Ⓐ Ⓑ Ⓒ Ⓓ	25 Ⓐ Ⓑ Ⓒ Ⓓ	33 Ⓐ Ⓑ Ⓒ Ⓓ
2 Ⓐ Ⓑ Ⓒ Ⓓ	10 Ⓐ Ⓑ Ⓒ Ⓓ	18 Ⓐ Ⓑ Ⓒ Ⓓ	26 Ⓐ Ⓑ Ⓒ Ⓓ	34 Ⓐ Ⓑ Ⓒ Ⓓ
3 Ⓐ Ⓑ Ⓒ Ⓓ	11 Ⓐ Ⓑ Ⓒ Ⓓ	19 Ⓐ Ⓑ Ⓒ Ⓓ	27 Ⓐ Ⓑ Ⓒ Ⓓ	35 Ⓐ Ⓑ Ⓒ Ⓓ
4 Ⓐ Ⓑ Ⓒ Ⓓ	12 Ⓐ Ⓑ Ⓒ Ⓓ	20 Ⓐ Ⓑ Ⓒ Ⓓ	28 Ⓐ Ⓑ Ⓒ Ⓓ	36 Ⓐ Ⓑ Ⓒ Ⓓ
5 Ⓐ Ⓑ Ⓒ Ⓓ	13 Ⓐ Ⓑ Ⓒ Ⓓ	21 Ⓐ Ⓑ Ⓒ Ⓓ	29 Ⓐ Ⓑ Ⓒ Ⓓ	37 Ⓐ Ⓑ Ⓒ Ⓓ
6 Ⓐ Ⓑ Ⓒ Ⓓ	14 Ⓐ Ⓑ Ⓒ Ⓓ	22 Ⓐ Ⓑ Ⓒ Ⓓ	30 Ⓐ Ⓑ Ⓒ Ⓓ	
7 Ⓐ Ⓑ Ⓒ Ⓓ	15 Ⓐ Ⓑ Ⓒ Ⓓ	23 Ⓐ Ⓑ Ⓒ Ⓓ	31 Ⓐ Ⓑ Ⓒ Ⓓ	
8 Ⓐ Ⓑ Ⓒ Ⓓ	16 Ⓐ Ⓑ Ⓒ Ⓓ	24 Ⓐ Ⓑ Ⓒ Ⓓ	32 Ⓐ Ⓑ Ⓒ Ⓓ	

SECTION 3

1 Ⓐ Ⓑ Ⓒ Ⓓ	9 Ⓐ Ⓑ Ⓒ Ⓓ	17 Ⓐ Ⓑ Ⓒ Ⓓ	25 Ⓐ Ⓑ Ⓒ Ⓓ	33 Ⓐ Ⓑ Ⓒ Ⓓ
2 Ⓐ Ⓑ Ⓒ Ⓓ	10 Ⓐ Ⓑ Ⓒ Ⓓ	18 Ⓐ Ⓑ Ⓒ Ⓓ	26 Ⓐ Ⓑ Ⓒ Ⓓ	34 Ⓐ Ⓑ Ⓒ Ⓓ
3 Ⓐ Ⓑ Ⓒ Ⓓ	11 Ⓐ Ⓑ Ⓒ Ⓓ	19 Ⓐ Ⓑ Ⓒ Ⓓ	27 Ⓐ Ⓑ Ⓒ Ⓓ	35 Ⓐ Ⓑ Ⓒ Ⓓ
4 Ⓐ Ⓑ Ⓒ Ⓓ	12 Ⓐ Ⓑ Ⓒ Ⓓ	20 Ⓐ Ⓑ Ⓒ Ⓓ	28 Ⓐ Ⓑ Ⓒ Ⓓ	36 Ⓐ Ⓑ Ⓒ Ⓓ
5 Ⓐ Ⓑ Ⓒ Ⓓ	13 Ⓐ Ⓑ Ⓒ Ⓓ	21 Ⓐ Ⓑ Ⓒ Ⓓ	29 Ⓐ Ⓑ Ⓒ Ⓓ	
6 Ⓐ Ⓑ Ⓒ Ⓓ	14 Ⓐ Ⓑ Ⓒ Ⓓ	22 Ⓐ Ⓑ Ⓒ Ⓓ	30 Ⓐ Ⓑ Ⓒ Ⓓ	
7 Ⓐ Ⓑ Ⓒ Ⓓ	15 Ⓐ Ⓑ Ⓒ Ⓓ	23 Ⓐ Ⓑ Ⓒ Ⓓ	31 Ⓐ Ⓑ Ⓒ Ⓓ	
8 Ⓐ Ⓑ Ⓒ Ⓓ	16 Ⓐ Ⓑ Ⓒ Ⓓ	24 Ⓐ Ⓑ Ⓒ Ⓓ	32 Ⓐ Ⓑ Ⓒ Ⓓ	

SECTION 4

1 Ⓐ Ⓑ Ⓒ Ⓓ	11 Ⓐ Ⓑ Ⓒ Ⓓ	21 Ⓐ Ⓑ Ⓒ Ⓓ	31 Ⓐ Ⓑ Ⓒ Ⓓ	41 Ⓐ Ⓑ Ⓒ Ⓓ
2 Ⓐ Ⓑ Ⓒ Ⓓ	12 Ⓐ Ⓑ Ⓒ Ⓓ	22 Ⓐ Ⓑ Ⓒ Ⓓ	32 Ⓐ Ⓑ Ⓒ Ⓓ	42 Ⓐ Ⓑ Ⓒ Ⓓ
3 Ⓐ Ⓑ Ⓒ Ⓓ	13 Ⓐ Ⓑ Ⓒ Ⓓ	23 Ⓐ Ⓑ Ⓒ Ⓓ	33 Ⓐ Ⓑ Ⓒ Ⓓ	43 Ⓐ Ⓑ Ⓒ Ⓓ
4 Ⓐ Ⓑ Ⓒ Ⓓ	14 Ⓐ Ⓑ Ⓒ Ⓓ	24 Ⓐ Ⓑ Ⓒ Ⓓ	34 Ⓐ Ⓑ Ⓒ Ⓓ	44 Ⓐ Ⓑ Ⓒ Ⓓ
5 Ⓐ Ⓑ Ⓒ Ⓓ	15 Ⓐ Ⓑ Ⓒ Ⓓ	25 Ⓐ Ⓑ Ⓒ Ⓓ	35 Ⓐ Ⓑ Ⓒ Ⓓ	45 Ⓐ Ⓑ Ⓒ Ⓓ
6 Ⓐ Ⓑ Ⓒ Ⓓ	16 Ⓐ Ⓑ Ⓒ Ⓓ	26 Ⓐ Ⓑ Ⓒ Ⓓ	36 Ⓐ Ⓑ Ⓒ Ⓓ	46 Ⓐ Ⓑ Ⓒ Ⓓ
7 Ⓐ Ⓑ Ⓒ Ⓓ	17 Ⓐ Ⓑ Ⓒ Ⓓ	27 Ⓐ Ⓑ Ⓒ Ⓓ	37 Ⓐ Ⓑ Ⓒ Ⓓ	47 Ⓐ Ⓑ Ⓒ Ⓓ
8 Ⓐ Ⓑ Ⓒ Ⓓ	18 Ⓐ Ⓑ Ⓒ Ⓓ	28 Ⓐ Ⓑ Ⓒ Ⓓ	38 Ⓐ Ⓑ Ⓒ Ⓓ	
9 Ⓐ Ⓑ Ⓒ Ⓓ	19 Ⓐ Ⓑ Ⓒ Ⓓ	29 Ⓐ Ⓑ Ⓒ Ⓓ	39 Ⓐ Ⓑ Ⓒ Ⓓ	
10 Ⓐ Ⓑ Ⓒ Ⓓ	20 Ⓐ Ⓑ Ⓒ Ⓓ	30 Ⓐ Ⓑ Ⓒ Ⓓ	40 Ⓐ Ⓑ Ⓒ Ⓓ	

Section 1
Verbal Reasoning

40 Questions	**Time: 20 Minutes**

This section is divided into two parts that contain two different types of questions. As soon as you have completed Part One, answer the questions in Part Two. You may write in your test booklet. For each answer you select, fill in the corresponding circle on your answer document.

Part One – Synonyms

Each question in Part One consists of a word in capital letters followed by four answer choices. Select the one word that is most nearly the same in meaning as the word in capital letters.

SAMPLE QUESTION:

    GENERIC:

        (A) effortless
        (B) general
        (C) strong
        (D) thoughtful

Sample Answer

Ⓐ ● Ⓒ Ⓓ

Go on to the next page. ⟶

Part Two – Sentence Completion

Each question in Part Two is made up of a sentence with one or two blanks. One blank indicates that a word is missing. Two blanks indicate that two words are missing. Each sentence is followed by four answer choices. Select the one word or pair of words that best completes the meaning of the sentence as a whole.

SAMPLE QUESTIONS:

Always ------, Edgar's late arrival surprised his friends.

(A)   entertaining
(B)   lazy
(C)   punctual
(D)   sincere

Sample Answer

Ⓐ Ⓑ ● Ⓓ

After training for months, the runner felt ------ that she would win the race, quite different from her ------ attitude initially.

(A)   confident . . . excited
(B)   indifferent . . . concern
(C)   secure . . . apprehensive
(D)   worried . . . excited

Sample Answer

Ⓐ Ⓑ ● Ⓓ

STOP. Do not go on until told to do so.

Part One – Synonyms

Directions: Select the word that is most nearly the same in meaning as the word in capital letters.

1. GRAVE:

   (A) deadly
   (B) final
   (C) open
   (D) solemn

2. FOMENT:

   (A) articulate
   (B) dissemble
   (C) instigate
   (D) praise

3. INARTICULATE:

   (A) creative
   (B) friendly
   (C) overly sensitive
   (D) tongue-tied

4. AMELIORATE:

   (A) enjoy
   (B) hinder
   (C) improve
   (D) restrain

5. THESIS:

   (A) belief
   (B) paper
   (C) report
   (D) study

6. DEBUNK:

   (A) build
   (B) discredit
   (C) impress
   (D) justify

7. DISDAIN:

   (A) annoy
   (B) contempt
   (C) find
   (D) hope

8. RETICENT:

   (A) anxious
   (B) aware
   (C) informed
   (D) reserved

9. PREVALENT:

   (A) fascinating
   (B) minority
   (C) old-fashioned
   (D) predominant

10. SATIATE:

    (A) deny
    (B) fill
    (C) serve
    (D) starve

Go on to the next page. ➡

11. CANDID:

(A) defiant
(B) dejected
(C) frank
(D) stingy

12. EMULATE:

(A) brush off
(B) imitate
(C) perplex
(D) permit

13. TAINT:

(A) annoy
(B) handle
(C) infect
(D) master

14. ENIGMA:

(A) effort
(B) mystery
(C) struggle
(D) tantrum

15. DETRIMENTAL:

(A) considerate
(B) desolate
(C) emphatic
(D) injurious

16. METICULOUS:

(A) favorable
(B) finicky
(C) gigantic
(D) maddening

17. JUXTAPOSE:

(A) keep away
(B) place side by side
(C) put behind
(D) question

18. CONGENIAL:

(A) friendly
(B) impressive
(C) inborn
(D) magical

19. MITIGATE:

(A) bend
(B) ease
(C) harden
(D) untangle

20. ELUSIVE:

(A) real
(B) slippery
(C) treacherous
(D) unhappy

Go on to the next page. ⟶

Part Two – Sentence Completion

Directions: Select the word or word pair that best completes the sentence.

21. Jane felt ------- about whether to go to the party or not; on one hand it seemed like fun, but on the other, she was very tired.

    (A) ambivalent
    (B) apathetic
    (C) happy
    (D) irritated

22. Like the more famous Susan B. Anthony, M. Carey Thomas ------- feminism and women's rights.

    (A) championed
    (B) defaced
    (C) found
    (D) gained

23. Morality is not -------; cultures around the world have different ideas about how people should be treated.

    (A) debatable
    (B) helpful
    (C) realistic
    (D) universal

24. Although Ms. Sanchez ------ the student that he needed a good grade on the final exam, he did not study at all.

    (A) admonished
    (B) congratulated
    (C) criticized
    (D) ridiculed

25. Thomas Jefferson was a man of ------- talents: he was known for his skills as a writer, a musician, an architect, and an inventor as well as a politician.

    (A) abundant
    (B) frugal
    (C) mundane
    (D) overblown

26. Monica could remain ------- no longer; the injustices she witnessed moved her to speak up.

    (A) active
    (B) furious
    (C) helpful
    (D) reticent

27. Louisa May Alcott's *Little Women* is really quite -------; much of the story is based on her experiences as a young woman growing up in Concord, Massachusetts.

    (A) autobiographical
    (B) fictional
    (C) moving
    (D) visual

Go on to the next page. ➡

28. Though his lectures could be monotonous, Mr. Cutler was actually quite ------- when he spoke to students in small, informal groups.

    (A) amiable
    (B) pious
    (C) prosaic
    (D) vapid

29. Craig had ------- that the day would not go well, and just as he'd thought, he had two pop quizzes.

    (A) an antidote
    (B) an interest
    (C) a premonition
    (D) a report

30. Far from shedding light on the mystery, Jason's ------- reponse left people unsure.

    (A) impartial
    (B) opaque
    (C) risky
    (D) systematic

31. Although Marie was a talented and ------- performer, her gifts were often ------- because she didn't know how to promote herself.

    (A) faithful . . . supported
    (B) insulting . . . overlooked
    (C) promising . . . satisfied
    (D) versatile . . . ignored

32. Although she was the daughter of a wealthy slaveholder, Angelina Grimke ------- slavery and ------- her whole life for the cause of abolition.

    (A) desired . . . picketed
    (B) detested . . . dedicated
    (C) hated . . . wasted
    (D) represented . . . fought

33. Rhubarb is actually quite -------, requiring a large amount of sugar to make it -------.

    (A) bitter . . . palatable
    (B) flavorful . . . fattening
    (C) nutritious . . . sickening
    (D) unpopular . . . sticky

34. Because Martha was naturally -------, she would see the bright side of any situation, but Jack had a ------- personality and always waited for something bad to happen.

    (A) cheerful . . . upbeat
    (B) frightened . . . mawkish
    (C) optimistic . . . dreary
    (D) realistic . . . unreasonable

35. Although Edgar was not telling the truth, his ------ succeeded: it ------- the crowd to demand that Edgar's competitor be rejected.

    (A) antipathy . . . questioned
    (B) condone . . . encouraged
    (C) fallacy . . . incited
    (D) lie . . . permitted

Go on to the next page. ➡

36. Even though the critics praised the author's ------- use of words, they found the text ------- at a mere 100 pages.

    (A) hackneyed . . . threadbare
    (B) improper . . . laconic
    (C) precise . . . short
    (D) sure . . . banal

37. Erica's mother could not ------- why Erica would study a subject as ------- as the culture of 13th century French winemakers.

    (A) fathom . . . esoteric
    (B) intend . . . bizarre
    (C) respond . . . gruesome
    (D) understand . . . interesting

38. The threat of the storm did not ------- Ernie's excitement for the race; he had no ------- running in even the most unpleasant of weather.

    (A) diminish . . . reservations about
    (B) improve . . . concerns about
    (C) lessen . . . inclination to go
    (D) understate . . . abilities for

39. Always -------, Mr. Sanford refused to spend any money on anything unnecessary; to him, even a meal at a restaurant was a ------- excess.

    (A) parsimonious . . . gratuitous
    (B) penurious . . . useful
    (C) spendthrift . . . respectable
    (D) stingy . . . selective

40. To her -------, Margie was given the unfair label of -------, even though her love of the arts was far from superficial.

    (A) chagrin . . . dilettante
    (B) frustration . . . adversary
    (C) irritation . . . performer
    (D) surprise . . . mentor

STOP. If there is time, you may check your work in this section only.

QR

Section 2
Quantitative Reasoning

37 Questions	Time: 35 Minutes

This section is divided into two parts that contain two different types of questions. As soon as you have completed Part One, answer the questions in Part Two. You may write in your test booklet. For each answer you select, remember to fill in the corresponding circle on your answer document.

Any figures that accompany the questions in this section may be assumed to be drawn as accurately as possible EXCEPT when it is stated that a particular figure is not drawn to scale. Letters such as *x, y,* and *n* stand for real numbers.

Part One – Word Problems

Each question in Part One consists of a word problem followed by four answer choices. You may write in your test booklet; however, you may be able to solve many of these problems in your head. Next, look at the four answer choices given and select the best answer.

EXAMPLE 1:

What is the value of the expression

$5 + 3 \times (10 - 2) \div 4$?

(A)   5
(B)   9
(C) 11
(D) 16

Sample Answer

Ⓐ Ⓑ ● Ⓓ

The correct answer is 11, so circle C is darkened.

Go on to the next page. ➞

Part Two – Quantitative Comparisons

All questions in Part Two are quantitative comparisons between the quantities shown in Column A and Column B. Using the information given in each question, compare the quantity in Column A to the quantity in Column B, and chose one of these four answer choices:

(A)   The quantity in Column A is greater.
(B)   The quantity in Column B is greater.
(C)   The two quantities are equal.
(D)   The relationship cannot be determined from the information given.

EXAMPLE 2:	Column A	Column B	Sample Answer
	50% of 40	20% of 100	Ⓐ Ⓑ ● Ⓓ

The quantity in <u>Column A</u> (20) is the same as the quantity in <u>Column B</u> (20), so circle C is darkened.

EXAMPLE 3:	*y* is any real non-zero number		Sample Answer
	Column A	Column B	Ⓐ Ⓑ Ⓒ ●
	y	$\frac{1}{y}$	

Since *y* can be any real number (including an integer or a fraction), there is not enough information given to determine the relationship, so circle D is darkened.

STOP. Do not go on until told to do so.

NO TEST MATERIAL ON THIS PAGE

Part One – Word Problems

Directions: Choose the best answer from the four choices given.

1. Which of the following is greatest?

   (A) 0.0100
   (B) 0.0099
   (C) 0.1900
   (D) 0.0199

2. Which of the following is NOT the product of two prime numbers?

   (A) 33
   (B) 35
   (C) 45
   (D) 91

3. If x, y, and z are consecutive even integers, then what is the difference between x and z ?

   (A) 0
   (B) 1
   (C) 2
   (D) 4

Questions 4-5 refer to the following chart.

Clothing Close-out

Dresses	Originally $120	Now $90
Coats	Originally $250	Now $180
Shoes	Originally $60	Now $40
Hats	Originally $40	Now $20

4. Which of the items for sale has the greatest percent discount?

   (A) Dresses
   (B) Coats
   (C) Shoes
   (D) Hats

5. Purchasing which item will save the buyer the most dollars?

   (A) Dresses
   (B) Coats
   (C) Shoes
   (D) Hats

Go on to the next page. →

6. Amy is three years older than Beth and five years younger than Jo. If Beth is b years old, how old is Jo, in terms of b ?

   (A) $2b + 3$
   (B) $2b - 3$
   (C) $b + 4$
   (D) $b + 8$

7. If x is divided by 5, the remainder is 4. If y is divided by 5, the remainder is 1. What is the remainder when $(x + y)$ is divided by 5 ?

   (A) 0
   (B) 1
   (C) 2
   (D) 3

8. If x is a factor of p and y is a factor of q, then which of the following is true?

   (A) pq is a factor of xy
   (B) pq is a multiple of xy
   (C) p is a factor of xy
   (D) p is a multiple of xy

9. Find the maximum value of y when $y = 3x^2 + 2$ and $-3 \leq x \leq 2$.

   (A) 2
   (B) 14
   (C) 29
   (D) 50

10. If b is a positive integer and $(x + 5)^2 = x^2 + bx + 25$, then b is equal to what value?

    (A) 5
    (B) 10
    (C) 20
    (D) 25

11. J is a whole number divisible by 4. J is also divisible by 3. Which of the following is NOT a possible value for J ?

    (A) 12
    (B) 24
    (C) 30
    (D) 36

12. The product of 0.48 and 100 is approximately

    (A) 0.5
    (B) 4.8
    (C) 5
    (D) 50

Go on to the next page.

13. If the length of a rectangle is increased by 20% and the width of the rectangle is decreased by 10%, what is the percent increase of the area of the rectangle?

(A) 8%
(B) 9%
(C) 10%
(D) 12%

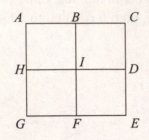

14. Square ACEG shown above is composed of 4 squares with sides of 1 meter each. Traveling only on the lines of the squares, how many different routes from A to D that are exactly 3 meters long are possible?

(A) 2
(B) 3
(C) 4
(D) 5

15. If, in triangle ABC, the measure of angle B is greater than 90°, and AB = BC, what is a possible measure for angle C in degrees?

(A) 35
(B) 45
(C) 60
(D) It cannot be determined from the information given.

16. Chumway Motors discounts the cost of a car by 10% and then runs another special one-day deal offering an additional 20% off the discounted price. What discount does this represent from the original price of the car?

(A) 28%
(B) 30%
(C) 40%
(D) 72%

17. David scored 82, 84, and 95 on his first three math tests. What score does he need on his fourth test to bring his average up to a 90?

(A) 90
(B) 92
(C) 96
(D) 99

Go on to the next page. ⟶

18. Howard has a coin jar filled with only quarters and nickels. If he has a total of 23 coins that equal $2.15, which of the following could be the number of nickels Howard has in the jar?

(A) 5
(B) 10
(C) 18
(D) 20

19. If $p^2 + q^2 = 25$ and $2pq = 10$, what is the value of $(p - q)^2$?

(A) 250
(B) 100
(C) 50
(D) 15

20. The ratio of yellow paint to red paint to white paint needed to make a perfect mixture of orange paint is 3 to 2 to 1. If 36 gallons of orange paint are needed to paint a cottage, how many gallons of red paint will be needed?

(A) 2
(B) 6
(C) 12
(D) 15

Go on to the next page. ➡

Part Two – Quantitative Comparisons

Directions: Using all information given in each question, compare the quantity in Column A to the quantity in Column B. All questions in Part Two have these answer choices:

(A) The quantity in Column A is greater.
(B) The quantity in Column B is greater.
(C) The two quantities are equal.
(D) The relationship cannot be determined from the information given.

	Column A	Column B
21.	25% of 50	50% of 25

A piggy bank is filled with nickels and pennies, totaling $2.10, and the number of pennies is double the number of nickels. (Note: 1 nickel = $0.05 and 1 penny = $0.01)

	Column A	Column B
22.	The total value of the nickels	$1.75

360 is the product of 4 consecutive integers.

	Column A	Column B
23.	The greatest of the 4 consecutive integers	6

	Column A	Column B
24.	x^2	x^3

	Column A	Column B
25.	$8 - 20 \div 2 \times 5 + 3$	20

Go on to the next page. →

QR

2

$$(x + 2)(x - 2) = 0$$

Column A	Column B
26. x	2

Column A	Column B
27. $\sqrt{36} + \sqrt{16}$	$\sqrt{52}$

Column A	Column B
28. 3^{12}	9^6

The volume of a solid cube is 27.

Column A	Column B
29. The height of the cube	3

$$\frac{x + 2}{y + 2} = \frac{x}{y}$$

Column A	Column B
30. x	$y + 2$

Column A	Column B
31. The sum of the integers from 1 to 100, inclusive	The sum of the even integers from 1 to 200, inclusive

$$\frac{x}{4} = 1.5$$

Column A	Column B
32. x	5

Go on to the next page. ➝

Column A	Column B

33. $\left(\dfrac{1}{5}\right)^{-\frac{1}{2}}$ $\left(\dfrac{1}{5}\right)^{4}$

A card is drawn from a standard deck and a 6-sided number cube, numbered 1 to 6, is rolled.

Column A	Column B

34. If a king is drawn from the deck, the probability of rolling an even number. / If a spade is drawn from the deck, the probability of rolling a number less than 4

When they are in season, a farmer sells turnips for $1.80 per bunch. At the beginning of the off-season, this farmer increases the price per bunch by 10%; however, at the end of the off-season the farmer decreases by 10% the price of turnips per bunch.

Column A	Column B

35. The price of turnips per bunch at the end of the off-season. / $1.80

A box contains 4 cookies, 5 brownies, and 6 doughnuts. Two items are removed from the bag.

Column A	Column B

36. The probability that both items are brownies / The probability that one item is a cookie and the other is a doughnut

A triangle has two sides measuring 4 and 6, respectively.

Column A	Column B

37. The greatest possible area of the triangle / 12

STOP. If there is time, you may check your work in this section only.

RC

Section 3
Reading Comprehension

36 Questions	Time: 35 Minutes

This section contains six short reading passages. Each passage is followed by six questions based on its content. Answer the questions following each passage on the basis of what is <u>stated</u> or <u>implied</u> in that passage. You may write in the test booklet.

**STOP. Do not go on
until told to do so.**

Questions 1–6

Line

1   New Orleans was the site of the last
2 major battle during the War of 1812,
3 a lengthy conflict between British and
4 American troops. The Battle of New
5 Orleans in January 1815 was one of the
6 greatest victories in American military
7 history. However, the great success of this
8 battle did not actually bring about the end of
9 the war. Surprisingly, the Treaty of Ghent,
10 which declared the end of the war, had
11 already been signed by both sides a month
12 earlier.
13   How was that possible? There were two
14 major reasons. The first is that New Orleans
15 was relatively isolated and communication
16 in the growing United States was not as
17 simple as it is today. Thus, it is possible that
18 the British commanders and the American
19 general, Andrew Jackson, did not realize a
20 treaty had been signed before they started
21 their battle. A second reason is that there is
22 a difference between a signed treaty and a
23 ratified treaty. Even if all soldiers fighting in
24 and around New Orleans had known of the
25 treaty, it had not yet been ratified by the U.S.
26 Senate. Thus, though the Treaty of Ghent
27 took place in December prior to the Battle of
28 New Orleans, the war did not officially end
29 until February 1815, when the Senate ratified
30 the treaty.

31   Had the combatants in New Orleans
32 known of the treaty, they might have
33 avoided a tough battle, especially the
34 British. In the battle, a force of about 4,000
35 American troops decisively defeated an
36 enemy of nearly twice its size. At stake for
37 the soldiers was control of the waterways of
38 the Mississippi, and the fighting was fierce.
39 A combination of tactical mistakes and bad
40 weather doomed the British attack, costing
41 them nearly 2,000 soldiers injured or killed.
42 The Americans lost fewer than 200. But
43 was the terrible battle all for nothing? Some
44 historians suggest that victory that day was
45 crucial for the American military in order
46 to enforce and help quickly ratify the peace
47 treaty. Potentially, with an American loss in
48 New Orleans, the British could have found
49 hope to continue the conflict.

Go on to the next page. ➞

1. The primary purpose of the passage is to

   (A) blame the British for fighting an unnecessary war
   (B) celebrate the tactical military maneuvers of Andrew Jackson
   (C) convince readers that peace treaties are often worthless
   (D) provide greater details about the end of a historical conflict

2. The passage suggests that all of the following occurred near the end of the War of 1812 EXCEPT

   (A) Andrew Jackson ignored the orders of President Madison
   (B) Communication with the battle line commanders was slow
   (C) The Treaty of Ghent was signed
   (D) Weather conditions hurt the efforts of the British soldiers

3. Which of the following is implied by the passage?

   (A) Andrew Jackson did not know the difference between a signed treaty and a ratified treaty.
   (B) President Madison did not realize the Battle of New Orleans was possible.
   (C) The British may have had a chance for victory with better conditions and preparation.
   (D) The British troops knew of the treaty but attacked anyway.

4. According to the passage, New Orleans was a strategic battle site because

   (A) it was the only location where American forces were better supplied than the British forces
   (B) the American forces would be trapped in the swamplands if they lost
   (C) the British were attempting to defeat a more numerous force
   (D) the Mississippi River was nearby and control of it was important

5. After which of the following was the War of 1812 officially at an end?

   (A) Both armies signing the Treaty of Ghent
   (B) British retreat from the Mississippi
   (C) The Battle of New Orleans
   (D) The Senate's ratification of the Treaty of Ghent

6. According to the passage, a treaty

   (A) cannot be signed by the President without the consent of the Senate
   (B) has sometimes been ignored by those in battle
   (C) is always used to end a war
   (D) is not effective until it is ratified by the Senate

Go on to the next page. ⟶

Questions 7–12

Line

1 According to game maker Hasbro,
2 approximately 750 million people have
3 played the well-known game *Monopoly*
4 since it was invented in the 1930s. Charles
5 Darrow is typically credited as the inventor
6 of the world's most famous board game.
7 However, he likely derived his version of
8 *Monopoly* from one of several other games
9 similarly involving realty buying and selling
10 that were already in existence prior to the
11 1930s when he got his patent for the game.

12 A probable reason that Darrow's
13 *Monopoly* became the hugely successful
14 game that still exists today is that he took
15 a diligent approach to producing it. Other
16 similar games existed, but some of them
17 had no board or regulation pieces. With
18 help from his wife and son who adorned the
19 sets with detail, Darrow personally created
20 the pieces and boards that became the first
21 *Monopoly* game sets. His extra work in
22 creating the entire environment that players
23 needed gave his game something extra that
24 other variations did not have.

25 Darrow had marginal success selling
26 his games in various parts of the country.
27 Several Philadelphia area stores were
28 the first to carry his game and sell it in
29 large quantities. Despite this, Darrow had
30 difficulty selling his game to the major
31 game manufacturer of the time, Parker
32 Brothers. He was told that his game was
33 too complex and had fundamental errors
34 in its design that would limit its appeal.
35 Ultimately, the continued sales he managed
36 on his own forced Parker Brothers to
37 reassess the worth of his game. Eventually,
38 the company agreed to produce the game
39 and shortly thereafter it became the
40 bestselling game in the country.

41 That success turned Charles Darrow
42 into a millionaire, which is the ultimate
43 irony. Darrow initially began work on
44 *Monopoly* to help support himself and his
45 family following the financial troubles tied
46 to the stock market crash of 1929.

47 Thus, Charles Darrow became a
48 millionaire by producing a game that allows
49 "regular" people to feel like they are buying
50 and selling homes and real estate like
51 millionaires.

Go on to the next page. ⟶

7. The best title for this passage would be

(A) "A Comparison of Several Early Real Estate Board Games"
(B) "How Hasbro Introduced *Monopoly* to the World"
(C) "The Early History of Charles *Monopoly*"
(D) "Two Views of Charles Darrow's Life"

8. It is suggested by the passage that

(A) Darrow decided to make his game less complex after initially meeting with Parker Brothers
(B) Darrow had no other skills to use after the stock market crash of 1929
(C) Parker Brothers probably doubted that a complex game could sell well
(D) Philadelphia was the only major city where he could sell his game

9. As used in line 48, "regular" refers to people who

(A) rent rather than own property
(B) are in the top 1% of wealthiest people
(C) love to play board games
(D) are in a lower economic class than millionaires

10. With which of the following would the author be LEAST likely to agree?

(A) Charles Darrow chose to continue to sell his game despite criticisms.
(B) Charles Darrow is not the first person to conceive of a board-based real estate game.
(C) Charles Darrow preferred to achieve his goals without the help of others.
(D) Some of the things Darrow chose to do helped make his game sell better than other games.

11. Which of the following was NOT mentioned by the author as contributing to the ultimate success of *Monopoly*?

(A) Darrow's efforts to initially sell the game on his own.
(B) The addition of specific pieces and a playing board in each set.
(C) The adjustments Parker Brothers made to the game.
(D) The enjoyment people get in pretending to be millionaires.

12. The author suggests in the third paragraph that

(A) certain errors in *Monopoly* served to limit its appeal
(B) Charles Darrow sold his game in Philadelphia because he knew it would be popular there
(C) *Monopoly* was initially too complex to be popular
(D) some people doubted that *Monopoly* would be popular

Go on to the next page. ➞

Questions 13–18

Line

1　Every year, hundreds of hopeful
2　students arrive in Washington, D.C., in
3　order to compete in the National Spelling
4　Bee. This competition has been held
5　annually since 1925 and is sponsored by
6　E.W. Scripps Company. The sponsors
7　provide both a trophy and a monetary award
8　to the champion speller. In the competition,
9　students under 16 years of age take turns
10　attempting to properly spell words as
11　provided by the moderator. The champion
12　is the sole remaining student who does not
13　make a mistake.

14　Most American students are familiar
15　with the concept of a spelling bee because
16　it is practiced in many schools throughout
17　the country. The National Spelling Bee,
18　however, is a much bigger setting and
19　showcases only the best spellers from all
20　parts of the nation. Students who appear
21　at the National Spelling Bee have already
22　won competitions at local and state levels.
23　Winning the competition nowadays requires
24　the ability to perform under intense pressure
25　against very talented students in front
26　of a large audience. A student who wins
27　the event in the twenty-first century will
28　experience a much different challenge than
29　the first winner, Frank Neuhauser, did in
30　1925 when he defeated only nine other
31　competitors.

32　Clearly, the 90 years of the National
33　Spelling Bee's existence attests to the
34　importance of spelling in the English
35　language. However, struggles with spelling
36　English words goes back much more than
37　80 years. The captivating thing about
38　spelling correctly in English is that it is in
39　many ways without rules. English language
40　has a powerful capacity to absorb new
41　words from other languages and in doing so
42　make them "English" words. As a result of
43　this ability to borrow from other languages,
44　the sheer number of words in English is
45　much higher than any other language. Thus,
46　spelling in many other languages involves
47　fewer words, fewer rules, and fewer odd
48　exceptions to those rules. It turns out that a
49　spelling bee in most other languages would
50　be a waste of time. Why is that? Well,
51　without the myriad exceptions to common
52　vocabulary, there would be very few words
53　that everyone didn't already know.

Go on to the next page. ➡

13. The author mentions "other languages" in line 41 in order to point out that

    (A) English-language spelling bees are unnecessarily complex
    (B) one challenge in English-language spelling bees is the number of words that can be tested
    (C) spelling bees are at least 90 years old
    (D) words are harder to spell in English than in any other language

14. According to the passage, what is a major difference between the first National Spelling Bee and today's competition?

    (A) Spellers in the past did not expect the competition to grow so large.
    (B) The competition no longer focuses on only English words.
    (C) There are more competitors.
    (D) The words used today are significantly harder.

15. In line 51, the word "myriad" most nearly means

    (A) confusing
    (B) dangerous
    (C) linguistic
    (D) numerous

16. Which of the following can be inferred from the passage?

    (A) A competitor at the National Spelling Bee has already won at least one smaller spelling bee.
    (B) E.W. Scripps Company desires to eliminate poor spelling in America.
    (C) Frank Neuhauser would not do well in today's competition.
    (D) The competition has grown too large.

17. The author of the passage intends to

    (A) compare the presentation of the current National Spelling Bee with the structure in the past
    (B) contrast the English language with other languages
    (C) investigate the role that vocabulary plays in our lives
    (D) review the history and current form of the National Spelling Bee

18. The author's attitude toward winners of the National Spelling Bee is

    (A) admiring
    (B) critical
    (C) indifferent
    (D) questioning

Go on to the next page. ⟶

Line

1   The idea of black holes was developed
2 by Karl Schwarzschild in 1916. Since then,
3 many different scientists have added to the
4 theory of black holes in space. A black hole
5 is usually defined as a very dense celestial
6 body from which nothing, not even light,
7 can escape. But from what do black holes
8 originate?
9   A black hole begins as a star. A star
10 burns hydrogen, and this process, called
11 fusion, releases energy. The energy released
12 outward works against the star's own
13 gravity pulling inward and prevents the star
14 from collapsing. After millions of years
15 of burning hydrogen, the star eventually
16 runs out of fuel. At this point, the star's
17 own gravity and weight cause it to start
18 contracting.
19   If the star is small and not very heavy it
20 will shrink just a little and become a white
21 dwarf when it runs out of fuel. White dwarf
22 stars do not emit much energy, so they are
23 usually not visible without a telescope.

24   If the star is bigger and heavier, it will
25 collapse very quickly in an implosion. If the
26 matter that remains is not much heavier than
27 our sun, it will eventually become a very
28 dense neutron star. However, if the matter
29 that remains is more than 1.7 times the mass
30 of our sun, there will not be enough outward
31 pressure to resist the force of gravity, and
32 the collapse will continue. The result is a
33 black hole.
34   The black hole will have a boundary
35 around it called the horizon. Light and
36 matter can pass over this boundary to enter,
37 but they cannot pass back out again—this is
38 why the hole appears black. The gravity and
39 density of the black hole prevent anything
40 from escaping.
41   Scientists are still adding to the black
42 hole theory. They think they may have
43 found black holes in several different
44 galaxies, and as they learn more about them,
45 scientists will be able to understand more
46 about how black holes are formed and what
47 happens as the holes change.

Go on to the next page. ➡

19. The purpose of the question in the first paragraph is to

   (A) illustrate how little we know about black holes
   (B) indicate the source of the facts quoted in the passage
   (C) interest the reader in the topic of the passage
   (D) set a goal for independent research

20. According to the passage, which of the following causes a collapsing star to become a neutron star?

   (A) Mass greater than 1.7 times that of our sun
   (B) Mass less than 1.7 times that of our sun
   (C) Remaining fuel that can be used in fusion
   (D) Slow, brief shrinkage process

21. The passage suggests that if we were to send a satellite to the horizon of a black hole, it would probably

   (A) begin spinning uncontrollably and fly apart
   (B) be immediately repelled from the black hole
   (C) be pulled into the black hole and not come back out
   (D) enter, then immediately exit, the black hole

22. According to the passage, which of the following is an effect of the process of fusion?

   (A) The star does not immediately collapse.
   (B) The star generates hydrogen.
   (C) The star survives millions of years longer than average.
   (D) The white dwarf fails to produce light.

23. Black holes appear black because

   (A) only a little energy escapes them
   (B) only one galaxy contains them
   (C) they are extraordinarily large
   (D) they do not eject light they have absorbed

24. Which of the following best describes the organization of the passage?

   (A) It discusses the biggest, heaviest celestial bodies before moving on to the smaller, lighter ones.
   (B) It introduces the topic and then narrates chronologically the process by which stars become black holes.
   (C) It uses a personal story to introduce the topic, then compares and contrasts black holes.
   (D) It uses the example of one specific black hole in order to generalize.

Go on to the next page. ➞

Questions 25–30

Line

1   The midterm elections of 2014 had
2 the lowest voter turnout of any American
3 election cycle since World War II, with only
4 36.4 percent of the eligible voting public
5 casting a ballot. What is most disturbing
6 about this number is that it was less than
7 100 years ago that 200 women marched on
8 the White House, incurring public scorn,
9 arrest, and even torture, to secure the vote
10 for half the American public.
11   Women's Suffrage, the movement
12 dedicated to securing women's right to
13 vote in the United States, began in earnest
14 in the 1840s. Several Women's Rights
15 Conventions were held throughout the 19th
16 century, beginning with the Seneca Falls
17 Convention of 1848, during which attendees
18 officially passed a resolution in favor of
19 Women's Suffrage. Over the next 70 years,
20 many brave women fought for the cause of
21 basic gender equality.
22   This fight came to a head in 1917,
23 when members of the National Women's
24 Party, led by Alice Paul, picketed outside
25 the White House in order to influence
26 President Wilson and Congress to pass
27 an amendment to the United States
28 Constitution that would enfranchise women
29 and guarantee their voting rights. This
30 was the first time in the history of the
31 United States that the White House was

32 picketed, and it was done so in an orderly
33 and peaceful fashion. After months of
34 nonviolent protest, police arrested over 200
35 women for blocking a public sidewalk in
36 July 1917.
37   Paul and many of her followers
38 underwent a hunger strike during their
39 incarceration to protest the deplorable
40 conditions of the prison, which resulted
41 in many women being force-fed and Paul
42 herself being moved to the psychiatric
43 ward of the hospital. The rest were sent
44 to the Occoquan Workhouse. It was at
45 this workhouse that the most terrible and
46 significant event of the Women's Suffrage
47 movement would occur. Dubbed the "Night
48 of Terror," 44 guards armed with clubs
49 attacked 33 women protesters as they
50 returned to the house. They were brutally
51 beaten, choked, and one was stabbed to
52 death. These events infuriated the nation
53 when they were exposed, and within two
54 weeks a judge had ordered the prisoners
55 released and cleared of all charges.
56   Due to the widespread gain of support
57 these women earned through their peaceful
58 protest and physical endurance, as well as
59 the work of countless men and women of
60 the previous 70 years, the 19th Amendment
61 was added to the Constitution three years
62 later, on August 20, 1920.

Go on to the next page. ➞

25. The main purpose of the passage is to

    (A) portray Alice Paul as an integral figure of the Women's Suffrage movement
    (B) attribute the adoption of the 19th Amendment solely to the Night of Terror
    (C) describe the actions taken by part of the American public to secure equal voting rights
    (D) demonstrate the terrible actions of guards against women's rights protestors

26. The word "exposed" as used in line 53 most closely means

    (A) unprotected
    (B) bare
    (C) revealed
    (D) buried

27. Which of the following best expresses the author's attitude toward the percentage of voter turnout mentioned in the first paragraph?

    (A) Shock
    (B) Reassurance
    (C) Pessimism
    (D) Terror

28. According to the author, the most probable legacy of the Night of Terror is

    (A) President Wilson's pardon of the protestors
    (B) the imprisonment of the 44 guards who attacked the protesters
    (C) the desired delay of the 19th amendment for several years
    (D) the right to vote for women

29. Which of the following does the passage imply was a reason for the protestor's hunger strike?

    (A) They were attempting to improve the environment of their captivity.
    (B) They were resisting being force-fed at the prison.
    (C) They wanted to be able to use the sidewalk for peaceful protest.
    (D) They were unable to eat after being choked during the Night of Terror.

30. The author believes that the National Women's Party's tactics are best described as

    (A) calm but pointless
    (B) disorderly but successful
    (C) violent and immediate
    (D) nonviolent and effective

Go on to the next page. ⟶

Questions 31–36

Line

1   He is one of the greatest living
2 scientists of this age. In fact, he is perhaps
3 one of the greatest scientists of any age.
4 Yet he owes much of his success not to
5 mathematics or physics or any other science
6 but to a disease. He is Stephen Hawking.
7   Born in 1942, three hundred years after
8 the death of Galileo, Stephen Hawking
9 had an unimpressive start to his scholarly
10 pursuits. At his revered English primary
11 school, St. Albans, he was considered by
12 his teachers a good, but not exceptional,
13 student. It was not evident at the time that
14 he would become internationally acclaimed
15 as a leader in several scientific fields.
16 He continued this moderately successful
17 academic trend at University College in
18 Oxford. Again, his professors thought him
19 to be intelligent, but not extraordinary in
20 his efforts. Both his cleverness and lack
21 of diligence were noticed by some of his
22 instructors.
23   After graduating from Oxford, he
24 continued to Cambridge, another excellent
25 school. Clearly, Hawking was moving
26 forward into a good science career.
27 However, it was at this time that he
28 encountered a life-changing challenge. He
29 was diagnosed with a disease that affects
30 and damages the nervous system. That

31 meant that he was eventually going to lose
32 control of his muscles and spend his life in
33 a wheelchair. Surprisingly though, Hawking
34 credits this event with making his outlook
35 on life strong again. He claims that until
36 then, he was often bored by life. For a man
37 with such a powerful mind, that makes
38 sense. He was talented, but he saw little use
39 for his talent and felt no pressure to work
40 hard. His diagnosis and impending physical
41 problems forced him to start living life to
42 the fullest.
43   Most of Stephen Hawking's
44 contributions to science have come after
45 learning of his disease. His work in the
46 field of physics has influenced the greatest
47 scientists alive. If the technology ever
48 becomes possible, he plans a trip into
49 space with the help of influential friends.
50 Though he now moves only with a special
51 wheelchair and speaks only with the help
52 of a computerized speech enhancer, he still
53 has the ability to contribute to the world. He
54 credits his disease with forcing him to face
55 the limited time available in one lifetime.
56 Stephen Hawking has made a crippling
57 disease the source of one of the greatest
58 scientific careers the world has known.
59 Through his misfortune, he learned to reach
60 his greatest potential.

Go on to the next page. ➞

31. The author's tone is best described as

    (A) nostalgic
    (B) admiring
    (C) pitying
    (D) scornful

32. The purpose of the last line of the first paragraph ("He is Stephen Hawking") is to

    (A) reveal an answer to a riddle
    (B) specify a subject who has already been introduced
    (C) answer a question the author asked earlier
    (D) name the greatest living scientist

33. Which of the following describes Stephen Hawking's attitude toward his disease?

    (A) Actively nonchalant
    (B) Bitterly irate
    (C) Ironically appreciative
    (D) Unreservedly giddy

34. According to the second paragraph, Stephen Hawking was seen by some as

    (A) often disrespectful
    (B) particularly brilliant
    (C) somewhat lazy
    (D) uniquely energetic

35. The passage does all of the following EXCEPT

    (A) demonstrate a connection between Stephen Hawking's disease and his success as a physicist
    (B) describe a goal Hawking hopes to achieve
    (C) note particular theories developed by Hawking
    (D) set forth educational institutions attended by Hawking

36. The passage can best be described as focusing primarily on

    (A) biographical details
    (B) medical diagnoses
    (C) scientific discoveries
    (D) technological advancements

STOP. If there is time, you may check your work in this section only.

Section 4
Mathematics Achievement

47 Questions	Time: 40 Minutes

Each question is followed by four suggested answers. Read each question and then decide which one of the four suggested answers is best.

Find the row of spaces on your answer document that has the same number as the question. In this row, mark the space having the same letter as the answer you have chosen. You may write in your test booklet.

SAMPLE QUESTION:

Sample Answer

Ⓐ ● Ⓒ Ⓓ

What is the perimeter of an isosceles triangle with two sides of 4 cm and one side of 6 cm?

(A) 10 cm
(B) 14 cm
(C) 16 cm
(D) 24 cm

The correct answer is 14 cm, so circle B is darkened.

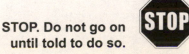

STOP. Do not go on
until told to do so.

NO TEST MATERIAL ON THIS PAGE

1. Which of the following pairs of numbers are the two different prime factors of 36 ?

   (A) 2 and 3
   (B) 3 and 4
   (C) 3 and 12
   (D) 4 and 9

2. For what nonzero value of x will the expression $\dfrac{x-3}{4x}$ be equal to 0 ?

   (A) −3
   (B) −2
   (C)   1
   (D)   3

3. Two positive whole numbers are in a ratio of 3 to 4. If the smaller of the two numbers is 9, what is the average of the two numbers?

   (A)   4
   (B) 10
   (C) 10.5
   (D) 12

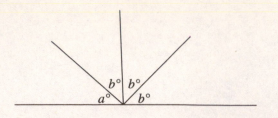

4. The four angles in the figure above share a common vertex on a straight line. What is the value of b when a equals 42°?

   (A) 38°
   (B) 40°
   (C) 42°
   (D) 46°

5. What is 85% of 50 ?

   (A) 150.75
   (B) 135
   (C)   42.5
   (D)   39

6. A set of three positive integers has a sum of 11 and a product of 36. If the smallest of the three numbers is 2, what is the largest?

   (A) 2
   (B) 4
   (C) 6
   (D) 9

Go on to the next page. ➞

7. What is two-thirds of one-half?

   (A) $\frac{1}{3}$

   (B) $\frac{7}{6}$

   (C) $\frac{1}{2}$

   (D) $\frac{2}{3}$

8. If the distance around an oval-shaped track is 400 meters, how many laps does a runner have to run to cover a distance of 4 kilometers?
   (1 kilometer = 1,000 meters)

   (A)   4
   (B)   10
   (C)   15
   (D) 1,000

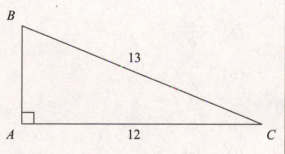

9. In triangle *ABC* shown above, the length of side *AB* is

   (A)   5
   (B)   7
   (C)   11
   (D)   14

10. Find the value of $\dfrac{2.7 \times 10^7}{3.0 \times 10^{-3}}$

    (A) 9.0×10^{10}
    (B) 9.0×10^{9}
    (C) 9.0×10^{4}
    (D) 9.0×10^{3}

11. MegaMusic decides to decrease the price of a digital song from $1.60 to $1.20. The percent decrease for this digital song is

    (A) 20%
    (B) 25%
    (C) $33\frac{1}{3}\%$
    (D) 40%

12. There are *x* students in Mrs. Sproul's class, 4 fewer than twice as many as are in Mrs. Puccio's class. If there are *y* students in Mrs. Puccio's class, then what is the value of *y* in terms of *x* ?

    (A) $\frac{x}{2} + 2$

    (B) $2x + 4$

    (C) $2x - 4$

    (D) $\frac{x}{2} - 4$

Go on to the next page. ⟶

Questions 13–14 refer to the following definition.

For all real numbers x,

$\#x = x^2$ if x is negative;
$\#x = 2x$ if x is positive.

13. $\#(-6) - \#(6) =$

(A) −24
(B)   16
(C)   24
(D)   30

14. What is the value of $\#[\#x - \#y]$ when $x = 3$ and $y = -4$?

(A) −10
(B)   12
(C)   32
(D)   100

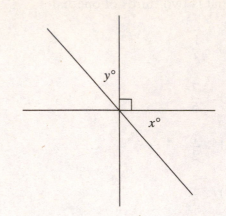

15. In the figure above, what is the value of x in terms of y ?

(A) y
(B) $90 - y$
(C) $90 + y$
(D) $180 - y$

16. $\dfrac{4a^4b^6c^3}{2a^3b^5c^2} =$

(A) $\dfrac{2ac}{b}$

(B) $\dfrac{ac}{b}$

(C) $\dfrac{2b}{c}$

(D) $2abc$

Go on to the next page. ➡

17. In Mr. Johanessen's class, $\frac{1}{4}$ of the students failed the final exam. Of the remaining students in the class, $\frac{1}{3}$ scored an A. What fraction of the whole class passed the test but scored below an A?

(A) $\frac{1}{4}$

(B) $\frac{5}{12}$

(C) $\frac{1}{2}$

(D) $\frac{7}{12}$

18. When buying new clothes for school, Rena spends $20 more than Karen and $50 more than Lynn does. If Rena spends r dollars, then what is the cost of all three of their purchases in terms of r ?

(A) $r + 70$

(B) $\frac{r + 70}{3}$

(C) $3r - 70$

(D) $r + 210$

19. In a group of 100 children, there are 34 more girls than there are boys. How many boys are in the group?

(A) 33
(B) 37
(C) 67
(D) 68

20. Samantha made a chart of her students' favorite types of books.

FAVORITE TYPE OF BOOK

Type of Book	Number of Students
Mystery	8
Fantasy	20
Sci-Fi	10
Other	2

A circle graph is made using the data. What is the central angle of the portion of the graph representing Sci-Fi?

(A) 10°
(B) 25°
(C) 45°
(D) 90°

Go on to the next page. ➡

21. At Nicholas's Computer World, computers usually sold for $1,500 are now being sold for $1,200. What fraction of the original price is the new price?

    (A) $\dfrac{1}{10}$

    (B) $\dfrac{1}{5}$

    (C) $\dfrac{3}{4}$

    (D) $\dfrac{4}{5}$

22. If $\dfrac{3}{x} = \dfrac{y}{4}$, then

    (A) $xy = 12$

    (B) $3y = 4x$

    (C) $\dfrac{x}{y} = \dfrac{4}{3}$

    (D) $3x = 4y$

23. The ratio of boys to girls at Delaware Township School is 3 to 2. If there is a total of 600 students at the school, how many are girls?

    (A) 120
    (B) 240
    (C) 360
    (D) 400

24. 150% of 40 is

    (A) 30
    (B) 40
    (C) 50
    (D) 60

25. Jane studied for her math exam for 4 hours last night. If she studied $\dfrac{3}{4}$ as long for her English exam, how many hours did she study all together?

    (A) 3

    (B) $4\dfrac{3}{4}$

    (C) 6

    (D) 7

26. $\dfrac{0.966}{0.42} =$

    (A) 0.23
    (B) 2.3
    (C) 23
    (D) 230

Go on to the next page. ➡

27. Nicole was able to type 35 words per minute. If she increased her speed to 42 words per minute, what was the percent increase in her typing speed?

    (A) $16\frac{2}{3}\%$

    (B) 20%

    (C) 70%

    (D) 71%

28. The first term in a series of numbers is 50. Each subsequent term is one-half the term before it if the term is even, or one-half rounded up to the next whole number if the term is odd. What is the third term in this sequence?

    (A) 13
    (B) 24
    (C) 30
    (D) 40

29. Sophia recorded the number of siblings each student in her class has in the table below.

    SIBLINGS OF EACH STUDENT

Number of Siblings	Number of Students with that Number of Siblings
0	6
1	10
2	8
3	6
4	1
5	1

    What is the mode of the data?

    (A) 1
    (B) 2
    (C) 6
    (D) 10

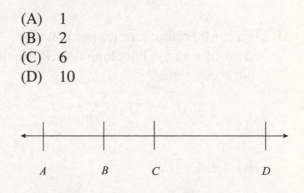

30. On the number line shown above, if segment BD has a length of 18, segment AB has a length of 5, and segment CD has a length of 12, then segment AC has a length of

    (A) 6
    (B) 11
    (C) 17
    (D) 23

Go on to the next page. ➡

31. The decimal representation of $2 + 40 + \frac{1}{100}$ is

    (A) 24.1
    (B) 24.01
    (C) 42.1
    (D) 42.01

32. What is the least possible integer divisible by 2, 3, 4, and 5 ?

    (A) 30
    (B) 40
    (C) 60
    (D) 90

33. If a car travels at x miles per hour, in terms of x and y, how long does it take it to travel y miles?

    (A) $\dfrac{2x}{y}$

    (B) xy

    (C) $\dfrac{y}{x}$

    (D) $\dfrac{x}{y}$

34. Triangles ABC and PQR are similar. The length of $\overline{BC}$ is 4 and the length of $\overline{QR}$ is 12. If the area of ABC is 6, what is the area of PQR?

    (A) 54
    (B) 24
    (C) 18
    (D) 15

35. James buys one halibut steak and two salmon steaks for $30.00. Dave buys two halibut steaks and four salmon steaks for $60.00. If halibut steaks cost x dollars each and salmon steaks cost y dollars each, what is the value of x ?

    (A) $5.00
    (B) $8.00
    (C) $10.00
    (D) It cannot be determined from the information given.

Question 36 refers to the following definition.

For all positive integer values of x,

$(x) = \frac{1}{2}x$ if x is even;

$(x) = 2x$ if x is odd.

36. $(1 + 5) =$

    (A) 2
    (B) 3
    (C) 4
    (D) 6

37. Which of the following equals $2(4z + 1)$?

    (A) $2z + \dfrac{1}{2}$

    (B) $2z + 1$

    (C) $4z + 2$

    (D) $8z + 2$

Go on to the next page. →

38. The stem-and-leaf plot shown represents the length, in minutes, of movies that Janet watched over the summer.

Stem	Leaf
10	8 9
11	1 2 2 5 5 6 7
12	0 3 4 8
13	2 4 6 6 7 7 9
14	2 3 3 8 9 9
15	7

What is the median length, in minutes, of the movies Janet watched?

(A) 130
(B) 132
(C) 133
(D) 136

39. Zoo A has 3 monkeys. Zoo B has 8 monkeys. Zoo C has 16 monkeys. What is the average number of monkeys at the three zoos?

(A) 3
(B) 7
(C) 9
(D) 27

40. A steak costs $4 more than a hamburger, and a hamburger costs $4 more than a grilled cheese sandwich. If six grilled cheese sandwiches cost $2x$ dollars, how much will 4 steaks and 2 hamburgers cost?

(A) $2x + 40$
(B) $2x + 48$
(C) $6x + 34$
(D) $12x + 40$

41. What is the solution set to the inequality $|3 - 2x| > 9$?

(A) $-3 < x < 6$
(B) $-6 < x < 3$
(C) $x < -3$ or $x > 6$
(D) $x < -6$ or $x > 3$

42. $100xy$ is what percent of xy ?

(A)   10
(B)   100
(C)   1,000
(D) 10,000

43. If Matt's home is four miles from school and Laura's home is eight miles from school, then the distance from Matt's home to Laura's home is

(A) 4 miles
(B) 8 miles
(C) 12 miles
(D) It cannot be determined from the information given.

44. Two partners divide a profit of $2,000 so that the difference between the two amounts is half of their average. What is the ratio of the larger to the smaller amount?

(A) 6:1
(B) 5:3
(C) 4:1
(D) 2:1

Go on to the next page. ➡

45. What is the total value, in cents, of j coins worth 10 cents each and $j + 5$ coins worth 25 cents each?

   (A) $35j + 125$
   (B) $35j + 5$
   (C) $10j + 130$
   (D) $2j + 5$

46. A box of coins has 6 pennies, 3 nickels, 4 dimes, and 5 quarters. If two coins are selected at random, what is the probability that the first coin is a penny and the second coin is a quarter?

   (A) $\dfrac{11}{18}$

   (B) $\dfrac{17}{18}$

   (C) $\dfrac{6}{18} \times \dfrac{5}{18}$

   (D) $\dfrac{6}{18} \times \dfrac{5}{17}$

47. The formula for the volume of a cone is $\dfrac{1}{3}\pi r^2 h$, where r is the radius of the circular base and h is the height of the cone.

   What is the radius of a cone with a volume of 12π and a height of 4 ?

   (A) 3
   (B) 4
   (C) 8
   (D) 9

STOP. If there is time, you may check your work in this section only.

Essay

You will have 30 minutes to plan and write an essay on the topic printed on the other side of this page. **Do not write on another topic. An essay on another topic is not acceptable.**

The essay is designed to give you an opportunity to show how well you can write. You should try to express your thoughts clearly. How well you write is much more important than how much you write, but you need to say enough for a reader to understand what you mean.

You will probably want to write more than a short paragraph. You should also be aware that a copy of your essay will be sent to each school that will be receiving your test results. You are to write only in the appropriate section of the answer sheet. Please write or print so that your writing may be read by someone who is not familiar with your handwriting.

You may make notes and plan your essay on the reverse side of the page. Allow enough time to copy the final form on to your answer sheet. You must copy the essay topic onto your answer sheet, on page 3, in the box provided.

Please remember to write only the final draft of the essay on pages 3 and 4 of your answer sheet and to write it in blue or black pen. Again, you may use cursive writing or you may print. Only pages 3 and 4 will be sent to the schools.

Directions continue on next page.

REMINDER: Please write this essay topic on the first few lines of page 3 of your answer sheet.

Essay Topic

If you could change one thing about your country, what would you change and why?

- Only write on this essay question
- Only pages 3 and 4 will be sent to the schools
- Only write in blue or black pen

NOTES

_____

_____

_____

_____

_____

_____

_____

_____

_____

_____

_____

Chapter 18
Upper Level ISEE
Practice Test:
Answers and
Explanations

ANSWER KEY

ISEE UL Verbal 1

1. D	5. A	9. D	13. C	17. B	21. A	25. A	29. C	33. A	37. A
2. C	6. B	10. B	14. B	18. A	22. A	26. D	30. B	34. C	38. A
3. D	7. B	11. C	15. D	19. B	23. D	27. A	31. D	35. C	39. A
4. C	8. D	12. B	16. B	20. B	24. A	28. A	32. B	36. C	40. A

ISEE UL Quantitative 2

1. C	5. B	9. C	13. A	17. D	21. C	25. B	29. C	33. A	37. C
2. C	6. D	10. B	14. B	18. C	22. B	26. D	30. B	34. C	
3. D	7. A	11. C	15. A	19. D	23. C	27. A	31. B	35. B	
4. D	8. B	12. D	16. A	20. C	24. D	28. C	32. A	36. B	

ISEE UL Reading 3

1. D	5. D	9. D	13. B	17. D	21. C	25. C	29. A	33. C
2. A	6. D	10. C	14. C	18. A	22. A	26. C	30. D	34. C
3. C	7. C	11. C	15. D	19. C	23. D	27. C	31. B	35. C
4. D	8. C	12. D	16. A	20. B	24. B	28. D	32. B	36. A

ISEE UL Math 4

1. A	6. C	11. B	16. D	21. D	26. B	31. D	36. B	41. C	46. D
2. D	7. A	12. A	17. C	22. A	27. B	32. C	37. D	42. D	47. A
3. C	8. B	13. C	18. C	23. B	28. A	33. C	38. B	43. D	
4. D	9. A	14. D	19. A	24. D	29. A	34. A	39. C	44. B	
5. C	10. B	15. B	20. D	25. D	30. B	35. D	40. A	45. A	

EXPLANATIONS

Section 1 Verbal

1. **D** Grave is defined as "serious" or "sober." An example phrase is "a grave silence," which would be a serious or sober silence. This makes (D) solemn the correct answer choice.

2. **C** To foment is defined as "to foster" or "to promote." An example phrase is to "foment trouble," which would be to promote or cause trouble. This makes (C) instigate the correct answer choice.

3. **D** Inarticulate is the opposite of articulate. Articulate can be defined as well expressed or clearly spoken. Since inarticulate is the opposite of articulate, it is defined as unclear, or not well understood or expressed. None of the first three choices, creative, friendly, or overly sensitive, are related to being well spoken or not. Choices (A), (B), and (C) can be eliminated. This makes (D) tongue-tied the best answer.

4. **C** One clue to finding the definition of ameliorate is the root "amo," which is Latin for love. In Spanish this is "amor" and in French it is "amore." This root establishes the correct word will be a positive word, which means that (B) hinder and (D) restrain can be eliminated. Ameliorate is defined as making something better, which makes (C) improve the correct answer.

5. **A** Thesis is another word for theory. A theory is best defined as an idea or belief, which best matches (A). One common use of the word "thesis" is to refer to the overarching piece of written work produced in a degree program, which might make (B), (C), or (D) appear to be likely answer choices. However, a written thesis is called a thesis because its aim is to explain or support the idea behind it, matching the true definition of the word thesis. Choice (A) is the correct answer.

6. **B** To debunk is defined as "to disprove." An example phrase is to "debunk a popular theory," which would be to disprove a popular theory. This makes (B) discredit the correct answer choice.

7. **B** Disdain contains the root word "dis," which means "apart," "asunder," "away," or "having a negative force." Since this is a negative root the answer choice should be negative as well, which eliminates (C) find and (D) hope. Since disdain is defined as a lack of respect, (B) contempt is the correct answer.

8. **D** Reticent is defined as withdrawn or introverted. An example phrase is "she was reticent about giving her answer aloud in class." This makes (D) reserved the best answer.

9. **D** Prevalent is defined as widespread. An example phrase would be "acronyms have become prevalent in text message and email communications." This makes (D) predominant the correct answer.

10. **B** Satiate comes from the root "sat" or "satis," which means "to satisfy" or "enough." Other words with this root include satisfaction, satisfactory, and satiable. All of these words have definitions related to being satisfied or having enough. Satiate is defined as being full, having a desire or appetite fulfilled. This makes (B) fill the correct answer.

11. **C** Candid is defined as truthful or straightforward. An example phrase would be "to speak candidly," which would be to speak truthfully. This makes (C) frank the correct answer.

12. **B** Emulate is related to the similar sounding word imitate. Emulate is defined as attempting to copy or imitate another's actions. This makes (B) imitate the correct answer.

13. **C** Taint is defined as to contaminate or pollute. An example phrase would be "the case involved tainted evidence, which resulted in a mistrial." This makes (C) infect the correct answer.

14. **B** Enigma is defined as a puzzle or a mystery. An example phrase would be "the unsolved disappearance of Amelia Earhart is one of the great enigmas of our time." This makes (B) mystery the correct answer.

15. **D** Detrimental is defined as harmful or resulting in a loss. It is the adjective form of the noun detriment, which is defined as a loss or harm. Loss or harm best matches (D) injurious, which is the correct answer.

16. **B** Meticulous is defined as overly attentive to detail, exact, or precise. An example phrase would be "the doctor was meticulous, she ran every test and examined her patient inch by inch." This makes (B) finicky the correct answer.

17. **B** Juxtapose comes from the Latin root juxta, which mean "next to." To juxtapose is defined as to place two items close to one another, in order to establish a contrast between them. The best match for this definition is (B) place side by side, which is the correct answer.

18. **A** Congenial has two main roots: con and gen. Con means with; examples of words with this root and meaning are connect, contract, congregate. Gen means race or kind of; in other words "relation." Examples of words with this root is genealogy, genetics, genes. Congenial is defined as something or someone pleasant due to being well-suited to a certain situation. This best matches answer (A) friendly, the correct answer.

19. **B** To mitigate is defined as to soften. An example phrase would be "the seriousness of Amy's injuries were mitigated by the immediate medical attention she received." This makes (B) ease the correct answer.

20. **B** Elusive is directly related to the word elude, which means to avoid or escape. This makes (B) slippery the correct answer.

21. **A** Pay attention to the clues in the sentence. The second half of the sentence indicates that Jane is torn between two feelings or sides, so the missing word should mean the same thing as torn. Choice (A),

ambivalent, means to have conflicted feelings, which matches the word you are looking for. Choice (B), apathetic, means to not care at all, so it can be eliminated. Neither happy nor irritated mean torn, so (C) and (D) can be eliminated as well. Choice (A) is the correct answer.

22. **A**   Pay attention to the clues in the sentence. The sentence states that M. Carey Thomas was like Susan B. Anthony, the famous women's rights activist. This indicates that Thomas also supported women's rights, and so the missing word must mean "supported." Choice (A), championed, is a synonym for supported. Choice (B) means to desecrate or vandalize; eliminate it. Neither (C) nor (D) mean supported, so they can be eliminated as well. Choice (A) is the correct answer.

23. **D**   Pay attention to the clues in the sentence. The second half of the sentence states that different cultures have different ideas about how people should be treated. This indicates that morality is not the same everywhere, so the missing word must mean not the same or not standardized. Choice (A), debatable, is the opposite meaning of the blank, so it can be eliminated. Neither (B) nor (C) mean not related or not standardized, so they can be eliminated as well. Only (D), universal, matches the meaning of the blank.

24. **A**   Pay attention to the clues in the sentence and the direction words. The sentence starts with although, and ends with the fact that the student did not study at all. This indicates that the opposite happened earlier in the sentence: Ms. Sanchez warned or advised the student that he should study. Since neither (B), (C), nor (D) mean "advised" or "warned," the only possible answer is (A).

25. **A**   Pay attention to the clues in the sentence. The sentence tells you that Thomas Jefferson was skilled at many things. This indicates that Jefferson was a man of many talents, so the missing word must mean many. The only choice that matches this answer choice is (A), abundant.

26. **D**   Pay attention to the clues in the sentence. The second part of the sentence states that Monica was moved to speak up. This indicates that Monica could no longer remain silent or quiet. Neither (A), (B), nor (C) mean silent or quiet, which makes (D) the only possible answer choice.

27. **A**   Pay attention to the clues in the sentence. The second part of the sentence states that *Little Women* was based on Louisa May Alcott's own life. This indicates that the missing word will mean personal. While the other three answer choices may seem related to a writing style or a novel, only (A), autobiographical, matches personal.

28. **A**   Pay attention to the clues in the sentence and the direction words. The sentence starts with "Though his lectures could be monotonous... ." "Though" is an opposite direction word, so the missing word will mean the opposite of monotonous. Look for a word that means interesting or captivating. Choice (A), amiable, matches this meaning. Choice (B) means religious or reverential, so it can be eliminated. Choices (C) and (D) are synonymous with boring or dull; eliminate those as well. Choice (A) is the correct answer.

29. C Pay attention to the clues in the sentence. The second part of the sentence states "…just as Craig had thought, he had two pop quizzes." Since having pop quizzes is generally considered a negative occurrence, the missing word most likely means he "felt" or had "known" the day would go badly right from the start. The only answer choice that is related to feeling or knowing how things would turn out is (C), a premonition.

30. B Pay attention to the clues in the sentence. The first part of the sentence says "Far from shedding light on the mystery," and the second part says Jason's response "left people unsure." This indicates that Jason's response was unclear, so the missing word must match that meaning. Choice (A), impartial, means to be unbiased, which does not match unclear. Eliminate it. Choice (B), opaque, means to be unclear or not transparent. Choice (C), risky, means to have the possibility of danger, which does not match unclear and so can be eliminated. Choice (D), systematic, means to be thorough or methodical, which is also incorrect. Choice (B) is the correct answer.

31. D On two-blank sentence completions, always start with one blank to work with first and eliminate answer choices based on that. The first blank matches the word "talented" in the sentence, so look for a word that means "talented" or "skilled." Neither "faithful" in (A) nor "insulting" in (B) match this meaning, so both choices should be completely eliminated. The rest of the sentence says that although Marie was talented, she didn't know how to promote herself. This indicates that her talents were overlooked, so the second word should match that meaning. Between (C) and (D), only "ignored" in (D) matches that meaning. Choice (D) is the correct answer.

32. B Pay attention to the clues in the sentence and the direction words. The first part of the sentence states that "Although she was the daughter of wealthy slaveholder… ." Since "although" is an opposite direction word, the remainder of the sentence most likely explains that Angelina Grimke was against slavery. If you start with the first word, the answer should match "against." Since (A) and (D) are the opposite of "against," those choices can be eliminated. The second blank most likely means "fought" or "dedicated," since she would have been for abolition. Only "dedicated" in (B) matches this meaning, making it the best answer choice.

33. A On two-blank sentence completions, always start with one blank to work with first and eliminate answer choices based on that. The second part of the sentence says that a great deal of sugar is required when cooking with rhubarb, indicating that it takes sugar to make the rhubarb taste "good" or "edible" for the second blank. Since neither fattening, sickening, nor sticky match this meaning, (A) is most likely the correct answer. However, you should still check the other blank. Since the second part of the sentence discusses how much sugar is needed when cooking rhubarb, rhubarb must be the opposite of sweet. Check (A)'s first word to make sure it means the opposite of sweet. Since "bitter" is the opposite of sweet (A) is the correct answer.

34. C On two-blank sentence completions, always start with one blank to work with first and eliminate answer choices based on that. The first half of the sentence states that Martha would see the bright side of any situation, so the missing blank would mean she is naturally "happy" or "cheerful."

Neither (B) nor (D) match this meaning, so those answer choices can be eliminated. The remainder of the sentence begins with the opposite direction word "but" and states that Jack was always waiting for something bad to happen. This indicates that the second blank means "negative" or "depressed." Choice (A) is the opposite meaning of negative, so it can be eliminated. Only (C) works for both blanks.

35. **C**   On two-blank sentence completions, always start with one blank to work with first and eliminate answer choices based on that. The first half of the sentence says that Edgar was not telling the truth, indicating that the missing word means "lies" or "falsehoods." Only (C) and (D) match this meaning, eliminating (A) and (B). The second part of the sentence indicates that Edgar's lies encouraged the crowd to reject Edgar's competitor, so the second blank must match "encouraged." Between "incited" and "permitted," "incited" is the best match. Choice (C) is the correct answer.

36. **C**   On two-blank sentence completions, always start with one blank to work with first and eliminate answer choices based on that. The second part of the sentence refers to the text as being "a mere 100 pages." The word "mere" indicates that the missing word must mean "short." Choices (A), (B), and (C) all match this meaning. "Banal" means lacking depth and is not related to length, and so (D) can be eliminated. The first part of the sentence discusses the critics praise for the author's use of words, so the first blank must mean something positive. Hackneyed means trite or overused, and improper means out of the norm or standard, neither of which are positive meanings. The only positive answer is (C), precise. Choice (C) is the correct answer.

37. **A**   On two-blank sentence completions, always start with one blank to work with first and eliminate answer choices based on that. The sentence starts by saying Erica's mother could not do something, followed by the word "why." Usually when someone does not know "why" something is happening or has happened, it means they do not understand. Look for the answer choices that match "understand" for the first word. Only (A) and (D) match; eliminate (B) and (C). The entire sentence is saying that Erica's mother couldn't understand why she would study the culture of thirteenth century French winemakers. Compare (A) and (D) to see which one makes the most sense in the context of the sentence. If this were an interesting subject, would Erica's mother not be able to understand why she wanted to study it? No; eliminate (D). The fact that the subject is very obscure, or esoteric, does make it more difficult to understand as a subject choice. Choice (A) is the correct answer.

38. **A**   On two-blank sentence completions, always start with one blank to work with first and eliminate answer choices based on that. The first part of the sentence states that Ernie was still excited about the race despite the storm. The missing word most likely means that the storm did not diminish or reduce Ernie's excitement. Only (A) and (C) match this meaning; eliminate (B) and (D) completely. Since Ernie remained excited about the race, he was not afraid of running it in bad weather. The second blank must mean he had no concerns or reservations about running in the storm. Since inclination is the opposite of concern or reservation, (C) cannot be correct. Choice (A) is the correct answer.

39.   A   On two-blank sentence completions, always start with one blank to work with first and eliminate answer choices based on that. The entire sentence is discussing how stingy Mr. Sanford is, and says "even a restaurant meal" was an excess. What kind of excess? Most likely an unnecessary or a wasteful expense. The only word in the answer choices that matches this meaning is (A), gratuitous. Ideally, you should check to make sure that the first word in (A) works as well. The sentence makes it clear that Mr. Sanford doesn't like to spend money, or is stingy. Parsimonious does mean stingy, so (A) is the correct answer. However, if you were unsure of what parsimonious meant you should feel confident in (A) due to process of elimination.

40.   A   Pay attention to clues and direction words in the sentence. The second part of the sentence starts with "even though," an opposite direction phrase. It continues to state that her love of art was far from superficial. Since the opposite direction phrase comes in front of this description, the missing second word must mean a superficial love of art. Neither mentor, performer, nor adversary match that meaning, and so (B), (C), and (D) can be eliminated. This leaves (A) as the most likely answer based on process of elimination. The first word describes how Margie felt about being told she has a superficial love of art, which is not true, so that word will most likely mean "unhappiness" or "frustration." Chagrin matches this meaning, making (A) the correct answer.

Section 2 Quantitative Reasoning

1.   C   The greatest number will be the one closest to 1. Choice (A) is equivalent to $\frac{1}{100}$, (B) is equivalent to $\frac{99}{10,000}$, (C) is equivalent to $\frac{19}{100}$, and (D) is equivalent to $\frac{199}{10,000}$. Thus, the correct answer is (C) since it is the closest to 1.

2.   C   Pay careful attention to the word *NOT*. Choice (A) is the product of two prime numbers: 3 and 11. Choice (B) is the product of two prime numbers: 5 and 7. Choice (D) is the product of two prime numbers: 7 and 13. Choice (C) is the product of 5 and 9, 3 and 15, or 1 and 45. Since 45 is not the product of 2 prime numbers, the correct answer is (C).

3.   D   Since the values of x, y, and z are not given, plug in. Let $x = 2$, $y = 4$, and $z = 6$. The difference between x and z is 4 since $z - x = 6 - 2 = 4$. The correct answer is (D).

4.   D   Use the chart to determine each amount. To find percent change, use the formula: % change = $\frac{\text{difference}}{\text{original}} \times 100$. For (A), the difference of the two prices is $30, so the percent discount is $\frac{120 - 90}{120} \times 100 = \frac{30}{120} \times 100 = 25$. For (B), the difference of the two prices is $70, so the percent discount is $\frac{250 - 180}{250} \times 100 = \frac{70}{250} \times 100 = 28$. For (C), the difference of the two prices is $20, so the percent discount is $\frac{60 - 40}{60} \times 100 = \frac{20}{60} \times 100 \approx 33$. For (D), the difference of the two

prices is \$20, so the percent discount is $\dfrac{40-20}{40} \times 100 = \dfrac{20}{40} \times 100 = 50$. Since 50% is the greatest

discount, the correct answer is (D).

5. **B** Use the chart to determine each amount. The buyer will save \$30 on dresses, \$70 on coats, \$20 on shoes, and \$20 on hats. Therefore, purchasing coats will save the buyer the most dollars, so the correct answer is (B).

6. **D** Since there are variables in the question and answers, plug in a value for b (Beth's age). If $b = 7$, then Amy is 10 years old and Jo is 15 years old. The correct answer will be the one that equals 15, so plug 7 in for b and check each answer choice. Choice (A) is $2(7) + 3 = 17$. Choice (B) is $2(7) - 3 = 11$. Choice (C) is $7 + 4 = 11$. Choice (D) is $7 + 8 = 15$. Since it is the only one that matches the target value, (D) is the correct answer.

7. **A** Since there are variables in the question, plug in values for x and y that will fit the restrictions of the problem. If $x = 9$, then $5 \overline{)9}^{\,1}$ with a remainder of 4. If $y = 6$, then $5 \overline{)6}^{\,1}$ with a remainder of 1. Plug in the values of x and y to get $x + y = 9 + 6 = 15$. 5 divides into 15 exactly three times (i.e. the remainder is 0), so the correct answer is (A).

8. **B** Since there are variables in the question and answers, plug in values for x, p, y, and q. If $x = 2$, then let $p = 6$. If $y = 5$, then let $q = 15$. Next, test these values in each answer choice to find the true statement. For (A), $pq = 6 \times 15 = 90$ and $xy = 2 \times 5 = 10$. 90 is not a factor of 10, so eliminate (A). In (B), $pq = 6 \times 15 = 90$ and $xy = 2 \times 5 = 10$. 90 is a multiple of 10, so keep (B). For (C), $p = 6$ and $xy = 2 \times 5 = 10$. 6 is not a factor of 10, so eliminate (C). In (D), $p = 6$ and $xy = 2 \times 5 = 10$. 6 is not a multiple of 10, so eliminate (D). Only (B) contains a true statement, so it is the correct answer.

9. **C** The range of x is given ($-3 \le x \le 2$), so test the highest and lowest values of x in the equation given to see what the maximum value of y is. If x = 2, then $3(2)^2 + 2 = 3(4) + 2 = 12 + 2 = 14$. Eliminate (A) because (B) contains a possible value of y that is higher than 2. If $x = -3$, then $3(-3)^2 + 2 = 3(9) + 2 = 27 + 2 = 29$. Eliminate (B) since (C) contains a greater value of y. There is not a value of x that will yield a higher value of y in this equation since the outermost values of x have been tested, so the correct answer is (C).

10. **B** To determine the value of b, FOIL (first, outer, inner, last) the left side of the equation: $(x + 5)^2 = (x + 5)(x + 5) = x^2 + 5x + 5x + 25 = x^2 + 10x + 25$. Since $x^2 + 10x + 25 = x^2 + bx + 25$, then $10x = bx$. Therefore, $b = 10$. The correct answer is (B).

11. **C** Pay careful attention to the word *NOT*. Since the answer choices represent possible values of J, plug in the answer choices (PITA). In choices (A), (B), and (C), J can equal 12, 24, or 36 since each one is divisible by both 4 and 3. However, in (C), while 30 is divisible by 3, it is not divisible by 4. Thus, J cannot equal 30, and the correct answer is (C).

12. **D** Estimation is a good way to solve this problem, since the question is asking for an approximation. 0.48 is close to 0.5 or $\frac{1}{2}$. The product of $\frac{1}{2}$ and 100 is 50 ($\frac{1}{2} \times 100 = 50$), so the correct answer is (D).

13. **A** Since the length and width of the rectangle are not provided, plug in values. Let $l = 20$ and $w = 10$.

If the length is increased by 20%, then the new length of the rectangle is 24 since $0.2 \times 20 = 4$ and $20 + 4 = 24$. If the width is decreased by 10%, then the new width of the rectangle is 9 since $0.1 \times 10 = 1$ and $10 - 1 = 9$. To find the area of a rectangle, use the formula $A = l \times w$. The area of the original rectangle is $20 \times 10 = 200$, and the area of the new rectangle is $2 \times 49 = 216$. Next, to determine percent change, use the formula: % change $= \dfrac{\text{difference}}{\text{original}} \times 100$. The difference of the areas is 16 since $216 - 200 = 16$, and the original area is 200. Thus, $\dfrac{216 - 200}{200} \times 100 = \dfrac{16}{200} \times 100 = 8$.

Therefore, the correct answer is (A).

14. **B** Since each segment is 1 meter and each route must be exactly 3 meters long, the only possible routes are $AH \rightarrow HI \rightarrow ID$, $AB \rightarrow BI \rightarrow ID$, and $AB \rightarrow BC \rightarrow CD$. With only 3 different routes possible, the correct answer is (B).

15. **A** There are 180° in a triangle. If angle B is greater than 90°, then the remaining two angles must have a sum less than 90°. The remaining two angles must also be equal to each other since the question states that $AB = BC$. Since the answer choices represent possible values of angle C, test the answer choices (PITA). If angle C is 35°, then angle A is 35°, and angle B would equal 110°. Since 35° is a possible value of angle C, (A) is the correct answer. Note the remaining choices are incorrect because angle B must be greater than 90°. Choice (B) is incorrect because if angle C is 45°, then angle A is 45°, and angle B would equal 90°. Choice (C) is incorrect because if angle C is 60°, then angle A is 60°, and angle B would equal 60°.

16. **A** Since the price of the car is not given, plug in. If the car costs $100, then a 10% discount is $10 since $0.1 \times 100 = 10$. The discounted price is $90 ($100 - 10 = 90$). After the one-day deal, the car is discounted another 20%, which is $18 since $0.2 \times 90 = 18$. The total amount of the discounts is $28 since $10 + 18 = 28$. The discount off the original price is 28% $\left(\dfrac{\text{discount}}{\text{original}} = \dfrac{28}{100} \right)$, so the correct answer is (A).

17.   **D**   Use an average pie.

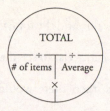

For this problem, draw 2 average pies. The first average pie will represent David's first three tests. The total can be determined by adding his first three test scores: 82 + 84 + 95 = 261. The number of items is the number of tests, which is 3. The second average pie will represent David's average for all four tests. The average (90) and the numbeer of items (4) are given. Multiply to find the total of all four tests: 4 × 90 = 360. To find the score needed on his fourth test, subtract the two totals from the two average pies. Therefore, in order to bring his average up to 90, David must get a 99 on his fourth test (360 – 291 = 99). The correct answer is (D).

18.   **C**   Since the answer choices represent possible values for the number of nickels, use the answer choice (PITA). If Howard has 10 nickels, he would have 50 cents since 10 × 0.05 = 0.5. He has 23 coins, so he would have 13 quarters, which would equal $3.25 since 13 × 0.25 = 3.25. Therefore, he would have well over $2.15, so (B) is too big. To bring the total down, he needs more nickels. Eliminate (A) and (B). If Howard has 18 nickels, he would have 90 cents since 18 × 0.05 = 0.9. He has 23 coins, so he would have 5 quarters, which would equal $1.25 since 5 × 0.25 = 1.25. Therefore, he would have $2.15 since 0.9 + 1.25 = 2.15. Thus, the correct answer is (C).

19.   **D**   Remember that $(p - q)^2 = (p - q)(p - q) = p^2 - pq - pq + q^2 = p^2 - 2pq + q^2$. Notice that the question stated that $p^2 + q^2 = 25$ and $2pq = 10$. Thus, $p^2 - 2pq + q^2$ can be rewritten as 25 – (10) which equals 15. The correct answer is therefore (D).

20.   **C**   Use a ratio box. The numbers for the ratio row are provided. Remember to add the 3 numbers to get the total. The total amount of orange paint needed is also given, so add that value to the ratio box.

	Yellow	Red	White	Total (Orange)
Ratio	3	2	1	6
Multiplier				
Real Value				36

What number does 6 need to be multiplied by to get 36? 6. Therefore, 6 goes in all the cells for the multiplier row.

	Yellow	Red	White	Total (Orange)
Ratio	3	2	1	6
Multiplier	6	6	6	6
Real Value		12		36

The question asks for the amount of red paint needed. Since 2 × 6 = 12, the correct answer is (C).

21. **C** To determine the value of Column A, multiply 0.25 and 50, which equals 12.5. For Column B, multiply 0.5 and 25, which equals 12.5. Since the two columns are equal, the correct answer is (C).

22. **B** Since Column B provides a specific value and the total value of nickels is not given, plug in $1.75 in for Column A (i.e. the total value of the nickels) to see if that could be the value of Column A. If $1.75 were the total value of the nickels, then there would be 35 nickels since $\frac{1.75}{.05} = \frac{175}{5} = 35$. The problems says that the number of pennies is double the number of nickels, so if there are 35 nickels, then there are 70 pennies, which is a total value of $0.70 since $0.01 \times 70 = 0.7$. Add the 2 totals to get $2.45 (1.75 + 0.7 = 2.45). However, the total amount of money inside the piggy bank was actually $2.10. Since $2.45 is greater than $2.10 and a smaller overall total is needed, then the value of the nickels must be smaller than $1.75. Therefore, the value of Column B is greater, and the correct answer is (B).

23. **C** Since Column B provides a specific value and the greatest of the 4 consecutive integers is not given, plug 6 in for Column A to see if 6 could work. If 6 were the greatest, then the other 3 integers would be 5, 4, and 3. The product of the four integers would be 360 since $6 \times 5 \times 4 \times 3 = 360$, which is what the problem stated. Therefore, since 6 is the greatest of the 4 consecutive integers and the two columns are equal, the correct answer is (C).

24. **D** Since the value of x is not given, plug in. If $x = 2$, then Column A would be $(2)^2 = 4$ and Column B would be $(2)^3 = 8$. Currently, Column B is greater. However, since the value of x was not given, remember to plug in more than once! If $x = -2$, then Column A would be $(-2)^2 = 4$ and Column B would be $(-2)^3 = -8$. This time Column A is greater. Since neither column is always greater, the correct answer is (D).

25. **B** Remember order of operations (PEMDAS). For Column A, multiplication and division should be performed in order from left to right: $80 - 20 \div 2 \times 5 + 3 \rightarrow 8 - 10 \times 5 + 3 \rightarrow 8 - 50 + 3$. Next, addition and subtraction should be performed in order from left to right: $8 - 50 + 3 \rightarrow -42 + 3 = -39$. Since $20 > -39$, Column B is greater, and the correct answer is (B).

26. **D** According to the equation given, x will be equal to whatever will make the equation equal to zero. Since the equation is already factored, set each binomial equal to zero: $(x + 2) = 0$ and $(x - 2) = 0$. Next, solve for x. For the first binomial, $x = -2$. For the second one, $x = 2$. Thus, Column A will equal -2 and 2, which is sometimes less than Column B and sometimes equal to Column B. Since Column B is not always greater, nor are the two columns always equal, the correct answer is (D).

27. **A** The value of Column A is 10 since $\sqrt{36} = 6$ and $\sqrt{16} = 4$ and $6 + 4 = 10$. Column B cannot be simplified since 52 is not a perfect square; therefore, the value of $\sqrt{52}$ will have to be approximated.

Since $\sqrt{49} = 7$ and $\sqrt{64} = 8$, then the value of $\sqrt{52}$ is between 7 and 8. Since that range is less than 10, Column A is greater. The correct answer is (A).

28. **C** When exponents do not have a common base, see if it is possible to rewrite the bases so they are the same. For example, in Column B, 9 can be rewritten as 3^2. Therefore, Column B can be rewritten as $(3^2)^6$. Remember MADPSM. Since there is an exponent being raised to another power, multiply. Thus, $(3^2)^6 = 3^{2 \times 6} = 3^{12}$. Therefore, the two columns are equal, and the correct answer is (C). Note that when in doubt with exponents, expand them out. Column A can be rewritten as $3 \times 3 \times 3 \times 3 \times 3 \times 3 \times 3 \times 3 \times 3 \times 3 \times 3 \times 3$, and Column B can be rewritten as $9 \times 9 \times 9 \times 9 \times 9 \times 9$. Each 9 is the same as 3×3, so $9 \times 9 \times 9 \times 9 \times 9 \times 9 = 3 \times 3 \times 3 \times 3 \times 3 \times 3 \times 3 \times 3 \times 3 \times 3 \times 3 \times 3$. As before, the two columns are equal, so (C) is the correct answer.

29. **C** All sides of a cube are equal, so to find the height of the cube, you need the side measure. The formula for the volume of a cube is $V = s \times s \times s$ or $V = s^3$. The volume of the cube is given as $V = 27$, so $s = 3$ since the $\sqrt[3]{27} = 3$. Therefore, the two columns are equal, and the correct answer is (C). Note that if you do not know cube roots, you should use the value in Column B to plug in for the height in Column A. If the height were 3, then the volume of the cube would be $3 \times 3 \times 3$ which equals 27. Since 27 is the volume of the cube, 3 is the correct height of the cube, so the columns are equal.

30. **B** Since the values of x and y are not given, plug in. If $x = 2$, then y would also need to equal 2 to make the equation true: $\dfrac{x + 2}{y + 2} = \dfrac{2 + 2}{2 + 2} = \dfrac{4}{4}$ and $\dfrac{4}{4} = \dfrac{2}{2}$. Therefore, Column A is 2 and Column B is 4 ($y + 2 = 2 + 2 = 4$). Currently, Column B is greater. Remember to plug in more than once since the values of the variables are not given. Try "weird" numbers like 0, 1, or fractions. However, x and y will always be equal to each other in order for the left and right sides of the equation to be equal. Since Column B will always be 2 greater than Column A, the correct answer is (B).

31. **B** One method for solving problems like these is to look for a pattern. For Column A, notice that if you pair up the numbers from either end, they all add up to 101: $1 + 100 = 101$, $2 + 99 = 101$, $3 + 98 = 101$, $4 + 97 = 101$, $5 + 96 = 101$, etc. Next, find the number of pairs. To do this, divide the biggest number (in this case 100) by 2: $\dfrac{100}{2} = 50$. Thus, there will be 50 pairs that add up to 101. Multiply to find the sum of the set of integers: $101 \times 50 = 5{,}050$. Column A is equal to 5,050. You can use the same method for Column B, but remember that this set is *even* integers. The pattern in Column B is the numbers add up to 202: $2 + 200 = 202$, $4 + 198 = 202$, $6 + 196 = 202$, $8 + 194 = 202$, $10 + 192 = 202$, $10 + 192 = 202$, etc. There will be 100 pairs that add up to 202 since $\dfrac{200}{2} = 100$. Remember to multiply to find the sum of this set of numbers:

$202 \times 100 = 20,200$. Thus, Column B equals 20,200. Since Column B is greater than Column A, the correct answer is (B).

32. A   Since the value of x can be determined, solve the equation to find the value of Column A. If $\frac{x}{4} = 1.5$, then multiply both sides by 4 to get $x = 6$. Column A is equal to 6. Since 6 is greater than 5, Column A will always be greater, and the correct answer is (A).

33. A   Use the exponent rules to simplify Column A. To simplify a negative exponent, rewrite as a positive exponent and take the reciprocal: $\left(\frac{1}{5}\right)^{-\frac{1}{2}} \Rightarrow \left(\frac{1}{\frac{1}{5}}\right)^{\frac{1}{2}} \Rightarrow \left(\frac{1}{\frac{1}{5}}\right)^{\frac{1}{2}}$. Next simplify inside the parentheses: $\left(\frac{1}{\frac{1}{5}}\right) = 1 \times \frac{5}{1} = 5$. Simplified, the equation looks a lot less intimidating: $(5)^{\frac{1}{2}}$.

Finally, a fractional exponent can be rewritten as a root. In this case, a number to the $\frac{1}{2}$ power is the same as the square root. Therefore, $(5)^{\frac{1}{2}} = \sqrt{5}$. Since 5 is not a perfect square, $\sqrt{5}$ will be between 2 and 3 because $\sqrt{4} = 2$ and $\sqrt{9} = 3$. Thus, Column A is between 2 and 3. In Column B, $\left(\frac{1}{5}\right)^{4} = \left(\frac{1^4}{5^4}\right) = \left(\frac{1 \times 1 \times 1 \times 1}{5 \times 5 \times 5 \times 5}\right) = \frac{1}{625}$. Since Column B is less than 1, Column A is greater, and the correct answer is (A).

34. C   To find the probability of an event, find the total of what is wanted out of the total possible outcomes: Probability $= \dfrac{\text{What you want}}{\text{What you've got}}$. In Column A, all that is wanted is to roll an even number. (Note the problem is NOT asking for the probability of both events, so the fact that a king is drawn from the deck of cards is extra information.) From 1 to 6, there are 3 even numbers: 2, 4, and 6. Therefore, the probability is $\dfrac{\text{even}}{\text{total}} = \dfrac{3}{6} = \dfrac{1}{2}$. Column A is equal to $\dfrac{1}{2}$. In Column B, all that is wanted is to roll a number less than 4 (again, note that drawing a spade from the deck is extra information). From 1 to 6, there are 3 numbers less than 4: 1, 2, and 3. Therefore, the probability is $\dfrac{\text{less than 4}}{\text{total}} = \dfrac{3}{6} = \dfrac{1}{2}$, and Column B is equal to $\dfrac{1}{2}$. Since the two columns are equal, the correct answer is (C).

35. **B** Break word problems into bite-sized pieces. To find the value of Column A, work through the information provided. If, in season, turnips are $1.80, then the increase at the beginning of the off-season will be $0.18 since 10% of 1.80 = 0.1 × 1.8 = 0.18. The new price is $1.98 since 1.8 + 0.18 = 1.98. When the farmer decreases the price at the end of the off-season, the discount amount is about $0.20 since 10% of 1.98 = 0.1 × 1.98 = 0.198. The final price is $1.78 since 1.98 − 0.2 = 1.78. Thus, Column A is equal to 1.78. This value is less than $1.80, so Column B is greater. The correct answer is (B).

36. **B** To find the probability of an event, find the total of what is wanted out of the total possible outcomes: Probability = $\dfrac{\text{What you want}}{\text{What you've got}}$. In Column A, choosing a brownie the first time would be $\dfrac{\text{brownie}}{\text{total}} = \dfrac{5}{15}$. On the second selection, there will be one brownie fewer and one item fewer overall, so the probability of choosing a brownie the second time would be $\dfrac{4}{14}$. To find the probability of BOTH events, multiply the fractions together: $\dfrac{5}{15} \times \dfrac{4}{14} = \dfrac{20}{210}$. (Note you can reduce prior to multiplying if you choose.) The value of Column A is $\dfrac{20}{210}$. For Column B, choosing a cookie the first time would be $\dfrac{\text{cookie}}{\text{total}} = \dfrac{4}{15}$. Making a second selection means that there is one fewer item overall to choose from, so the total decreases by 1. The probability of choosing a doughnut the second time is $\dfrac{\text{doughnut}}{\text{total}} = \dfrac{6}{14}$. To find the probability of BOTH events, multiply the fractions together: $\dfrac{4}{15} \times \dfrac{6}{14} = \dfrac{24}{210}$. (Note you can reduce prior to multiplying if you choose.) The value of Column B is $\dfrac{24}{210}$. Since the value of Column B is greater, the correct answer is (B).

37. **C** To find the area of a triangle, use the formula $A = \left(\dfrac{1}{2}\right)bh$. Since the problem provides two of the three sides lengths of the triangle, plug those values in for the base and height of the triangle. After all, if the triangle were a right triangle, the legs could be 4 and 6. Therefore, $A = \left(\dfrac{1}{2}\right)(4)(6) = 12$, and Column A could equal 12. This would be equal to Column B. How do you know if this is the greatest possible area? If the triangle were not a right triangle (i.e. the angle between sides 4 and 6 were less than 90° or greater than 90°), then the height would decrease. Making the triangle a right triangle allows for the greatest possible height. Therefore, the two columns are equal, and the correct answer is (C).

Section 3 Reading

1.   **D**   For general purpose questions, ask yourself "Why did the author write this?" The passage describes a battle that took place between the Americans and the British, after a treaty was signed but before it was ratified. The author explains the different possible reasons the timing worked out that way, and what the timing of those events actually meant in historical context. The author at no point casts blame on the British, nor does he say the war was unnecessary. Eliminate (A). The author does state that the British made tactical errors, but never mentions the tactical maneuvers of Andrew Jackson, eliminating (B). The author does not indicate that peace treaties are worthless, only that there are several steps to finalizing them, so eliminate (C). The author does explain the confusing way the War of 1812 ended, which supports (D).

2.   **A**   On Except/Not/Least questions cross check each answer choice and write a "T" for true and an "F" for false for each answer choice, based on the passage. The false answer will be the correct choice. This question asks about what is mentioned in the passage as occurring near the end of the war. President Madison is never mentioned in the passage, so (A) is false. Lines 14–17 state that communication was more complicated at this time, so (B) is true. Lines 9–12 state that the Treaty of Ghent was signed, so (C) is true. Lines 39–41 state that bad weather doomed the British, so (D) is true. Choice (A) is the correct answer.

3.   **C**   On specific questions, make sure you are going back to the passage to find the answer. Since this is an open-ended question, take the answer choices one by one. Although Andrew Jackson is mentioned in the passage, it only says that it is possible he was unaware a treaty was signed, not that he didn't understand the difference between a signed and a ratified treaty. Eliminate (A). President Madison is never mentioned in the passage, eliminating (B). Lines 39–41 state that tactical mistakes and bad weather were the reason for the loss by the British, so it may have been that more time and better conditions would have resulted in a different outcome of the battle. Keep (C). The passage never states one way or the other if it was known to the British that the treaty was signed. Eliminate (D). Choice (C) is the correct answer.

4.   **D**   On specific questions go find the answer! The question asks why New Orleans was a strategic battle point. Lines 36–38 state that the battle would determine who controlled the waterways of the Mississippi. This best supports (D). There is no mention of the American being better supplied, so eliminate (A). There is no mention of anyone being trapped if they lost, eliminating (B). It was the Americans who were attempting to defeat a more numerous force, not the British, so eliminate (C). Choice (D) is the correct answer.

5.   **D**   On specific questions go find the answer! Lines 26–30 state that the war ended after the Treaty of Ghent was ratified by the Senate in February 1815. This best supports (D). Although all the other answers contain information mentioned in the passage, they are not the answer to this question.

6.   **D**   On specific questions, make sure you are going back to the passage to find the answer. Since this is an open-ended question, take the answer choices one by one. The President is never mentioned in

the passage, eliminating (A). Since the author does not know if the commanders ignored the treaty or were unaware of its existence, (B) is not necessarily true. Eliminate it. Choice (C) contains extreme language; this passage only discusses one war a treaty played a part in, not that treaties are always used. Eliminate (C). Choice (D) is supported by lines 21–30, which explain that a treaty is not officially effective until it is ratified, not after it is signed. Choice (D) is the correct answer.

7.　**C**　This question is a "main idea" question in disguise. Ask yourself the "so what?" of the story. This story is about Charles Darrow, and the history of how he created and sold the board game *Monopoly*. Although other realty-based board games are mentioned, (A) is much too specific for a main idea answer. Eliminate it. Hasbro is never mentioned in the passage. Eliminate (B). The passage is focused on Charles Darrow's creation of *Monopoly*, not his life in general, and there is only one view presented in the passage. This eliminates (D). Only (C) supports the main idea, which is a review of Charles Darrow's development of *Monopoly*.

8.　**C**　On specific questions, make sure you are going back to the passage to find the answer. Since this is an open-ended question, take the answer choices one by one. The passage never mentions Darrow changing his game, which eliminates (A). There is also no mention of Charles Darrow's lack of skills, so eliminate (B). Lines 29–34 state that Parker Brothers thought Darrow's game was too complex to become widely popular, which supports (C). Although Philadelphia is mentioned in lines 27–29, the passage states that it was the first city to have stores carry the game, not the only city, eliminating (D). Choice (C) is the correct answer.

9.　**D**　On specific questions, make sure you are going back to the passage to find the answer. This question asks about what kind of people the word "regular" refers to. The people in this sentence are those who buy a game that lets them feel as though they are behaving like "millionaires." It can be inferred then that these regular people are not in fact millionaires. This best supports answer (D). There is no mention of renting versus owning, the 1%, or the love of playing board games in this part of the passage. The only possible answer is (D).

10.　**C**　On Except/Not/Least questions cross check each answer choice and write a "T" for true and an "F" for false for each answer choice, based on the passage. The false answer will be the correct choice. Lines 35–37 clearly state that Charles Darrow continued to sell his game, so (A) is true. Lines 7–10 state that Darrow most likely based his game on already existing realty-based games, so (B) is true. Choice (C) is false; the third paragraph states that he made multiple attempts to sell his game to a larger company. Choice (D) is true, the second paragraph describes the extra details Darrow created to make his game more successful compared to others. As (C) is the false answer, it is the correct answer.

11.　**C**　On Except/Not/Least questions cross check each answer choice and write a "T" for true and an "F" for false for each answer choice, based on the passage. The false answer will be the correct choice. Choice (A) is mentioned in the second paragraph, so it is true. Choice (B) is mentioned at the end of the second paragraph, so it is true. Choice (D) is mentioned in lines 47–51, so it is true. At no point are any adjustments to the game by Parker Brothers mentioned, making (C) false. Therefore, (C) is the correct answer.

12. **D** This question asks what the author suggests in the third paragraph, so make sure to check the answers with that part of the passage. The author does not believe that *Monopoly* had limited appeal, either for complexity or errors, but Parker Brothers did. Eliminate (A) and (C). Although Philadelphia is mentioned in this paragraph, the author does not say why Darrow sold his games there. Eliminate (B). Choice (D) is supported by the passage in that the author says the Parker Brothers were not convinced the game would be popular. Choice (D) is the correct answer.

13. **B** This question asks why the author mentions "other languages" in line 41; go back to the passage and find the answer. In this sentence, the author is explaining that the English language is adept at absorbing words from other languages. The other languages are likely mentioned in order to stress the pool of words that the English language draws from when absorbing new words. This best supports (B). This sentence does not discuss the complexity of spelling bees, only the complexity of the English language, so eliminate (A). This sentence does not mention time at all, eliminating (C). And there is no mention of spelling in this sentence, eliminating (D). Choice (B) is the correct choice.

14. **C** On specific questions, make sure you are going back to the passage to find the answer. This question asks what the major difference is between the first National Spelling Bee and those of today. The first National Spelling Bee is mentioned only in lines 26–31. The only major detail discussed about the first Spelling Bee in these lines is that the winner only had to beat nine other contestants. This most strongly supports (C), that there are more competitors now than originally. There is no mention of what the expectations for the spelling bee were, eliminating (A). The words that were included in the original spelling bee were not discussed, eliminating (D). And there is no mention that the spelling bee has switched to testing a different language than English. The correct answer is (C).

15. **D** When asked a vocabulary in context question, focus on what the word means in the sentence. In line 47, the author states that other languages have fewer rules than English. In lines 50–53, the author states that without all these rules there wouldn't be a point in having a spelling bee at all. This implies the English language has many spelling rules, so myriad must mean many. The only answer choice that matches this meaning is (D), numerous.

16. **A** This is a very open ended questions, so make sure to check each answer choice with the passage. According to lines 20–22, students who reach the National Spelling Bee have won other lower-level spelling bees first. This supports (A), so keep it. There is no discussion of the motivation behind the sponsors of the spelling bee, so eliminate (B). The passage states that Frank Neuhauser would have a very different experience in today's spelling bee than he had in the original, not that

he would do poorly. Eliminate (C). And the author never states that the spelling bee has grown too large, only that it is larger today than the original event, eliminating (D). Choice (A) is the correct answer.

17. **D** This is a general purpose question in disguise. Why did the author write this passage, what point is he or she trying to make? The author focuses on two main points: the evolution of the spelling bee and why the English language makes the spelling bee interesting. Choice (A) is not supported by the passage; the author does not focus on the presentation or structure of the spelling bee. Choice (B) is too specific, the author does much more than merely contrast English with other languages. The role of vocabulary in our lives is never mentioned, so (C) is also incorrect. Choice (D) touches both on the history and the form of the spelling bee, making it the correct answer.

18. **A** On tone questions, eliminate answer choices that are too extreme or don't make sense based on the passage. The author is most likely interested in the spelling bee if he or she is writing about it, so (C), indifferent, cannot be correct. The author is neither questioning nor critical of the spelling bee, eliminating (B) and (D). This leaves (A), admiring, as the best answer choice.

19. **C** In order to answer this question, ask yourself "Why does the author include this question? What purpose does this question serve in the passage?" The question, from what does a black hole originate, is asked at the end of the first paragraph. The beginning of the next paragraph discusses the origins of a black hole, a description which is continued through the remainder of the passage. This best supports (C). The details presented in the passage indicate we know a great deal about black holes, eliminating (A). This question does not include a source, eliminating (B). There is no mention of independent research, so (D) is also incorrect. Choice (C) is the correct answer.

20. **B** This is a specific question, so go back to the passage and find the answer. The question asks what causes a collapsing star to become a neutron star. This process is discussed at the beginning of the fourth paragraph, which states that a collapsing star will become a neutron star if it is big, heavy, and collapses very quickly in an implosion. It goes on to say that the mass matters; it will only become a neutron star if it is not much heavier than our sun, but if it more than 1.7 times that it will become a black hole. This best supports (B). Choice (A) is the opposite of what is stated in the passage, and (C) and (D) are not mentioned in this part of the passage.

21. **C** This is a specific question, so go back to the passage and find the answer. The horizon of a black hole is discussed in the fifth paragraph. It states that matter can pass over the horizon of a black hole, but it cannot pass back out. This suggests that a satellite would pass into a black hole but not come back out. The only answer that matches this is (C).

22. **A** This is a specific question, so go back to the passage and find the answer. The question asks what is a mentioned effect of the process of fusion. According to lines 9–11, fusion is the result of a star burning hydrogen. The energy this creates prohibits the star from collapsing. This supports (A). Although (B) may seem correct at first, it is a deceptive answer choice. Fusion is the result of a star burning hydrogen; a star burning hydrogen is not the result of fusion. Eliminate (B). There is no

mention of the average life of a star or a white dwarf in these lines, so (C) and (D) cannot be correct. Choice (A) is the correct answer.

23. **D** This is a specific question, so go back to the passage and find the answer. The question asks why a black hole appears black, which is discussed in lines 35–38. The passage states that a black hole appears black because no light or matter can escape from it. The only choice that matches this answer is (D).

24. **B** This question asks about the organization of the passage, so go back and examine the main idea of each paragraph and how they connect. At the beginning, the topic of black holes is introduced; the next three paragraphs discuss the process of stars changing into other forms of matter, ending with black holes. This best supports (B). Choice (A) is too general, so it can be eliminated. There is no personal story, only a historical reference, and no black holes are compared and contrasted, so eliminate (C). No single black hole is used in the story to generalize, eliminating (D). Choice (B) is the correct answer.

25. **C** For general purpose questions, ask yourself "Why did the author write this?" The passage describes the fight of the Women's Suffrage movement to earn the right to vote. This best matches (C). Choice (A) is too specific: Although Alice Paul is mentioned in the passage the focus is not solely on her. Choice (B) is too extreme; it was not solely the Night of Terror that prompted the Nineteenth Amendment. And while the deplorable actions of the guards are mentioned in the passage, it is also too specific to be the correct answer. Choice (C) is correct.

26. **C** When asked a vocabulary in context question, focus on what the word means in the sentence. This sentence discusses how outraged the public was over the events of the Night of Terror. In this context, "exposed" most nearly means made known to the public. The only choice that matches this meaning is (C), revealed.

27. **C** This question is asking what the author's attitude is toward a specific event, low voter turnout. In the first paragraph, after the author discusses the low voter turnout, he or she then refers to that number as "disturbing," since so many fought so hard to secure voting rights for all. This is certainly a negative attitude, which eliminates (B). Although (A) and (D) are negative, they are too extreme for this story. Only (C), pessimism, matches the tone of the passages.

28. **D** This is a specific question, so go back to the passage and find the answer. The passage describes the Night of Terror, and then goes on to say that these events infuriated the nation when they were discovered. The following paragraph then discusses how this new support eventually helped in the creation of the Nineteenth Amendment. This best supports (D). There is no mention of either President Wilson or the punishment of the guards in this part of the passage, eliminating (A) and (B), and (C) is the opposite of what was stated in the passage. Choice (D) is the correct answer.

29.   **A**   This is a specific question, so go back to the passage and find the answer. The hunger strike is discussed in lines 37–43, where it is stated that the women went on a hunger strike led by Alice Paul to protest the deplorable conditions of the prison. This best matches (A), they were trying to make the prison better. Choice (B) may seem correct, but it is deceptive. The prisoners were not force fed until after they began the strike, not before. Choices (C) and (D) also contain deceptive wording as they are on subjects mentioned in the passage, but neither is the answer to this question. The correct answer is (A).

30.   **D**   This is an attitude question in disguise; you are being asked what the author thought of the women's tactics. Ask yourself how the author described the women and the activities they engaged in. Look through the passage for descriptive phrases. The author states in lines 29–36 that the women protested in an orderly and peaceful fashion. In the last paragraph, the women's peacefulness and physical endurance are noted. Not only should the answer touch on these topics, but the answer should be generally positive as the author's attitude is positive. This eliminates all choices but (D), since only (D) does not contain any negative ideas in it.

31.   **B**   On tone questions, eliminate answer choices that are too extreme or don't make sense based on the passage. The passage opens by saying that Stephen Hawking is one of the greatest living scientists, and then goes on to discuss how he overcame physical hardship to excel in his field. This eliminates (C) and (D), as they are too negative. The author is not displaying any longing for the past, which eliminates (A). Only admiring, (B), works with the passage.

32.   **B**   When asked the purpose of a sentence or phrase in the passage, ask yourself "Why is this included? What point does the author make with this line?" Up until this point, it is unclear what scientist the author is discussing. At this point the author makes it clear whom he or she has been talking about. This best supports (B). There is no riddle or question prior to this, only a description, eliminating (A) and (C). Choice (D) is deceptive and extreme; the passage says Hawking is one of the greatest living scientists, not the greatest. The correct answer is (B).

33.   **C**   This is a specific question, so go back to the passage and find the answer. Hawking's attitude towards his disease is discussed in lines 53–60, where it states he credits his disease with forcing him to face the limitations of his life and time. According to the last lines of the passage, because of his disease he reached his greatest potential. This best supports (C), that he is appreciative of his disease, which is somewhat ironic. He is not giddy, irate, nor uncaring about his disease, eliminating (A), (B), and (D).

34.   **C**   This is a specific question, so go back to the passage and find the answer. The second paragraph discusses Hawking as a child and young man, and includes the descriptions "lack of diligence," "moderately successful," "not extraordinary," etc. This best supports (C). There is no mention of Hawking being disrespectful or energetic, eliminating (A) and (D). And it was not until later that he became considered brilliant, which makes (B) incorrect. Choice (C) is the correct answer.

35. **C** On Except/Not/Least questions cross check each answer choice and write a "T" for true and an "F" for false for each answer choice, based on the passage. The false answer will be the correct choice. The last paragraph does discuss the connection between Hawking's disease and his success in science, so (A) is true. The last paragraph also includes the goal of Hawking to travel to space someday, so (B) is true as well. No specific theory of Hawking's is ever mentioned, making (C) false. The educational institutions Hawking attended are reviewed in the second and third paragraphs of the passage, so (D) is true. Only (C) is false, and therefore the correct answer.

36. **A** This question is a "main idea" question in disguise. Ask yourself the "so what?" of the story. This story is reviewing biographical details of Stephen Hawking, and focusing on the role his disease played in his life. There are no scientific discoveries discussed in the passage, eliminating (C). Although the author mentions Hawking's medical diagnosis and the technology he uses with his disease, these answers are much too specific for this question. Only (A) matches the biographical description of the passage. Choice (A) is the correct answer.

Section 4 Mathematics Achievement

1. **A** Draw a factor tree of 36.

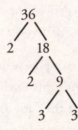

The prime factorization of 36 is $2 \times 2 \times 3 \times 3$ or $2^2 \times 3^2$. The two different prime factors of 36 are 2 and 3, so the correct answer is (A). Note that (B), (C), and (D) contain numbers that are not prime (4, 12, and 9).

2. **D** Use the answer choices (PITA) to find a value of x that will make the expression equal to 0. If $x = 3$, as in (D), then $\frac{x-3}{4x} = \frac{3-3}{4(3)} = \frac{0}{12} = 0$. No other answer choice contains a value of x that will make the expression equal 0. Thus, the correct answer is (D).

3. **C** If the numbers are in a ratio of 3 to 4 and the smaller of the two numbers is 9, then $\frac{3}{4} = \frac{9}{x}$. Cross multiply and solve for x, and $x = 12$. Therefore, the larger number is 12. (Note you can also use a ratio box to find the larger number.) To find the average, use an average pie.

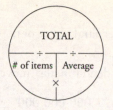

TOTAL

$\div$ $\div$

\# of items | Average

$\times$

The total will be the sum of the two integers: $9 + 12 = 21$. There are 2 numbers, so the number of items is 2. Divide to find the average: $\frac{138}{3} = 46°$. Thus, the average is 10.5, and the correct answer is (C).

4. **D** There are 180° in a straight line. If $a = 42°$, then the remaining angles ($b + b + b$) will equal 138° since $180 - 42 = 138$. Since the remaining three angles are all equal, divide to find the value of b: $\frac{138}{3} = 46°$. The correct answer is (D).

5. **C** 85% of 50 will be greater than 25 (50% of 50) but less than 50 (100% of 50). Therefore, eliminate (A) and (B). One way to find 85% of 50 is to find the product: $0.85 \times 50 = 42.5$. Therefore, the correct answer is (C).

6. **C** To find the largest of the three numbers, use the answer choices (PITA). Start with (B) or (C). If the largest number is 6, then $x = 2$ and $z = 6$. Thus, y would have to be 3 since $2 + y + 6 = 11 \Rightarrow 8 + y = 11 \Rightarrow y = 3$. Check the other equation: $xyz = 2 \times 3 \times 6 = 36$. This works, so the largest number is 6, and the correct answer is (C).

7. **A** Translate the words into their math equivalents: two-thirds of one-half is the same as $\frac{2}{3} \times \frac{1}{2}$. Multiply the numerators together and multiply the denominators together to get $\frac{2}{6}$. Reduce to $\frac{1}{3}$. Therefore, the correct answer is (A).

8. **B** If there is 1 km in 1,000 m and the runner wants to run 4 km, then set up a proportion to solve for the total number of meters: $\frac{1 \text{ km}}{1,000 \text{ m}} = \frac{4 \text{ km}}{x}$. Cross multiply to get $x = 4,000$. The question asks for the number of laps, so if 1 lap equals 400 m, then $\frac{1 \text{ lap}}{400 \text{ m}} = \frac{x}{4,000 \text{ m}}$. Cross multiply and solve for x to get $x = 10$. Therefore, 4,000 m is equal to 10 laps, so the correct answer is (B).

9. **A** Use the figure provided. Since this is a right triangle and side BC is the hypotenuse, eliminate (D) since the hypotenuse is the longest side of a right triangle. Use the Pythagorean Theorem to solve for the missing side: $a^2 + b^2 = c^2$, where c is the hypotenuse. Thus, $a^2 + 12^2 = 13^2 \Rightarrow a^2 + 144 = 169 \Rightarrow a^2 = 25 \Rightarrow a = 5$. Side AB is 5, so the correct answer is (A). Note: this is a 5-12-13 right triangle. Memorizing the Pythagorean triples can make questions like these faster.

10. **B** When in doubt with exponents, expand them out. $\dfrac{2.7 \times 10^7}{3.0 \times 10^{-3}}$ can be rewritten as $\dfrac{27,000,000}{0.003}$.

To get rid of the decimals in the denominator, move the decimal in the numerator and denominator to the right 3 spaces to get $\dfrac{27,000,000,000}{3}$. Divide to get $3\overline{)27,000,000,000}$ with quotient $3,000,000,000$. To rewrite 3,000,000,000 in scientific notation, move the decimal 9 places to the left. The result is 3.0×10^9, or answer (B).

11. **B** To determine percent change, use the formula: % change $= \dfrac{\text{difference}}{\text{original}} \times 100$. The difference between the two prices is \$0.40 since $1.6 - 1.2 = 0.4$, and the original price of the digital song was \$1.60. Therefore, $\dfrac{0.4}{1.6} \times 100 = \dfrac{40}{1.6} = \dfrac{400}{16} = 25$. The digital song decreased in price by 25%, so the correct answer is (B).

12. **A** Since there are variables in the question and answers, plug in a value for y (the number of students in Mrs. Puccio's class). If $y = 10$, then twice as many would be 20, and 4 less than 20 would be 16. Therefore, $x = 16$ (the number of students in Mrs. Sproul's class). Since the question asks for the value of y, the correct answer will be the one that equals 10. Plug 16 in for x and check each answer choice. Choice (A) is $\dfrac{16}{2} + 2 = 8 + 2 = 10$. Choice (B) is $2(16) + 4 = 32 + 4 = 36$. Choice (C) is $2(16) - 4 = 32 - 4 = 28$. Choice (D) is $\dfrac{16}{2} - 4 = 8 - 4 = 4$. Since it is the only one that matches the target value, (A) is the correct answer.

13. **C** Don't be intimidated by weird symbols! Use the definitions provided and plug in the given values for x. For the first part of the equation, #(–6), $x = -6$ so use the definition for x is negative: $\#(x) = x^2$. Thus, $\#(-6) = (-6)^2 = 36$. For the second part of the equation, #(6), $x = 6$ so use the definition for x is positive: $\#(x) = 2x$. Thus, $\#(6) = 2(6) = 12$. Now replace #(–6) with 36 and #(6) with 12, so the equation looks like $36 - 12 =$, which is 24. The correct answer is (C).

14. **D** Don't be intimidated by weird symbols! Use the definitions provided and plug in the given values for x and y. #[#x – #y] can be rewritten as #[#(3) – #(–4)]. Start inside the brackets. For #(3), $x = 3$ so use the definition for x is positive $\#(x) = 2x$. Thus, $\#(3) = 2(3) = 6$. For #(–4), $x = -4$ so use the definition for x is negative: $\#(x) = x^2$. (Don't let the different variables confuse you. Remember now the number inside the parentheses is an x value according to the definitions.) Thus, $\#(-4) = (-4)^2$. Now the equation looks like #[6 – 16]. Simplify inside the brackets ($6 - 16 = -10$) to get #(–10). Since $x = -10$, use the definition for x is negative. Thus, $\#(-10) = (-10)^2 = 100$. The final answer is 100, so the correct answer is (D).

15. **B** Since there are variables in the question and answers, plug in a value for x or y. If $x = 45$ and $x + 90 + y = 180$, then $y = 45$. The question asks for the value of x, so the correct answer will be the one that equals 45. Plug 45 in for y and check each answer choice. Choices (A) and (B) equal 45. Choice (C) equals 135 ($90 + 45 = 135$), and (D) equals 135 ($180 - 45 = 135$). Eliminate (C) and (D). Since two answers worked, plug in another value for x. If $x = 50$ and $x + 90 + y = 180$, then $y = 40$. The correct answer will be the one that equals 50 since $x = 50$. Plug in 40 for y and check the two remaining answer choices. Choice (A) equals 40; eliminate it. Choice (B) equals 50 ($90 - 40 = 50$). Since it is the only option that still works, the correct answer is (B).

16. **D** First, start by dividing the integers: $\frac{4}{2} = 2$. Eliminate (B) since it does not contain 2. Next, simplify the exponents using the exponent rules (MADSPM). Since the bases are being divided, subtract the exponents. $\frac{a^4}{a^3} = a^{4-3} = a^1 = a$. Eliminate (C) since it does not contain a. $\frac{b^6}{b^5} = b^{6-5} = b^1 = b$. Eliminate (A) since it does not contain b in the numerator. Note that b in the denominator is equal to b^{-1}. Therefore, the correct answer is (D).

17. **C** Since the number of students in the class is not provided, plug in. If there were 12 students in the class, then $\frac{1}{4}$ of 12 is 3 $\left(\frac{1}{4} \times 12 = 3\right)$, which means that 3 students failed the exam. The remaining number of students in the class (those who passed the exam) is 9 since $12 - 3 = 9$. Of those 9 passing students, $\frac{1}{3}$ scored an A. Thus, 3 students scored an A: $\left(\frac{1}{3} \times 9 = 3\right)$. The number of students who passed the exam but scored below an A is 6 ($9 - 3 = 6$). Therefore, the fraction of the whole class that passed but scored below an A is $\frac{6}{12} = \frac{1}{2}$. The correct answer is (C).

18. **C** Since there are variables in the question and answers, plug in a value for r. If $r = 100$, then Karen spends \$80 since Rena spends \$20 more than Karen ($100 - 20 = 80$). If Rena spends \$100, then Lynn spends \$50 since $100 - 50 = 50$. The question asks for the total cost of their purchases, which is \$230: $100 + 80 + 50 = 230$. The question asks for the total cost, so the correct answer will be the one that equals 230. Plug 100 in for r and check each answer choice. Choice (A) equals $100 + 70 = 170$. Choice (B) equals $\frac{100 + 70}{3} = \frac{170}{3}$. Choice (C) equals $3(100) - 70 = 300 - 70 = 230$. Choice (D) equals $100 + 210 = 310$. Since it is the only one that matches the target value, (C) is the correct answer.

19. **A** Since the answer choices represent possible values for the number of boys in the group, use the answer choices (PITA). If there are 37 boys in the group, then there are 71 girls in the group since $37 + 34 = 71$. Thus, there would be 108 children in the group since $37 + 71 = 108$, which is too big.

Eliminate (B), (C), and (D) because a smaller number is needed for the number of boys. Therefore, (A) is the correct answer. Note that if there were 33 boys in the group, there would be 67 girls (33 + 34 = 67) and 100 total children in the group (33 + 67 = 100).

20.   **D**   Use the chart provided to find the total number of students and the number of students whose favorite type of book is Sci-Fi. There are 40 students (8 + 20 + 10 + 2 = 40) and 10 chose Sci-Fi. Thus, 10 out of the 40 students, or $\frac{1}{4}\left(\frac{10}{40}=\frac{1}{4}\right)$, like Sci-Fi books the best. If this information were presented in a pie graph, then the central angle would be $\frac{1}{4}$ out of 360° since circles have 360°. $\frac{1}{4}\times 360=\frac{360}{4}=90$, so the central angle would be 90°. The correct answer is (D).

21.   **D**   To find what fraction the new price is compared to the original price, set up a fraction: $\frac{\text{new price}}{\text{old price}}=\frac{1,200}{1,500}=\frac{12}{15}=\frac{4}{5}$. Therefore, the correct answer is (D).

22.   **A**   Since there are variables in the question and answers, plug in a value for x or y. If $x = 3$, then $y = 4$ since $\frac{3}{3}=\frac{4}{4}$. Plug 3 in for x and 4 in for y and check each answer choice to see which statement is true. Choice (A) equals 3(4) = 12. Choice (B) equals 3(4) = 4(3), or 12 = 12. Choice (C) equals $\frac{3}{4}=\frac{4}{3}$, which is not true. Choice (D) equals 3(3) = 4(4), or 9 = 16, which is not true. Since there are two answer choices that work, plug in again. This time if $x = 4$, then $y = 3$ since $\frac{3}{4}=\frac{3}{4}$. Now plug 4 in for x and 3 in for y to see which of the remaining two answer choices is true. Choice (A) equals 4(3) = 12. Choice (B) equals 3(3) = 4(4), or 9 = 16, which is not true. Since it is the only option that is still true, the correct answer is (A). Another way to solve this problem would be to cross multiply: $\frac{3}{x}=\frac{y}{4}\rightarrow x(y)=3(4)\rightarrow xy=12$. This matches (A), which is the correct answer.

23.   **B**   Use a ratio box. The numbers for the ratio row are provided. Remember to add the 2 numbers to get the total. The total number of students at the school is also given, so add that value to the ratio box.

	Boys	Girls	Total
Ratio	3	2	5
Multiplier			
Real Value			600

What number does 5 need to be multiplied by to get 600? 120. Therefore, 120 goes in all the cells for the multiplier row.

	Boys	Girls	Total
Ratio	3	2	5
Multiplier	120	120	120
Real Value		240	600

The question asks for the number of girls. Since $2 \times 120 = 240$, the correct answer is (B).

24. **D** 150% of 40 will be greater than 40 since 100% of 40 is 40 ($1 \times 40 = 40$). Eliminate (A) and (B). Since 50% of 40 is 20 ($0.5 \times 40 = 20$), then 150% of 40 will equal 60. The correct answer is (D).

25. **D** The question is asking for the number of hours she studied all together. Eliminate (A) since the time she spent studying math alone was 4 hours. To find the number of hours she spent studying English, find $\frac{3}{4}$ of 4, which is $\frac{3}{4}(4) = \frac{12}{4} = 3$. If she spent 4 hours studying math and 3 hours of studying English, she spent a total of 7 hours studying. Therefore, the correct answer is (D).

26. **B** Long division is one way to approach division with decimals. $\frac{0.966}{0.42}$ can be written as $0.42\overline{)0.966}$. Move the decimal to the right three times to get rid of the decimal in the divisor and the dividend: $420\overline{)966}$. The result is $420\overline{)966.0}^{\,2.3}$, so the correct answer is (B). Another option is use the answer choices (PITA). Multiply the answer choices by 0.42 to see which one equals 0.966. Choice (B) is the only option that works.

27. **B** To determine percent change, use the formula: % change $= \dfrac{\text{difference}}{\text{original}} \times 100$. The difference between her two typing speeds is 7 since $42 - 35 = 7$, and her original speed was 35 words per minute. Therefore, $\dfrac{42 - 35}{35} \times 100 = \dfrac{7}{35} \times 100 = \dfrac{700}{35} = 20$. Her typing speed increased by 20%, so the correct answer is (B).

28. **A** The first term in the series is given: 50. To find the second number (which is an even term), multiply the first term by $\frac{1}{2}$. Thus, the second term equals 25 ($\frac{1}{2} \times 50 = 25$). To find the third number (which is an odd term), multiply the second term by $\frac{1}{2}$ and round to the nearest whole number. The third term equals 13 since $\frac{1}{2} \times 25 = 12.5$ and 12.5 rounds up to 13. Therefore, the correct answer is (A).

29. **A** Use the table provided to determine the mode of the data. The mode of a list of numbers is the number that appears most frequently. Note that the information is presented in a deceptive manner. Note that (D) is a trap. For example, 0 should be listed 6 times, since the number of students who have 0 siblings is 6. If the list were written out like this {0, 0, 0, 0, 0, 0, 1, 1, 1, 1, 1, 1, 1, 1, 1, 1, 1, 2, 2, 2, 2, 2, 2, 2, 2, 3, 3, 3, 3, 3, 3, 4, 5}, it would be easier to see that the mode is 1 since the number of students who have 1 sibling occurs the most times (10). The correct answer is (A).

30. **B** Mark the given lengths on the figure provided to see what other lengths can be determined. Segment BC is not provided; however, if segment $BD = 18$ and segment $CD = 12$, then $BC = 6$ since $18 - 12 = 6$. Segment AB is also given (5), so add it to the value found for segment BC to get the length of segment AC: $5 + 6 = 11$. The correct answer is (B).

31. **D** Eliminate (A) and (B) since $2 + 40 = 42$, not 24. $\dfrac{1}{100} = 0.01$. Eliminate (C) because $0.1 = \dfrac{1}{10}$. Therefore, (D) is the correct answer.

32. **C** Since the question asks for a specific value, use the answer choices (PITA). Start with (A) because the *least* possible value is wanted. Choice (A) is incorrect because it is not divisible by 4. Choice (B) is incorrect because it is not divisible by 3. Choice (C) is divisible by all 4 numbers: $\dfrac{60}{2} = 30$, $\dfrac{60}{3} = 20$, $\dfrac{60}{4} = 15$, and $\dfrac{60}{5} = 12$. Since there is not a smaller possible integer, the correct answer is (C).

33. **C** Since there are variables in the question and answers, plug in values for x and y. If $x = 30$, then the car travels 30 mph. If $y = 90$, then find the time it will take a car traveling 30 mph to go 90 mph. Set up a proportion to solve: $\dfrac{30 \text{ miles}}{1 \text{ hour}} = \dfrac{90 \text{ miles}}{x}$. Cross-multiply and solve for x to get $30x = 90 \Rightarrow x = 3$. It will take 3 hours, so the correct answer will be the one that equals 3. Plug 30 in for x and 90 in for y and check each answer choice. Choice (A) equals $\dfrac{2(30)}{90} = \dfrac{60}{90} = \dfrac{2}{3}$. Choice (B) equals $30 \times 90 = 2{,}700$. Choice (C) equals $\dfrac{90}{30} = 3$. Choice (D) equals $\dfrac{30}{90} = \dfrac{1}{3}$. Since it is the only one that matches the target value of 3, (C) is the correct answer.

34. **A** Similar triangles are triangles that have the same angle measures and corresponding sides have the same ratio. Thus, if in triangle ABC, side BC has a side measure of 4 and the side QR of triangle PQR has a side measure of 12, those sides correspond and have a ratio of 4:12. Therefore, the sides of triangle PQR will all be 3 times the size of the sides in triangle ABC. To find the area of a triangle, use the formula $A = \dfrac{1}{2}(b)(h)$. The area of triangle ABC is given (6), and any side can be the

base, so let side BC (4) be the base. Therefore, $\frac{1}{2}$ (4)(h) = 6. Simplify to get $2h$ = 6, and divide to get h = 3. The height of triangle ABC is 3. The height of triangle PQR is not given; however, it will be 3 times the height of triangle ABC, so it will be 9 (3 × 3 = 9). Let the base of triangle PQR be side QR (12). Therefore, $A = \frac{1}{2}$ (12)(9) = 6(9) = 54. The area of triangle PQR is 54, so the correct answer is (A).

35. **D** The answer choices represent possible values of x (i.e. the cost of each halibut steak), so plug in (PITA). If x = 5, then one halibut steak ($5) plus 2 salmon steaks cost $30, which means that each salmon steak (y) costs $12.50: 5 + 2$y$ = 30 → 2y = 25 → y = 12.5. Check to see if those values work for what Dave pays: if x = 5 and y = 12.5, then 2 halibut steaks cost $10 (2 × 5 = 10) and 4 salmon steaks cost $50 (4 × 12.5 = 50), so he spends a total of $60, which is true. So is (A) the answer? Be careful! What if you had tried (C) first? If x = 10, then y = 10 because 10 + 2y = 30 → 2y = 20 → y = 10. These numbers for x and y also work in the second equation: 2 halibut steaks are $20 (2 × 10 = 20) and 4 salmon steaks are $40 (4 × 10 = 40), so Dave spends a total of $60 (20 + 40 = 60), which is true. There can't be multiple correct answers, so since there is not enough information provided about the price of the fish steaks, the correct answer is (D). Note: normally you don't need to check all the answers when you use PITA. This one is a tricky question!

36. **B** Pay attention to the information above the problem. Choice (D) is a trap answer. (1 + 5) = (6). Since the value inside the parentheses is even, use the definition for x is even: (x) = $\frac{1}{2}$ (x). Plug in 6 for x and simplify: $\frac{1}{2}$ (6) = 3. Since (6) = 3, the correct answer is (B).

37. **D** Since there are variables in the question and answers, plugging in for x, calculating a target value, and finding the answer choice that matches would be an option. However, another way to solve the problem would be to distribute the 2: 2(4z + 1) = (2 × 4z) + (2 × 1) = 8z + 2. This matches (D), which is the correct answer.

38. **B** On a stem-and-leaf plot, the values in the "stem" column are tens digits and the values in the "leaf" column are the ones digits. For example, a stem of 10 and a leaf of 8 represent 108. To find the median of this data set, locate the number in the middle. There are 27 numbers in this set, so the middle number will be the 14th number, which is the 2 in the leaf column in stem row 13, which equals 132. The correct answer is (B). Note: if you have trouble trying to determine the middle number, just use the leaf numbers and cross off one number from the beginning and one number from the end of the list until you reach the middle term. Don't forget to add the stem part to the beginning of the number.

39. C To find the average, use an average pie.

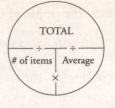

The total will be the sum of the monkeys at the 3 zoos: 3 + 8 + 16 = 27. There are 3 zoos, so the number of items is 3. Divide to find the average: $\frac{27}{3} = 9$. Thus, the average is 9, and the correct answer is (C).

40. A Since there are variables in the question and answers, plug in a value for the cost of one of the items to determine the cost of the other items. If a steak costs $10 and it is $4 more than a hamburger, then a hamburger costs $6. If a hamburger costs $6 and it is $4 more than a grilled cheese sandwich, then a grilled cheese sandwich is $2. Six grilled cheese sandwiches cost $12 since 2 × 6 = 12. If 6 grilled cheese sandwiches cost $2x$, then $x = 6$ because $2x = 12$ and $\frac{12}{2} = 6$. The question asks how much 4 steaks and 2 hamburgers cost. Steaks are $10 each and hamburgers are $6 each, so the total cost will be $52 since (4 × 10) + (2 × 6) = 40 + 12 = 52. The correct answer will be the one that equals 52. Plug 6 in for x and check each answer choice. Choice (A) equals 2(6) + 40 = 12 + 40 = 52. Choice (B) equals 2(6) + 48 = 12 + 48 = 60. Choice (C) equals 6(6) + 24 = 36 + 34 = 70. Choice (D) equals 12(6) + 40 = 72 + 40 = 112. Since it is the only one that matches the target value of 52, (A) is the correct answer.

41. C A solution set is the set of all numbers that make the inequality true. One method of solving this question is to plug in values from the answer choices (PITA). For example, if $x = 0$, then $|3 - 2(0)| > 9$. Multiply to get $|3 - 0| > 9$, and then subtract to get $|3| > 9$. The absolute value of 3 is 3, so 3 > 9, which is not true. Eliminate any answer choices that include 0 as a possible value for x—(A) and (B). Try another number. If $x = 4$, then $|3 - 2(4)| > 9$. Multiply to get $|3 - 8| > 9$, and then subtract to get $|-5| > 9$. The absolute value of −5 is 5, so 5 > 9, which is also not true. Therefore, eliminate (D), which would include $x = 4$ as a possible solution. The correct answer is (C), which includes the complete solution set for this inequality. Note: another way to do this problem is to solve the inequality for x. If you chose to solve this way, don't forget to flip the sign if you multiply or divide by a negative number.

42. **D** Since there are variables in the question, plug in values for x and y. If $x = 2$ and $y = 3$, then

$100xy = 100(2)(3) = 600$ and $xy = (2)(3) = 6$. Now the question reads 600 is what percent of

6. Translate the English words into their math equivalents: $600 = \dfrac{x}{100} \times 6$ and solve for

x: $600 = \dfrac{x}{100} \times 6 \rightarrow 600 = \dfrac{6x}{100}$. Multiply both sides of the equation by 100 to get $60{,}000 = 6x$.

Divide both sides by 6 to get $x = 10{,}000$. The correct answer is (D). Note: setting up a proportion

$\left(\dfrac{600}{6} = \dfrac{x}{100}\right)$, cross-multiplying, and solving for x works too.

43. **D** If Matt's home and Laura's home are in the same direction from the school, then their homes would be 4 miles apart since $8 - 4 = 4$. However, if Matt lives 4 miles west of the school and Laura lives 8 miles east of the school, then their homes are 12 miles apart since $8 + 4 = 12$. There are other possibilities as well, so without knowing which direction they both live, there is not enough information to determine the distance between their homes. The correct answer is (D).

44. **B** Use a ratio box. The numbers for the ratio row are provided in the answer choices, so use the answers (PITA). Remember to add the 2 numbers in the ratio row to get the total. Since the ratio total has to be a number that is divisible by the real value total ($2,000), eliminate (A) and (D) since $6 + 1 = 7$ (A) and $2 + 1 = 3$ (D) yield totals that are not divisible by 2,000. Start with one of the remaining choices and fill in the values into a ratio box. For (B),

	Larger	Smaller	Total
Ratio	5	3	8
Multiplier			
Real Value			2,000

What number does 8 need to be multiplied by to get 2,000? 250. Therefore, 250 goes in all the cells for the multiplier row.

	Larger	Smaller	Total
Ratio	5	3	8
Multiplier	250	250	250
Real Value	1,250	750	2,000

The question states that the difference between the two amounts is half of their average. Remember to find average, use an average pie. The total ($2,000) and the number of things (2 partners) is given. Therefore, divide the total by the number of things to get the average: $\dfrac{2{,}000}{2} = 1{,}000$.

If $1,000 is the average, then half the average is $500 $\left(\dfrac{1{,}000}{2} = 500\right)$. The difference between the larger and smaller amounts should be $500, which is true for this answer choice since

1,250 − 750 = 500. Thus, the correct answer is (B). Note that (C) will not work because the difference between the larger and smaller amounts will be $1,200, which does not fit the restrictions of the problem.

45. A   Since there are variables in the question and answers, plug in a value for j. If $j = 2$, then $j + 5 = 2 + 5 = 7$. Next, calculate the values. Two coins each worth 10 cents is a total value of 20 cents since $2 \times 10 = 20$. Seven coins each worth 25 cents each is a total value of 175 cents since $7 \times 25 = 175$. Thus, all 9 coins have a value of 195 cents ($20 + 175 = 195$). The question asks for the total value, so the correct answer will be the one that equals 195. Plug 2 in for j and check each answer choice. Choice (A) equals $35(2) + 125 = 195$. Choice (B) equals $35(2) + 5 = 75$. Choice (C) equals $10(2) + 130 = 150$. Choice (D) equals $2(2) + 5 = 9$. Since it is the only one that matches the target value, (A) is the correct answer.

46. D   To find the probability of an event, find the total of what is wanted out of the total possible outcomes:

$$\text{Probability} = \frac{\text{What you want}}{\text{What you've got}}.$$ If the first randomly selected coin is a penny, the probability would be $\frac{\text{penny}}{\text{total}} = \frac{6}{18}$. Making a second selection means that there is one fewer item overall to choose from, so the total decreases by 1. The probability of choosing a quarter as the second coin would be $\frac{\text{quarter}}{\text{total}} = \frac{5}{17}$. To find the probability of BOTH events, multiply the fractions together: $\frac{6}{18} \times \frac{5}{17}$. There is no need to actually multiply the fractions—pay attention to how the answer choices are written. The correct answer is (D).

47. A   Use the formula provided and plug in the given values to solve for the radius. $V = \frac{1}{3}\pi r^2 h \rightarrow 12\pi = \frac{1}{3}\pi r^2(4)$. Divide both sides by π to get $12 = \frac{1}{3}r^2(4)$. Multiply both sides by $\frac{3}{1}$ to cancel the fraction on the right side to get $36 = r^2(4)$. Divide both sides by 4 to get $9 = r^2$. Finally, take the square root of both sides to find $r = 3$. The correct answer is (A). Note: Another way to approach this problem is to use the answer choices rather than solve for r. Remember that the answer choices represent possible values of the radius. Use PITA to see which value of r will make the equation equal to 12π. Only (A) will work.

Chapter 19
Middle Level
ISEE Practice Test

Middle Level Practice Test

Be sure each mark *completely* fills the answer space.

SECTION 1

1 Ⓐ Ⓑ Ⓒ Ⓓ	9 Ⓐ Ⓑ Ⓒ Ⓓ	17 Ⓐ Ⓑ Ⓒ Ⓓ	25 Ⓐ Ⓑ Ⓒ Ⓓ	33 Ⓐ Ⓑ Ⓒ Ⓓ
2 Ⓐ Ⓑ Ⓒ Ⓓ	10 Ⓐ Ⓑ Ⓒ Ⓓ	18 Ⓐ Ⓑ Ⓒ Ⓓ	26 Ⓐ Ⓑ Ⓒ Ⓓ	34 Ⓐ Ⓑ Ⓒ Ⓓ
3 Ⓐ Ⓑ Ⓒ Ⓓ	11 Ⓐ Ⓑ Ⓒ Ⓓ	19 Ⓐ Ⓑ Ⓒ Ⓓ	27 Ⓐ Ⓑ Ⓒ Ⓓ	35 Ⓐ Ⓑ Ⓒ Ⓓ
4 Ⓐ Ⓑ Ⓒ Ⓓ	12 Ⓐ Ⓑ Ⓒ Ⓓ	20 Ⓐ Ⓑ Ⓒ Ⓓ	28 Ⓐ Ⓑ Ⓒ Ⓓ	36 Ⓐ Ⓑ Ⓒ Ⓓ
5 Ⓐ Ⓑ Ⓒ Ⓓ	13 Ⓐ Ⓑ Ⓒ Ⓓ	21 Ⓐ Ⓑ Ⓒ Ⓓ	29 Ⓐ Ⓑ Ⓒ Ⓓ	37 Ⓐ Ⓑ Ⓒ Ⓓ
6 Ⓐ Ⓑ Ⓒ Ⓓ	14 Ⓐ Ⓑ Ⓒ Ⓓ	22 Ⓐ Ⓑ Ⓒ Ⓓ	30 Ⓐ Ⓑ Ⓒ Ⓓ	38 Ⓐ Ⓑ Ⓒ Ⓓ
7 Ⓐ Ⓑ Ⓒ Ⓓ	15 Ⓐ Ⓑ Ⓒ Ⓓ	23 Ⓐ Ⓑ Ⓒ Ⓓ	31 Ⓐ Ⓑ Ⓒ Ⓓ	39 Ⓐ Ⓑ Ⓒ Ⓓ
8 Ⓐ Ⓑ Ⓒ Ⓓ	16 Ⓐ Ⓑ Ⓒ Ⓓ	24 Ⓐ Ⓑ Ⓒ Ⓓ	32 Ⓐ Ⓑ Ⓒ Ⓓ	40 Ⓐ Ⓑ Ⓒ Ⓓ

SECTION 2

1 Ⓐ Ⓑ Ⓒ Ⓓ	9 Ⓐ Ⓑ Ⓒ Ⓓ	17 Ⓐ Ⓑ Ⓒ Ⓓ	25 Ⓐ Ⓑ Ⓒ Ⓓ	33 Ⓐ Ⓑ Ⓒ Ⓓ
2 Ⓐ Ⓑ Ⓒ Ⓓ	10 Ⓐ Ⓑ Ⓒ Ⓓ	18 Ⓐ Ⓑ Ⓒ Ⓓ	26 Ⓐ Ⓑ Ⓒ Ⓓ	34 Ⓐ Ⓑ Ⓒ Ⓓ
3 Ⓐ Ⓑ Ⓒ Ⓓ	11 Ⓐ Ⓑ Ⓒ Ⓓ	19 Ⓐ Ⓑ Ⓒ Ⓓ	27 Ⓐ Ⓑ Ⓒ Ⓓ	35 Ⓐ Ⓑ Ⓒ Ⓓ
4 Ⓐ Ⓑ Ⓒ Ⓓ	12 Ⓐ Ⓑ Ⓒ Ⓓ	20 Ⓐ Ⓑ Ⓒ Ⓓ	28 Ⓐ Ⓑ Ⓒ Ⓓ	36 Ⓐ Ⓑ Ⓒ Ⓓ
5 Ⓐ Ⓑ Ⓒ Ⓓ	13 Ⓐ Ⓑ Ⓒ Ⓓ	21 Ⓐ Ⓑ Ⓒ Ⓓ	29 Ⓐ Ⓑ Ⓒ Ⓓ	37 Ⓐ Ⓑ Ⓒ Ⓓ
6 Ⓐ Ⓑ Ⓒ Ⓓ	14 Ⓐ Ⓑ Ⓒ Ⓓ	22 Ⓐ Ⓑ Ⓒ Ⓓ	30 Ⓐ Ⓑ Ⓒ Ⓓ	
7 Ⓐ Ⓑ Ⓒ Ⓓ	15 Ⓐ Ⓑ Ⓒ Ⓓ	23 Ⓐ Ⓑ Ⓒ Ⓓ	31 Ⓐ Ⓑ Ⓒ Ⓓ	
8 Ⓐ Ⓑ Ⓒ Ⓓ	16 Ⓐ Ⓑ Ⓒ Ⓓ	24 Ⓐ Ⓑ Ⓒ Ⓓ	32 Ⓐ Ⓑ Ⓒ Ⓓ	

SECTION 3

1 Ⓐ Ⓑ Ⓒ Ⓓ	9 Ⓐ Ⓑ Ⓒ Ⓓ	17 Ⓐ Ⓑ Ⓒ Ⓓ	25 Ⓐ Ⓑ Ⓒ Ⓓ	33 Ⓐ Ⓑ Ⓒ Ⓓ
2 Ⓐ Ⓑ Ⓒ Ⓓ	10 Ⓐ Ⓑ Ⓒ Ⓓ	18 Ⓐ Ⓑ Ⓒ Ⓓ	26 Ⓐ Ⓑ Ⓒ Ⓓ	34 Ⓐ Ⓑ Ⓒ Ⓓ
3 Ⓐ Ⓑ Ⓒ Ⓓ	11 Ⓐ Ⓑ Ⓒ Ⓓ	19 Ⓐ Ⓑ Ⓒ Ⓓ	27 Ⓐ Ⓑ Ⓒ Ⓓ	35 Ⓐ Ⓑ Ⓒ Ⓓ
4 Ⓐ Ⓑ Ⓒ Ⓓ	12 Ⓐ Ⓑ Ⓒ Ⓓ	20 Ⓐ Ⓑ Ⓒ Ⓓ	28 Ⓐ Ⓑ Ⓒ Ⓓ	36 Ⓐ Ⓑ Ⓒ Ⓓ
5 Ⓐ Ⓑ Ⓒ Ⓓ	13 Ⓐ Ⓑ Ⓒ Ⓓ	21 Ⓐ Ⓑ Ⓒ Ⓓ	29 Ⓐ Ⓑ Ⓒ Ⓓ	
6 Ⓐ Ⓑ Ⓒ Ⓓ	14 Ⓐ Ⓑ Ⓒ Ⓓ	22 Ⓐ Ⓑ Ⓒ Ⓓ	30 Ⓐ Ⓑ Ⓒ Ⓓ	
7 Ⓐ Ⓑ Ⓒ Ⓓ	15 Ⓐ Ⓑ Ⓒ Ⓓ	23 Ⓐ Ⓑ Ⓒ Ⓓ	31 Ⓐ Ⓑ Ⓒ Ⓓ	
8 Ⓐ Ⓑ Ⓒ Ⓓ	16 Ⓐ Ⓑ Ⓒ Ⓓ	24 Ⓐ Ⓑ Ⓒ Ⓓ	32 Ⓐ Ⓑ Ⓒ Ⓓ	

SECTION 4

1 Ⓐ Ⓑ Ⓒ Ⓓ	11 Ⓐ Ⓑ Ⓒ Ⓓ	21 Ⓐ Ⓑ Ⓒ Ⓓ	31 Ⓐ Ⓑ Ⓒ Ⓓ	41 Ⓐ Ⓑ Ⓒ Ⓓ
2 Ⓐ Ⓑ Ⓒ Ⓓ	12 Ⓐ Ⓑ Ⓒ Ⓓ	22 Ⓐ Ⓑ Ⓒ Ⓓ	32 Ⓐ Ⓑ Ⓒ Ⓓ	42 Ⓐ Ⓑ Ⓒ Ⓓ
3 Ⓐ Ⓑ Ⓒ Ⓓ	13 Ⓐ Ⓑ Ⓒ Ⓓ	23 Ⓐ Ⓑ Ⓒ Ⓓ	33 Ⓐ Ⓑ Ⓒ Ⓓ	43 Ⓐ Ⓑ Ⓒ Ⓓ
4 Ⓐ Ⓑ Ⓒ Ⓓ	14 Ⓐ Ⓑ Ⓒ Ⓓ	24 Ⓐ Ⓑ Ⓒ Ⓓ	34 Ⓐ Ⓑ Ⓒ Ⓓ	44 Ⓐ Ⓑ Ⓒ Ⓓ
5 Ⓐ Ⓑ Ⓒ Ⓓ	15 Ⓐ Ⓑ Ⓒ Ⓓ	25 Ⓐ Ⓑ Ⓒ Ⓓ	35 Ⓐ Ⓑ Ⓒ Ⓓ	45 Ⓐ Ⓑ Ⓒ Ⓓ
6 Ⓐ Ⓑ Ⓒ Ⓓ	16 Ⓐ Ⓑ Ⓒ Ⓓ	26 Ⓐ Ⓑ Ⓒ Ⓓ	36 Ⓐ Ⓑ Ⓒ Ⓓ	46 Ⓐ Ⓑ Ⓒ Ⓓ
7 Ⓐ Ⓑ Ⓒ Ⓓ	17 Ⓐ Ⓑ Ⓒ Ⓓ	27 Ⓐ Ⓑ Ⓒ Ⓓ	37 Ⓐ Ⓑ Ⓒ Ⓓ	47 Ⓐ Ⓑ Ⓒ Ⓓ
8 Ⓐ Ⓑ Ⓒ Ⓓ	18 Ⓐ Ⓑ Ⓒ Ⓓ	28 Ⓐ Ⓑ Ⓒ Ⓓ	38 Ⓐ Ⓑ Ⓒ Ⓓ	
9 Ⓐ Ⓑ Ⓒ Ⓓ	19 Ⓐ Ⓑ Ⓒ Ⓓ	29 Ⓐ Ⓑ Ⓒ Ⓓ	39 Ⓐ Ⓑ Ⓒ Ⓓ	
10 Ⓐ Ⓑ Ⓒ Ⓓ	20 Ⓐ Ⓑ Ⓒ Ⓓ	30 Ⓐ Ⓑ Ⓒ Ⓓ	40 Ⓐ Ⓑ Ⓒ Ⓓ	

Section 1
Verbal Reasoning

| **40 Questions** | **Time: 20 Minutes** |

This section is divided into two parts that contain two different types of questions. As soon as you have completed Part One, answer the questions in Part Two. You may write in your test booklet. For each answer you select, fill in the corresponding circle on your answer document.

Part One – Synonyms

Each question in Part One consists of a word in capital letters followed by four answer choices. Select the one word that is most nearly the same in meaning as the word in capital letters.

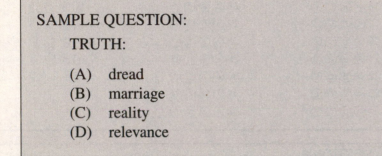

SAMPLE QUESTION:

TRUTH:

Sample Answer

Ⓐ Ⓑ ● Ⓓ

(A)   dread
(B)   marriage
(C)   reality
(D)   relevance

Go on to the next page. ⟶

VR

Part Two – Sentence Completion

Each question in Part Two is made up of a sentence with one blank. Each blank indicates that a word is missing. The sentence is followed by four answer choices. Select the word that best completes the meaning of the sentence as a whole.

SAMPLE QUESTIONS:

The question was so ------- that the best
student in class got it wrong.

(A) coarse
(B) difficult
(C) funny
(D) long

Sample Answer

Ⓐ ● Ⓒ Ⓓ

STOP. Do not go on
until told to do so.

Part One – Synonyms

Directions: Select the word that is most nearly the same in meaning as the word in capital letters.

1. UNUSUAL:

   (A) friendly
   (B) happy
   (C) new
   (D) peculiar

2. ASSISTANCE:

   (A) call
   (B) disability
   (C) service
   (D) teaching

3. REALITY:

   (A) dream
   (B) fact
   (C) rarity
   (D) security

4. DIMINUTION:

   (A) assessment
   (B) leniency
   (C) reduction
   (D) restitution

5. CONTENTED:

   (A) diplomatic
   (B) disgusted
   (C) mammoth
   (D) satisfied

6. BOUND:

   (A) badgered
   (B) confused
   (C) obliged
   (D) relieved

7. FALTER:

   (A) drop
   (B) hesitate
   (C) question
   (D) replenish

8. CONTAINED:

   (A) eliminated
   (B) held
   (C) raging
   (D) wooden

9. REVERE:

   (A) disdain
   (B) esteem
   (C) faith
   (D) reliance

10. DILIGENT:

    (A) defensive
    (B) hardworking
    (C) lazy
    (D) obsessive

Go on to the next page. ➡

11. DETRIMENTAL:

    (A) harmful
    (B) knowledgeable
    (C) tentative
    (D) worrisome

12. VOW:

    (A) argue
    (B) claim
    (C) please
    (D) pledge

13. ASPIRATION:

    (A) focus
    (B) hope
    (C) injury
    (D) trend

14. BASHFUL:

    (A) argumentative
    (B) serious
    (C) shy
    (D) tolerant

15. SINISTER:

    (A) elderly
    (B) erratic
    (C) uncomfortable
    (D) wicked

16. DISCLOSE:

    (A) hide
    (B) remove
    (C) reveal
    (D) undress

17. CONGEAL:

    (A) coagulate
    (B) help
    (C) recede
    (D) weaken

18. INUNDATE:

    (A) enter
    (B) flood
    (C) migrate
    (D) strive

19. STEADFAST:

    (A) constant
    (B) optional
    (C) quick
    (D) restful

20. RUTHLESS:

    (A) counterfeit
    (B) unofficial
    (C) unsparing
    (D) victorious

Go on to the next page. ➡

Part Two – Sentence Completion

Directions: Select the word that best completes the sentence.

21. Myron was able to remain completely
 -------; he never took sides in any of the
 disagreements around the house.

 (A) biased
 (B) interested
 (C) neutral
 (D) thoughtful

22. Since the great drought left the soil completely useless, the people of that country
 were forced to ------- food from other
 countries.

 (A) export
 (B) import
 (C) report on
 (D) sell

23. Because he was annoyed by even the
 smallest grammatical error, Mr. Jones
 reviewed all the students' papers -------
 before grading them.

 (A) crudely
 (B) helplessly
 (C) inefficiently
 (D) meticulously

24. Eric doesn't merely dislike racism; he
 ------- it.

 (A) abhors
 (B) moderates
 (C) questions
 (D) studies

25. Sharon's anger was too great: David simply could not ------- her with his charm.

 (A) irritate
 (B) manipulate
 (C) pacify
 (D) terrify

26. Even though the accident led to serious
 damage to our property, our ------- lawyer
 didn't present a convincing argument and
 we received no compensation.

 (A) discerning
 (B) fatalistic
 (C) incompetent
 (D) professional

27. After months of petty disputes, the two
 countries finally decided to sit down at a
 table and have a ------- discussion.

 (A) friendly
 (B) hostile
 (C) lengthy
 (D) pressing

28. Although the thief claimed that he accidentally picked up the stolen watch, the
 jury judged his action -------.

 (A) deliberate
 (B) frantic
 (C) impractical
 (D) misguided

Go on to the next page. ➞

29. In order to be a good doctor, you don't need to be ------- yourself, just as a good architect does not have to live in a fancy house.

    (A) educated
    (B) handsome
    (C) healthy
    (D) thoughtful

30. Pete ------- his coach when he followed up his winning season with an even better performance this year.

    (A) disappointed
    (B) gratified
    (C) relieved
    (D) upset

31. While many species, such as wolves, travel in groups, the cheetah is a ------- animal.

    (A) dangerous
    (B) pack
    (C) solitary
    (D) territorial

32. During his years in the Senate, Jones felt ------- about speaking up at all, while most of the other senators were aggressive and argumentative.

    (A) blithe
    (B) contented
    (C) favorable
    (D) timid

33. The politician's speech was so ------- that nearly everyone in the room decided not to vote for him.

    (A) feeble
    (B) monotonous
    (C) persuasive
    (D) unique

34. The corporation did not have a ------- system for promotions; each department was free to use its own discretion in advancing employees.

    (A) dignified
    (B) favorable
    (C) forgiving
    (D) uniform

35. Only from years of training can a gymnast hope to become ------- enough to master Olympic-level techniques.

    (A) agile
    (B) mature
    (C) passive
    (D) strict

36. Though Mr. Fenster was known to be ------- toward his neighbors, he always welcomed their children as trick-or-treaters at Halloween.

    (A) belligerent
    (B) cheerful
    (C) courteous
    (D) direct

Go on to the next page. ➡

37. The ------- young man talked back to his parents and teachers alike.

    (A) dreary
    (B) insolent
    (C) nervous
    (D) respectful

38. While the painting's brushstrokes seem -------, they are actually carefully planned out.

    (A) flagrant
    (B) haphazard
    (C) intricate
    (D) paltry

39. The Declaration of Independence is premised upon ------- principles, such as protecting life, liberty, and the pursuit of happiness.

    (A) united
    (B) lofty
    (C) predictable
    (D) variable

40. Our teacher advised us not to get too caught up in the ------- of information in the textbook, or we could lose the "big picture" of its theory.

    (A) minutiae
    (B) principles
    (C) scope
    (D) thought

STOP. If there is time, you may check your work in this section only.

Section 2
Quantitative Reasoning

37 Questions	Time: 35 Minutes

This section is divided into two parts that contain two different types of questions. As soon as you have completed Part One, answer the questions in Part Two. You may write in your test booklet. For each answer you select, remember to fill in the corresponding circle on your answer document.

Any figures that accompany the questions in this section may be assumed to be drawn as accurately as possible EXCEPT when it is stated that a particular figure is not drawn to scale. Letters such as *x, y,* and *n* stand for real numbers.

Part One – Word Problems

Each question in Part One consists of a word problem followed by four answer choices. You may write in your test booklet; however, you may be able to solve many of these problems in your head. Next, look at the four answer choices given and select the best answer.

EXAMPLE 1:

What is the value of the expression

$1 + 3 \times (4 \div 2) - 5$?

(A) 2
(B) 3
(C) 4
(D) 8

The correct answer is 2, so circle A is darkened.

Sample Answer

● Ⓑ Ⓒ Ⓓ

Go on to the next page. ➡

Part Two – Quantitative Comparisons

All questions in Part Two are quantitative comparisons between the quantities shown in Column A and Column B. Using the information given in each question, compare the quantity in Column A to the quantity in Column B, and chose one of these four answer choices:

(A)　The quantity in Column A is greater.
(B)　The quantity in Column B is greater.
(C)　The two quantities are equal.
(D)　The relationship cannot be determined from the information given.

EXAMPLE 2:	Column A	Column B	Sample Answer
	$\frac{2}{3}$ of 9	$\frac{1}{3}$ of 18	Ⓐ Ⓑ ● Ⓓ

The quantity in <u>Column A</u> (6) is the same as the quantity in <u>Column B</u> (6), so circle C is darkened.

EXAMPLE 3:

Sample Answer

Ⓐ Ⓑ Ⓒ ●

When integer x is multiplied by 2, the result is greater than 10 but less than 16.

Column A	Column B
x	7

Since $10 < 2x < 16$, $5 < x < 8$. Thus, as x can equal 6 or 7, there is not enough information given to determine the relationship. Circle D is darkened.

STOP. Do not go on until told to do so.

NO TEST MATERIAL ON THIS PAGE

Part One – Word Problems

Directions: Choose the best answer from the four choices given.

1. $54 \times 3 =$

   (A) 123
   (B) 150
   (C) 162
   (D) 172

2. What is the area of a square with a side of length 2 ?

   (A) 2
   (B) 4
   (C) 6
   (D) 8

3. $3 \times 2 \times 1 - (4 \times 3 \times 2) =$

   (A) 18
   (B) 6
   (C) −6
   (D) −18

4. Vicky scored 80, 90, and 94 on her three tests. What was her average score?

   (A) 81
   (B) 88
   (C) 90
   (D) 93

Questions 5–6 refer to the following graph.

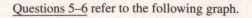

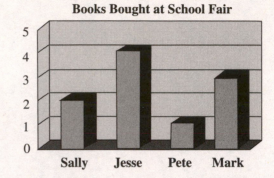

Books Bought at School Fair

5. Who bought the most books at the school fair?

   (A) Sally
   (B) Jesse
   (C) Pete
   (D) Mark

6. Sally and Mark together bought how many more books than Jesse?

   (A) 1
   (B) 2
   (C) 3
   (D) 5

Go on to the next page. ➡

QR

7. $\frac{1}{2} + \frac{3}{4} =$

    (A) $\frac{3}{8}$

    (B) $\frac{5}{4}$

    (C) $\frac{3}{2}$

    (D) $\frac{5}{2}$

8. What is the value of the digit 7 in the number 4,678.02 ?

    (A)   7
    (B)   70
    (C)   700
    (D) 7,000

9. Jason has several books in his room, 20% of which are fiction. The other books are nonfiction. If he has 5 fiction books, how many nonfiction books does he have?

    (A)   5
    (B) 10
    (C) 20
    (D) 25

10. $\frac{7}{0.35} =$

    (A)   0.2
    (B)   2
    (C) 20
    (D) 200

11. Which of the following is closest in value to 5 ?

    (A) 4.5
    (B) 5.009
    (C) 5.01
    (D) 5.101

12. Janice went to the butcher and bought six pounds of hamburger. If the bill was $18.50, which of the following is closest to the cost per pound of the hamburger?

    (A) $2.00
    (B) $3.00
    (C) $5.00
    (D) $6.00

13. Which of the following numbers is closest to the square root of 175 ?

    (A)   9
    (B) 13
    (C) 22
    (D) 30

14. Laurie was reading a book that had an illustration on every odd-numbered page. If there are 32 numbered pages in the book, how many illustrations are there?

    (A) 15
    (B) 16
    (C) 17
    (D) 31

Go on to the next page. →

15. If $6y + 8 = 20$, what is the value of $3y + 4$?

(A)   2
(B)   8
(C)   10
(D)   12

16. A lecture hall's maximum capacity of 56 has increased by 75%. What is the new seating capacity after the increase?

(A)   42
(B)   70
(C)   98
(D)   112

17. When a number is divided by 8, the quotient is 11 and the remainder is 2. What is the number?

(A)   11
(B)   22
(C)   72
(D)   90

The following graph shows the amount of rainfall in Miller County for the years 1942–1946.

Average Inches of Rainfall in Miller County, 1942–1946

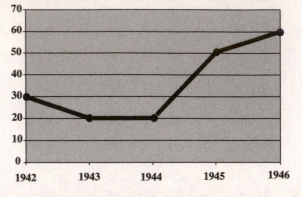

18. When did the greatest increase in rainfall occur in Miller County?

(A)   Between 1942 and 1943
(B)   Between 1943 and 1944
(C)   Between 1944 and 1945
(D)   Between 1945 and 1946

19. The temperature at 6 A.M. was 32 degrees. If the temperature increased at a constant rate of 3 degrees per hour all day, what was the temperature at 1 P.M.?

(A)   35 degrees
(B)   43 degrees
(C)   47 degrees
(D)   53 degrees

20. What is the volume of a box with length 4 cm, width 3 cm, and height 2 cm?

(A)   6 cubic centimeters
(B)   9 cubic centimeters
(C)   12 cubic centimeters
(D)   24 cubic centimeters

Go on to the next page. ⟶

QR

Part Two – Quantitative Comparisons

Directions: Using all information given in each question, compare the quantity in Column A to the quantity in Column B. All questions in Part Two have these answer choices:

(A) The quantity in Column A is greater.
(B) The quantity in Column B is greater.
(C) The two quantities are equal.
(D) The relationship cannot be determined from the information given.

Column A	Column B
23. $\sqrt{9}+\sqrt{25}$	$\sqrt{9+25}$

125° / x

	Column A	Column B
21.	x	55

A rectangle with sides x and y has an area of 12.

	Column A	Column B
22.	The length of x	The length of y

The quadrilateral $ABCD$ has an area of 12

	Column A	Column B
24.	The perimeter of $ABCD$	15

Go on to the next page. ➡

Answer choices for all questions on this page.

(A) The quantity in Column A is greater.
(B) The quantity in Column B is greater.
(C) The two quantities are equal.
(D) The relationship cannot be determined from the information given.

Martha had $20. She gave half of her money to her sister, Linda. Linda now has $30.

Column A	Column B

25. The amount of money Martha now has | The amount of money Linda had originally

---

$$4x + 7 = 63$$

$$\frac{y}{3} + 6 = 15$$

Column A	Column B

26. x y

Column A	Column B

27. The area of a rectangle with length 3 and width 4 | The area of a square with a side of 3

Number of Cookies Eaten Each Day

Wednesday	3
Thursday	2
Friday	1
Saturday	3

Column A	Column B

28. The average number of cookies eaten each day | The number of cookies eaten on Thursday

---

Column A	Column B

29. $\sqrt{0.64}$ $\sqrt{6.4}$

Go on to the next page. ➡

QR

Answer choices for all questions on this page.

(A) The quantity in Column A is greater.
(B) The quantity in Column B is greater.
(C) The two quantities are equal.
(D) The relationship cannot be determined from the information given.

Amy bought 5 oranges and 6 peaches. The total price of the fruit was $1.10.

Column A	Column B
30. The cost of one orange	The cost of one peach

Column A	Column B
31. $-(5)^6$	$(-5)^6$

a represents an odd integer greater than 9 and less than 15.

b represents an even integer greater than 9 and less than 15.

Column A	Column B
32. $a \times 3$	$b \times 4$

A 12-sided die with faces numbered 1 through 12 is rolled.

Column A	Column B
33. The probability that the result is even	The probability that the result is prime

Go on to the next page. ➞

Answer choices for all questions on this page.

(A) The quantity in Column A is greater.
(B) The quantity in Column B is greater.
(C) The two quantities are equal.
(D) The relationship cannot be determined from the information given.

The original price of a shirt now on sale was $50.

	Column A	Column B
36.	The price of the shirt after two 20% discounts	The price of the shirt after a single 40% discount

	Column A	Column B
34.	The fractional part of the figure that is shaded	$\dfrac{3}{20}$

	Column A	Column B
37.	The slope of the line with points (3, 8) and (5, 2)	The slope of the line $6x - 2y = -8$

Melvin brought home a large pizza with 12 slices.

	Column A	Column B
35.	The number of slices left if Melvin eats 50% of the pizza	The number of slices left if Melvin eats one-third of the pizza

STOP. If there is time, you may check your work in this section only.

Section 3
Reading Comprehension

This section contains six short reading passages. Each passage is followed by six questions based on its content. Answer the questions following each passage on the basis of what is <u>stated</u> or <u>implied</u> in that passage. You may write in the test booklet.

STOP. Do not go on
until told to do so.

Questions 1–6

Line

1   When most people think of the history
2   of transportation, they think of the invention
3   of the wheel as the starting point. The
4   wheel was invented around 3,500 B.C.E.,
5   more than 5,000 years ago. Before then,
6   transportation was a difficult process,
7   especially for those who had anything to
8   carry. During prehistoric times, the only
9   way to get around was to walk. Children
10 and possessions were strapped to someone's
11 back if they needed to be carried. If the
12 load was too heavy for one person, it could
13 be strapped to a pole and carried by two.
14 The sledge was developed as a way to
15 drag a heavy load. Sledges were originally

16 just logs or pieces of animal skin upon
17 which a load was strapped and dragged.
18 In time, runners were put on the sledge,
19 and it evolved to what is now called a sled.
20 Around 5,000 B.C.E., the first animals were
21 domesticated, or tamed. Then, donkeys and
22 oxen were used to carry heavy loads and
23 pull sledges. It wasn't until almost 1,500
24 years later that wheeled vehicles appeared.
25 It is believed that the wheel was invented
26 in Mesopotamia, in the Middle East. About
27 300 years later, the Egyptians invented the
28 sailboat. These two inventions changed
29 transportation forever.

Go on to the next page. ➡

1. The primary purpose of the passage is to

   (A) describe some of the things people used for transportation long ago
   (B) describe the reasons that led to transportation discoveries
   (C) explain the evolution of the sled
   (D) give a detailed history of transportation

2. The passage suggests that prehistoric man used all of the following for carrying things EXCEPT

   (A) animals
   (B) children
   (C) poles
   (D) primitive sleds

3. The passage implies that early man

   (A) was incapable of inventing the wheel any earlier than 3,500 B.C.E.
   (B) was interested in farming
   (C) was interested in finding ways to help carry things
   (D) was outgoing and friendly

4. It can be inferred from the passage that the reason animals were domesticated was

   (A) to help carry large loads
   (B) to move people and possessions around quickly
   (C) to provide family pets
   (D) to ward off danger

5. Which of the following describes the author's attitude toward the invention of the wheel?

   (A) Admiration
   (B) Disdain
   (C) Indifference
   (D) Regret

6. The passage suggests that the sledge was

   (A) a precursor to the sled
   (B) invented in conjunction with the wheel
   (C) made exclusively of animal skin
   (D) the only tool used for transportation at the time

Go on to the next page. ➞

Questions 7–12

Line

1   Bison and buffalo are not the same
2 animal. For years, American bison were
3 mistakenly referred to as buffalo. Due to
4 this confusion there are many references
5 to buffalo in the United States. There is the
6 city of Buffalo in northwestern New York
7 state. In addition, the buffalo appeared
8 on the U.S. nickel for many years at the
9 beginning of the twentieth century. This is
10 often referred to as the "Buffalo Nickel" to
11 distinguish it from the current nickel with
12 Thomas Jefferson on the front. Buffalo are
13 actually found in Asia, Africa, and South
14 America. Bison roamed the North American
15 western plains by the millions just a couple
16 of centuries ago. Because the bison were so
17 widely hunted, however, their numbers fell
18 greatly. In fact, as of a century ago, there
19 were only about 500 left. They were deemed
20 near extinction, but due to conservation
21 efforts, their numbers have increased. There
22 are approximately 50,000 bison living today
23 in protected parks. Though they may never
24 be as abundant as they once were, they are
25 not in danger of extinction as long as they
26 remain protected.

Go on to the next page. ➞

7. The primary purpose of the passage is to

    (A) applaud conservation efforts
    (B) explain the genetic difference between the bison and the buffalo
    (C) explain why people confuse the buffalo and the bison
    (D) give some background on the American bison

8. The passage implies that the primary difference between the buffalo and the bison is

    (A) their geographic location
    (B) their number
    (C) their size
    (D) when they existed

9. As used in line 19, the word "deemed" most closely means

    (A) found
    (B) hunted
    (C) ruled
    (D) eaten

10. According to the passage, what can be hoped for as long as the American bison is protected?

    (A) They will be as plentiful as they once were.
    (B) They will disturb the delicate ecological balance in the plains.
    (C) They will face even greater dangers.
    (D) They will probably not die out.

11. According to the passage, the primary reason that the American bison is no longer near extinction is

    (A) conservation efforts
    (B) lack of interest in hunting them
    (C) loss of value of their fur
    (D) the migration of the animals

12. In line 6, the author mentions the city of Buffalo in order to

    (A) criticize a hunting practice
    (B) establish the reason for a particular currency
    (C) illustrate a common misunderstanding
    (D) pinpoint the first sighting of buffalo in New York

Go on to the next page. ➡

Questions 13–18

Line

1   The Greek philosopher Aristotle
2 had many students, but perhaps none so
3 famous as Alexander the Great. As a child,
4 Alexander was known for his intelligence
5 and bravery. The lessons he learned from
6 Aristotle left him with a lifelong love of
7 books and learning. But it was not his love
8 of books that made him famous. Alexander,
9 in 336 B.C., became the king of a small
10 Greek kingdom called Macedonia. He was
11 only twenty at the time. He went on to

12 invade country after country: Persia (now
13 known as Iran), Egypt, and all the way
14 to parts of India and Pakistan. Alexander
15 conquered most of what was then the
16 "civilized world." He brought with him the
17 Greek way of thinking and doing things. He
18 is considered one of the great generals and
19 kings of history and is responsible for the
20 spread of Greek culture throughout much of
21 the world.

Go on to the next page. ⟶

13. Which of the following would be the best title for the passage?

    (A) "Alexander the Great: King and Conqueror"
    (B) "Aristotle: Teacher of the Kings"
    (C) "Greek Culture"
    (D) "The History of Macedonia"

14. As used in line 16, the word "civilized" most closely means

    (A) barbaric
    (B) educated
    (C) friendly
    (D) well-mannered

15. The tone of the passage is most like that found in

    (A) a diary entry from an historian
    (B) a letter from an archeologist
    (C) a philosophy journal
    (D) a reference book

16. According to the passage, one of the things that was so impressive about Alexander was

    (A) his ability to teach
    (B) his great integrity
    (C) his handsome features
    (D) his intelligence and culture

17. The passage suggests that Aristotle

    (A) encouraged Alexander to spread culture
    (B) helped foster Alexander's love of books
    (C) supported Alexander's military career
    (D) taught Alexander military strategy

18. According to the passage, when Alexander invaded a country, he

    (A) enslaved citizens
    (B) freed oppressed people
    (C) spread Greek ideas
    (D) toppled monuments

Go on to the next page. ➞

Questions 19–24

Line

Everyone has had attacks of the hiccups, or hiccoughs, at one point in his or her life. Few people, however, think about what is happening to them and how hiccups begin and end.

The diaphragm is a large muscle, shaped like a dome, that sits at the base of the chest cavity. As one breathes, the diaphragm gently contracts and relaxes to help the process. Occasionally, an irritation near the diaphragm or a disease may cause the muscle to spasm, or contract suddenly. The spasm will suck air into the lungs past the vocal cords. A small flap called the epiglottis tops the vocal cords so that food will not accidentally enter into the windpipe. The sudden spasm of the diaphragm causes the epiglottis to close quickly. Imagine the pull of air into the vocal cords from the spastic diaphragm hitting the closed epiglottis. This moves the vocal cords, causing the "hic" sound of the hiccup. Although most people don't really worry about the hiccups, attacks may last for days. The exhaustion of hiccuping for days on end has been fatal in certain rare cases. Home remedies abound—from breathing into paper bags to squeezing on pressure points that supposedly relax the diaphragm.

Go on to the next page. ➡

19. The primary purpose of the passage is to

    (A) describe a common occurrence
    (B) prescribe a treatment
    (C) settle a dispute
    (D) warn about a danger

20. According to the passage, one possible cause of hiccups is

    (A) a sudden rush of air
    (B) an irritant near the diaphragm
    (C) breathing in and out of a paper bag
    (D) the closing of the epiglottis

21. As used in line 24, "attacks" most closely means

    (A) advances
    (B) assaults
    (C) bouts
    (D) threats

22. The passage suggests that which of the following makes the "hic" sound of the hiccup?

    (A) The diaphragm
    (B) The lungs
    (C) The stomach
    (D) The vocal cords

23. According to the passage, the hiccups can be fatal due to

    (A) fatigue from days of hiccuping
    (B) home remedies that are toxic
    (C) the humiliation of hiccuping for days on end
    (D) the irritant to the diaphragm

24. The author mentions "hiccoughs" in line 2 in order to

    (A) correct an improper usage
    (B) define a technical term
    (C) indicate an alternate spelling
    (D) weaken a misguided argument

Go on to the next page. ➡

Questions 25–30

Line
1   During the winter months in many
2 regions, food can be extremely scarce. For
3 the wildlife of these areas, this can be a
4 great problem unless animals have some
5 mechanism that allows them to adapt. Some
6 animals migrate to warmer climates. Others
7 hibernate to conserve energy and decrease
8 the need for food. Prior to hibernation, an
9 animal will generally eat a lot to build up a
10 store of fat. The animal's system will "feed"
11 off the fat stores throughout the long cold
12 winter months. When the animal hibernates,
13 its body temperature decreases and its body
14 functions slow down considerably. The
15 dormouse's heartbeat, for example, slows
16 down to just a beat every few minutes. Its

17 breathing also becomes slow and its body
18 temperature drops to just a few degrees
19 above the temperature of the ground around
20 it. All these changes decrease the need for
21 fuel and allow the animal to survive long
22 periods without any food. It is a mistake
23 to think that all hibernating animals sleep
24 for the whole winter. In fact, many animals
25 hibernate for short spurts during the winter.
26 They may wake for an interval of mild
27 weather. Scientists have now discovered
28 the chemical that triggers hibernation. If
29 this chemical is injected in an animal in the
30 summer months, it can cause the animal to
31 go into summer hibernation.

Go on to the next page. ➔

25. The primary purpose of the passage is to

    (A) compare the hibernating dormouse to other hibernating animals
    (B) debunk some common myths about hibernation
    (C) discuss the discovery of the chemical that causes hibernation
    (D) explore some basic information about hibernation

26. As used in line 7, the word "conserve" most closely means

    (A) expend
    (B) help
    (C) reserve
    (D) waste

27. According to the author, each of the following happens to a hibernating animal EXCEPT

    (A) it goes into a dream state
    (B) its body temperature drops
    (C) its breathing slows
    (D) its heartbeat slows

28. Which of the following can be inferred as a reason a hibernating animal may interrupt its hibernation?

    (A) A day or two of stormy weather
    (B) An overabundance of food
    (C) A week in which there was no snow
    (D) A week in which the temperature was well above freezing

29. According to the author, if the chemical that triggers hibernation is injected into an animal when it would not normally hibernate, the chemical may

    (A) allow the animal to shed extra fat stores
    (B) cause an out-of-season hibernation
    (C) cause body functions to slow to a halt
    (D) decrease an animal's need for food

30. The tone of the passage is best described as

    (A) amazed
    (B) concerned
    (C) indifferent
    (D) informative

Go on to the next page. ⟶

Questions 31–36

Line

1   The theater is one of the richest art
2   forms. The excitement of opening night
3   can be felt by the people waiting to watch
4   a performance and by the performers and
5   workers backstage waiting for the curtain
6   to go up. Live theater is thrilling because
7   no one really knows how well the play
8   will go until it is performed. Many people
9   collaborate to bring a play to life. There
10 are playwrights, directors, set designers,
11 costumers, lighting technicians, and,
12 of course, actors. If the performance is
13 a musical, the skills of a songwriter, a
14 choreographer (the person who composes
15 the dances), and musicians are also
16 required. The word *theater* comes from the
17 Greek *theatron*, which means "a place for
18 seeing." One concept from Greek theater
19 that is still seen in some plays today is the
20 "Greek Chorus." This consists of several
21 actors/characters watching the action of the

22 play (almost like the audience) and then
23 commenting on what they just saw with
24 either reactions or dialogue. Although most
25 people think of the theater in terms of a play
26 performed on the stage, theater has taken
27 on a much broader meaning in the modern
28 world. You may find yourself walking into
29 a theater with no seats in the rows. Instead,
30 you are seated among the set pieces, which
31 makes you part of the setting. Sometimes
32 theater may come to life on a street corner,
33 or in a classroom. The excitement of theater
34 is in its very nature—it is an art form that
35 changes as it is interpreted in different
36 ways by different people. That is probably
37 why the works of the greatest playwright
38 of all time, William Shakespeare, are still
39 performed and enjoyed today, both in
40 classic and new interpretations.

Go on to the next page. ➞

31. The best title for the passage might be

    (A) "A Brief History of Theatrical Productions"
    (B) "Modern Theater: Adventures in Acting"
    (C) "Shakespeare: Our Greatest Playwright"
    (D) "The Excitement of Theater"

32. According to the passage, the primary reason that theater is so exciting is that

    (A) it derives from a Greek custom
    (B) it is performed live
    (C) plays are often well written
    (D) there are so many people working on it

33. The passage suggests which of the following about modern theater?

    (A) It always draws great attention from the audience.
    (B) It has been interpreted in a more varied fashion.
    (C) It is less exciting than classic theater.
    (D) There are mostly Shakespearean plays performed.

34. The author's attitude toward theater can best be described as

    (A) admiring
    (B) ambivalent
    (C) apathetic
    (D) neutral

35. In line 1, the word "richest" is best understood to mean most

    (A) diverse
    (B) entertaining
    (C) terrifying
    (D) wealthy

36. The passage suggests that the plays of Shakespeare

    (A) are more often given new interpretations today than at any other time
    (B) are more popular today than during Shakespeare's time
    (C) have been performed in a variety of ways
    (D) will always be considered the world's greatest

STOP. If there is time, you may check your work in this section only.

Section 4
Mathematics Achievement

Each question is followed by four suggested answers. Read each question and then decide which one of the four suggested answers is best.

Find the row of spaces on your answer document that has the same number as the question. In this row, mark the space having the same letter as the answer you have chosen. You may write in your test booklet.

SAMPLE QUESTION:

Sample Answer
Ⓐ ● Ⓒ Ⓓ

What is the perimeter of an equilateral triangle with a side length of 4 in?

(A) 8 in
(B) 12 in
(C) 16 in
(D) 24 in

The correct answer is 12 in, so circle B is darkened.

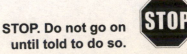

STOP. Do not go on until told to do so.

NO TEST MATERIAL ON THIS PAGE

1. In the decimal 0.0987, the digit 9 is equivalent to which of the following?

   (A) $\dfrac{9}{10}$

   (B) $\dfrac{9}{100}$

   (C) $\dfrac{9}{1,000}$

   (D) $\dfrac{9}{10,000}$

2. What is the least common multiple of 6, 9, and 12 ?

   (A) 3
   (B) 36
   (C) 72
   (D) 324

3. Which of the following equals 5 ?

   (A) $30 - 12 \div 2 \times (3 + 7)$
   (B) $30 - 12 \div (2 \times 3 + 7)$
   (C) $(30 - 12) \div 2 \times 3 + 7$
   (D) $30 - 12 \div 2 \times 3 - 7$

4. $\dfrac{5}{7} + \dfrac{2}{11} =$

   (A) $\dfrac{10}{17}$

   (B) $\dfrac{10}{77}$

   (C) $\dfrac{7}{18}$

   (D) $\dfrac{69}{77}$

5. $7\dfrac{1}{2}$ hours is how many minutes more than $6\dfrac{1}{4}$ hours?

   (A) 45
   (B) 60
   (C) 75
   (D) 90

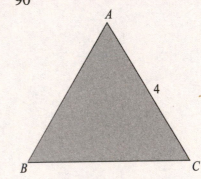

6. What is the perimeter of equilateral triangle *ABC* shown above?

   (A) 12
   (B) 15
   (C) 18
   (D) It cannot be determined from the information given.

Go on to the next page. ➡

7. Which of the following is 20% of 200 ?

   (A)   20
   (B)   30
   (C)   40
   (D)   100

Questions 8–10 refer to the following chart.

Day	Temperature (in degrees Celsius)	Snowfall (in centimeters)
Monday	2	3
Tuesday	6	3
Wednesday	3	4
Thursday	13	1

8. What was the total amount of snowfall for the four-day period shown?

   (A)   44 cm
   (B)   40 cm
   (C)   11 cm
   (D)   10 cm

9. On which day was the snowfall the greatest?

   (A)   Thursday
   (B)   Wednesday
   (C)   Tuesday
   (D)   Monday

10. What was the average temperature for each day in the four-day period?

    (A)   24 degrees
    (B)   20 degrees
    (C)   11 degrees
    (D)   6 degrees

11. $\dfrac{100}{0.25} =$

    (A)   4
    (B)   40
    (C)   400
    (D)   4000

12. $5 \times 31 = 100 +\_$

    (A)   55
    (B)   51
    (C)   50
    (D)   36

13. Gwen planted six tomato plants. Half of them died. She then planted one more. How many tomato plants does Gwen have now?

    (A)   3
    (B)   4
    (C)   5
    (D)   6

Go on to the next page. ➡

14. The public library charges one dollar to rent a video game overnight, with a fifty-cent charge for each day the video game is late. If Tracey returns a video game three days late, how much does she owe all together?

(A) $1.50
(B) $2.00
(C) $2.50
(D) $3.50

15. 0.45 × 100 =

(A) 4,500
(B) 450
(C) 45
(D) 4.5

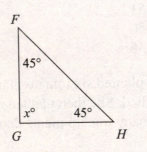

16. In triangle *FGH* shown above, the value of angle *x*, in degrees, is

(A) 30
(B) 45
(C) 50
(D) 90

17. If a dozen eggs cost $1.20, then 3 eggs cost

(A) 30¢
(B) 36¢
(C) 40¢
(D) $3.60

18. Boris and his friend Bruce collect baseball cards. If Bruce has 12 baseball cards and Boris has three times as many baseball cards as Bruce, what is the average number of cards in the boys' collections?

(A) 7.5
(B) 18
(C) 24
(D) 48

19. What is the perimeter of a rectangle with length 3 and width 2 ?

(A) 6
(B) 8
(C) 10
(D) 12

20. $\frac{3}{5} \times \frac{2}{7} =$

(A) $\frac{3}{8}$

(B) $\frac{6}{35}$

(C) $\frac{31}{35}$

(D) $\frac{21}{35}$

Go on to the next page. ➡

21. If Kenny can run three miles in 45 minutes, how long will it take him to run five miles?

   (A) 1 hour
   (B) 1 hour 15 minutes
   (C) 1 hour 30 minutes
   (D) 2 hours

22. Which fraction is greater than $\frac{5}{11}$?

   (A) $\frac{3}{8}$
   (B) $\frac{2}{7}$
   (C) $\frac{4}{9}$
   (D) $\frac{4}{7}$

23. If the perimeter of a square is 36, what is its area?

   (A) 16
   (B) 36
   (C) 64
   (D) 81

24. Maureen studied for two hours before school. After school she studied for twice as long as she had before school. What was the total number of hours she studied in the day?

   (A) 4
   (B) 6
   (C) 8
   (D) 12

25. $\dfrac{40(37+63)}{8} =$

   (A) 450
   (B) 500
   (C) 1,250
   (D) 4,000

26. 0.347 =

   (A) $\frac{7}{10} + \frac{4}{100} + \frac{3}{1,000}$
   (B) $\frac{3}{100} + \frac{4}{10} + \frac{7}{100}$
   (C) $\frac{4}{100} + \frac{3}{10} + \frac{7}{1,000}$
   (D) $\frac{3}{10} + \frac{4}{1,000} + \frac{7}{100}$

27. Which is the prime factorization of 36 ?

   (A) $3 \times 3 \times 3 \times 2$
   (B) $3 \times 3 \times 2 \times 2$
   (C) $3 \times 2 \times 2 \times 2$
   (D) $6 \times 3 \times 2$

Go on to the next page. ⟶

Questions 28–30 refer to the following chart.

Train Fares from Monroeville to Perkins' Corner

Fares	Weekday Peak	Weekday Off-Peak	Weekend & Holiday
One Way	$6.00	$5.00	$4.50
Round-Trip	$12.00	$10.00	$9.00
10-Trip Ticket	$54.00	$45.00	$40.00
Children Under 11	$1.00	$0.50	Free with Paying Adult

28. How much would it cost two adults and one child under the age of 11 to travel one way from Monroeville to Perkins' Corner on a weekend?

    (A) $25.00
    (B) $20.50
    (C) $18.00
    (D) $9.00

29. The price of a weekday peak fare ten-trip ticket is what percent less than the cost of purchasing ten one-way weekday peak fare tickets?

    (A) 10%
    (B) 20%
    (C) 50%
    (D) 100%

30. How much more does it cost for one adult to travel one way during the weekday peak fare period than for one adult to make the trip on the weekend?

    (A) $0.50
    (B) $0.75
    (C) $1.00
    (D) $1.50

31. Mr. Schroder swims laps at the community pool. It takes him 5 minutes to swim one lap. If he swims for 60 minutes without stopping, how many laps will he swim?

    (A)   8
    (B) 10
    (C) 12
    (D) 14

32. $10^3 =$

    (A) 10×3

    (B) $10 + 10 + 10$

    (C) $10 \times 10 \times 10$

    (D) $\dfrac{10}{3}$

Go on to the next page. ➞

33. A DVD player initially cost $100. During a sale, the store reduced the price by 10%. Two days later, the store reduced the new price by 20%. What was the final price?

    (A) $68
    (B) $70
    (C) $72
    (D) $80

34. Mr. Hoffman has a rectangular box that is 10 centimeters wide, 30 centimeters long, and 4 centimeters high. What is the volume of the box?

    (A)   44 cm³
    (B)   120 cm³
    (C)   300 cm³
    (D)   1,200 cm³

35. Dr. Heldman sees an average of nine patients an hour for eight hours on Monday and for six hours on Tuesday. What is the average number of patients she sees on each day?

    (A)   54
    (B)   63
    (C)   72
    (D)   126

36. If $q + 9 = 7 - p$, what is the value of $q + p$?

    (A)   −16
    (B)   −2
    (C)   2
    (D)   16

37. Which of the following is the product of two consecutive even integers?

    (A)   0
    (B)   15
    (C)   22
    (D)   30

38. Two triangles, *ABC* and *XYZ* are similar. Triangle *ABC* has lengths of 3, 4, and 5. Which of the following could be the corresponding lengths of triangle *XYZ* ?

    (A)   3, 3, and 3
    (B)   4, 5, and 6
    (C)   6, 8, and 10
    (D)   13, 14, and 15

39. The perimeter of a square whose area is 169 centimeters is

    (A)   52
    (B)   48
    (C)   44
    (D)   42

40. If three-fourths of the 240 employees at Tigger's Toys are at a party, how many of the employees are NOT at the party?

    (A)   60
    (B)   80
    (C)   120
    (D)   180

Go on to the next page. ➡

41. Jose and Greg are going on a 20-mile walk for charity. If they walk $\frac{1}{4}$ of the distance in the first two hours, and $\frac{1}{5}$ of the entire distance in the next hour and a half, how many miles do they have left to walk?

    (A)   9
    (B)   10
    (C)   11
    (D)   12

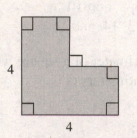

42. What is the perimeter of the shaded area in the figure above?

    (A)   15
    (B)   16
    (C)   24
    (D)   It cannot be determined from the information given.

43. A field hockey player scored an average of 3 goals per game for 12 games. How many points did she score in all 12 games?

    (A)   4
    (B)   20
    (C)   24
    (D)   36

44. What is the volume of a box with length 8, width 4, and height $\frac{1}{4}$?

    (A)   8
    (B) $12\frac{1}{4}$
    (C)   32
    (D)   128

45. The price of a $30 hat is decreased by 20%. What is the new price of the hat?

    (A) $10.00
    (B) $12.00
    (C) $20.00
    (D) $24.00

Go on to the next page. ➔

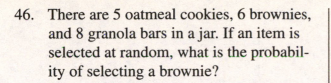
46. There are 5 oatmeal cookies, 6 brownies, and 8 granola bars in a jar. If an item is selected at random, what is the probability of selecting a brownie?

(A) $\dfrac{1}{6}$

(B) $\dfrac{6}{19}$

(C) $\dfrac{8}{19}$

(D) $\dfrac{6}{13}$

47. Which of the following is equivalent to $\dfrac{2}{3}x = 6 - y$?

(A) $2x = 6 - 3y$
(B) $3y - x = 6$
(C) $2x + 3y = 18$
(D) $2(x + 3y) = 18$

STOP. If there is time, you may check your work in this section only.

Essay

You will have 30 minutes to plan and write an essay on the topic printed on the other side of this page. **Do not write on another topic. An essay on another topic is not acceptable.**

The essay is designed to give you an opportunity to show how well you can write. You should try to express your thoughts clearly. How well you write is much more important than how much you write, but you need to say enough for a reader to understand what you mean.

You will probably want to write more than a short paragraph. You should also be aware that a copy of your essay will be sent to each school that will be receiving your test results. You are to write only in the appropriate section of the answer sheet. Please write or print so that your writing may be read by someone who is not familiar with your handwriting.

You may make notes and plan your essay on the reverse side of the page. Allow enough time to copy the final form on to your answer sheet. You must copy the essay topic onto your answer sheet, on page 3, in the box provided.

Please remember to write only the final draft of the essay on pages 3 and 4 of your answer sheet and to write it in blue or black pen. Again, you may use cursive writing or you may print. Only pages 3 and 4 will be sent to the schools.

Directions continue on next page.

Essay Topic

If you could change one thing about your school, what would you change and why?

- Only write on this essay question
- Only pages 3 and 4 will be sent to the schools
- Only write in blue or black pen

NOTES

_____

_____

_____

_____

_____

_____

_____

_____

_____

_____

_____

_____

_____

Chapter 20
Middle Level ISEE
Practice Test:
Answers and
Explanations

ANSWER KEY

ISEE ML Verbal 1

1. D	5. D	9. B	13. B	17. A	21. C	25. C	29. C	33. A	37. B
2. C	6. C	10. B	14. C	18. B	22. B	26. C	30. B	34. D	38. B
3. B	7. B	11. A	15. D	19. A	23. D	27. A	31. C	35. A	39. B
4. C	8. B	12. D	16. C	20. C	24. A	28. A	32. D	36. A	40. A

ISEE ML Quantitative 2

1. C	5. B	9. C	13. B	17. D	21. C	25. B	29. B	33. A	37. B
2. B	6. A	10. C	14. B	18. C	22. D	26. B	30. D	34. C	
3. D	7. B	11. B	15. C	19. D	23. A	27. A	31. B	35. B	
4. B	8. B	12. B	16. C	20. D	24. B	28. A	32. B	36. A	

ISEE ML Reading 3

1. A	5. A	9. C	13. A	17. A	21. C	25. D	29. B	33. B
2. B	6. A	10. D	14. B	18. C	22. D	26. C	30. D	34. A
3. C	7. D	11. A	15. D	19. A	23. A	27. A	31. D	35. B
4. A	8. A	12. C	16. D	20. B	24. C	28. D	32. B	36. C

ISEE ML Math 4

1. B	6. A	11. C	16. D	21. B	26. C	31. C	36. B	41. C	46. B
2. B	7. C	12. A	17. A	22. D	27. B	32. C	37. A	42. B	47. C
3. D	8. C	13. B	18. C	23. D	28. D	33. C	38. C	43. D	
4. D	9. B	14. C	19. C	24. B	29. A	34. D	39. A	44. A	
5. C	10. D	15. C	20. B	25. B	30. D	35. B	40. A	45. D	

EXPLANATIONS

Section 1 Verbal

1. **D** Unusual is the opposite of usual, which is defined as regular or normal. The answer should match the opposite of usual or normal. Only (D), peculiar, matches this meaning.

2. **C** If you are unsure of the meaning of this word, try to use it in a sentence. An example would be "the pedestrian could not stand up after his fall without assistance." Assistance is defined as help or aide. The only choice that matches this definition is (C), service.

3. **B** Reality comes from the word "real"—it has to do with facts and what is happening in real life. The only choice that matches this meaning is (B), fact.

4. **C** Try to think of other words that sound like diminution: diminish. To diminish something means to tear it down or lessen it in some way. The best match to this meaning is (C), reduction.

5. **D** Contented is a form of content, which is defined as a state of happiness. The best match to happiness in these choices is (D), satisfied.

6. **C** Bound can be used in several different ways, so try it in a few different sentences. For example: The oath of office bound the President to stay within the law; in my dream I was bound to a skateboard and couldn't get off! In both of these examples, the meaning of bound means to be obligated or tied down to something. This best matches (C).

7. **B** To falter is defined as to hesitate or to waver. The best match for this definition is (B), hesitate.

8. **B** What does it mean to contain something? It means to keep it closed off or boxed in. This best matches (B), held.

9. **B** Try to think of other words that are related to or sound like revere: reverential, reverence, reverend. A reverend, for example, is a religious official whose job is to offer reverence to a deity. Reverence means to honor or worship; to revere someone or something means to honor or think highly of that person or thing. The best match for this meaning is (B), esteem.

10. **B** What does it mean to work diligently? To work tirelessly or very hard. The best match for the meaning of diligent is hardworking, (B).

11. **A** Detrimental is defined as harmful or destructive. The best match for this definition is (A), harmful.

12. **D** What are phrases that you heard the word "vow" used in? Marriage vows, a vow of silence, I vow revenge. A vow is a type of promise or pact. This meaning best matches (D), pledge.

13. **B** To have aspirations is to aspire to something. To aspire means to reach for or to dream of. The best match for this meaning is (B), hope.

14. **C** Where have you heard the word bashful before? One of Snow White's Seven Dwarves was named Bashful; the shy one. Bashful is defined as shy or retiring. This best matches (C), shy.

15. **D** Sinister is defined as having evil intent. This best matches (D), wicked.

16. **C** To disclose information means to share or provide information. This best matches (C), reveal.

17. **A** Congeal might be a word you have heard in science class or when you have had a cut; congeal means to become thicker, as in when the blood from a cut congeals and the cut stops bleeding. This best matches the meaning of (A), coagulate, another word for congeal.

18. **B** To inundate means to overwhelm or overcome. The best match for this meaning is (B), flood.

19. **A** Steadfast is related to steady, which means to stay the course or remain firm. This best matches the meaning of constant, (A).

20. **C** Ruthless is defined as without sympathy or concern. This best matches the definition of unsparing, (C).

21. **C** Pay attention to the clues in the sentence. The second half of the sentence indicates that Myron never took sides in any disagreements. The missing word most likely means unbiased or undecided. This best matches (C), neutral. Choices (A) and (B) are the opposite of this meaning, and (D) does not relate to being undecided. Choice (C) is the correct answer.

22. **B** Pay attention to the clues in the sentence. The first half of the sentence indicates that the drought left the soil completely useless. The second half of the sentence discusses food. Since food can't come from useless soil, the missing word must mean requested or brought in. This best matches (B), imported. Choice (A) means to send out, so it cannot be correct. Choices (C) and (D) do not mean to bring in, so they can also be eliminated. Choice (B) is the correct answer.

23. **D** Pay attention to the clues in the sentence. The first part of the sentence indicates that Mr. Jones does not like even small grammatical errors, which means that he likely checked the students' papers closely. The missing word must mean closely. The only choice that matches this meaning is (D), meticulously. Choices (A) and (C) are the opposite of this meaning, and (B) does not relate to the sentence. Choice (D) is the correct answer.

24. **A** Pay attention to the clues in the sentence. The first part of the sentence indicates that Eric is strongly against racism, so the missing word must mean something like "strongly against" or "hates." The only answer that matches this meaning is (A), abhors. Although it may be true that Eric questions racism, as in (C), abhors more strongly matches "dislikes." Choice (A) is the correct answer.

25. **C** Pay attention to the clues in the sentence. The first part of the sentence states that Sharon's anger was "too great." David couldn't do something because of it in the second part of the sentence. This indicates David couldn't overcome her anger, so the missing word must mean "overcome her anger." The best match for this meaning is (C), pacify.

26. **C** Pay attention to the clues and direction words in the sentence. The first part of the sentence indicates that serious damage to property occurred. But that part of the sentence starts with "even though," indicating an opposite meaning later in the sentence. So even though there was damage, the lawyers did not do a convincing job. So the lawyers did not to a good job. The missing word must match the meaning "did not do a good job," which best matches incompetent, (C).

27.   A   Pay attention to the clues in the sentence. It states that after months of disputes the countries finally decided to sit down and do something. The time shift indicates they made some kind of change, so they are no longer in a dispute when they sit down. The missing word must mean the opposite of dispute, which best matches (A), friendly.

28.   A   Pay attention to the clues and direction words in the sentence. The first part of the sentence indicates that the thief claimed his crime was an accident. But that part of the sentence starts with "Although," indicating an opposite result later in the sentence. The missing word must mean "on purpose," the opposite of accident. This best matches (A), deliberate.

29.   C   This sentence is making an analogy. The second part of the sentence says that to be a good architect you don't need to live in a fancy house, which is something architects build as part of their jobs. The first part of the sentence is about doctors. What do doctors do for part of their jobs? They try to make or keep people healthy. The missing word must be healthy, (C).

30.   B   Based on the clues in this sentence, Paul is doing a better and better job as time goes on. This indicates that he is most likely impressing his coach with his performance. The missing word must mean impressed, which best matches (B), gratified.

31.   C   Pay attention to the clues and direction words in the sentence. The first part of the sentence states that wolves travel in packs, but starts that idea with the word "while" and goes on to discuss what cheetahs do. The use of the word "while" indicates a difference between wolves and cheetahs, so it is likely that cheetahs do not travel in packs. The missing word must mean "lone" or "individual." This meaning best matches (C), solitary.

32.   D   Pay attention to the clues and direction words in the sentence. The second part of the sentence states that the senators were argumentative, but starts that idea with the word "while." The use of the word "while" indicates a difference between these senators and Jones, who is mentioned earlier in the sentence. So most likely Jones is not argumentative. The missing word must mean "not argumentative," which best matches (D), timid.

33.   A   Pay attention to the clues in the sentence. The sentence says that no one ended up voting for the politician, so it sounds as though his speech was not very good. The missing word must mean "not very good." This best matches (A), feeble. Choices (C) and (D) are both positive words, so they cannot be the answer. Although monotonous, (B), is a negative word it is more related to the physical sound of the speech as opposed to how good it was. Choice (A) is the correct answer.

34.   D   Pay attention to the clues in the sentence. The second part of the sentence states that each department was free to advance employees as it saw fit. The missing word must mean that there was no standard system for promotions. The best match to this meaning is (D), uniform.

35.   A   Pay attention to the clues in the sentence. The sentence says it takes years of training for a gymnast to become something. What would likely happen after a gymnast trains for years? He or she would be very good. The missing word must mean very good at gymnastics. The best match for this meaning is (A), agile, as agility is a very good quality for gymnasts to have.

36.   **A**   Pay attention to the clues and direction words in the sentence. The second part of the sentence states that Mr. Fenster was welcoming to children on Halloween, but starts that idea with the word "though." The use of the word "though" indicates a difference between how Mr. Fenster treats the children versus how he treats his neighbors in general. It seems that he treats his neighbors differently than he treats the children, so the missing word must mean "mean" or "angry." This best matches (A), belligerent.

37.   **B**   Pay attention to the clues in the sentence. The sentence says the young man talked back to his parents and teachers, so the missing word must mean "rude" or "disrespectful." The best match for this meaning is (B), insolent.

38.   **B**   Pay attention to the clues and direction words in the sentence. The second part of the sentence states that the brushstrokes are actually carefully planned. The first part of the sentence starts with "while," which indicates a shift within the sentence. This must mean that while they seem the opposite of planned, they are in fact planned. So the missing word must mean the opposite of planned. The only word that matches this meaning is (B), haphazard.

39.   **B**   Pay attention to the clues in the sentence. The sentence says the Declaration of Independence is based on principles, which it then lists. The principles listed are very important ones to our society, so the missing word must mean important. The only choice that matches this meaning is (B), lofty.

40.   **A**   Pay attention to the clues in the sentence. The teacher does not want the students to lose the "big picture." Therefore the students shouldn't get too lost in the details or nuances of the information. The missing word must mean "details" or "nuances." The only word that means details or nuances is (A), minutiae.

Section 2 Quantitative Reasoning

1.   **C** $54 \times 3 = 162$, so the correct answer is (C). The stacking method works well or you can break the problem into two steps: $50 \times 3 = 150$ and $4 \times 3 = 12$. When you add 150 and 12 together, you get 162.

2.   **B**   To find the area of square multiply two sides together. Since each side of the square is equal, use the formula $A = s^2$. The side length of this particular square is 2, so the area of the square would be 4: $A = s^2 = 2^2 = 4$. The correct answer is (B).

3.   **D**   Remember to use order of operations (PEMDAS). First, simplify inside the parentheses multiplying from left to right: $(4 \times 3 \times 2) \Rightarrow (12 \times 2) \Rightarrow (24)$. Next, multiply from left to right: $3 \times 2 \times 1 - 24 \Rightarrow 6 \times 1 - 24 \Rightarrow 6 - 24$. Finally, subtract from left to right: $6 - 24 = -18$. The correct answer is (D).

4. **B** Use the average pie:

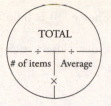

Find the total by adding all of Vicky's test scores together: 80 + 90 + 94 = 264. She took 3 tests, so 3 is the # of items. Divide to find her average: $\frac{264}{3} = 88$. The correct answer is (B).

5. **B** Use the graph provided to find out which student bought the most books at the school fair. The tallest bar indicates which student bought the most books. Sally bought 2 books, Jesse bought 4 books, Pete bought 1 book, and Mark bought 3 books. Since Jesse bought the most books at the school fair, (B) is the correct answer.

6. **A** Use the graph provided to find the number of books the students bought. Sally bought 2 books and Mark bought 3 books, so together they bought 5 books. Jess bought 4 books. Therefore, Sally and Mark together bought 1 more book than Jesse did (5 − 4 = 1). The correct answer is (A).

7. **B** When adding fractions with unlike denominators, find a common denominator first. For this question, multiply the first fraction by 2 so that $\frac{1}{2}$ becomes $\frac{2}{4}$. Next add the numerators together to get the final sum: $\frac{2}{4} + \frac{3}{4} = \frac{5}{4}$. The correct answer is (B).

8. **B** For the number given, 7 is two spots to the left of the decimal which is the tens place. Seven 10s (or 7 groups of 10) is equal to 70, so the correct answer is (B).

9. **C** If 20% of Jason's books are fiction and he has 5 fiction books, then 20% of something is equal to 5: $20\%(x) = 5$ or $0.20x = 5$

   Divide 0.20 from both sides to get $x = 25$. Therefore, Jason has a total of 25 books. To find out the number of nonfiction books he has subtract 5 from 25. The result is 20, making the correct answer (C). Another way to solve the problem is to determine that if 20% are fiction, then 80% are nonfiction. If 5 books equals 20%, then four times that would equal 80%: 4 × 5 = 20. Note that answer (D) represents the total number of books Jason has.

10. **C** Long division is one way to approach division with decimals. $\frac{7}{0.35}$ can be written as $0.35\overline{)7}$. Move the decimal to the right two times to get rid of the decimal in the divisor and also move the decimal to the right two times in the dividend: $35\overline{)700}$. The result is $35\overline{)700}^{\,20}$, so the correct answer is (C). Another option is use the answer choices (PITA). Multiply the answer choices by 0.35 to see which one equals 7. Choice (C) is the only option that works.

11. **B** To find the answer closest in value to 5, find the answer that has the smallest distance between itself and 5. Choice (A) is 0.5 from 5. Choice (B) is 0.009 from 5. Choice (C) is 0.01 from 5. Choice (D) is 0.101 from 5. Therefore, the one closest to 5 is (B) since $\dfrac{9}{1,000}$ is a shorter distance than $\dfrac{5}{10}$, $\dfrac{1}{100}$, and $\dfrac{101}{1,000}$.

12. **B** Use the answers (PITA) to determine the closest cost per pound. Janice bought 6 pounds of hamburger. If each pound cost \$2.00 (A), then she paid \$12.00. If each pound cost \$3.00, then she paid \$18.00 (B). If each pound cost \$5.00, then she paid \$30.00 (C). If each pound cost \$6.00, then she paid \$36.00 (D). The closest option to \$18.50 is (B), which is the correct answer.

13. **B** Use the answers (PITA) to determine number that is closest to $\sqrt{175}$ since 175 is not a perfect square. In (A), 9 would be $\sqrt{81}$. In (B), 13 would be $\sqrt{169}$. In (C), 22 would be $\sqrt{484}$. Stop after (C) because (D) will be even greater. The closest to the $\sqrt{175}$ is (B), which is the correct answer.

14. **B** If there are 32 numbered pages in Laurie's book, then there are 16 odd-numbered pages (odd numbers from 1–31) and 16 even-numbered pages (even numbers from 2–32). Since illustrations appear on every odd-numbered page, there are 16 total illustrations. The correct answer is (B).

15. **C** One way to solve this problem is to solve for y in the first equation: $6y + 8 = 20$. Subtract 8 from both sides to get $6y = 12$. Divide both sides by 6 to get $y = 2$. Next, plug 2 in for y in the second equation: $3y + 4 = 3(2) + 4 = 6 + 4 = 10$. The correct answer is (C). If you noticed that $3y + 4$ is half of $6y + 8$, then $3y + 4$ will equal half of what $6y + 8$ equals. $\dfrac{20}{2} = 10$, which is the correct answer.

16. **C** If the lecture hall's current capacity is 56 seats, then the increased capacity will be greater than 56. Eliminate (A). The capacity only increased by 75%, so eliminate (D), which represents a 100% increase. $\dfrac{3}{4}(56) = 42$, so the lecture hall's capacity increased by 42 seats. $56 + 42 = 98$. Therefore, the correct answer is (C).

17. **D** Use long division to check each answer. In (A), 8 goes into 11 once with a remainder of 3. In (B), 8 goes into 22 twice with a remainder of 6. In (C), 8 goes into 72 exactly nine times, so the remainder is 0. In (D), 8 goes into 90 eleven times with a remainder of 2. Therefore, (D) is the correct answer.

18. **C** Use the graph provided and the answer choices (PITA) to determine when the greatest increase in rainfall occurred. There was no increase between 1942 and 1944, so eliminate (A) and (B). From 1944 to 1945, there was an average increase of 30 inches. Keep (C). From 1945 to 1946, there was an average increase of 10 inches. Since the increase in (C) is greater, it is the correct answer.

19. **D** There are 7 hours between 6 a.m. and 1 p.m. Therefore, if the temperature increases at a constant rate of 3 degrees per hour, then the temperature at 1 p.m. will be 21 degrees higher than it was at

6 a.m. ($3 \times 7 = 21$). If it was 32 degrees at 6 a.m., then the temperature at 1 p.m. is 53 degrees ($32 + 21 = 53$). The correct answer is (D).

20. **D** To find the volume of a box, use the formula $V = l \times w \times h$. Plug the given dimensions into the formula: $V = 4$ in $\times$ 3 in $\times$ 2 in $= 24$ in^3. Therefore, (D) is the correct answer.

21. **C** There are 180° in a straight line. Subtract 125 from 180 to find the degree measure of x: $180 - 125 = 55$, so $x = 55°$. Since both columns are equal, the correct answer is (C).

22. **D** To find the area of a rectangle, use the formula $A = l \times w$. Since the side lengths are x and y, plug in values that will equal 12 when multiplied together. For example, if Column A equals 1, then Column B would equal 12, and Column B would be greater. However, if Column A equals 12, then Column B would equal 1, making Column A greater. Since neither column is *always* greater, the correct answer is (D).

23. **A** The value of Column A is 8 since $\sqrt{9} = 3$ and $\sqrt{25} = 5$ and $3 + 5 = 8$. Column B can be rewritten as $\sqrt{34}$; however, 34 is not a perfect square so the value of $\sqrt{34}$ will have to be approximated. Since $\sqrt{25} = 5$ and $\sqrt{36} = 6$, then the value of $\sqrt{34}$ is between 5 and 6. Since that range is less than 8, Column A is greater. The correct answer is (A).

24. **B** The area formula of the quadrilateral is $A = l \times w$. The area of the figure (12) and one side (3) are given. Therefore, the missing side length is 4 since $12 = 3 \times w$ and $\frac{12}{3} = 4 = w$. To find the perimeter of a shape, add up all the sides. In a rectangle, opposite sides are equal, so since $AD = 3$, then $BC = 3$, and since $AB = 4$, then $DC = 4$. $3 + 4 + 3 + 4 = 14$, so Column A equals 14. Since 14 is less than 15, Column B is greater. The correct answer is (B).

25. **B** If Martha has \$20, then half of her money is \$10: $\frac{1}{2}(20) = 10$. If Martha gives away \$10, then she has \$10 left which is the value of Column A. If, after receiving \$10 from her sister, Linda now has \$30, then Linda originally had \$20: $30 - 10 = 20$. Thus, Column B equals \$20. Since Column B is greater, the correct answer is (B).

26. **B** To determine the value of Column A, solve for x in the equation: $4x + 7 = 63$. Subtract 7 from both sides to get $4x = 56$. Then divide both sides by 4 to get $x = 14$. Column A equals 14. To determine the value of Column B, solve for y in the equation: $\frac{y}{3} + 6 = 15$. Subtract 6 from both sides to get $\frac{y}{3} = 9$. Then multiply both sides by 3 to get $y = 27$. Column B equals 27. Since Column B is greater, the correct answer is (B).

27. **A** To find the area of a rectangle, use the formula $A = l \times w$. Since $l = 3$ and $w = 4$, then $A = 3 \times 4 = 12$. Thus, Column A equals 12. To find the area of square multiply two sides together.

Since each side of the square is equal, use the formula $A = s^2$. The side length of this square is 3, so $A = 3^2 = 9$. Thus, Column B equals 9. Since Column A is greater, the correct answer is (A).

28. **A** Use the table provided to find the values of the two columns. To find the average number of cookies eaten each day, use the average pie:

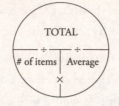

The total is the sum of all the cookies eaten: $3 + 2 + 1 + 3 = 9$. The number of items is 4 since there are 4 days. Divide the total and the number of items to get the average: $\frac{9}{4} = 2.25$. Therefore, Column A equals 2.25. According to the table, the number of cookies eaten on Thursday is 2. Since Column A is greater, the correct answer is (A).

29. **B** Estimation will work well for this problem. For Column A, 0.64 is less than 1, so $\sqrt{0.64} < \sqrt{1}$. Since $\sqrt{1} = \sqrt{1}$, then $\sqrt{0.64} < 1$. Therefore, Column A is less than 1. For Column B, 6.4 is between perfect squares 4 and 9. Since $\sqrt{4} = 2$ and $\sqrt{9} = 3$, then $2 < \sqrt{6.4} < 3$. Therefore, Column B is between 2 and 3. Since that range is greater than any number less than 1, Column B is greater. The correct answer is (B).

30. **D** Since the prices of an orange and a peach are not given, plug in values. If 1 orange costs 4 cents, then 5 oranges cost 20 cents: $5 \times 0.04 = 0.20$. Since 6 peaches would cost 90 cents ($1.10 - 0.20 = 0.90$), then 1 peach would cost 15 cents: $0.90 \times 6 = 0.15$. Column A equals 4, and Column B equals 15. Currently, Column B is greater. However, since the prices of the fruit are not given, remember to plug in more than once! If 1 orange costs 10 cents, then 5 oranges cost 50 cents: $5 \times 0.10 = 0.50$. Since 6 peaches would cost 60 cents ($1.10 - 0.50 = 0.60$), then 1 peach would cost 10 cents: 0.60 6 = 0.10. In this instance, Columns A and B both equal 10. Since Column B is not always greater, nor are the two columns always equal, the correct answer is (D).

31. **B** Pay attention to the parentheses and remember order of operations (PEMDAS). For Column A, 5 will be raised to the 6th power first and then multiplied by –1, so Column A will be a negative number. For Column B, –5 will be raised to the 6th power, so the result is positive number. Since Column A is negative and Column B is positive, the correct answer is (B). Note that it is not necessary to calculate $5 \times 5 \times 5 \times 5 \times 5 \times 5$. Simply knowing that one column is negative and one column is positive will allow you to answer the question correctly!

32. **B** If a represents an odd integer greater than 9 and less than 15, a could be 11 or 13. If b represents an even integer greater than 9 and less than 15, b could be 10, 12, or 14. Therefore, Column A could equal 33 (11×3) or 39 (13×3). Column B could equal 40 (10×4), 48 (12×4), or 46 (14×4). In every instance, Column B is greater than Column A, so the correct answer is (B).

33. A To find the probability of an event, find the total of what is wanted out of the total possible outcomes: Probability = $\dfrac{\text{What you want}}{\text{What you've got}}$. If the die has 12 sides numbered 1 through 12, then there are 6 even-numbered sides (2, 4, 6, 8, 10, and 12). Thus, Column A equals $\dfrac{6}{12}$. From 1 to 12, there are 4 prime numbers (2, 3, 5, and 7), so Column B equals $\dfrac{4}{12}$. Since Column A is greater, the correct answer is (A).

34. C For column A, there are 20 total squares and 3 that are shaded, so the fractional part that is shaded is $\dfrac{3}{20}$. Since the two columns are equal, the correct answer is (C).

35. B If Melvin eats 50% of 12 slices, then he will eat 6 out of 12 slices or $\dfrac{1}{2}$ of the pizza, so there will be 6 slices left (12 − 6 = 6). Column A equals 6. If Melvin eats $\dfrac{1}{3}$ of the pizza, then he will eat 4 out of 12 slices, so there will be 8 slices left (12 − 4 = 8). Column B equals 8. Since Column B is greater, the correct answer is (B).

36. A If the shirt was originally $50, the first 20% discount would be $10 off: 0.2(50) = 10. The new price of the shirt is $40 (50 − 10 = 40). After a second 20% discount, which is a discount of $8 since 0.2(40) = 8, the shirt will be $32 (40 − 8 = 32). Column A equals 32. If the shirt had only been discounted once by 40%, the discount would be $20: 40% of 50 is 0.4(50) =20. The new price of the shirt would be $30 since 50 − 20 = 30. Column B equals 30. Since Column A is greater, the correct answer is (A).

37. B To find the slope of a line with two given points, use the slope formula: $\dfrac{y_2 - y_1}{x_2 - x_1}$. For Column A, the slope equals $\dfrac{2 - 8}{5 - 3} = \dfrac{-6}{2} = -3$. Therefore, Column A equals −3. To find the slope of a line with a given equation, rewrite the equation in slope-intercept form: $y = mx + b$, where m represents the slope. For Column B, isolate y in the equation $6x - 2y = 8$. Subtract $6x$ from both sides to get $-2y = -6x + 8$. Next, divide both sides by −2 to get $y = 3x - 4$. Therefore, the slope is 3, and Column B equals 3. Since Column B is greater, the correct answer is (B).

Section 3 Reading

1. A On primary purpose questions, ask yourself "Why did the author write this story? What is the main takeaway for this story?" The story is focused on the history of early modes of travel. Choice (C) is focused only on one form of transportation, so it is too specific. Choice (D) is too general; this story is about the history of early transportation, not transportation in general. And (B) is incorrect as the focus is not on the motivation for travel but rather on modes of travel. Choice (A) is the correct answer.

2. **B** On Except/Not/Least questions cross check each answer choice and write a "T" for true and an "F" for false for each answer choice, based on the passage. The false answer will be the correct choice. Lines 21–23 mention donkeys and oxen being used to pull sledges, so (A) is true. Although children are mentioned in line 9, they are not being used to carry things, so (B) is false. Poles are mentioned as being used to carry goods in line 13, so (C) is true. And primitive sleds are discussed in lines 15–19 as a form of transport for goods, so (D) is true. Choice (B) is the only false answer, and so is therefore correct.

3. **C** This is a very open-ended question, so check each answer with the information in the passage. Answer (A) is too extreme, the passage never indicates that early man was incapable of anything. Farming is not mentioned in the passage, which eliminates (B). There is also no mention of early man being outgoing or friendly, so (D) is wrong as well. Only (C) is supported by the passage, since the entire focus is on man's history of different ways of transporting goods.

4. **A** This is a specific question, so make sure to go back to the passage and find the answer. Animals are mentioned in lines 20–23. The only information provided is that they were first tamed around 5,000 B.C.E., and they were used for transporting heavy loads and pulling sledges. This best supports (A). Although (B), (C), and (D) may seem like likely answer choices, they are never explicitly stated in the passage. Choice (A) is the correct answer.

5. **A** This question asks about the author's attitude towards the invention of the wheel, so pay attention to what the author says about that particular invention. Then eliminate choices that don't match the story. The author begins and ends the passage discussing the wheel. Quite clearly he or she finds this to be an important invention, which eliminates (C). The author says positive things about the wheel, so neither (B) or (D) makes sense. The only possible answer is (A), admiration.

6. **A** This is a relatively open ended question about a specific subject in the passage, so make sure to check each answer choice with the passage. Lines 18–19 state that the sledge evolved into the sled, which supports (A). The sledge was invented before the wheel, so (B) is incorrect. Choice (C) is too extreme; the passage says early sledges were made from logs as well as animal skins. Eliminate (C). Choice (D) is also too extreme due to the word "only" and so is not supported by the passage. The correct answer is (A).

7. **D** On primary purpose questions, ask yourself "Why did the author write this story? What is the main takeaway for this story?" The story is focused on providing factual information about the American bison. This best matches (D). Choice (A) is much too specific; (B) and (C) are not mentioned in the passage. Choice (D) is the correct answer.

8. **A** This is a specific question, so make sure to find the answer in the story. The actual buffalo is only mentioned twice in the story, lines 1–2 and lines 12–14. The passage states that buffalo and bison are different animals, and that they are found on different continents. This best matches (A), they differ by geographical location. The author does not mention the size or number of buffalo, which eliminates (B) and (C). Both buffalo and bison are found today, so (D) is not a difference. Choice (A) is the correct answer.

9. C When asked a vocabulary in context question, focus on what the word means in the sentence. In line 19, deemed most nearly means "categorized" or "listed," which best matches answer (C). No other choice matches the context of the sentence.

10. D This is a specific question, so make sure to find the answer in the story. Protection of the bison is discussed in the last lines of the passage, where it states that the bison is not in danger of extinction as long as it is protected, although they may never be as plentiful as they were. This refutes (A), so it can be eliminated. Choice (C) is the opposite of what is stated in these lines, so it can be eliminated. The ecological balance of the plains is not mentioned, so (C) can be eliminated. Only (D) matches the passage.

11. A This is a specific question, so make sure to find the answer in the story. Lines 19–21 state that due to conservation efforts the bison has been saved from near extinction. This best supports (A). Choice (B) is the opposite of this; they were near extinction due to being hunted. Choices (C) and (D) are not mentioned in the passage, so (A) is the correct answer.

12. C When a question asks why an author includes a line in the passage, ask yourself "What purpose does this line serve?" The author mentions the city of Buffalo as part of a list of the things in America that are named after buffalo. The other items on this list show the different ways in which we used the buffalo when we were really referring to bison. This best supports (C). Choice (B) is deceptive as it refers to the next example of the nickel, not the city of Buffalo. Choice (A) comes from a different area of the passage and does not answer this question. And (D) is never mentioned in the passage. Choice (C) is the correct answer.

13. A This question is a "main idea" question in disguise. Ask yourself the "so what?" of the story. This story is about the life and influences of Alexander the Great. The only answer choice that focuses on Alexander the Great is (A), making it the best and only correct answer choice.

14. B When asked a vocabulary in context question, focus on what the word means in the sentence. In line 16, civilized most nearly means advanced or forward thinking, based on the following sentences that stress "ways of thinking." This best matches (B), educated.

15. D On tone questions, eliminate answer choices that are too extreme or don't make sense based on the passage. This passage is very informative and fact based. It not from a personal perspective, which eliminates (A) and (B). The story is focused on historical facts rather than philosophical aspects, which best supports (D) over (C). Choice (D) is the correct answer.

16. D This is an open-ended question, as there are many impressive things discussed about Alexander. Check each answer choice with the information in the passage. The passage says that Aristotle is the teacher, not Alexander, so eliminate (A). Integrity is never mentioned in the passage, so eliminate (B). Alexander is never described as being handsome, eliminating (C) as well. The passage does discuss Alexander's intelligence in lines 4–5 and his culture in lines 16–17 (his ways of thinking and doing things), making (D) the best answer.

17. **B** This question asks about Aristotle, who is discussed in the first few lines of the passage. Lines 5–7 state that Aristotle's teachings left Alexander with a lifelong love of books, which best supports (B). There is no indication that Aristotle influenced Alexander's military approach or strategy, so eliminate (C) and (D). There is also no indication that Aristotle encouraged Alexander to do anything, let alone something as specific as spreading culture, eliminating (A). Choice (B) is the correct answer.

18. **C** This is a specific question, so make sure to find the answer in the story. Alexander's conquering is discussed in lines 11–21, where it states he conquered most of the "civilized world" and brought the "Greek way of thinking and doing things" to those places. This best supports (C). None of the things listed in (A), (B), and (D) are mentioned in the passage.

19. **A** On primary purpose questions, ask yourself "Why did the author write this story? What is the main takeaway for this story?" The story is focused on what hiccups are and how they occur in the human body. This best supports (A), describe a common occurrence. Although the subject of remedies are mentioned at the end of the passage, the passage does not prescribe a treatment so eliminate (B). There is no dispute mentioned, eliminating (C) as well. Although the potential danger of hiccups is mentioned, that is not the primary purpose of the passage, which eliminates (D). Choice (A) is the correct answer.

20. **B** This is a specific question, so make sure to go back and find the answer in the passage. As the passage begins to describe how hiccups occur in line 8, it is an irritant that begins the process of developing hiccups. This best matches (B). A paper bag is mentioned as a remedy to the hiccups, not the cause, eliminating (C). Choices (A) and (D) include information mentioned in the passage, but they come after an irritant has already prompted a spasm. Choice (B) is the best answer.

21. **C** When asked a vocabulary in context question, focus on what the word means in the sentence. In line 24, "attacks" is referring to the hiccups mentioned early in the sentence. The best meaning of the word attacks then is most likely "fits". This best matches (C), bouts. Choices (A), (B), and (D) are all synonyms of attacks, but do not work in the context of the sentence.

22. **D** This is a specific question, so make sure to go back and find the answer in the passage. The "hic" noise is mentioned specifically in line 22, and states that it is the movement of the vocal chords that prompts this sound. This supports (D) as the correct answer.

23. **A** This is a specific question, so make sure to go back and find the answer in the passage. The passage discusses the fatal possibility of hiccups in lines 25–27, due to exhaustion. This best matches (A), fatigue from hiccups. None of other answers are supported by the passage.

24. **C** When asked why the author includes a word or phrase in the passage, ask yourself "Why is this word or phrase there? What point does this make?" The inclusion of the word "hiccoughs" is a very brief aside that merely demonstrates another word used to refer to the same phenomenon. This best supports (C). It is not a correction, definition, nor an attack on an argument, so (A), (B), and (D) can all be eliminated. Choice (C) is the correct answer.

25.   D   On primary purpose questions, ask yourself "Why did the author write this story? What is the main takeaway for this story?" The story is focused on the phenomenon of hibernation. Although all four answer choices contain information that is provided in the passage, all are too specific other than (D). The passage is focused on the general information regarding hibernation, making (D) the correct answer.

26.   C   When asked a vocabulary in context question, focus on what the word means in the sentence. In line 7, conserve most nearly means to "store" or "save up". This best matches (C), reserve. Choices (A) and (D) are the opposite meaning, and (B) does not match the context of the sentence as well as (C).

27.   A   On Except/Not/Least questions cross check each answer choice and write a "T" for true and an "F" for false for each answer choice, based on the passage. The false answer will be the correct choice. There is no reference to a "dream state" in the passage, so (A) is false. Lines 12–14 discuss the possible drop in body temperature for some animals, which makes (B) true. The following lines also discuss the possibility of slower heartbeats and breathing in some animals, so (C) and (D) are also true. Choice (A) is the only false answer, and is therefore correct.

28.   D   This is a specific question, so make sure to go back and find the answer in the passage. In lines 26–27, it states that an animal may wake from hibernation when there is mild weather. This best supports (D). Food is not mentioned as a motivation to break hibernation in the passage, only weather, which eliminates (B). Choice (A) is the opposite of mild weather, so it can be eliminated. Although (C) may seem like a good choice, just because there isn't snow doesn't mean the weather is favorable. Choice (D) is the best answer.

29.   B   This is a specific question, so make sure to go back and find the answer in the passage. The chemical that causes hibernation is discussed in lines 27–31, where it states that if the chemical were injected into an animal in the summer months it might cause the animal to go into summer hibernation. This best supports (B). None of the other answer choices are supported from these lines.

30.   D   On tone questions, eliminate answer choices that are too extreme or don't make sense based on the passage. This passage is a very fact-based review, which best supports (D), informative. The author does not come off as overly impressed with hibernation, which eliminates (A), nor does he or she seem concerned, which eliminates (B). It is unlikely that the author would write a passage about something that doesn't interest him or her, which eliminates (C). Choice (D) is the correct answer.

31.   D   This question is a "main idea" question in disguise. Ask yourself the "so what?" of the story. The passage focuses on the experience of theater. Although Shakespeare is mentioned in the passage, (C) is much too specific an answer for a main idea question; eliminate it. Choices (A) and (B) are also much too specific; the passage is not focused on any specific productions, modern or otherwise. The only choice that matches the overall main idea of the passage is (D).

32.   B   This is a specific question, so make sure to go back and find the answer in the passage. The author discusses why the theater is "thrilling" in lines 6–8. According to the author, it is the live nature of the theater that makes it so thrilling. This best matches (B). The author goes on to discuss the Greek origin of the word theater, but that does not answer this question so (A) is incorrect. There

is no mention of plays being thrilling because they are well written or have several people working on them, which also eliminated (C) and (D). Choice (B) is correct.

33.   **B**   This is an open-ended question, so make sure to check all four answer choices and remember your process of elimination guidelines. Choice (A) has extreme language; there is no indication that modern theory always does anything. Eliminate that choice. The passage does not state that one form of theater is better than another, which eliminates (C). Although Shakespeare is mentioned in the passage, it does not say modern theater is mostly comprised of those plays. Eliminate (D). The only possible answer is (B), which is supported by the information in lines 24–33, in which the variety of modern forms of theater are discussed.

34.   **A**   On tone questions, eliminate answer choices that are too extreme or don't make sense based on the passage. The author is very positive about the theater in this passage, which eliminates (B), (C), and (D) since those are all neutral words. Only (A), admiring, works based on the passage.

35.   **B**   When asked a vocabulary in context question, focus on what the word means in the sentence. In the first line, "richest" is being used in a positive manner by the author. He or she goes on to say that live theater is very exciting and thrilling. "Exciting" and "thrilling" best match (B), entertaining. Choice (D), wealthy, is too literal a meaning for "richest". Choice (C) is very negative, which doesn't match the tone of the passage. And (A) doesn't fit with the topic discussed in the first lines of the passage. Choice (B) is the correct answer.

36.   **C**   This is a specific question, so make sure to go back and find the answer in the passage. Shakespeare's plays are mentioned in the last lines of the passage. These lines state that the works of Shakespeare are still performed today in a variety of interpretations. This best matches (C). Choices (A) and (D) contain extreme language; eliminate them. The passage never states that Shakespeare is more popular today than during his time, eliminating (B) as well. Choice (C) is the correct answer.

Section 4 Mathematics Achievement

1.   **B**   Since the digit 9 is two places to the right of the decimal, it is in the hundredths place and would be equivalent to nine one-hundredths or $\dfrac{9}{100}$. The correct answer is (B). Choice (A) is nine tenths and would be one place to the right of the decimal. Choice (C) is nine one-thousandths and would be three places to the right of the decimal. Finally, (D) is nine ten-thousandths and would be four places to the right of the decimal.

2.   **B**   The least common multiple of a set of numbers is the smallest number that is divisible by all members of the set. Use the answer choices (PITA). Choice (A) can be eliminated because 3 is a factor, not a multiple, of 6, 9, and 12. In (B), 36 goes into 6, 9, and 12 evenly (6 times, 4 times, and 3 times). Since there is no smaller number that works, (B) is the correct answer.

3. **D** Remember to use order of operations (PEMDAS) and check each answer choice. Choice (A) equals $30 - 12 \div 2 \times (3 + 7) = 30 - 12 \div 2 \times (10) = 30 - 6 \times 10 = 30 - 60 = -30$. Choice (B) equals $30 - 12 \div (2 \times 3 + 7) = 30 - 12 \div (6 + 7) = 30 - 12 \div (13) = 30 - \frac{12}{13}$, which is not an integer and therefore not equal to 5. Choice (C) equals $(30 - 12) \div 2 \times 3 + 7 = (18) \div 2 \times 3 + 7 = 9 \times 3 + 7 = 27 + 7 = 34$. Finally, (D) equals $30 - 12 \div 2 \times 3 - 7 = 30 - 6 \times 3 - 7 = 30 - 18 - 7 = 12 - 7 = 5$. Therefore, the correct answer is (D).

4. **D** When adding fractions with unlike denominators, find a common denominator first. For this question, multiply $\frac{5}{7}$ by 11 and multiply $\frac{2}{11}$ by 7. Add the numerators of the fraction to get the final sum: $\frac{55}{77} + \frac{14}{77} = \frac{69}{77}$. The correct answer is (D).

5. **C** Remember that when subtracting mixed numbers, make sure the fractions have a common denominator. For this question, multiply $\frac{1}{2}$ by 2 to get $\frac{2}{4}$. Subtract the numerators of the fractions: $\frac{2}{4} - \frac{1}{4} = \frac{1}{4}$. Next, subtract the whole numbers: $7 - 6 = 1$. Be careful! The question is looking for minutes, not hours, so convert $1\frac{1}{4}$ hours to minutes. There are 60 minutes in 1 hour and 15 minutes in $\frac{1}{4}$ hours, so there is a total of 75 more minutes: $60 + 15 = 75$. The correct answer is (C).

6. **A** To find the perimeter of a shape, add up all the sides. In an equilateral triangle, all sides are equal, so if one side is 4, all three sides are equal to 4. Thus, the correct answer is (A), since $4 + 4 + 4 = 12$.

7. **C** To find 20% of 200, multiply 0.2 and 200 to get the result: $0.20 \times 200 = 40$. Therefore, the correct answer is (C). Choice (A) would be 10% of 200, (B) would be 15% of 200, and (D) would be 50% or half of 200.

8. **C** Use the chart provided to find the total snowfall for the four-day period. Add the amount of snowfall for each day: $3 + 3 + 4 + 1 = 11$. The correct answer is (C).

9. **B** Use the chart provided to determine which day had the greatest amount of snowfall. Both Monday and Tuesday each had 3 inches of snowfall. On Wednesday, there was 4 inches of snow. On Thursday, there was 1 inch of snow. Therefore, the greatest amount of snow was on Wednesday. The correct answer is (B).

10. **D** To find the average temperature, use an average pie:

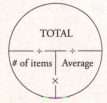

The total is the sum of all temperatures: 2 + 6 + 3 + 13 = 24. The number of items is 4 since there are 4 days. Divide the total and the number of items to get the average: $\frac{24}{4} = 6$. The correct answer is (D). Note that (A) is incorrect because 24 is the total degrees for the four-day period.

11.   C   Long division is one way to approach division with decimals. You can write $\frac{100}{0.25}$ as $0.25\overline{)100}$. Move the decimal to the right two times to get rid of the decimal in the divisor and also move the decimal to the right two times in the dividend: $25\overline{)10000}$. The result is $25\overline{)10000}^{400}$, so the correct answer is (C). Another option is use the answer choices (PITA). Multiply the answer choices by 0.25 to see which one equals 100. Choice (C) is the only option that works.

12.   A   To find the missing part of this equation, simplify the left side of the equation first: 5 × 31 = 155. The equation now looks like 155 = 100 + ___ . To determine what goes in the blank, subtract 100 from 155 or use the answer choice (PITA). Try (A): 155 = 100 + 55. Since this is the only answer choice that makes the right side of the equation equal to 155, the correct answer is (A).

13.   B   If half of the 6 tomato plants that Gwen planted died, then she lost 3 tomato plants: $\left(\frac{1}{2} \times 6 = 3\right)$. If Gwen then planted another tomato plant, she would have 4 total tomato plants: 3 + 1 = 4. Therefore, the correct answer is (B).

14.   C   To rent the video game, Tracey had to spend $1. Since she returned the video game 3 days late, she had to pay $0.50 for each late day, so she owed another $1.50 since 0.5 × 3 = 1.5. The total amount she paid for the video game rental is $2.50 because 1 + 1.5 = 2. Thus, the correct answer is (C).

15.   C   When multiplying a decimal by 100, simply move the decimal two places to the right so that 0.45 becomes 45, making the correct answer (C). Multiplying by stacking will also work. 45 times 100 equals 4,500. Don't forget to move the decimal two places to the left to get 45.

16.   D   There are 180° in a triangle. The given angles are each 45°, so they represent a total of 90°. Subtract 90 from 180 to get 90°, so the correct answer is (D) because 90° + 45° + 45° = 180°.

17.   A   There are 12 in a dozen, so 12 eggs cost $1.20. Therefore, the cost of 1 egg is 10 cents: $\frac{1.2}{12} = 0.1$. If 1 egg costs 10 cents, then 3 eggs cost 30 cents: 0.1 × 3 = 0.3. The correct answer is (A).

18.   C   If Boris has three times as many baseball cards as Bruce and Bruce has 12, then Boris has 36 cards: 12 × 3 = 36. To find the average number of cards between the two boys, use the average pie:

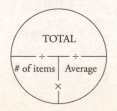

The total will be the sum of the boys' baseball cards: 36 + 12 = 48. The number of items is 2 since there are 2 boys. Divide the total and the number of items to get the average: $\frac{48}{2} = 24$. The correct answer is (C). Note that (D) is incorrect because 48 is total number of baseball cards between the 2 boys.

19. **C** To find the perimeter of a shape, add up all the sides. In a rectangle, opposite sides are equal, so if the length is 3, then the side opposite of it will also be 3. If the width is 2, then the side opposite of it will also be 2. Add all the sides: 3 + 2 + 3 + 2 = 10. Thus, (C) is the correct answer. Note that (A) is incorrect because 6 would be the area of this rectangle: $l \times w = 3 \times 2 = 6$.

20. **B** To multiply fractions, multiply the numerators together and multiply the denominators together: $\frac{3}{5} \times \frac{2}{7} = \frac{6}{35}$. The correct answer is (B).

21. **B** If Kenny can run 3 miles in 45 minutes, then he can run 1 mile in 15 minutes since $\frac{45}{3} = 15$. If he runs 5 miles, then it will take him 75 minutes ($15 \times 5 = 75$) or 1 hour and 15 minutes since there are 60 minutes in 1 hour. Therefore, the correct answer is (B). Note that estimation can help eliminate some of the answer choices. Since Kenny runs 3 miles in 45 minutes, 6 miles would take him twice that amount of time. The questions asks for the time it would take him to run 5 miles, so eliminate (C) because 1 hour and 30 minutes is twice as long as 45 minutes (the time to run 6 miles), and eliminate (D) because in 2 hours he would run farther than 6 miles.

22. **D** There are several ways to solve this problem (e.g. using the Bowtie method or finding a common denominator for the fractions). Another option would be to convert the fractions to decimal form: $\frac{5}{11} = 0.45\overline{45}$. Choice (A) equals 0.375, (B) is about 0.286, (C) equals $0.4\overline{4}$, and (D) is about 0.571. The only answer that is greater than $\frac{5}{11}$ or $0.45\overline{45}$ is 0.571, or (D).

23. **D** The perimeter of a shape is the sum of all the sides. In a square, all four sides are equal, so if the perimeter is equal to 36, then each side equals 9 because $\frac{36}{4} = 9$. To find the area of square multiply two sides together. Since each side of the square is equal, use the formula $A = s^2$. Therefore, the area is 81 because $9^2 = 81$. The correct answer is (D).

24. **B** If Maureen studied twice as long after school than she did before school, she studied for 4 hours after school: $2 \times 2 = 4$. For that day, she studied a total of 6 hours because 2 + 4 = 6. The correct answer is (B). Note that (A) is incorrect since it only represents the number of hours she studied after school.

25. **B** Remember to use order of operations (PEMDAS). Start with parentheses first!
$$\frac{40(37+63)}{8} = \frac{40(100)}{8} = \frac{4,000}{8} = 500.$$ The correct answer is (B).

26. **C** Use process of elimination. 0.3 is equivalent to $\frac{3}{10}$, so eliminate (A) and (B). 0.04 is equivalent to $\frac{4}{100}$, so eliminate (D). Therefore, the correct answer is (C).

27. **B** Draw a factor tree of 36.

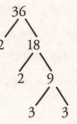

The prime factorization of 36 is $2 \times 2 \times 3 \times 3$ or $2^2 \times 3^2$. Therefore, (B) is the correct answer. Note that (D) contains a number that is not prime (6).

28. **D** Use the figure to determine each price. If one adult buys a one-way weekend train ticket, it will cost $4.50. Therefore, two one-way adult tickets cost $9.00. Children do not pay to ride the train on the weekend, so the total cost is $9.00 (4.5 + 4.5 + 0 = 9). The correct answer is (D).

29. **A** Use the figure to determine each price. The cost of 1 weekday peak fare ten-trip ticket is $54.00. The cost of purchasing 1 one-way weekday peak fare ticket is $6.00, so the cost of 10 such tickets is $60.00 (6 × 10 = 60). To find percent change, use the formula: % change = $\frac{\text{difference}}{\text{original}} \times 100$. The difference of the two prices is $6.00, and the original price is $60.00. Note that when the question says *percent less*, the *original* will be the larger number.
$$\frac{\text{difference}}{\text{original}} \times 100 = \frac{60-54}{60} \times 100 = \frac{6}{60} \times 100 = \frac{600}{60} = 10$$
Therefore, the correct answer is (A).

30. **D** Use the figure to determine each price. The price for 1 adult to travel one way during the weekday peak fare period is $6.00. The price for 1 adult to travel one way on the weekend is $4.50. The question asks how much more it costs this adult to travel during a weekday peak time versus to travel on the weekend. It costs $1.50 less since 6 × 4.5 = 1.5. Thus, the correct answer is (D).

31. **C** If Mr. Schroder can swim 1 lap in 5 minutes, then set up a proportion to find how many laps he can swim in 60 minutes: $\frac{1 \text{ lap}}{5 \text{ min}} = \frac{x}{60 \text{ min}}$. Cross-multiply to get $5x = 60$. Then divide both sides by 5 to get $x = 12$. Therefore, he can swim 12 laps in 60 minutes. The correct answer is (C).

32. **C** When in doubt with exponents, expand them out. $10^3 = 10 \times 10 \times 10$. Therefore, the correct answer is (C).

33. **C** If the DVD player originally cost \$100, a 10% discount would be \$10 off: $0.1 \times 100 = 10$. The new price of the DVD player is \$90 ($100 - 10 = 90$). When the new price of the DVD player is reduced by 20%, which is a discount of \$18 since $0.2 \times 90 = 18$, the final price will be \$72 ($90 - 18 = 72$). Therefore, the correct answer is (C).

34. **D** To find the volume of a box, use the formula $V = l \times w \times h$. Plug the given dimensions into the formula: $V = 30 \text{ cm} \times 10 \text{ cm} \times 4 \text{ cm} = 1{,}200 \text{ cm}^3$. Therefore, (D) is the correct answer.

35. **B** Use an average pie.

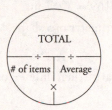

For this problem, draw 3 average pies. The first average pie will represent Monday. The average (9) and the number of items (8 hours) are given. Multiply to find the total number of patients seen that day: $9 \times 8 = 72$. The second average pie will represent Tuesday. The average (9) and the number of items (6 hours) are given. Multiply to find the total number of patients seen that day: $9 \times 6 = 54$. Finally, the third average pie will represent the average number of patients she sees each day. To find the total, add the total patients seen on Monday and the total patients seen on Tuesday to get $72 + 54 = 126$. To find the number of items, pay attention to the question. It asks for the average number of patients she sees on each *day*. There were 2 days, so the number of items is 2. Divide the total and the number of items to find the average: $\dfrac{126}{2} = 63$. Therefore, the correct answer is (B). Note that (A) is incorrect because 54 is the total patients seen on Tuesday, (C) is incorrect because 72 is the total patients seen on Monday, and (D) is incorrect because 126 is the total number of patients seen on the two days.

36. **B** Since there are variables in the question and answers, plug in a value for q or p. If $q = 2$, then $2 + 9 = 7 - p$. Simplify the left side of the equation to get $11 = 7 - p$. Isolate p to get $p = -4$. The value of $q + p = -2$ because $2 + (-4) = -2$. Therefore, the correct answer is (B).

37. **A** Use the answer choices (PITA) to determine which one is the product of two consecutive even integers. Choice (A) could be the product of 0 and 2, so it is the correct answer. Note that in (B) is incorrect because 15 is the product of 3 and 5, which are consecutive *odd* integers. Choice (D) is incorrect because 30 is the product of 5 and 6, which are consecutive but not both even integers. Choice (C) is not the product of consecutive integers.

38. **C** Similar triangles are triangles that have the same angle measures and corresponding sides have the same ratio. Thus, if triangle *ABC* has side measures of 3, 4, and 5, then the sides of triangle *XYZ* should have the same ratio. Only (C) will work. If the sides of triangle *ABC* are each multiplied by 2, the result is 6, 8, and 10, which are possible side lengths for triangle *XYZ*. Therefore, the correct answer is (C). Note that (A) is incorrect because triangle *ABC* is not equilateral, so triangle *XYZ* will not be either.

39. **A** If the area of the square is 169 cm, then use the area formula to find the length of one side of the square: $A = s^2$. If $169 = s^2$, then $\sqrt{169} = s^2$. Thus, $s = 13$. Since all four sides of a square are equal, each side equals 13. To find the perimeter of a shape, add up of all the sides: $13 + 13 + 13 + 13 = 52$. The correct answer is (A).

40. **A** If $\frac{3}{4}$ of the employees are at the party, then only $\frac{1}{4}$ of the employees are NOT at the party. Eliminate (C) and (D) since the answer should be less than half of 240. Note that (C) equals $\frac{1}{2}$ of 240 and (D) equals $\frac{3}{4}$ of 240. If $\frac{1}{4}$ of the employees are NOT at the party, then 60 employees did not attend because $\frac{1}{4} \times 240 = 60$. The correct answer is (A).

41. **C** Break word problems into bite-sized pieces. If Jose and Greg walk $\frac{1}{4}$ of the distance in the first 2 hours, they will walk 5 miles since $\frac{1}{4} \times 20 = 5$. If they walk $\frac{1}{5}$ of the entire distance (20 miles) in the next 1.5 hours, then they will walk 4 miles: $\frac{1}{5} \times 20 = 4$. The number of miles remaining is 11 since $20 - 5 - 4 = 11$. Therefore, (C) is the correct answer.

42. **B** To find the perimeter of a shape, add up all the sides. Even though the shape is odd looking and not all sides are labeled, the sides opposite of a labeled side can still be determined because opposite sides will still be equal.

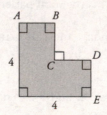

Thus, *AB* + *CD* = 4 since they are opposite the base, which is equal to 4. Furthermore, *BC* + *DE* = 4 since they are opposite the left side of the shape, which is equal to 4. Therefore, the perimeter is 16 since $4 + 4 + 4 + 4 = 16$. The correct answer is (B).

43. **D** Use an average pie.

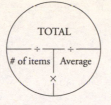

The average (3) and the number of items (12 games) are given. Multiply to find the total number of points scored: $12 \times 3 = 36$. Therefore, the correct answer is (D).

44. **A** To find the volume of a box, use the formula $V = l \times w \times h$. Plug the given dimensions into the formula: $V = 8 \times 4 \times \dfrac{1}{4} = 8$. Therefore, (A) is the correct answer.

45. **D** If the hat costs \$30, then a 20% decrease would be \$6 since $0.2 \times 30 = 6$. The new price of the hat would be \$24 because $30 - 6 = 24$. The correct answer is (D).

46. **B** To find the probability of an event, find the total of what is wanted out of the total possible outcomes: Probability $= \dfrac{\text{What you want}}{\text{What you've got}}$. The item wanted is a brownie, so any 6 could be chosen. The total number of items in the jar is 19 since $5 + 6 + 8 = 19$. Therefore, the probability of selecting a brownie is $\dfrac{6}{19}$. The correct answer is (B). Note that (C) is incorrect since $\dfrac{8}{19}$ is the probability of choosing a granola bar.

47. **C** Since there are variables in the question and answers, plug in a value for x or y. If $x = 3$, then $\dfrac{2}{3}(3) = 6 - y$. Simplify the left side of the equation to get $2 = 6 - y$. Isolate y to get $y = 4$. Using these values for x and y, check each answer choice to see which one works. In (A), $2(3) \neq 6 - 3(4)$ since $6 \neq -6$. In (B), $3(4) - 3 \neq 6$ since $9 \neq 6$. In (C), $2(3) + 3(4) = 18$ since $18 = 18$. Finally, in (D), $2(3 + 3(4)) \neq 18$ since $30 \neq 18$. Therefore, the correct answer is (C). Another option is to multiply both sides of the equation by 3 to get rid of the fraction: $\left(\dfrac{2}{3}\right)x = 6 - y$ becomes $2x = 3(6 - y)$. Distribute the 3 to get $2x = 18 - 3y$. Finally, add $3y$ to both sides to get $2x + 3y = 18$, which is (C).

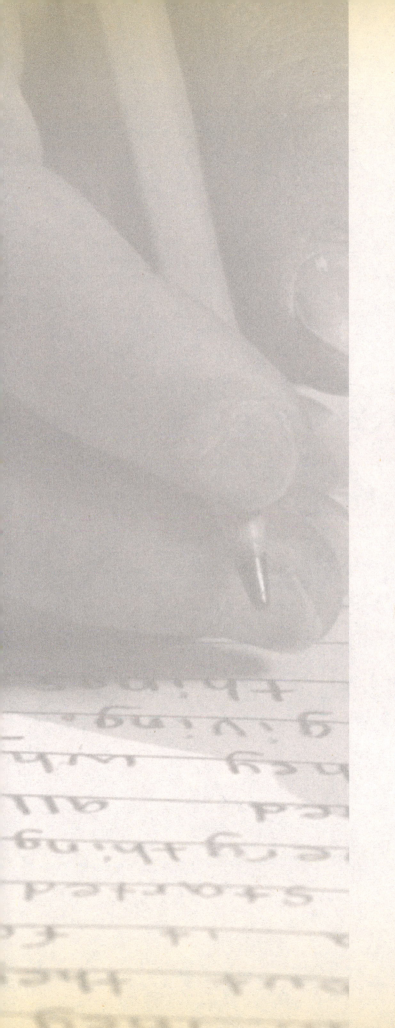

Chapter 21
Lower Level
ISEE Practice Test

Lower Level Practice Test

Be sure each mark *completely* fills the answer space.

SECTION 1

1 (A)(B)(C)(D)	9 (A)(B)(C)(D)	17 (A)(B)(C)(D)	25 (A)(B)(C)(D)	33 (A)(B)(C)(D)
2 (A)(B)(C)(D)	10 (A)(B)(C)(D)	18 (A)(B)(C)(D)	26 (A)(B)(C)(D)	34 (A)(B)(C)(D)
3 (A)(B)(C)(D)	11 (A)(B)(C)(D)	19 (A)(B)(C)(D)	27 (A)(B)(C)(D)	
4 (A)(B)(C)(D)	12 (A)(B)(C)(D)	20 (A)(B)(C)(D)	28 (A)(B)(C)(D)	
5 (A)(B)(C)(D)	13 (A)(B)(C)(D)	21 (A)(B)(C)(D)	29 (A)(B)(C)(D)	
6 (A)(B)(C)(D)	14 (A)(B)(C)(D)	22 (A)(B)(C)(D)	30 (A)(B)(C)(D)	
7 (A)(B)(C)(D)	15 (A)(B)(C)(D)	23 (A)(B)(C)(D)	31 (A)(B)(C)(D)	
8 (A)(B)(C)(D)	16 (A)(B)(C)(D)	24 (A)(B)(C)(D)	32 (A)(B)(C)(D)	

SECTION 2

1 (A)(B)(C)(D)	9 (A)(B)(C)(D)	17 (A)(B)(C)(D)	25 (A)(B)(C)(D)	33 (A)(B)(C)(D)
2 (A)(B)(C)(D)	10 (A)(B)(C)(D)	18 (A)(B)(C)(D)	26 (A)(B)(C)(D)	34 (A)(B)(C)(D)
3 (A)(B)(C)(D)	11 (A)(B)(C)(D)	19 (A)(B)(C)(D)	27 (A)(B)(C)(D)	35 (A)(B)(C)(D)
4 (A)(B)(C)(D)	12 (A)(B)(C)(D)	20 (A)(B)(C)(D)	28 (A)(B)(C)(D)	36 (A)(B)(C)(D)
5 (A)(B)(C)(D)	13 (A)(B)(C)(D)	21 (A)(B)(C)(D)	29 (A)(B)(C)(D)	37 (A)(B)(C)(D)
6 (A)(B)(C)(D)	14 (A)(B)(C)(D)	22 (A)(B)(C)(D)	30 (A)(B)(C)(D)	38 (A)(B)(C)(D)
7 (A)(B)(C)(D)	15 (A)(B)(C)(D)	23 (A)(B)(C)(D)	31 (A)(B)(C)(D)	
8 (A)(B)(C)(D)	16 (A)(B)(C)(D)	24 (A)(B)(C)(D)	32 (A)(B)(C)(D)	

SECTION 3

1 (A)(B)(C)(D)	9 (A)(B)(C)(D)	17 (A)(B)(C)(D)	25 (A)(B)(C)(D)
2 (A)(B)(C)(D)	10 (A)(B)(C)(D)	18 (A)(B)(C)(D)	
3 (A)(B)(C)(D)	11 (A)(B)(C)(D)	19 (A)(B)(C)(D)	
4 (A)(B)(C)(D)	12 (A)(B)(C)(D)	20 (A)(B)(C)(D)	
5 (A)(B)(C)(D)	13 (A)(B)(C)(D)	21 (A)(B)(C)(D)	
6 (A)(B)(C)(D)	14 (A)(B)(C)(D)	22 (A)(B)(C)(D)	
7 (A)(B)(C)(D)	15 (A)(B)(C)(D)	23 (A)(B)(C)(D)	
8 (A)(B)(C)(D)	16 (A)(B)(C)(D)	24 (A)(B)(C)(D)	

SECTION 4

1 (A)(B)(C)(D)	9 (A)(B)(C)(D)	17 (A)(B)(C)(D)	25 (A)(B)(C)(D)
2 (A)(B)(C)(D)	10 (A)(B)(C)(D)	18 (A)(B)(C)(D)	26 (A)(B)(C)(D)
3 (A)(B)(C)(D)	11 (A)(B)(C)(D)	19 (A)(B)(C)(D)	27 (A)(B)(C)(D)
4 (A)(B)(C)(D)	12 (A)(B)(C)(D)	20 (A)(B)(C)(D)	28 (A)(B)(C)(D)
5 (A)(B)(C)(D)	13 (A)(B)(C)(D)	21 (A)(B)(C)(D)	29 (A)(B)(C)(D)
6 (A)(B)(C)(D)	14 (A)(B)(C)(D)	22 (A)(B)(C)(D)	30 (A)(B)(C)(D)
7 (A)(B)(C)(D)	15 (A)(B)(C)(D)	23 (A)(B)(C)(D)	
8 (A)(B)(C)(D)	16 (A)(B)(C)(D)	24 (A)(B)(C)(D)	

Section 1
Verbal Reasoning

This section is divided into two parts that contain two different types of questions. As soon as you have completed Part One, answer the questions in Part Two. You may write in your test booklet. For each answer you select, fill in the corresponding circle on your answer document.

Part One – Synonyms

Each question in Part One consists of a word in capital letters followed by four answer choices. Select the one word that is most nearly the same in meaning as the word in capital letters.

SAMPLE QUESTION:

AGGRAVATE:

(A) apply
(B) enjoy
(C) irritate
(D) present

Sample Answer

Ⓐ Ⓑ ● Ⓓ

Go on to the next page. ➝

VR

Part Two – Sentence Completion

Each question in Part Two is made up of a sentence with one blank. Each blank indicates that a word or phrase is missing. The sentence is followed by four answer choices. Select the one word or phrase that best completes the meaning of the sentence as a whole.

SAMPLE QUESTIONS:

Because Edgar enjoyed seeing new places, every winter he went on a ------ to a place he had never been.

(A) debate
(B) puzzle
(C) restoration
(D) voyage

<u>Sample Answer</u>
Ⓐ Ⓑ Ⓒ ●

Doctors recommend that Americans exercise more in order to stay healthy, but unfortunately many people ------.

(A) watch, rather than play, professional sports
(B) do not eat enough fruits and vegetables
(C) do not choose to follow that advice
(D) work too many hours to enjoy leisure time

<u>Sample Answer</u>
Ⓐ Ⓑ ● Ⓓ

STOP. Do not go on until told to do so.

Part One – Synonyms

Directions: Select the word that is most nearly the same in meaning as the word in capital letters.

1. BASIN:

   (A) desk
   (B) frame
   (C) mound
   (D) sink

2. DRENCH:

   (A) clean
   (B) rain
   (C) soak
   (D) twist

3. HASTILY:

   (A) happily
   (B) passively
   (C) quickly
   (D) quietly

4. HEAP:

   (A) grain
   (B) imprint
   (C) pile
   (D) volume

5. ADORN:

   (A) average
   (B) decorate
   (C) sew
   (D) visit

6. UNFURL:

   (A) close
   (B) flap
   (C) gather up
   (D) spread out

7. NOVICE:

   (A) beginner
   (B) player
   (C) sickness
   (D) story

8. COMPREHEND:

   (A) compare
   (B) speak
   (C) understand
   (D) wonder

9. MALICE:

   (A) fear
   (B) hatred
   (C) joy
   (D) opinion

10. UNKEMPT:

   (A) free
   (B) frequent
   (C) messy
   (D) obvious

Go on to the next page. ➝

11. RUSE:

   (A) laugh
   (B) partner
   (C) sale
   (D) trick

12. OBSOLETE:

   (A) historical
   (B) old-fashioned
   (C) popular
   (D) uncommon

13. WILY:

   (A) careful
   (B) crafty
   (C) loud
   (D) thin

14. BRITTLE:

   (A) breakable
   (B) lumpy
   (C) sharp
   (D) small

15. ORATOR:

   (A) curator
   (B) listener
   (C) orchestra
   (D) speaker

16. POLL:

   (A) argument
   (B) discussion
   (C) election
   (D) survey

17. PLEA:

   (A) appeal
   (B) explanation
   (C) remark
   (D) response

Go on to the next page. ⟶

Part Two – Sentence Completion

Directions: Select the word that best completes the sentence.

---

18. Sasha's friends think she is outgoing and talkative, but when she meets people for the first time she is often -------.

    (A) friendly
    (B) privileged
    (C) shy
    (D) sociable

19. Ms. Lin reviewed all the essays so that she could ------- each student's writing.

    (A) deny
    (B) emphasize
    (C) evaluate
    (D) ignore

20. A snapping turtle's neck can ------- to catch fish far away from its body.

    (A) blend
    (B) extend
    (C) retract
    (D) wander

21. The young man dressed carefully for his job interview because he wanted to ------- the interviewer.

    (A) annoy
    (B) discourage
    (C) employ
    (D) impress

22. Scientists spend a lot of time studying ants, bees, and other ------- insects that live and work together in large groups.

    (A) aquatic
    (B) social
    (C) uninteresting
    (D) wingless

23. Because the domestic cat cleans its fur thoroughly with its rough tongue, it rarely becomes -------.

    (A) distracted
    (B) soiled
    (C) tidy
    (D) washed

24. Everyone said Jaquinta was an ------- person because she always asked a lot of questions.

    (A) inquisitive
    (B) intense
    (C) organized
    (D) unpredictable

25. Although Wanda has taken violin lessons for three years, her ------- is actually to play sports.

    (A) possibility
    (B) preference
    (C) question
    (D) routine

Go on to the next page. ➜

26. People who obey the law and try not to hurt anyone are not likely to become -------.

    (A) happy
    (B) infamous
    (C) quiet
    (D) serene

27. At one time, Western movies were released -------, but now they are hardly ever made.

    (A) frequently
    (B) informally
    (C) quickly
    (D) seldom

28. Mr. Thomas placed celery in colored water in order to ------- the way plants can absorb liquids.

    (A) compress
    (B) cover
    (C) demonstrate
    (D) ignore

29. Most goods were produced in people's homes before industrialization, but as the factory system became common, ------- production of goods decreased.

    (A) domestic
    (B) energetic
    (C) foreign
    (D) high-speed

30. Frederick Church built a large Moorish home that was ------- as a visitor came up the long driveway, but came into view suddenly at the end.

    (A) beautiful
    (B) concealed
    (C) uninteresting
    (D) visible

31. To keep Cassidy's baby sister safe once she begins to crawl, her family will -------.

    (A) take lots of pictures
    (B) stay close to the ground
    (C) buy new baby shoes
    (D) baby-proof the house

32. Even though most of the students looked confused, the teacher -------.

    (A) wondered what she would have for lunch
    (B) explained the solution to the problem a second time
    (C) sent a student to the principal's office for misbehaving
    (D) moved on to a new topic without asking whether anyone had questions

Go on to the next page. ➡

33. Although the weather forecast predicted freezing temperatures and wet snow, Jason -------.

    (A)   decided to learn how to ski
    (B)   did not wear a coat when he went outside
    (C)   worked twice as hard as he usually does
    (D)   put on his favorite wool sweater

34. Because Ronnie was terrified of the ocean and never learned to swim, -------.

    (A)   she did not accept an invitation to her friend's beach house
    (B)   her parents never took her on their vacations to Kansas
    (C)   she became an A student and was the president of two clubs
    (D)   her brother decided to try out for the Olympic swimming team

STOP. If there is time, you may check your work in this section only.

QR

Section 2
Quantitative Reasoning

38 Questions	Time: 35 Minutes

Part One – Word Problems

Each question consists of a word problem followed by four answer choices. Read each question and then decide which one of the four suggested answers is best.

Find the row of spaces on your answer document that has the same number as the question. In this row, mark the space having the same letter as the answer you have chosen. You may write in your test booklet.

EXAMPLE 1:

What is the value of the expression

$6 + (8 \div 2)$?

(A) $2 + 5$
(B) 2×5
(C) $3 + 4$
(D) 3×4

Sample Answer

Ⓐ ● Ⓒ Ⓓ

The correct answer is 10, so circle B is darkened.

EXAMPLE 2:

Which could be the dimensions of a rectangle with an area of 34 cm² ?

(A) 2 cm × 17 cm
(B) 3 cm × 12 cm
(C) 4 cm × 8 cm
(D) 5 cm × 7 cm

Sample Answer

● Ⓑ Ⓒ Ⓓ

The correct answer is 2 cm × 17 cm, so circle A is darkened.

STOP. Do not go on until told to do so.

1. Which is seven hundred ninety thousand twelve?

    (A)   7,912
    (B)   79,012
    (C)   709,012
    (D)   790,012

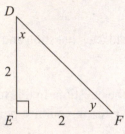

2. Which of the following must be true of triangle *DEF* above, which is drawn to scale?

    (A) $x = 45$
    (B) $\overline{DF} = 2$
    (C) $\overline{DF} = 4$
    (D) $x + y > 90$

3. Which number shows 9 in the thousands place?

    (A)   1,039
    (B)   7,920
    (C)   9,437
    (D)   94,016

4. Which of the following is the product of two distinct prime numbers?

    (A)   1
    (B)   4
    (C)   8
    (D)   14

5. Which is the smallest fraction?

    (A) $\dfrac{2}{5}$

    (B) $\dfrac{3}{8}$

    (C) $\dfrac{3}{4}$

    (D) $\dfrac{4}{9}$

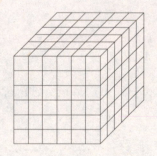

6. The number of smaller cubes that make up the solid object above is

    (A)   36
    (B)   108
    (C)   216
    (D)   46,656

Go on to the next page. ➡

7. It takes Ms. Weiss ten minutes to drive 4 miles. If she continues to drive at the same speed for 25 more minutes, how many more miles will she have driven?

   (A)   4
   (B)   10
   (C)   14
   (D)   25

8. A painter uses 3 gallons of paint to cover 2 square yards on the inside of a house. How many gallons will it take for him to cover a wall that is 12 feet tall and 60 feet long? <u>Note</u>: 3 feet = 1 yard.

   (A)   40
   (B)   120
   (C)   180
   (D)   240

9. Which of the following is equal to $\frac{1}{6}$?

   (A) $\frac{3}{6}$

   (B) $\frac{3}{9}$

   (C) $\frac{3}{18}$

   (D) $\frac{3}{24}$

10. When a number is divided by 8, the remainder is 3. Which could be the number?

    (A)   11
    (B)   14
    (C)   17
    (D)   21

11. Which of the following equals 90 ?

    (A) 5×18
    (B) 5×16
    (C) 4×15
    (D) 9^{10}

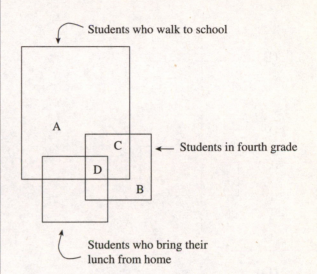

12. In which region of the figure above would you find Stephanie, a fourth-grade student who walks to school and buys her lunch in the cafeteria?

    (A)   A
    (B)   B
    (C)   C
    (D)   D

Go on to the next page. ➡

13. Which of the following shows a line of symmetry?

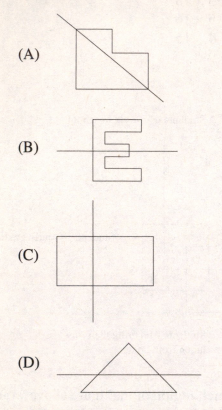

(A)

(B)

(C)

(D)

14. What is the area of the shaded region in the figure above?

(A) 12
(B) 13
(C) 14
(D) 24

$$16$$
$$\times M$$
$$\overline{A0}$$

15. In the multiplication problem shown above, if A and M represent distinct positive integers, which of the following is the value of A ?

(A) 0
(B) 4
(C) 8
(D) 9

Go on to the next page. ➞

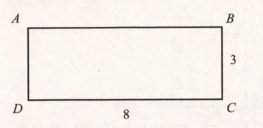

16. What is the perimeter of rectangle *ABCD* above?

(A) 5
(B) 11
(C) 22
(D) 24

17. Which shows 7 in the hundreds and thousandths places?

(A) 2,793.4701
(B) 5,704.2371
(C) 7,421.9783
(D) 8,072.7634

18. Which is seventy two thousand fourteen?

(A) 7,214
(B) 72,014
(C) 72,140
(D) 720,014

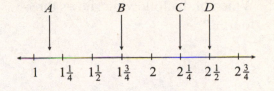

19. Which point on the number line above indicates the correct placement of $\frac{10}{4}$?

(A) A
(B) B
(C) C
(D) D

20. Which of the following is closest in value to 7 ?

(A) 6.8
(B) 7.009
(C) 7.01
(D) 7.1

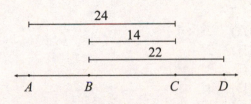

21. The length of *AD* in the figure shown above is

(A) 30
(B) 32
(C) 38
(D) 46

Go on to the next page. ➡

22. Which of the following shows three-fourths?

(A)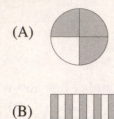

(B)

(C)

(D) ▲

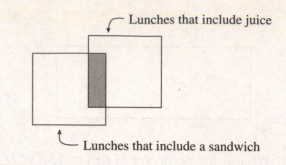

Lunches that include juice

Lunches that include a sandwich

25. Which lunch menu can be found in the shaded part of the figure above?

(A) yogurt and soda
(B) ham sandwich and apple juice
(C) pizza and milk
(D) cheese sandwich and water

23. Which of the following is NOT equal to 16 ?

(A) $2^2 \times 4$
(B) 2^3
(C) 2^4
(D) 4^2

24. Which is the largest fraction?

(A) $\dfrac{3}{5}$

(B) $\dfrac{2}{3}$

(C) $\dfrac{1}{6}$

(D) $\dfrac{1}{2}$

Go on to the next page. ➡

26. Which of the following shows a reflection?

(A)

(B)

(C)

(D)

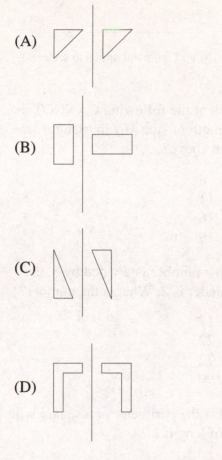

27. Which of the following produces a remainder of 3 ?

(A) $72 \div 9$
(B) $57 \div 6$
(C) $49 \div 9$
(D) $39 \div 7$

28. Sam's Pizza uses 24 slices of pepperoni on 8 pieces of pizza. How many slices of pepperoni would be used on 6 pieces of pizza?

(A)   3
(B)   12
(C)   18
(D)   48

29. Evan is making a quilt out of 6-inch squares of material. How many squares will he need to make a quilt that is 6 feet long and 5 feet wide?
Note: 1 foot = 12 inches.

(A)   15
(B)   30
(C)   60
(D)   120

Go on to the next page. ⟶

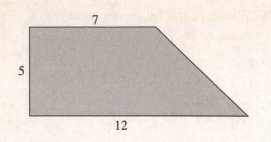

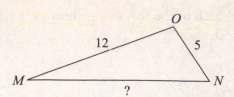

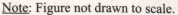

Note: Figure not drawn to scale.

30. What is the area of the figure shown above?

    (A) 24
    (B) 35
    (C) 47.5
    (D) 60

31. Which of the following shows 48 as a product of primes?

    (A) 3×8
    (B) $2^4 \times 3$
    (C) $2^3 \times 6$
    (D) 2×3

32. Which of the following CANNOT be the length of side *MN* in triangle *MNO*, shown above?

    (A) 8
    (B) 11
    (C) 16
    (D) 19

33. When a number is divided by 8, the remainder is 2. What is the number?

    (A) 11
    (B) 22
    (C) 72
    (D) 90

34. What is the perimeter of a square with a side of length 2 ?

    (A) 8
    (B) 6
    (C) 4
    (D) 2

Go on to the next page. →

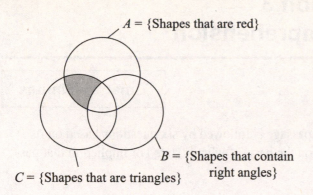

A = {Shapes that are red}

B = {Shapes that contain right angles}

C = {Shapes that are triangles}

35. Which of these shapes would fall into the shaded region of the figure shown above?

(A) a red right triangle
(B) a red equilateral triangle
(C) a green rectangle
(D) a blue circle

36. Melissa had 20 words on her spelling test. If she spelled $\frac{1}{4}$ of the words incorrectly, how many words did she spell correctly?

(A) 4
(B) 5
(C) 15
(D) 16

37. $\frac{2}{3} \times \frac{1}{8} =$

(A) $\frac{1}{12}$

(B) $\frac{1}{24}$

(C) $\frac{19}{24}$

(D) $\frac{1}{4}$

38. The distance from Amy's home to Los Angeles is 2,281 miles. The distance from Dave's house to Los Angeles is 1,912 miles. How much closer is Dave's house to Los Angeles than Amy's house?

(A) 379
(B) 369
(C) 359
(D) 269

STOP. If there is time, you may check your work in this section only.

Section 3
Reading Comprehension

25 Questions	Time: 25 Minutes

This section contains six short reading passages. Each passage is followed by six questions based on its content. Answer the questions following each passage on the basis of what is <u>stated</u> or <u>implied</u> in that passage. You may write in the test booklet.

STOP. Do not go on until told to do so.

NO TEST MATERIAL ON THIS PAGE

Questions 1–5

Line

1   "What's that noise?" my brother asked.
2   I listened carefully. Just when I thought
3 I heard a small noise, the thunder crashed
4 again. The rain was hitting the roof hard,
5 too, making it difficult to hear anything. "I
6 don't hear it," I said.
7   "What do you mean you don't hear
8 it? It's so loud!" my brother whispered.
9 Then I heard it. It was a *click-click-click*,
10 and it sounded like it was coming from the
11 bathroom.
12   "Maybe it's a monster. We should go
13 get Mom," my brother said. I didn't want
14 to be a scaredy-cat, and I knew Mom was
15 probably asleep. Besides, I'd have to walk
16 past the bathroom to get to her.
17   *Click-click-click*. I told my brother to
18 go to sleep, but he said, "I can't. We have to
19 see what it is."

20   "Okay," I said. I pretended I was
21 very brave, and got up and marched to the
22 bathroom. When I saw what was making the
23 noise, I laughed out loud. My brother came
24 running down the hall, asking, "What is it?"
25   Then, he poked his head in the door and
26 looked in the bathtub. There was our dog,
27 Mack. He was so scared of the thunder that
28 he was hiding in the tub! He sat there with
29 his head down, shivering. His toenails went
30 *click-click-click* against the ceramic tub as
31 he turned to look at us.
32   "Poor Mack! He's more scared than
33 we were," I said. We brought Mack into our
34 bedroom and petted him until he stopped
35 shaking. Then, we all went to sleep.

Go on to the next page. ⟶

1. At the beginning of the story, the narrator's brother thinks the noise is made by

    (A) a monster
    (B) his mother
    (C) the dog
    (D) the narrator

2. When the narrator says, "Besides, I'd have to walk past the bathroom," (lines 15–16), you know that he

    (A) is afraid of getting in trouble
    (B) is not familiar with the house
    (C) is scared to go near the noise
    (D) would rather go to the kitchen

3. In line 21, "marched" most nearly means

    (A) hopped loudly
    (B) ran sneakily
    (C) sang a military song
    (D) walked with a purpose

4. Why does the narrator "laugh out loud" (line 23) when he gets to the bathroom?

    (A) He is amused because he sees that it is just the dog making a noise.
    (B) He is happy that there is nothing making a noise in the bathroom.
    (C) He is nervous about opening the door.
    (D) His brother has just told him a good joke.

5. According to the passage, the dog was in the bathtub because

    (A) he needed a bath
    (B) he was hungry
    (C) he was trying to hide from the brothers
    (D) he was trying to hide from the thunder

Go on to the next page. ➡

Questions 6–10

This story is adapted from an African folktale that explains why the sun and moon are in the sky.

Line

1   Long ago, the sun and the moon and the
2 water all lived on Earth. The sun and moon
3 were married and they were friends with
4 the water. The sun and moon often went to
5 visit the water where he lived, but the water
6 never returned their visits.
7   One day, the moon said to the water,
8 "Why do you never come to visit us?"
9   The water replied, "My people and I
10 take up a lot of room. I do not think you have
11 enough room in your house for all my people
12 and me. I would like to visit you, but I do not
13 want to crowd your home."
14   The moon said, "Well, then we shall
15 build a bigger house so that you can visit."
16   "I would like that," said the water, "but
17 it must be a very big place."
18   So the moon and the sun built a huge
19 palace. It took many months, but finally it
20 was finished. They sent word to the water to
21 come and visit.
22   The next day, the water came. It stayed
23 outside the gates and called inside. "I have
24 arrived, my friends. Shall I come in?"

25   The sun and moon said together, "Yes,
26 of course. Come in." So the water came
27 through the gates. So, too, came the fishes
28 and the crabs and the other water-dwelling
29 creatures.
30   The water filled the palace so much that
31 the sun and moon were forced to move up
32 to the top floor. "Are you sure you want me
33 to continue?" the water asked.
34   "Of course, come in," said the sun and
35 moon. So the water continued.
36   Soon the water had filled the house
37 completely, and the sun and moon were
38 perched on the roof. "Are you sure?" asked
39 the water.
40   "Yes, yes. You are welcome here," said
41 the moon and sun. And so the water flowed
42 more, until the moon and sun had to jump
43 into the sky. They have stayed there ever
44 since.

Go on to the next page. ➡

6. The primary purpose of this passage is to

    (A) describe how to build a large and expensive palace
    (B) describe how water flows in a flood
    (C) explain how the sun and moon got into the sky
    (D) provide information about sea creatures

7. The sun and moon can best be described as

    (A) assertive
    (B) friendly
    (C) grumpy
    (D) selfish

8. In the beginning of the story, why does the water never come to visit the sun and moon?

    (A) The sun and moon have never invited the water to their home.
    (B) The water does not really like the sun and moon.
    (C) The water lives too far away from the sun and moon to make the trip.
    (D) The water thinks there is not enough space where the sun and moon live.

9. When the water says "my people" in line 9, he is referring to

    (A) the creatures that live in the trees
    (B) the creatures that live in the water
    (C) the sun and the moon
    (D) the workers who build the palace

10. In line 38, "perched" most nearly means

    (A) got very thirsty
    (B) laughed heartily
    (C) looked like a fish
    (D) sat on the edge

Go on to the next page. ⟶

Questions 11–15

Line

1   Not all bees live in colonies. Some
2 bees live all alone in a nest built for one.
3 Most of us, however, when we think of bees
4 and wasps, think of huge groups of insects,
5 working together in a cohesive social
6 unit. The hive is, in many ways, a perfect
7 example of a social system. Inside the hive,
8 bees raise their young and store honey. The
9 queen honeybee, for example, may lay up to
10 1,500 eggs a day in the summer. The drone
11 bees mate with the queen and die. The
12 worker bees gather food, care for the hive
13 and the young, and protect the hive. The
14 stored pollen and honey will feed the colony
15 throughout the cold winter months. Inside
16 a hive there is one queen, a few hundred
17 drones, and as many as 40,000 workers.
18 The expression "busy as a bee" is certainly
19 appropriate when you consider the work
20 that bees perform.

Go on to the next page. ➡

11. According to the passage, the purpose of the drones is to

  (A) care for the hive
  (B) gather food
  (C) mate with the queen
  (D) supervise the workers

12. According to the passage, the purpose of the honey and pollen is to

  (A) attract a queen to the hive
  (B) fertilize flowers
  (C) provide a place for the queen to lay her eggs
  (D) provide food for the hive

13. According to the passage, the hive is an example of a social system because

  (A) different members of the hive perform different jobs, yet they work together
  (B) the queen rules over all the bees
  (C) there are workers to do all the work
  (D) there is no conflict in the hive

14. The word "cohesive" in line 5 most nearly means

  (A) connected
  (B) hardworking
  (C) sacred
  (D) sticky

15. The tone of the passage is most like that found in a

  (A) diary entry of a modern naturalist
  (B) general science textbook
  (C) laboratory report
  (D) letter to a friend

Go on to the next page. ⟶

Questions 16–20

Line
1   A wealthy contributor to the arts,
2 Isabella Stewart Gardner was born in New
3 York in 1840. She married John Lowell
4 Gardner, a wealthy heir, and settled in
5 Boston, Massachusetts. When her only son
6 died as a young child, she devoted her life
7 to the arts. Assisted by Bernard Berenson,
8 a young art critic, she began collecting
9 important works of art. After her husband
10 died in 1898, she purchased land for the
11 construction of a museum and worked for
12 years overseeing its creation. She actually
13 lived in the museum until her death in 1924.
14 Her museum became a gathering place for
15 artists, writers, and celebrities. She was
16 considered quite eccentric, often shunning
17 Boston "society" in favor of more colorful
18 characters. She gave her wonderful museum
19 to the city of Boston, to be preserved as a
20 public museum. Today, if you visit Boston,
21 you can admire the work of Isabella Stewart
22 Gardner.

Go on to the next page. ➞

16. Which title would be most appropriate for the passage?

    (A) "An Eccentric Woman"
    (B) "Isabella Stewart Gardner— Museum Maker"
    (C) "The Beginnings of a Museum"
    (D) "Two Deaths in a Family"

17. In line 17, the word "colorful" most nearly means

    (A) beautiful
    (B) brilliant
    (C) unusual
    (D) vivid

18. The passage suggests that Isabella Stewart Gardner began collecting art

    (A) after the death of her husband
    (B) after the death of her son
    (C) to impress art critics
    (D) to spend her husband's money

19. According to the passage, the museum built by Isabella Stewart Gardner was used for all of the following EXCEPT

    (A) a place for artists to congregate
    (B) a place for art to be viewed
    (C) a school for aspiring artists
    (D) her home

20. The author's attitude toward Isabella Stewart Gardner can best be described as

    (A) admiring
    (B) critical
    (C) jealous
    (D) skeptical

Go on to the next page. ➞

Questions 21–25

Line

1   Charlotte Perkins Gilman lived from
2 1860 to 1935. She lived during a time when
3 most women in America and Europe had
4 few educational opportunities. For most of
5 Gilman's life, women could not even vote.
6 Gilman had many ideas for how to improve
7 women's lives.
8   Because she grew up in a family that
9 was not wealthy, Gilman read a lot in order
10 to educate herself. When she was eighteen,
11 however, she attended the Rhode Island
12 School of Design. She worked her way
13 through school by tutoring and teaching.

14   Gilman eventually began publishing
15 books, articles, poems, and even a monthly
16 magazine of her own. She also lectured
17 to large groups. Much of her writing and
18 speaking focused on allowing women to
19 use their natural talents and intelligence by
20 giving them access to education and jobs
21 that paid well. By offering lots of different
22 ideas and ways to change society, Gilman
23 helped women gain the right to live full,
24 productive lives.

Go on to the next page. ⟶

21. The primary purpose of the passage is to

    (A) convince the reader that women are able to work and study outside the home
    (B) describe how one woman focused on helping to improve others' lives
    (C) prove that people who are not wealthy can still gain access to education
    (D) show that everyone needs to find a way to help others

22. According to the passage, during Gilman's life women did not have

    (A) any ideas about how to change things
    (B) any way to publish their writing
    (C) a way to travel between America and Europe
    (D) many options for school and work

23. It can be inferred from lines 8–10 that Gilman

    (A) did not like to read by herself
    (B) planned to become a writer and speaker when she was young
    (C) preferred to spend time alone
    (D) was not able to attend school very often as a child

24. The main point of the third paragraph (lines 14–24) is that

    (A) Gilman enjoyed writing and speaking to large groups
    (B) Gilman worked to spread ideas about how women could live fuller lives
    (C) it was very easy to publish your own magazine at the turn of the century
    (D) most women did not have access to education and well-paying jobs

25. Based on the information in the passage, you could most likely expect one of Gilman's books to be titled

    (A) *Europe: A History*
    (B) *Growing Up Rich*
    (C) *Why Women Don't Need to Vote*
    (D) *Women and Economics*

STOP. If there is time, you may check your work in this section only.

Section 4
Mathematics Achievement

Each question is followed by four suggested answers. Read each question and then decide which one of the four suggested answers is best.

Find the row of spaces on your answer document that has the same number as the question. In this row, mark the space having the same letter as the answer you have chosen. You may write in your test booklet.

SAMPLE QUESTION:

Sample Answer
Ⓐ ● Ⓒ Ⓓ

Which number is divisible by 7 without a remainder?

(A) 26
(B) 35
(C) 18
(D) 60

The correct answer is 35, so circle B is darkened.

STOP. Do not go on until told to do so.

NO TEST MATERIAL ON THIS PAGE

1. $6\frac{1}{2}$ hours is how many minutes more than 5 hours?

   (A) $1\frac{1}{2}$

   (B) 30

   (C) 60

   (D) 90

2. Which numeral represents twenty-four thousand, six hundred and three?

   (A) 2,463
   (B) 20,463
   (C) 24,603
   (D) 24,630

3. $\frac{2}{3}+\frac{8}{9}=$

   (A) $\frac{14}{9}$

   (B) $\frac{28}{27}$

   (C) $\frac{10}{9}$

   (D) $\frac{9}{14}$

Questions 4–6 refer to the pictograph shown below.

Letters Delivered on Mrs. Adler's Mail Route

Monday	
Tuesday	
Wednesday	

Note: Each represents 2 letters.

4. How many letters did Mrs. Adler deliver on Tuesday?

   (A) None
   (B) 2
   (C) 3
   (D) 6

5. How many more letters did Mrs. Adler deliver on Monday than on Wednesday?

   (A) 1
   (B) 2
   (C) 3
   (D) 4

6. How many letters did Mrs. Adler deliver on Monday and Tuesday?

   (A) 24
   (B) 18
   (C) 16
   (D) 8

Go on to the next page. ➡

7. In the decimal 0.42537, the digit 2 is equivalent to which of the following?

(A) $\dfrac{2}{10}$

(B) $\dfrac{2}{100}$

(C) $\dfrac{2}{1,000}$

(D) $\dfrac{2}{10,000}$

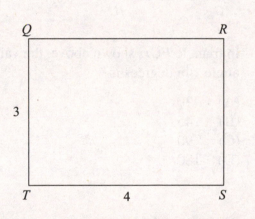

8. What is the perimeter of rectangle *QRST* shown above?

(A)   7
(B)   10
(C)   12
(D)   14

9. $\dfrac{1,000}{25} =$

(A)   400
(B)   40
(C)   4
(D) $\dfrac{1}{4}$

10. $3 \times 64 =$

(A)   128
(B)   182
(C)   192
(D)   256

11. $3 \times 2 + 4 =$

(A)   7
(B)   10
(C)   14
(D)   16

12. Wu had 18 marbles. He lost half of them, and then his friend gave him 3 more marbles. How many marbles does Wu have now?

(A)   6
(B)   9
(C)   12
(D)   21

Go on to the next page. ➡

```
┌─────────────────────────────────┐
│         School Supplies         │
│  Pad of Paper.............$1.25  │
│  Notebook................$1.50  │
│  Box of Pencils..........$2.00  │
│  Pens....................$1.00  │
└─────────────────────────────────┘
```

13. Ian visits the store and buys 2 pads of paper, 1 notebook, and 3 boxes of pencils. How much money does he spend?

   (A) $10.00
   (B) $8.00
   (C) $5.75
   (D) $4.75

14. $\frac{1}{5} \times 400 =$

   (A) 20
   (B) 40
   (C) 80
   (D) 120

15. Evan has 26 comic books. Mark has twice as many comic books as Evan has. How many comic books does Mark have?

   (A) 13
   (B) 26
   (C) 42
   (D) 52

16. If 12 eggs cost $1.80, then how much will 36 eggs cost?

   (A) $0.60
   (B) $1.80
   (C) $3.60
   (D) $5.40

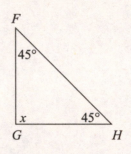

17. In triangle *FGH* shown above, the value of angle *x* in degrees is

   (A) 30
   (B) 45
   (C) 90
   (D) 180

Go on to the next page. ⟶

Questions 18–19 refer to the following graph.

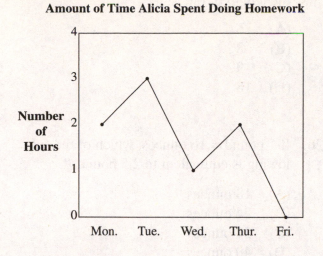

Amount of Time Alicia Spent Doing Homework

Number of Hours

Mon. Tue. Wed. Thur. Fri.

18. On which day did Alicia spend the same amount of time doing homework as she spent on Monday?

(A) Tuesday
(B) Wednesday
(C) Thursday
(D) Friday

19. How many more hours did Alicia spend doing her homework on Tuesday than on Wednesday?

(A) 1
(B) 2
(C) 3
(D) 4

20. $6 \times 20 = 150 - \underline{\hspace{1cm}}$

(A) 130
(B) 90
(C) 30
(D) 10

21. Which fraction is less than $\frac{3}{4}$?

(A) $\frac{2}{3}$

(B) $\frac{5}{6}$

(C) $\frac{7}{8}$

(D) $\frac{9}{10}$

22. All of the following are multiples of 3 EXCEPT

(A) 120
(B) 210
(C) 462
(D) 512

Go on to the next page. ➡

Questions 23–24 refer to the graph shown below.

Favorite Ice Cream Flavors of Helen's Class

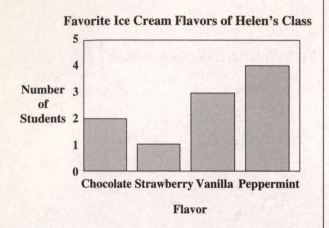

23. How many students chose vanilla ice cream as their favorite?

(A) 1
(B) 2
(C) 3
(D) 4

24. Which flavor was the favorite of the greatest number of students?

(A) Peppermint
(B) Vanilla
(C) Chocolate
(D) Strawberry

25. If the perimeter of a square is 36, what is the length of one side?

(A) 6
(B) 8
(C) 9
(D) 18

26. If 1 pound = 16 ounces, which of the following is equivalent to 2.5 pounds?

(A) 18 ounces
(B) 24 ounces
(C) 32 ounces
(D) 40 ounces

27. Jessica worked $5\frac{1}{2}$ hours on Tuesday and $3\frac{3}{4}$ hours on Wednesday. How many hours did she work on Tuesday and Wednesday?

(A) $1\frac{3}{4}$

(B) $2\frac{1}{2}$

(C) $8\frac{1}{4}$

(D) $9\frac{1}{4}$

Go on to the next page. ➞

Questions 28–30 refer to the price list shown below.

Fast Ferry Price List

	ADULTS	CHILDREN
Weekday Mornings	$15.00	$9.00
Weekday Afternoons	$12.00	$6.00
Weekends	$10.00	FREE

28. How much will it cost for 2 adults and 1 child to ride the Fast Ferry on a weekday afternoon?

    (A) $30.00
    (B) $27.00
    (C) $24.00
    (D) $18.00

29. How much less will it cost 1 adult and 2 children to ride the Fast Ferry on a weekday afternoon than it would cost them to ride on a weekday morning?

    (A) $6.00
    (B) $8.00
    (C) $9.00
    (D) $18.00

30. The price for 2 adults and 1 child to ride the Fast Ferry on a weekend is what fractional part of the price for 2 adults and 1 child to ride the Fast Ferry on a weekday afternoon?

    (A) $\frac{1}{2}$

    (B) $\frac{1}{3}$

    (C) $\frac{2}{3}$

    (D) $\frac{3}{4}$

STOP. If there is time, you may check your work in this section only.

Essay

You will have 30 minutes to plan and write an essay on the topic printed on the other side of this page. **Do not write on another topic. An essay on another topic is not acceptable.**

The essay is designed to give you an opportunity to show how well you can write. You should try to express your thoughts clearly. How well you write is much more important than how much you write, but you need to say enough for a reader to understand what you mean.

You will probably want to write more than a short paragraph. You should also be aware that a copy of your essay will be sent to each school that will be receiving your test results. You are to write only in the appropriate section of the answer sheet. Please write or print so that your writing may be read by someone who is not familiar with your handwriting.

You may make notes and plan your essay on the reverse side of the page. Allow enough time to copy the final form on to your answer sheet. You must copy the essay topic onto your answer sheet, on page 3, in the box provided.

Please remember to write only the final draft of the essay on pages 3 and 4 of your answer sheet and to write it in blue or black pen. Again, you may use cursive writing or you may print. Only pages 3 and 4 will be sent to the schools.

Directions continue on next page.

Essay Topic

If you could plan your perfect vacation, what would you do?

- Only write on this essay question
- Only pages 3 and 4 will be sent to the schools
- Only write in blue or black pen

NOTES

_____

_____

_____

_____

_____

_____

_____

_____

_____

_____

_____

_____

Chapter 22
Lower Level ISEE
Practice Test:
Answers and
Explanations

ANSWER KEY

ISEE LL Verbal 1

1. D	5. B	9. B	13. B	17. A	21. D	25. B	29. A	33. B
2. C	6. D	10. C	14. A	18. C	22. B	26. B	30. B	34. A
3. C	7. A	11. D	15. D	19. C	23. B	27. A	31. D	
4. C	8. C	12. B	16. D	20. B	24. A	28. C	32. D	

ISEE LL Quantitative 2

1. D	5. B	9. C	13. B	17. B	21. B	25. B	29. D	33. D	37. A
2. A	6. C	10. A	14. C	18. B	22. A	26. D	30. C	34. A	38. B
3. C	7. B	11. A	15. C	19. D	23. B	27. B	31. B	35. B	
4. D	8. B	12. C	16. C	20. B	24. B	28. C	32. D	36. C	

ISEE LL Reading 3

1. A	5. D	9. B	13. A	17. C	21. B	25. D
2. C	6. C	10. D	14. A	18. B	22. D	
3. D	7. B	11. C	15. B	19. C	23. D	
4. A	8. D	12. D	16. B	20. A	24. B	

ISEE LL Math 4

1. D	5. B	9. B	13. A	17. C	21. A	25. C	29. C
2. C	6. C	10. C	14. C	18. C	22. D	26. D	30. C
3. A	7. B	11. B	15. D	19. B	23. C	27. D	
4. D	8. D	12. C	16. D	20. C	24. A	28. A	

EXPLANATIONS

Section 1 Verbal

1. **D** If you are unsure of the meaning of a word, try to think of a context you have heard it used in. For example, washbasin. A washbasin is used for washing. A basin is a type of tub. This best matches (D), sink.

2. **C** To drench means to completely soak through; an example sentence is "I became completely drenched after walking home during the rainstorm". This best matches (C), soak.

3. **C** To perform an act hastily is to perform it swiftly, with little attention to detail. This best matches (C), quickly.

4. **C** To heap means to add on or pile; an example phrase is "a heap of trouble", which means a pile or load of trouble. This best matches (C), pile.

5. **B** To adorn means to decorate; this best matches (B).

6. **D** If you are unsure of the meaning of a word, try to think of a context you have heard it used in. For example, you may have heard of someone "unfurling a banner" in a book set in older times. To unfurl means to uncurl or unfold. This best matches (D), spread out.

7. **A** Novice is defined as beginner or apprentice. This best matches (A), beginner.

8. **C** To comprehend means to understand or process intellectually. This best matches (C), understand.

9. **B** Malice is a feeling of hatred or extreme anger. This best matches (B), hatred.

10. **C** Unkempt means disorderly or untidy. This best matches (C), messy.

11. **D** A ruse is a story or con used to deceive someone. This best matches (D), trick.

12. **B** If you are unsure of the meaning of a word, try to think of a context you have heard it used in. For example, "the pace of technology will make many of our devices obsolete in a few years". Obsolete means out-of-date or no longer useful. This best matches (B), old-fashioned.

13. **B** If you are unsure of the meaning of a word, try to think of a context you have heard it used in. For example, the "wily coyote" in the cartoons was always trying to trick the roadrunner. "Wily" means clever. This best matches (B), crafty.

14. **A** If you are unsure of the meaning of a word, try to think of a context you have heard it used in. For example, "brittle bones". Brittle bones are bones that are likely to fracture or break; so brittle most nearly means breakable, (A).

15. **D** If you are unsure of the meaning of a word, try to think of a context you have heard it used in. For example, a "great orator" was a great speaker or speechmaker. This best matches (D).

16. **D** If you are unsure of the meaning of a word, try to think of a context you have heard it used in. For example, in an election year many people are polled about the candidates. Polls are surveys or questionnaires, which best matches (D), survey.

17. **A** A plea is a request; this best matches (A), appeal.

18. **C** Pay attention to the clues in the sentence and the direction words. The first part of the sentence states that Sasha's friends think she is outgoing and talkative. The sentence then says "but," which indicates opposite information in the second half of the sentence. The missing word must mean the opposite of "outgoing" and "talkative." This best matches (C), shy.

19. **C** Pay attention to the clues in the sentence. The only thing we know about Ms. Lin is that she reviewed all the essays in her class. The missing word must mean "review." This best matches (C), evaluate.

20. **B** Pay attention to the clues in the sentence. The turtle is using its neck to catch fish far away from its body. What action is usually performed to reach things far away? Stretching. This means the missing word must mean stretches, which best matches (B), extends. Choice (C) is a deceptive answer choice, turtles can retract their necks but that is the opposite meaning the sentence is looking for.

21. **D** Pay attention to the clues in the sentence. The sentence says that the young man dressed carefully for his interview. Why would one dress carefully, especially for an interview? Probably to impress someone. The missing word must mean "impress," which best matches (D).

22. **B** Pay attention to the clues in the sentence. The only information the sentence tells you about this list of insects is that they "live and work together in large groups." The only information you know then is that these are group or social insects. The missing word must mean group or social, which best matches (B).

23. **B** Pay attention to the clues in the sentence. The only information the sentence tells you is that the cat cleans itself regularly. The missing word must mean dirty. This best matches (B), soiled.

24. **A** Pay attention to the clues in the sentence. The only information the sentence tells us about Jaquinta is that she asks a lot of questions. The missing word must mean "curious." This best matches (A), inquisitive.

25. **B** Pay attention to the clues in the sentence and the direction words. The sentence starts by saying "Although Wanda has taken violin lessons for three years;" "although" indicates that the second half of the sentence will be opposed to this information. This means that the missing word must mean Wanda preferred sports to violin. This best matches (B).

26. **B** Pay attention to the clues in the sentence. This sentence is about people who obey the law and don't try to hurt anyone. Such people are unlikely to become several things, but specifically they are unlikely to become criminals or notorious for bad deeds. This best matches (B), infamous.

27. **A** Pay attention to the clues in the sentence and the direction words. The second part of the sentence says that now Western movies are hardly ever made. This part of the sentence started with "but," indicating it is the opposite of what is stated in the first part of the sentence. So the missing word must mean the opposite of "hardly ever made." The best match for this meaning is (A), frequently.

28. **C** Pay attention to the clues in the sentence. The sentence says Mr. Thomas was showing the students how plants absorb liquid, so the missing word most likely means "show" or "illustrate." This best matches (C), demonstrate.

29. **A** Pay attention to the clues in the sentence and the direction words. The first part of the sentence says that most goods were produced in people's homes previously. The second part of the sentence begins with "but," indicating it is the opposite of what is stated in the first part of the sentence. The missing word must mean "home," which best matches (A), domestic.

30. **B** Pay attention to the clues in the sentence and the direction words. The second part of the sentence says that came into view suddenly. This part of the sentence started with "but," indicating it is the opposite of what is stated in the first part of the sentence. So the missing word must mean the opposite of "came into view," something matching "hidden." The best match for this meaning is (B), concealed.

31. **D** Pay attention to the clues in the sentence. The only information the sentence tells you is about the baby's safety. The answer must be related to safety. The only choice that involves safety is (D), baby-proof the house.

32. **D** Pay attention to the clues in the sentence and the direction words. The first part of the sentence says that the students were confused. This part of the sentence starts with "Even though," indicating that the second part of the sentence won't align with this information. So, even though the students are confused, the teacher must not be concerned about their confusion. The missing word or phrase must match the teacher not being concerned. This best matches (D), the teacher moved on to a new topic.

33. **B** Pay attention to the clues in the sentence and the direction words. The first part of the sentence says freezing temperatures and wet snow were predicted. This part of the sentence started with "Although," indicating that the second part of the sentence won't align with this information. So, even though the weather would be cold and snowy, Jason must not be concerned about the weather. The missing word or phrase must match Jason not caring about the weather. This best matches (B), he did not wear a coat.

34. **A** Pay attention to the clues in the sentence. The only information the sentence tells you is that Ronnie is terrified of the ocean and never learned to swim. The missing part of the sentence must be related to this information. The only answer choice that is related to the ocean is (A), she did not accept an invitation to the beach house.

Section 2 Quantitative Reasoning

1. **D** Seven hundred thousand is written out as 700,000, and ninety thousand is written out as 90,000. Therefore, the correct answer is (D). Choice (A) is seven thousand nine hundred and twelve, (B) is seventy-nine thousand and twelve, and (C) is seven hundred nine thousand and twelve.

2. **A** There are 180° in a triangle. Since this is a right triangle, the two remaining angles (x and y) must add up to 90°. Eliminate (D). Since the sides opposite of angles x and y are both equal to 2, the angles themselves are both equal. $\frac{90}{2} = 45$, so the correct answer is (A). Choices (B) and (C) cannot be correct since side $\overline{DF}$ is $2\sqrt{2}$.

3. **C** The thousands place is four spots to the left of the decimal. The only choice that has nine in the thousands place is (C). Choice (A) contains a nine in the units or ones place. Choice (B) contains a nine in the hundreds place. Choice (D) contains a nine in the ten thousands place.

4. **D** The important math vocabulary words in this question are *product* (the result of multiplication), *distinct* (different), and *prime* (the only factors are 1 and the number itself). Choice (D) is the correct answer since 14 is the product of two prime, distinct numbers: 2 and 7. Choices (A) and (C) cannot be found by multiplying two prime numbers. 1, 4, and 8 are not prime. Choice (B) would be the product of 2 and 2, which would not be the product of two *distinct* numbers.

5. **B** There are several ways to solve this problem (e.g. using the Bowtie method or finding a common denominator for the fractions). Another option would be to convert the fractions to decimal form. Choice (A) equals 0.4, (B) equals 0.375, (C) equals 0.75, and (D) equals $0.4\overline{4}$. Since 0.375 is the smallest number, the correct answer is (B).

6. **C** Rather than counting all of the squares (which could take a *long* time!), use multiplication. The front face of the cube has 6 rows and 6 columns, which equals 36 smaller cubes. The large cube is 6 rows deep (i.e. 6 rows each containing 36 cubes, lined up one in front of the other). Multiply 36 by 6, and the answer is 216, or (C).

7. **B** If it takes Ms. Weiss 10 minutes to drive 4 miles and she needs to drive 25 more minutes, set up a proportion to find how much farther she will drive: $\frac{10 \text{ min}}{4 \text{ miles}} = \frac{25 \text{ min}}{x}$

Use cross multiplication to solve: $10x = 4(25)$

Divide both sides by 10, and $x = 10$. She will drive 10 additional miles (B). Be sure to read the question carefully! Choice (C) represents the total number of miles she drove, not *how many more miles she drove*.

8. **B** First, convert the dimensions of the wall from feet to yards. If the wall is 12 feet tall by 60 feet long, then the wall is 4 yards tall by 20 yards long $\left(\dfrac{12}{3} = 4 \text{ and } \dfrac{60}{3} = 20 \right)$. Next, find the area of the wall: $4 \times 20 = 80$. If the wall is 80 yd^2 and 3 gallons of paint can cover 2 yd^2, set up a proportion to find the total number of gallons needed to paint the wall: $\dfrac{3 \text{ gal}}{2 \text{ yd}^2} = \dfrac{x}{90 \text{ yd}^2}$

Cross multiply to solve: $3(80) = 2x$. Then divide both sides by 2, and $120 = x$. He will need 120 gallons of paint to cover the wall, so (B) is the correct answer.

9. **C** To find the fraction that equals $\dfrac{1}{6}$, reduce the answer choices. Choice (A) is $\dfrac{1}{2}$, which is too big. Choice (B) is $\dfrac{1}{3}$, which is also too big. Choice (C) reduces to $\dfrac{1}{6}$, which is correct. Finally, (D) is $\dfrac{1}{8}$, which is too small. Only (C) equals $\dfrac{1}{6}$.

10. **A** Use the answer choices (PITA) for this question. If you start with (A), $8\overline{)11}$ with 1 above, which leaves a remainder of 3 ($1 \times 8 = 8$ and $11 - 8 = 3$). Therefore, the correct answer is (A). Note that no other answer choice has a remainder of 3: (B) has a remainder of 6, (C) has a remainder of 1, and (D) has a remainder of 5.

11. **A** Only (A) works: $5 \times 18 = 90$. Choice (B) equals 80, (C) equals 60, and (D) is much too large ($9^{10} = 9 \times 9 \times 9 \times 9 \times 9 \times 9 \times 9 \times 9 \times 9 \times 9$).

12. **C** Use process of elimination. If Stephanie is in 4th grade, eliminate (A) because 4th grade students are only in regions B, C, and D. Stephanie also walks to school, so eliminate (B) since only regions C and D contain students that walk to school. Stephanie buys her lunch in the cafeteria, so she can't be in region D (eliminate (D)) since those students bring lunch from home. Therefore, the correct answer is (C), region C.

13. **B** A line of symmetry is a line drawn through an image creating two identical halves on each side. Imagine folding the image on that line. The one with a line of symmetry would be the one that has two parts that match up exactly. The only image that fits this description is (B).

14. **C** To find the area of the shaded region, count all the shaded squares. There are 13. There are two shaded triangles that if you matched them together, they would create one full shaded square. Therefore, since there are 14 shaded squares, the shaded area is 14, or (C).

15. **C** Since A and M must be distinct, they cannot be the same number. Use the answer choices (PITA) to test out values of A. If A equals 0 (A), then M would have to equal 0. Eliminate (A) since A and M are not distinct values. If A equals 4 (B), then M would have to be 2.5, which is not an integer. Eliminate (B). If A equals 8 (C), then M would have to equal 5 because $16 \times 5 = 90$. Since A and M are not the same and the equation is true, the correct answer is (C).

16. **C** To find the perimeter of a shape, add up all the sides. In a rectangle, opposite sides are equal, so $AD = 3$ and $AB = 8$. $3 + 8 + 3 + 8 = 22$. Thus, (C) is the correct answer. Note that (D) is incorrect because 24 is the area of this rectangle: $l \times w = 3 \times 8 = 24$.

17. **B** The hundreds place is three spots to the left of the decimal, and the thousandths place is three spots to the right of the decimal. The only choice that has seven in the correct places is (B). Choice (A) contains seven in the hundreds and hundredths places. Choice (C) contains seven in the thousands and hundredths places. Choice (D) contains a seven in the tens and tenths places.

18. **B** Seventy two thousand is written out as 72,000, and fourteen is written out as 14. Therefore, the correct answer is (B). Choice (A) is seven thousand two hundred and fourteen, (C) is seventy two thousand one hundred and forty, and (D) is seven hundred twenty thousand and fourteen.

19. **D** Since $\frac{10}{4} = 2.5$, then (D) is correct. Choices (A) and (B) are incorrect because both are less than 2. Choice (C) would equal 2.25, which is also less than 2.5.

20. **B** To find the answer closest in value to 7 find the answer that has the smallest distance between itself and 7. Choice (A) is 0.2 from 7. Choice (B) is 0.009 from 7. Choice (C) is 0.01 from 7. Choice (D) is 0.1 from 7. Therefore, the one closest to 7 is (B) since $\frac{9}{1,000}$ is a shorter distance than $\frac{2}{10}, \frac{1}{100}$, and $\frac{1}{10}$.

21. **B** Since the distances for $\overline{AC}$ and $\overline{BC}$ are given, the difference will be the distance for $\overline{AB}$: $24 - 14 = 10$. Since the distance for $\overline{BD}$ is also given, the difference of it and $\overline{BC}$ will be the distance of $\overline{CD}$: $22 - 14 = 8$. Next add up the segments $\overline{AB}, \overline{BC}$, and $\overline{CD}$: $10 + 14 + 8 = 32$. Thus, $\overline{AD}$ equals 32, which is (B).

22. **A** Only (A) represents a shaded region of $\frac{3}{4}$. Choice (B) equals $\frac{5}{9}$. Choice (C) equals $\frac{1}{2}$. Choice (D) equals $\frac{3}{3}$ or 1.

23. **B** When in doubt with exponents, expand them out! Choice (A) can be written as $2 \times 2 \times 4$, which equals 16. Choice (B) can be written as $2 \times 2 \times 2$, which equals 8. Choice (C) can be written as $2 \times 2 \times 2 \times 2$, which equals 16. Finally, (D) can be written as 4×4, which equals 16. Therefore, the answer that does NOT equal 16 is (B).

24. **B** There are several ways to solve this problem (e.g. using the Bowtie method or finding a common denominator for the fractions). Another option would be to convert the fractions to decimal form. Choice (A) equals 0.6, (B) equals $0.\overline{66}$, (C) equals $0.1\overline{66}$, and (D) equals 0.5. Since $0.\overline{66}$ is the largest number, the correct answer is (B).

25. **B** In the figure, the shaded region includes lunches that contain juice AND a sandwich. Only (B) has a menu that includes both a sandwich and juice. Choices (A) and (C) do not contain either option. Choice (D) does not contain a juice.

26. **D** An image that has been reflected has been "flipped" over a line, resulting in a mirror image of the original. Imagine if a fold could be made where each line is, the two images would then fold together and appear as one image. The only answer choice that makes this description is (D).

27. **B** Use long division to check each answer. In (A), 72 is divisible by 9, so the remainder is 0. In (B), 6 goes into 57 9 times evenly with 3 as a remainder. Therefore, (B) is the correct answer. Note that (C) and (D) both have a remainder of 4.

28. **C** If Sam is dividing 24 slices of pepperoni among the 8 pieces of pizza, each piece of pizza will have 3 slices of pepperoni since $\frac{24}{8} = 3$. If one piece has 3 slices of pepperoni, then six pieces of pizza will have 6×3 or 18 slices of pepperoni. Thus, the correct answer is (C).

29. **D** First convert the dimensions of the quilt from feet to inches. If the quilt is 6 feet long and 5 feet wide, then the quilt is 72 inches long and 60 inches wide ($6 \times 12 = 72$ and $5 \times 12 = 60$). Next, find the area of the quilt and the area of each square: $72 \times 60 = 4{,}320$ and $6 \times 6 = 36$. To see how many squares will be needed for the quilt, divide 36 into 4320. The results is 120, so 120 squares will be needed (D).

30. **C** To find the area of a trapezoid, use the formula: $\left(\frac{1}{2}\right)(b_1 + b_2)(h)$, where b_1 and b_2 represent the two bases (top and bottom) and h represents the height. Thus, $\left(\frac{1}{2}\right)(7 + 12)(5) = 47.5$. Choice (C) is the correct answer.

31. **B** Draw a factor tree of 48.

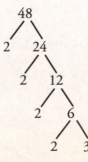

The prime factorization of 48 is $2 \times 2 \times 2 \times 2 \times 3$ or $2^4 \times 3$. Therefore, (B) is the correct answer. Note that (A) and (C) contain numbers that are not prime (8 and 6) and (D) is not a complete factorization of 48.

32. **D** The third side of a triangle must always be greater than the difference and less than the sum of the other two sides. In this case, the third side must be greater than 7 (12 – 5) and less than 17 (12 + 5). Since (A), (B), and (C) all fall within this range ($7 < x < 17$), they could be possible values for the third side. Since (D) is greater than 17, it is the only choice that CANNOT be the length of side *MN* and is the correct answer to this question.

33. **D** Use the answer choices (PITA) for this question. If you start with (A), 8 goes into 11 once with a remainder of 3. In (B), 8 goes into 22 twice with a remainder of 6. In (C), 8 goes into 72 evenly and has a remainder of 0. For (D), 8 goes into 90 11 times with a remainder of 2. Therefore, the correct answer is (D).

34. **A** To find the perimeter of a shape, add up all the sides. In a square, all sides are equal, so if one side is 2, all 4 sides are equal to 2. Thus, (A) is the correct answer since 2 + 2 + 2 + 2 = 8. Note that (C) is incorrect because 4 is the area of this square ($A = s^2 = 2^2 = 4$).

35. **B** In the figure, the shaded region includes shapes that are red triangles that do not have right angles. Only (B) has a shape that includes those features. Choice (A) does not contain a shape without a right angle. Choices (C) and (D) do not contain a triangular shape.

36. **C** If Melissa spelled $\frac{1}{4}$ of the words incorrectly, then she spelled $\frac{3}{4}$ of the words correctly. $\frac{3}{4}$ of 20 words (or 75% of 20 words) is 15 words. Thus, the correct answer is (C). Be sure to read the question carefully! Choice (B) is incorrect because it has the number of words she spelled *incorrectly*.

37. **A** To multiply fractions, multiply the numerators together and then multiply the denominators together. Then reduce. $\frac{2}{3} \times \frac{1}{8} = \frac{2 \times 1}{3 \times 8} = \frac{2}{24} = \frac{1}{12}$ The correct answer is (A).

38. **B** To see how much closer Dave's house is to Los Angeles than Amy's house, find the difference of the two distances. 2,281 – 1,912 = 369, which makes (B) the correct answer.

Section 3 Reading

1. **A** This is a specific question, so go back to the passage and find the answer. According to lines 12–13, the brother suggests that the noise might be a monster. The only choice that matches this information is (A). The brother suggests they go ask their mom, not that the noise is their mother, eliminating (B). The brother is speaking to the narrator about the noise, so he can't think that the narrator is the one making the noise. Eliminate (D). Although it turns out the noise is the dog, that is not what this question asks, eliminating (C). The correct answer is (A).

2. **C** This is a specific question, so go back to the passage and find the answer. At the beginning of the sentence, the author says he does not want to be a "scaredy-cat," and that he would have to walk past where the noise is coming from to even get to his mother's room. This supports the idea that the narrator is afraid of what could be making the noise his brother hears. This matches (C), the narrator is afraid of going near the noise. There is no indication that the other answers are true based on the passage.

3. **D** When asked a vocabulary in context question, focus on what the word means in the sentence. In line 21, "marched" is being used to describe how the author walked to the bathroom, with a put on sense of bravery. The best meaning for this word in the context of the sentence is (D), walked with a purpose, since he was pretending to be brave and that's how he walked. There is no indication of loudness or sneakiness, eliminating (A) and (B). Choice (C) is deceptive as it references the military, which the word "march" might make you think of but isn't correct in this context.

4. **A** This is a specific question, so go back to the passage and find the answer. The author laughs after seeing what is in the bathroom. What was in the bathroom? The dog! This best matches (A). Neither (B) nor (D) is mentioned in the passage, and although the narrator is nervous to open the door that is not what this question asks. The correct answer is (A).

5. **D** This is a specific question, so go back to the passage and find the answer. Lines 27–28 state that the dog was so afraid of the thunder that he had hidden in the tub. The only answer that matches these lines is (D). Choices (A), (B), and (C) are not mentioned in the passage and so cannot be correct.

6. **C** On primary purpose questions, ask yourself "Why did the author write this story? What is the main takeaway for this story?" The passage is focused on telling the story of how the moon and sun came to live in the sky. This best matches (C). The passage does not describe how to build a palace, how water flows in a flood, or specific sea creatures. This eliminates (A), (B), and (D). Choice (C) is the correct answer.

7. **B** The main descriptions of the sun and the moon center on their desire to have the sea come and visit them. They build a new palace and keep moving higher and higher to fit the water and all its friends in. This sounds like very friendly behavior, which best supports (B). There is no negative description of the sun and moon included in the story, which eliminates (C) and (D). Choice (A) does not match the information listed in the passage, so (B) is the correct answer.

8. **D** This is a specific question, so go back to the passage and find the answer. Lines 9–13 explain that the water does not want to visit the sun and the moon because he is afraid that he and his people will take up too much room in the sun and moon's house. This best matches (D). Choices (A), (B), and (C) are never mentioned in the passage. Choice (D) is the correct answer.

9. **B** This is a specific question, so go back to the passage and find the answer. Lines 27–29 list all of the guests that the water brought along with it: the fishes, crabs, and other water-dwelling creatures. This best matches (B), the creatures that live in the water. The water is visiting the sun and the moon, they are not "his people" he brings. Eliminate (C). There are never any trees or workers mentioned in the passage, which eliminates (A) and (D). Choice (B) is the correct answer.

10. **D** When asked a vocabulary in context question, focus on what the word means in the sentence. In line 38, "perched" most nearly means teetering on or balanced on. This best matches (D), sat on the edge.

11. **C** This is a specific question, so go back to the passage and find the answer. The drone bee is mentioned in lines 10–11, which state that their purpose is to mate with the queen and then die. This best matches (C). It is the worker bees that gather food and care for the hive; eliminate ((A) and (B). There is no mention of which bees supervise the workers, so (D) cannot be correct. The correct answer is (C).

12. **D** This is a specific question, so go back to the passage and find the answer. The honey and pollen are mentioned in lines 13–15, in which it states that they will go to feeding to colony throughout the winter months. This best matches (D), to provide food for the hive. There is no discussion of attracting a queen in the passage, which eliminates (A). There is also no discussion of flower fertilization or where the queen lays her eggs in the passage, eliminating (B) and (C) as well. The correct answer is (D).

13. **A** This is a relatively general question, since the entire passage addresses this answer. When asked a general question, remember your process of elimination rules. Notice that (B), (C), and (D) all have extreme language—"all" and "no." These are very strongly-worded answers that are not supported by the passage, so they should be eliminated. Choice (A) does not contain extreme language, and it summarizes the description of the various bees' jobs in the passage. Choice (A) is the correct answer.

14. **A** When asked a vocabulary in context question, focus on what the word means in the sentence. In line 5, "cohesive" most nearly means the phrase "working together," which was used earlier in the sentence. The best match for this meaning is (A), connected. Although bees may be hardworking, as in (B), this sentence is focused on how they work as a group, which supports (A). Choices (C) and (D) are not supported by the text of the passage.

15. **B** On tone questions, eliminate answer choices that are too extreme or don't make sense based on the passage. This is a very fact-based passage, which eliminates ((A) and (D) as too personal. Since the

information included in the passage is focused on bees in general rather than any specific observations, (B) is the best answer.

16. **B**   This question is a "main idea" question in disguise. Ask yourself the "so what?" of the story. The story is focused on the dedication Isabella Stewart Gardner had to art and her establishment of a museum. This best matches (B). Although the information included in other answer choices may be mentioned in the passage, they are all much too narrow to be the main idea of the passage.

17. **C**   When asked a vocabulary in context question, focus on what the word means in the sentence. In line 17, "colorful" most nearly means uncommon or outside of social norms. This best fits with (C), unusual. The other choices go along with the topic of art, and so may seem attractive but those are deceptive answers and don't fit the context of this specific sentence.

18. **B**   This is a specific question, so go back to the passage and find the answer. The passage states in lines 5–9 that it was after the death of her young son that she devoted her life to the arts. This best supports (B). It was after her husband died that she purchased land for a museum, so eliminate (A). Neither (C) nor (D) is mentioned, eliminating those answers as well. Choice (B) is the correct answer.

19. **C**   On Except/Not/Least questions, cross-check each answer choice and write a "T" for true and an "F" for false for each answer choice, based on the passage. The false answer will be the correct choice. Lines 14–15 support (A), so it is true. Lines 18–22 support (B), so it is true. Lines 12–13 support (D), so it is true. The only choice that is not supported by the passage is (C), as there is no mention of a school in the passage. This makes (C) the false answer, and therefore the correct one.

20. **A**   On attitude questions, eliminate answer choices that are too extreme or don't make sense based on the passage. The passage is very positive about Isabella Stewart Gardner. This best supports (A), admiring. All other answer choices are negative, which does not fit with the tone of the passage.

21. **B**   For general purpose questions, ask yourself "Why did the author write this?" The passage describes the work of Charlotte Perkins Gilman to improve the lives of women through her writing and speaking. This best supports (B). The passage is not focused on women working outside the home, which eliminates (A). Although the passage mentions that Gilman's family was not wealthy, this was not the focus of the passage in general, which eliminates (C). Choice (D) is much too broad and extreme to be the correct answer. Choice (B) is correct.

22. **D**   This is a very open-ended question, so check each answer with the information provided in the passage. Choice (A) is not a good answer as it is insulting to women and is not supported by the passage, since Gilman was a woman who had ideas about how to change things. Since Gilman was able to publish her writing, (B) is also incorrect. Choice (C) also is not supported by the passage. Choice (D) is supported by lines 2–4, educational opportunities were limited for women in Gilman's lifetime. Choice (D) is the correct answer.

23. **D** Remember that on inference questions it is important to stick as closely to the text of the passage as possible. Lines 8–10 are focused on the fact that Gilman was self-educated as her family was not wealthy. This best matches (D). There is no indication in these lines that she preferred to be alone, nor what she planned to be in the future, which eliminates (B) and (C). Since it sounds like she read on her own, (A) is the opposite of what the passage says. The correct answer is (D).

24. **B** This is a specific question, so go back to the passage and find the answer. The third paragraph is focused on the work Gilman did to spread her ideas. This best supports (B). There is no mention of whether or not Gilman enjoyed speaking to large groups, so (A) is not supported. It does not say that publishing a magazine was easy, eliminating (C). And although the passage does indicate the information included in (D), it does not do so in the third paragraph. Choice (B) is the correct answer.

25. **D** This question is a "main idea" question in disguise. Ask yourself the "so what?" of the story. This story is about Gilman's work to encourage women to educate themselves and become productive. This best matches (D), since her focus was on women and their productivity. The passage only briefly mentioned Europe, and does not indicate that Gilman ever went there or cared about it, which eliminates (A). The passage states that Gilman did not grow up rich, eliminating (B). And Gilman is described as being for the advancement of women, which eliminates (C). Only (D) works with the information provided in the passage.

Section 4 Mathematics Achievement

1. **D** The difference between $6\frac{1}{2}$ hours and 5 hours is $1\frac{1}{2}$ hours. Be careful! The question is asking for minutes. Eliminate (A). There are 60 minutes in 1 hour and 30 minutes in $\frac{1}{2}$ hour, so there are 90 more minutes. Therefore, (D) is the correct answer.

2. **C** Twenty-four thousand is written out as 24,000, and six hundred and three is written out as 603. Therefore, the correct answer is (C). Choice (A) is two thousand, four hundred and sixty three. Choice (B) is twenty thousand, four hundred and sixty three. Choice (D) is twenty-four thousand, six hundred and thirty.

3. **A** When adding fractions with unlike denominators, find a common denominator first. For this question, multiply the first fraction by 3 so that $\frac{2}{3}$ becomes $\frac{6}{9}$. Next add the numerators together to get the final sum: $\frac{6}{9} + \frac{8}{9} = \frac{14}{9}$. The correct answer is (A).

4. **D** Note that each symbol represents 2 letters. Therefore, the 3 mailbox symbols will equal 6 letters delivered on Tuesday ($2 \times 3 = 6$ or $2 + 2 + 2 = 6$), and the correct answer is (D).

5. **B** Note that each symbol represents 2 letters. On Monday, Mrs. Adler delivered 10 letters ($2 \times 5 = 10$ or $2 + 2 + 2 + 2 + 2 = 10$), and on Wednesday she delivered 8 letters ($2 \times 4 = 8$ or $2 + 2 + 2 + 2 = 8$). Thus, she delivered 2 more letters on Monday than she did on Wednesday. The correct answer is (B).

6. **C** Note that each symbol represents 2 letters. On Monday, Mrs. Adler delivered 10 letters ($2 \times 5 = 10$ or $2 + 2 + 2 + 2 + 2 = 10$), and on Tuesday she delivered 6 letters ($2 \times 3 = 6$ or $2 + 2 + 2 = 6$). Therefore, she delivered a total of 16 letters over those two days, and the correct answer is (C).

7. **B** Since the digit 2 is two places to the right of the decimal, it is in the hundredths place and would be equivalent to two one-hundredths or $\dfrac{2}{100}$. The correct answer is (B). Choice (A) is two tenths and would be one place to the right of the decimal. Choice (C) is two one-thousandths and would be three places to the right of the decimal. Finally, (D) is two ten-thousandths and would be four places to the right of the decimal.

8. **D** To find the perimeter of a shape, add up all the sides. In a rectangle, opposite sides are equal, so $QR = 4$ and $RS = 3$. $3 + 4 + 3 + 4 = 14$. Thus, (D) is the correct answer. Note that (C) is incorrect because 12 is the area of this rectangle: $l \times w = 3 \times 4 = 12$.

9. **B** Solve by using long division or use the answers choice (PITA). $25\overline{)1,000}$ with 40 above, or $25 \times 40 = 1,000$, so the correct answer is (B).

10. **C** $3 \times 64 = 192$, so the correct answer is (C). The stacking method works well or you can break the problem into two steps: $3 \times 60 = 180$ and $3 \times 4 = 12$. When you add 180 and 12 together, you get 192.

11. **B** Remember to use order of operations (PEMDAS). For this problem, multiply first; then add:

$3 \times 2 = 6$

$6 + 4 = 10$

The correct answer is (B).

12. **C** If Wu originally had 18 marbles and loses half of them, he is left with 9 marbles ($18 - 9 = 9$). If his friend gives him 3 more marbles, then Wu has 12 marbles ($9 + 3 = 12$). Therefore, the correct answer is (C).

13. **A** Use the figure to determine the price of each item. If Ian bought 2 pads of paper, he spent $2.50, since each pad of paper costs $1.25 ($1.25 + $1.25 = $2.50). He purchased 1 notebook, which cost $1.50. Each box of pencils costs $2.00, so if Ian purchased 3 boxes, he spent $6.00 total ($3 \times $2.00 = $6.00). Add up the 3 totals to get the final amount that Ian spent: $2.50 + $1.50 + $6.00 = $10.00. The correct answer is (A).

14. **C** Solve by using multiplication and division: $\frac{1}{5} \times 400 = \frac{1}{5} \times \frac{400}{1} = \frac{400}{5} = 80$. The correct answer is (C).

15. **D** If Evan has 26 comic books and Mark has twice as many as Evan does, then Mark has 52 comic books (26 + 26 = 52 or 2 × 26 = 52). The correct answer is (D). Note that (A) represents *half* as many comic books as Evan has and (B) represents the number of comic books that Evan has.

16. **D** If 12 eggs cost $1.80, then 36 eggs will be 3 times more: if 12 × 3 = 36, then $1.80 × 3 = $5.40. You can also set up a proportion to solve: $\frac{12 \text{ eggs}}{\$1.80} = \frac{36 \text{ eggs}}{x}$. Another method would be to estimate. If 12 eggs cost about $2.00, then 36 eggs would cost about $6.00. The closest option to $6.00 is (D), which is the correct answer.

17. **C** There are 180° in a triangle, so eliminate (D) since the question asks for the missing angle. The given angles are each 45°, so they represent a total of 90°. Subtract 90 from 180 to get 90°, so the correct answer is (C) because 90° + 45° + 45° = 180°.

18. **C** Use the graph provided to find the number of hours Alicia spent doing homework. On Monday she spent 2 hours. Draw a horizontal line to see which other day she spent 2 hours on homework. The only other day that will touch this line is Thursday, so the correct answer is (C). Note that she spent 3 hours doing homework on Tuesday, 1 hour doing homework on Wednesday, and 0 hours doing homework on Friday.

19. **B** Use the graph provided to find the number of hours Alicia spent doing homework. On Tuesday, she spent 3 hours doing homework, and on Wednesday she spent 1 hour doing homework. Therefore, Alicia spent 2 more hours doing homework on Tuesday than she did on Wednesday (3 − 1 = 2). The correct answer is (B).

20. **C** To find the missing part of this equation, simplify the left side of the equation first: 6 × 20 = 120. The equation now looks like 120 = 150 − ___. To determine what goes in the blank, subtract 120 from 150 or use the answer choice (PITA). Try (C): 120 = 150 − 30. Since this is the only answer choice that makes the right side of the equation equal to 120, the correct answer is (C).

21. **A** There are several ways to solve this problem (e.g. using the Bowtie method or finding a common denominator for the fractions). Another option would be to convert the fractions to decimal form. Choice (A) equals $0.\overline{66}$, (B) equals $0.8\overline{3}$, (C) equals 0.875, and (D) equals 0.9. The only one that is less than $\frac{3}{4}$ or 0.75 is $0.\overline{66}$, or (A).

22. **D** A multiple means that a number can be divided by another number without a remainder. For a question like this, it is helpful to know divisibility rules. For the number 3, the rule is to add all the digits of the number together. If that sum is divisible by 3, then the number will be divisible by 3. For example, in (A) take 120 and find the sum of the digits: $1 + 2 + 0 = 3$. Since 3 is divisible by 3, 120 is a multiple of 3. In (B), $2 + 1 + 0 = 3$. Since 3 is divisible by 3, 210 is a multiple of 3. For (C), $4 + 6 + 2 = 12$. Since 12 is divisible by 3, 462 is a multiple of 3. Finally, in (D), $5 + 1 + 2 = 8$. Since 8 is *not* divisible by 3, 512 is *not* a multiple of 3. Therefore, the correct answer is (D).

23. **C** Use the graph provided to find the number of students who chose vanilla ice cream as their favorite. Since 3 students chose vanilla, the correct answer is (C). Note that the remaining answer choices are incorrect because they represent a different ice cream flavor: 2 students chose chocolate, 1 student chose strawberry, and 4 students chose peppermint.

24. **A** Use the graph provided to find which flavor the greatest number of students chose. Based on the graph, 2 students chose chocolate, 1 student chose strawberry, 3 students chose vanilla, and 4 students chose peppermint. Since peppermint was chosen by the most number of students, the correct answer is (A).

25. **C** The perimeter of a shape is the sum of all the sides. In a square, all sides are equal, so if the perimeter is equal to 36, then each side equals 9 because $\frac{36}{4} = 9$ (or $9 + 9 + 9 + 9 = 36$). Thus, (C) is the correct answer.

26. **D** If 1 pound equals 16 ounces, then 2 pounds would equal 32 ounces and 0.5 pounds would equal 8 ounces, so 2.5 pounds would be 40 ounces ($32 + 8 = 40$). Therefore, the correct answer is (D). Another way to solve this problem would be estimation. Since the question is asking for what would be equivalent to 2.5 pounds, the number of ounces has to be larger than 32. Therefore, only (D) could be the correct answer.

27. **D** Since Jessica worked at least 5 hours on Tuesday and at least 3 hours on Wednesday, she worked at least 8 hours, so eliminate (A) and (B) because they are too small. Since $\frac{1}{2}$ and $\frac{3}{4}$ will add up to be greater than one whole, the correct answer must be (D). Remember that when adding mixed numbers, you need to make sure that the fractions have a common denominator. For this question, multiply $\frac{1}{2}$ by 2 so that it becomes $\frac{2}{4}$. Add the numerators of the fractions: $\frac{2}{4} + \frac{3}{4} = \frac{5}{4}$. Convert the improper fraction into a mixed number: $\frac{5}{4} = 1\frac{1}{4}$. Next combine all the whole numbers: $5 + 3 + 1 = 9$. Finally, add 9 to $\frac{1}{4}$. Thus, the final sum is $9\frac{1}{4}$.

28.	**A**	Use the figure to determine each price. If one adult rides the ferry on a weekday afternoon, it will cost $12.00. Therefore, two adult tickets cost $24.00. It costs $6.00 for one child to ride the ferry on a weekday afternoon. Thus, the total cost will be $30.00 (12 + 12 + 6 = 30). The correct answer is (A).

29.	**C**	Use the figure to determine each price. One adult ticket to ride the ferry on a weekday afternoon costs $12.00. One child ticket to ride the ferry on a weekday afternoon costs $6.00, so two children's tickets cost $12.00. The total cost is $24.00 (12 + 12 = 24). One adult ticket to ride the ferry on a weekday morning costs $15.00. One child ticket to ride the ferry on a weekday morning costs $9.00, so two children's tickets cost $18.00. The total cost is $33.00 (15 + 18 = 33). The question asks how much more it costs these people to ride the ferry in the morning versus in the afternoon. It costs $9 less to ride in the afternoon since 33 − 24 = 9. Thus, the correct answer is (C).

30.	**C**	Use the figure to determine each price. One adult ticket to ride the ferry on a weekend costs $10.00, so two adult tickets cost $20.00. Children do not pay to ride the ferry on the weekend, so the total cost is $20.00 (20 + 0 = 20). One adult ticket to ride the ferry on a weekday afternoon is $12.00. Therefore, two adult tickets cost $24.00. It costs $6.00 for one child to ride the ferry on a weekday afternoon. Thus, the total cost will be $30.00 (24 + 6 = 30). Next set up the two total costs as a fraction: $\dfrac{\text{total cost on weekend}}{\text{total cost on weekday afternoon}} = \dfrac{20}{30} = \dfrac{2}{3}$. Therefore, the correct answer is (C).

International Offices Listing

China (Beijing)
1501 Building A,
Disanji Creative Zone,
No.66 West Section of North 4th Ring Road Beijing
Tel: +86-10-62684481/2/3
Email: tprkor01@chol.com
Website: www.tprbeijing.com

China (Shanghai)
1010 Kaixuan Road
Building B, 5/F
Changning District, Shanghai, China 200052
Sara Beattie, Owner: Email: sbeattie@sarabeattie.com
Tel: +86-21-5108-2798
Fax: +86-21-6386-1039
Website: www.princetonreviewshanghai.com

Hong Kong
5th Floor, Yardley Commercial Building
1-6 Connaught Road West, Sheung Wan, Hong Kong
(MTR Exit C)
Sara Beattie, Owner: Email: sbeattie@sarabeattie.com
Tel: +852-2507-9380
Fax: +852-2827-4630
Website: www.princetonreviewhk.com

India (Mumbai)
Score Plus Academy
Office No.15, Fifth Floor
Manek Mahal 90
Veer Nariman Road
Next to Hotel Ambassador
Churchgate, Mumbai 400020
Maharashtra, India
Ritu Kalwani: Email: director@score-plus.com
Tel: + 91 22 22846801 / 39 / 41
Website: www.score-plus.com

India (New Delhi)
South Extension
K-16, Upper Ground Floor
South Extension Part-1,
New Delhi-110049
Aradhana Mahna: aradhana@manyagroup.com
Monisha Banerjee: monisha@manyagroup.com
Ruchi Tomar: ruchi.tomar@manyagroup.com
Rishi Josan: Rishi.josan@manyagroup.com
Vishal Goswamy: vishal.goswamy@manyagroup.com
Tel: +91-11-64501603/ 4, +91-11-65028379
Website: www.manyagroup.com

Lebanon
463 Bliss Street
AlFarra Building - 2nd floor
Ras Beirut
Beirut, Lebanon
Hassan Coudsi: Email: hassan.coudsi@review.com
Tel: +961-1-367-688
Website: www.princetonreviewlebanon.com

Korea
945-25 Young Shin Building
25 Daechi-Dong, Kangnam-gu
Seoul, Korea 135-280
Yong-Hoon Lee: Email: TPRKor01@chollian.net
In-Woo Kim: Email: iwkim@tpr.co.kr
Tel: + 82-2-554-7762
Fax: +82-2-453-9466
Website: www.tpr.co.kr

Kuwait
ScorePlus Learning Center
Salmiyah Block 3, Street 2 Building 14
Post Box: 559, Zip 1306, Safat, Kuwait
Email: infokuwait@score-plus.com
Tel: +965-25-75-48-02 / 8
Fax: +965-25-75-46-02
Website: www.scorepluseducation.com

Malaysia
Sara Beattie MDC Sdn Bhd
Suites 18E & 18F
18th Floor
Gurney Tower, Persiaran Gurney
Penang, Malaysia
Email: tprkl.my@sarabeattie.com
Sara Beattie, Owner: Email: sbeattie@sarabeattie.com
Tel: +604-2104 333
Fax: +604-2104 330
Website: www.princetonreviewKL.com

Mexico
TPR México
Guanajuato No. 242 Piso 1 Interior 1
Col. Roma Norte
México D.F., C.P.06700
registro@princetonreviewmexico.com
Tel: +52-55-5255-4495
+52-55-5255-4440
+52-55-5255-4442
Website: www.princetonreviewmexico.com

Qatar
Score Plus
Office No: 1A, Al Kuwari (Damas)
Building near Merweb Hotel, Al Saad
Post Box: 2408, Doha, Qatar
Email: infoqatar@score-plus.com
Tel: +974 44 36 8580, +974 526 5032
Fax: +974 44 13 1995
Website: www.scorepluseducation.com

Taiwan
The Princeton Review Taiwan
2F, 169 Zhong Xiao East Road, Section 4
Taipei, Taiwan 10690
Lisa Bartle (Owner): lbartle@princetonreview.com.tw
Tel: +886-2-2751-1293
Fax: +886-2-2776-3201
Website: www.PrincetonReview.com.tw

Thailand
The Princeton Review Thailand
Sathorn Nakorn Tower, 28th floor
100 North Sathorn Road
Bangkok, Thailand 10500
Thavida Bijayendrayodhin (Chairman)
Email: thavida@princetonreviewthailand.com
Mitsara Bijayendrayodhin (Managing Director)
Email: mitsara@princetonreviewthailand.com
Tel: +662-636-6770
Fax: +662-636-6776
Website: www.princetonreviewthailand.com

Turkey
Yeni Sülün Sokak No. 28
Levent, Istanbul, 34330, Turkey
Nuri Ozgur: nuri@tprturkey.com
Rona Ozgur: rona@tprturkey.com
Iren Ozgur: iren@tprturkey.com
Tel: +90-212-324-4747
Fax: +90-212-324-3347
Website: www.tprturkey.com

UAE
Emirates Score Plus
Office No: 506, Fifth Floor
Sultan Business Center
Near Lamcy Plaza, 21 Oud Metha Road
Post Box: 44098, Dubai
United Arab Emirates
Hukumat Kalwani: skoreplus@gmail.com
Ritu Kalwani: director@score-plus.com
Email: info@score-plus.com
Tel: +971-4-334-0004
Fax: +971-4-334-0222
Website: www.princetonreviewuae.com

Our International Partners

The Princeton Review also runs courses with a variety of
partners in Africa, Asia, Europe, and South America.

Georgia
LEAF American-Georgian Education Center
www.leaf.ge

Mongolia
English Academy of Mongolia
www.nyescm.org

Nigeria
The Know Place
www.knowplace.com.ng

Panama
Academia Interamericana de Panama
http://aip.edu.pa/

Switzerland
Institut Le Rosey
http://www.rosey.ch/

All other inquiries, please email us at
internationalsupport@review.com